# Contents

# List of figures and tables

Numbers in brackets refer to similar items appearing in *Social Trends 35*

Page

## The different experiences of the United Kingdom's ethnic and religious populations

## 1: Population

## 4: Labour market

## 5: Income and wealth

## 6: Expenditure

## 7: Health

## 8: Social protection

## 9: Crime and justice

## 10: Housing

## 11: Environment

## 12: Transport

## 13: Lifestyles and social participation

# List of contributors

| | |
|---|---|
| Authors: | Karin Bosveld |
| | Siân Bradford |
| | Simon Burtenshaw |
| | Jenny Church |
| | Aleks Collingwood Bakeo |
| | Craig Corbet |
| | Melissa Coulthard |
| | Figen Deviren |
| | Konstantina Dimou |
| | Caroline Hall |
| | David Harper |
| | Steve Howell |
| | Kwabena Owusu-Agyemang |
| | Chris Randall |
| | Matthew Richardson |
| | Adrian Shepherd |
| | |
| Production manager: | Mario Alemanno |
| | |
| Production team: | Lola Akinrodoye |
| | Elizabeth Attree |
| | Kirsty Burns |
| | John Chrzczonowicz |
| | Joseph Goldstein |
| | Usuf Islam |
| | Shiva Satkunam |
| | Steve Whyman |

# Acknowledgements

The Editors would like to thank all their colleagues in contributing Departments and other organisations for their generous support and helpful comments, without which this edition of *Social Trends* would not have been possible. Thanks also go to the following for their help in the production process:

| | |
|---|---|
| Reviewers: | Sharon Adhikari |
| | Mat Charlton |
| | Simon Huxstep |
| | Henriette Johansen |
| | Francis Jones |
| | Sam Xavier |
| | |
| Design and artwork: | Tony Castro |
| | Genevieve Chapman |
| | Michelle Franco |
| | Andy Leach |
| | Desk Top Publications |
| | |
| Publishing management: | Paul Hyatt |
| | Phil Lewin |
| | |
| Maps: | Jeremy Brocklehurst |
| | Alistair Dent |
| | |
| Data: | Nicola Amaranayake |
| | Michael Crawley |
| | Trish Duffy |
| | Jonathan Elphick |
| | David Penny |
| | Sunita Rajput |
| | Sathees Sivagnanam |
| | Brian Yin |

# Introduction

This is the 36th edition of *Social Trends* – one of the flagship publications from the Office for National Statistics (ONS). *Social Trends* draws together statistics from a wide range of government departments and other organisations to paint a broad picture of our society today, and how it has been changing. It is also the main means of reporting on the General Household Survey (GHS), although GHS datasets continue to be published on the National Statistics website as soon as they are available. This year *Social Trends* features an article exploring the different experiences of the ethnic and religious populations in the United Kingdom.

*Social Trends* is aimed at a wide audience: policy makers in the public and private sectors; service providers; people in local government; journalists and other commentators; academics and students; schools; and the general public.

The editorial team welcomes views on how *Social Trends* could be improved. Please write to the Editor at the address shown below with your comments or suggestions.

## New material and sources

To preserve topicality, over half of the 307 tables and figures in the 13 chapters of *Social Trends 36* are new compared with the previous edition. These draw on the most up-to-date available data.

In all chapters the source of the data is given below each table and figure, and where this is a survey the name of the survey is also included. A list of contact telephone numbers, including the contact number for each chapter author and a list of useful website addresses, can be found on pages 201 to 208. A list of further reading is also given, beginning on page 209. Regional and other sub-national breakdowns of much of the information in *Social Trends* can be found in the ONS publication *Regional Trends*.

## Definitions and terms

Symbols and conventions used in this publication can be found on page 217 and the Appendix gives definitions and general background information, particularly on administrative and legal structures and frameworks. Anyone seeking to understand the tables and figures in detail will find it helpful to read the corresponding entries in the Appendix. An index to this edition starts on page 236.

## Availability on electronic media

*Social Trends* 36 is available electronically on the National Statistics website, www.statistics.gov.uk/socialtrends. *Social Trends* brings a range of statistics together in one place and is updated once a year. There are also links from the web version of *Social Trends* to topic-based summaries, which contain a key chart and short interpretative commentary. These are updated as new data become available. By adding these summaries over time, a continually updated version of the key topics in *Social Trends* will become available. A PDF file can also be found on the website, containing links to Excel spreadsheets giving the data for all tables, figures and maps.

## Contact

### Hayley Butcher

Social Analysis and Reporting Division
Office for National Statistics
Room: B5/02
1 Drummond Gate
London
SW1V 2QQ

Email: social.trends@ons.gov.uk

# The different experiences of the United Kingdom's ethnic and religious populations

By Helen Connolly and Amanda White

## Introduction

The United Kingdom is an area of increasing ethnic and religious diversity. The majority of the population are White British, but a pattern of migration since the middle of the 20th century has produced a number of recognisable minority ethnic groups. Many have their own distinct appearance, language, religion and culture.

The 1950s and 1960s were periods of mass immigration from the New Commonwealth countries, in particular the Caribbean, India and Pakistan. Migrants from Bangladesh, Hong Kong and Africa followed. The 1980s onwards witnessed a dramatic increase in the number of asylum seekers.[1] More recently there has been an increase in migration from eastern European countries.

The 1991 Censuses in England, Wales and Scotland presented the first opportunity to accurately measure the size of the ethnic minority populations in Great Britain. Ethnic group data were not collected on the 1991 Census in Northern Ireland. Prior to the 1991 Census, estimates of the size of ethnic groups relied upon survey data or upon using country of birth as a proxy for ethnic group. Estimates from both sources were prone to error. Between 1991 and 2001 Great Britain's ethnic minority population grew from 3.1 million people to 4.6 million. It also increased as a proportion of the population, from 5.6 per cent to 8.1 per cent over the decade. During this period there was growth in each of the ethnic minority populations, particularly in the Black African population which doubled (Figure A.1 overleaf).

Ethnic minority groups are diverse. The original migrants entered the UK speaking a range of languages, adhering to different religious and cultural beliefs, and their socio-economic backgrounds, educational backgrounds and economic resources were often as different from each other as their countries of origin. Some groups have experienced economic success and seen their children make substantial gains in education and employment. Others have found themselves and their children comparatively disadvantaged – both in comparison to the majority White British population and in comparison to other ethnic minority groups.

While the article discusses labour market and educational outcomes of different ethnic and religious populations, other topics are discussed in the Focus on Ethnicity and Focus on Religion online reports see: www.statistics.gov.uk/focuson.

Figures for the United Kingdom are presented where available but due to the lack of directly comparable data for Northern Ireland, data for Great Britain are used to describe each ethnic group.

## Who, When and Where: Ethnic and religious populations in the UK

The ethnic minority population comprised 8 per cent of the UK population in 2001. Ethnic minority populations are characterised by a number of factors including their particular group characteristics, the younger age structure of their populations and the geographical regions in which they live.

Indians formed the largest ethnic minority group in 2001. They comprised nearly 2 per cent of the UK population (1,053,000 people) but accounted for almost one in four (23 per cent) of the UK ethnic minority population (Table A.2). The next largest group were the Pakistanis, who accounted for 16 per cent of the ethnic minority population, followed by the Black Caribbeans (12 per cent), Black Africans (10 per cent), Bangladeshis (6 per cent) and Chinese (5 per cent).

Most ethnic minority groups in Great Britain have young populations compared with the White British population. The Mixed group are the youngest, half (50 per cent) being under 16 years of age in 2001, followed by the Bangladeshi (38 per cent), Pakistani (35 per cent) and Black African (30 per cent) populations. The Black Caribbean population have the oldest age structure of the non-White groups – 20 per cent were under 16 years of age in 2001 and 11 per cent were over 65 years of age. This distribution was closest to the White British age structure. The White Irish population have the oldest age structure of all ethnic groups, having the smallest proportion of under 16 year olds (6 per cent) and the largest proportion of people aged 65 and over (25 per cent) (see Population chapter; Figure 1.5).

### Figure A.1

### Growth of the main ethnic minority groups, 1991[1] and 2001

**Great Britain**

Thousands

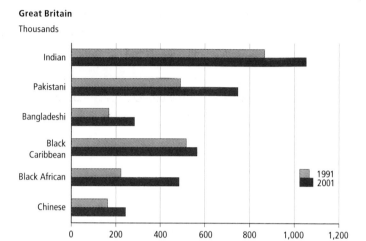

1 Data for 1991 have been adjusted for census under enumeration.

*Source: Census 2001, Office for National Statistics; Census 2001, General Register Office for Scotland; Ethnicity in the 1991 Census: Volume One, Office for National Statistics*

### Table A.2

### Population: by ethnic group, 2001

**United Kingdom** — Numbers and percentages

| | Total population | | Non-White population (percentages) |
|---|---|---|---|
| | Numbers | Percentages | |
| **White** | 54,153,898 | 92.1 | . |
| **Mixed** | 677,117 | 1.2 | 14.6 |
| **Asian or Asian British** | | | |
|   Indian | 1,053,411 | 1.8 | 22.7 |
|   Pakistani | 747,285 | 1.3 | 16.1 |
|   Bangladeshi | 283,063 | 0.5 | 6.1 |
|   Other Asian | 247,664 | 0.4 | 5.3 |
| All Asian or Asian British | 2,331,423 | 4.0 | 50.3 |
| **Black or Black British** | | | |
|   Black Caribbean | 565,876 | 1.0 | 12.2 |
|   Black African | 485,277 | 0.8 | 10.5 |
|   Other Black | 97,585 | 0.2 | 2.1 |
| All Black or Black British | 1,148,738 | 2.0 | 24.8 |
| **Chinese** | 247,403 | 0.4 | 5.3 |
| **Other ethnic groups** | 230,615 | 0.4 | 5.0 |
| **All minority ethnic population** | 4,635,296 | 7.9 | 100.0 |
| **All ethnic groups** | 58,789,194 | 100.0 | . |

*Source: Census 2001, Office for National Statistics; Census 2001, General Register Office for Scotland; Census 2001, Northern Ireland Statistics and Research Agency*

Although the post-war period is associated with ethnic minority migration, Britain has a long history of White migration prior to the 1950s, including waves of economic migrants from Ireland, and Jewish and other migrants from across Europe. These groups have characteristics that distinguish them from the majority White British population. However, the groups usually considered to make up the UK ethnic minority population are the non-White groups.

In 2001 most of the UK ethnic minority population lived in England (96 per cent), with smaller proportions in Scotland (2 per cent) and Wales (1 per cent), and less than 0.5 per cent living in Northern Ireland. The White population was much more geographically dispersed – 82 per cent lived in England, 9 per cent in Scotland, 5 per cent in Wales and 3 per cent in Northern Ireland. Ethnic minority populations were concentrated in certain government office regions. In 2001, 45 per cent of the UK ethnic minority population lived in London, compared with 10 per cent of the White population. Ethnic minority populations were also concentrated in the midlands, 13 per cent living in the West Midland and 6 per cent in the East Midland regions. There were smaller ethnic minority populations in the North West and South East regions (8 per cent in each case) and in the Yorkshire and the Humber region (7 per cent).

There were geographic differences between ethnic minority groups across the United Kingdom, with Black Africans, Black Caribbeans and Bangladeshis being most likely to live in London. More than three quarters of Black Africans (78 per cent), and more than half of Black Caribbeans (61 per cent) and Bangladeshis (54 per cent) lived in London in 2001. This compared with four in ten Indians (41 per cent) and three in ten Chinese (32 per cent). The Pakistani population were more evenly dispersed than many other non-White groups, with similar proportions living in the government office regions of the North West of England (16 per cent), London (19 per cent), Yorkshire and the Humber (20 per cent) and the West Midlands (21 per cent) in 2001. The West Midlands was also home to a large proportion of the Indian (17 per cent), Black Caribbean (15 per cent) and Bangladeshi (11 per cent) populations.

In addition to differences between the main ethnic groups, there is often diversity within groups. The Indian and African populations in particular include a number of distinct groups who originate from different regions, speak different languages, observe different religious practices, and have different socio-economic backgrounds. There is also diversity within the non-specific ethnic group categories such as the 'Other White', 'Other Black', 'Other Asian' and 'Other ethnic group' categories.[2] The rest of this article discusses some of the diversity within, and differences between, Great Britain's ethnic populations. Ethnicity is not fixed, being both subjective and

evolving, but the groups described are those considered to be the main ethnic groups in Great Britain at the present time.[3]

## White British

Historically Great Britain has been populated by an indigenous White population. In 2001 there were 50 million White British people in Great Britain. The majority shared a common religious background, Great Britain being historically Christian. While most recognised themselves as belonging to the 'White British' ethnic group, their sense of 'national identity' reflected the particular country with which they identified. Respondents to the 2004 Annual Population Survey were asked what they considered their national identities to be, choosing from British, English, Scottish, Welsh, Irish or some other identity. They could choose more than one if they wished. People from the White British group were more likely to describe their national identity as English (58 per cent) rather than British (36 per cent). Nine per cent reported a 'Scottish' national identity and 5 per cent 'Welsh'. In addition the White British population includes people from very different socio-economic backgrounds. Among the working-age White British population in 2001, 30 per cent belonged to a managerial or professional occupation, while 24 per cent belonged to a routine or semi-routine occupation. Experiences and outcomes vary greatly between the different socio-economic occupational groups.

## White Irish

Great Britain has a long history of Irish migration following the Irish potato famines in the 19th century. This migration continued throughout the 20th century. Those who came shared a common language and Christian religious background with the White British population. The White Irish population accounted for 691,000 people and 1.2 per cent of Great Britain's population in 2001. They were less geographically concentrated than some of the non-White ethnic groups. About three in ten (32 per cent) lived in the London region and one in ten respectively lived in the South East (12 per cent), the West Midlands (11 per cent), the North West (11 per cent) and the East of England (9 per cent) regions. A further 7 per cent lived in Scotland which was greater than the proportion for the non-White groups (2 per cent). In 2004 White Irish respondents mainly described their national identity as 'Irish', but some also reported an additional identity – 'British' (12 per cent), 'English' (14 per cent), 'Scottish' (3 per cent) and 'Welsh' (1 per cent). The White Irish had a relatively advantaged socio-economic position in 2001, with more than one in three of the working-age population belonging to a managerial or professional occupation (35 per cent) and a smaller proportion belonging to a routine or semi-routine occupation (20 per cent).

## Black Caribbean

The 1950s and 1960s were periods of mass migration from the Caribbean in response to labour shortages in Great Britain.[4] Caribbean migrants differed from many South Asian migrants by often sharing the language and the Christian religious background of the White British population. In 2001 the Black Caribbean population included the second and third generation descendents of the original migrants and accounted for 566,000 people in Great Britain. Six in ten (58 per cent) were born in the UK but the proportion who regarded themselves as British, English, Scottish or Welsh was greater – more than eight out of ten (86 per cent) Black Caribbean respondents reported one of these British identities in 2004. The original migrants came to fill employment gaps in mainly semi-skilled or unskilled manual occupations, but the Black Caribbean group has experienced occupational mobility since the 1950s. Among the working-age population in 2001 the proportion in a managerial or professional occupation (28 per cent) was greater than the proportion belonging to a routine or semi-routine occupation (23 per cent). These proportions were similar to those of the White British ethnic group.

## Indians

There has been an Indian presence in the United Kingdom since the 18th century but mass migration from the Indian sub-continent began in the 1950s and 1960s.[5] The migrant population was made up of many groups, including Sikhs and Hindus from the Punjab region in north west India and Hindus and Muslims from the Gujarat area in the western part of India. They were joined in the 1970s by Indians from East Africa including Uganda, Kenya and Tanzania. They had previously migrated to East Africa from India. In 2001 the Indian population was one of the most religiously diverse, including Hindus (45 per cent), Sikhs (29 per cent), Muslims (13 per cent) and Christians (5 per cent). Together with their British-born descendents, they formed the largest ethnic minority group in Great Britain, accounting for 23 per cent of the ethnic minority population. Almost half (46 per cent) had been born in the UK but a greater proportion felt they had a British national identity (75 per cent). Indians had a relatively more advantaged socio-economic position compared with other ethnic groups of South Asian origin (Pakistanis and Bangladeshis). Among the Indian working-age population in 2001, almost three in ten were in a managerial or professional occupation (28 per cent), while two in ten were in a routine or semi-routine occupation (20 per cent).

## Pakistanis

Pakistan came into existence in 1947 when the Indian subcontinent was partitioned following independence from British rule.[6] Mass migration from Pakistan took place from the 1960s with the arrival of male economic migrants to the UK. It continued through the 1970s and 1980s with wives and children joining their husbands and fathers. By 2001 the Pakistani population accounted for 747,000 people and over half (55 per cent) had been born in the UK. Eight in ten (83 per cent) reported having a British national identity in 2004. The Pakistani population is overwhelmingly Muslim, a characteristic it shares with the Bangladeshi population. Pakistanis have a relatively disadvantaged socio-economic position. In 2001 the proportion of the working-age population in a managerial or professional occupation (14 per cent) was smaller than the proportion in a routine or semi-routine occupation (20 per cent).

## Bangladeshis

Bangladesh came into existence in 1971 when it became independent from Pakistan. The majority of the Bangladeshi population originate from one single district, Sylhet, in the north east of Bangladesh. Migration from this region began before the 1960s but increased thereafter. Male economic migrants arrived first and were joined later by their wives and dependents from Bangladesh.[7] In 2001 the Bangladeshi population accounted for 283,000 people and was considerably smaller than the Indian and Pakistani populations. Bangladeshis, like Pakistanis, are overwhelmingly Muslim. The proportion born in the United Kingdom (46 per cent) was slightly smaller than the proportion of the Pakistani group, due to their later arrival in Great Britain. However in 2004, they were just as likely as the Pakistani or Indian ethnic groups to consider their national identity to be British (82 per cent). Bangladeshis had the most disadvantaged socio-economic position in 2001, with just over one in ten (11 per cent) of the working-age population belonging to a managerial or professional occupation and twice that proportion belonging to a routine or semi-routine occupation (22 per cent).

## Black Africans

Black Africans have a long history of small-scale settlement in Great Britain with communities established from the late 1940s onwards in the seaports of Liverpool, Cardiff and London. Since the 1970s, political instability across the African continent has contributed to increased migration.[8] The 2001 Black African population included people from Nigeria, Ghana, Somalia, Zimbabwe, Uganda, Sierra Leone and Kenya, as well as their British-born descendents. This range of countries of origin has contributed to the formation of distinct populations within the Black African ethnic group, with different characteristics including religious affiliation and socio-economic background. They include those seeking asylum, students and economic migrants. Seven in ten (69 per cent) were Christian in 2001 and two in ten (20 per cent) were Muslim. The Black African population in 2001, 485,000 people, was a similar size to the Black Caribbean population, though the proportion born in the UK, 34 per cent, was much smaller than the Black Caribbean or South Asian ethnic groups. The proportion reporting a British national identity was also smaller (53 per cent). The proportion who had a managerial or professional occupation (26 per cent) was greater than the proportion in a routine or semi-routine occupation (18 per cent).

### Chinese

The Chinese population has a relatively long history of settlement in Great Britain. Since the late 20th century there has been further growth in the Chinese population due to increasing migration and large numbers of overseas students. The Chinese population in Great Britain was almost a quarter of a million people (243,000) in 2001. Just three in ten (29 per cent) had been born in the United Kingdom but a greater proportion considered their national identity to be British (52 per cent) in 2004. One in five of the working-age population had a managerial or professional occupation (24 per cent), while those in a routine or semi-routine occupation (14 per cent) were the smallest proportion of any ethnic group. The Chinese working-age population included the largest proportion of full-time students (30 per cent) and the largest proportion of small employers or own account workers (13 per cent).

### New minority ethnic groups

The last 50 years has seen the emergence of new, British-born, ethnic minority groups. These are the children of inter-ethnic partnerships, primarily partnerships between people from the White British population and people from ethnic minority groups. In 2001 there were 674,000 people from mixed groups in Great Britain. The different mixed groups cannot be identified from the Scotland Census as the ethnic group question provided a single Mixed group category. The more extensive ethnic group question asked in England and Wales identified three distinct mixed groups. The largest was the Mixed White and Black Caribbean ethnic group which accounted for almost a quarter of a million people (237,000 people) in England and Wales. The next largest mixed groups were the Mixed White and Asian group (189,000 people) and the Mixed White and African group (79,000 people). The majority of people from a Mixed ethnic group share some things in common such as having a White parent and being born in Great Britain. Their cultural attitudes, socio-economic backgrounds and religion may vary, reflecting to some extent their parentage.

In 2004, 88 per cent of the Mixed group reported having one of the British national identities. They were more likely than any other ethnic minority group to describe themselves as 'English'

as opposed to 'British'. Thirty seven per cent of the Mixed group described themselves as English compared with no more than 19 per cent in any other ethnic minority group. Many in the ethnic minority population are children and their national identity will have been reported by their parents. People from a Mixed group may feel that they are English to a greater extent than their ethnic minority counterparts but equally White parents may be more likely than ethnic minority parents to describe their children's national identity as English.

## Women making choices: households, children and work

Culture and religion are important influences on how women organise their lives. They affect the choices women make when it comes to their role within the family, as mothers and partners, and their activity in the labour market. Women's labour market behaviour may also be affected by their age, structural factors such as the local economy, and the skills they can bring to the labour market.

Bangladeshi and Pakistani women have the highest rates of economic inactivity (for definitions see the labour market glossary on page 51). In 2004, 75 per cent of working-age Bangladeshi women and 69 per cent of working-age Pakistani women were neither working nor seeking work (Figure A.3). The majority were looking after their families within the home. The groups with the next highest economic inactivity rates were Chinese (44 per cent) and Black African (43 per cent) women. Economic inactivity rates were lower for Indian women (34 per cent) than the other South Asian groups, Indian women having

### Figure A.3

### Economic inactivity rates of women: by ethnic group, 2004[1]

**Great Britain**

Percentages

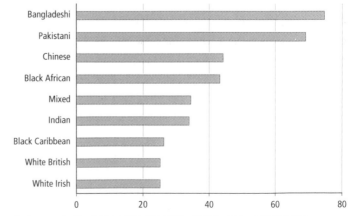

1 January to December. See Appendix, Part 4: Annual Population Survey.

*Source: Annual Population Survey, Office for National Statistics*

the same economic inactivity rates as women from the Mixed group (34 per cent). The women least likely to be economically inactive were from White British (25 per cent), White Irish (25 per cent) and Black Caribbean (26 per cent) ethnic groups.

The differences in economic inactivity rates for women reflect a number of factors, including age and life stage. The Pakistani and Bangladeshi female populations are relatively young and they contain a larger proportion of women of child-bearing age. Women from these ethnic groups are more likely to have child-rearing responsibilities than women from other groups. In 2001, 74 per cent of Bangladeshi households contained dependent children, as did 66 per cent of Pakistani households. This compared with half of Indian (50 per cent) and Black African (48 per cent) households. The households least likely to contain dependent children were White British (28 per cent) and White Irish (21 per cent).[9]

Religious or cultural attitudes may also play some part in the differences in economic inactivity rates. The majority of Pakistani and Bangladeshi women and one in five Black African women came from Muslim backgrounds, while White British, White Irish and Black Caribbean women had predominantly Christian backgrounds. Muslim women have the highest rates of economic inactivity. In 2004 almost seven in ten (69 per cent) Muslim women of working age were economically inactive, a rate twice that of Hindu (31 per cent) and Sikh (36 per cent) women. The lowest economic inactivity rates were among Christian women (25 per cent) and women with no religion (28 per cent).

Culture and religion may affect people's views regarding their desired number of children. Between 1979 and 2001, Pakistani and Bangladeshi women expressed a preference for larger families. The average intended number of children for Pakistani and Bangladeshi women was 3.4 and 3.6 respectively, compared with 2.1 for White women of child-bearing age.[10]

Differences in the levels of skills and qualifications may also contribute to differences in the economic inactivity rates of different ethnic groups. Women with children have to weigh up the economic advantages of paid work versus the cost of childcare and this will in part depend on the skills they can bring to the labour market. Pakistani and Bangladeshi women have lower educational levels than other women and many additionally may have English language difficulties. These may impact on the viability of seeking paid work outside the home.

Decisions about whether and when to have children, how many children to have and whether to work, are faced by women of all ethnic and religious groups. Women's choices do not occur in isolation but with regard to strongly held and contested views about women's roles. Which path they take will reflect economic realities, as well as cultural influences.

## Men at work: ethnicity, unemployment and education

Unemployment rates have traditionally shown variation by ethnic group with all ethnic minority groups experiencing higher unemployment rates than White British people. In 2004 White British and White Irish men had the lowest unemployment rates at 5 per cent (Figure A.4). The highest unemployment rates were among Black Caribbean men (14 per cent) and men from Black African, Mixed and Bangladeshi groups (each 13 per cent). Unemployment rates were slightly lower for Pakistani and Chinese men (11 per cent and 10 per cent respectively). Indian men had the lowest unemployment rates among the ethnic minority groups at 7 per cent – closer to those for White British men. (See also Figure 4.21.)

Differences can also be seen when unemployment rates are compared by religion. In 2004 the unemployment rate among economically active Muslim men (13 per cent) was twice the rate of Sikh (7 per cent) or Hindu (5 per cent) men. Christian and Jewish men had the lowest unemployment rates (4 per cent and 3 per cent respectively). Variations in male unemployment rates are unlikely to reflect religious or cultural attitudes as all ethnic and religious groups emphasise the importance of male economic productivity.

Early migrants may have been disadvantaged by language difficulties, a lack of recognisable qualifications and racial prejudice among the general population, which may in part explain some of the differences in unemployment rates. Over time these differences may be expected to disappear.

## Figure A.4

### Unemployment rates of men: by ethnic group, 2004[1]

**Great Britain**

Percentages

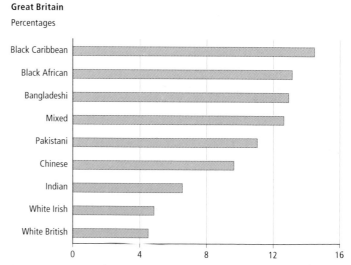

1 January to December. See Appendix, Part 4: Annual Population Survey.

**Source: Annual Population Survey, Office for National Statistics**

However, research suggests that they still exist, and that second generation ethnic minorities continue to experience higher unemployment rates than the White British population.[11]

Ethnic minority groups are concentrated in particular geographic areas and variations in the availability of different types of employment may explain some of the differences in unemployment rates. In general, ethnic minority communities tend to live in urban areas, which have higher unemployment rates. In addition, the decline of manufacturing industries in the midlands and the north of England impacted upon a number of ethnic minority communities.

The differences in unemployment rates may also reflect the younger age of the different populations, unemployment being particularly high among young men. The Mixed, Bangladeshi, Pakistani and Black African populations have particularly young populations. However, age does not account for all the difference. Indian men have a younger age profile than Black Caribbean men but have lower unemployment rates.

Variations in rates of unemployment may reflect different skills and qualifications each ethnic group brings to the labour market. Among Indian men, who had low unemployment rates in 2004, a relatively high proportion possessed a degree level qualification (30 per cent) and a relatively low proportion had no qualifications (15 per cent) (See Table 3.17). Among Pakistani and Bangladeshi men, who had high rates of unemployment, relatively small proportions possessed a degree level qualification (11 per cent and 15 per cent respectively), while relatively high proportions had no qualifications (29 per cent and 40 per cent respectively). However, qualifications do not fully account for variations in unemployment. Among Black African men, a high proportion (24 per cent) possessed a degree level qualification in 2004 and a small proportion had no qualifications (12 per cent), yet they also had high rates of unemployment. The pattern among Black Caribbean men is also inconsistent. While a small proportion possessed a degree (or equivalent) in 2004 (11 per cent), the proportion with no qualifications (18 per cent) was similar to that for White British men (14 per cent), yet Black Caribbean men had the highest unemployment rates of all groups.

Racial and religious discrimination may also contribute to the higher unemployment rates of many ethnic minority groups. Despite the introduction of the Race Relations Act in 1968, which made it illegal for employers to discriminate on the grounds of race, ethnic or national origins, various studies have suggested that discrimination persists. Studies in 1974, 1982 and 1994 reported the continuing perception among people from non-White groups that they had been refused a job for reasons associated with race or religion.[12] More recently, the Home Office Citizenship Survey reported that perceptions of discrimination persisted in 2003. People from all ethnic minority groups were more likely than those from White ethnic groups to have been refused a job within the previous five years. Of these, large proportions believed that they had been refused a job because of their race, ranging from 12 per cent of Pakistanis to 35 per cent of Black Africans. The proportions believing they had been refused a job because of their religion were highest for Pakistanis (9 per cent) and Bangladeshis (13 per cent), virtually all being Muslim.[13]

## A promising future? Educational attainment among today's young ethnic populations

Over the last decade, all ethnic groups have seen rising educational attainment among the younger populations. This is true for both boys and girls, and is reflected by increasing numbers going on to study in universities and colleges. Between 1992 and 2004 the greatest gains in educational attainment were among the Bangladeshi population who traditionally had the lowest educational qualifications.

The latest GCSE results for all 15 year old pupils in England showed the highest GCSE attainment among Indian and Chinese pupils, with grades higher than those from the White British ethnic group (Figure A.5). Three quarters (74 per cent) of Chinese pupils and 67 per cent of Indian pupils gained five or more grades A* to C at GCSE (or equivalent) in 2004. White Irish (58 per cent) and White British (52 per cent) pupils attained the next highest results. Bangladeshi (48 per cent) pupils had similar attainment levels to White British pupils, followed by Pakistani (45 per cent) and Black African (43 per cent) pupils. The lowest grades were achieved by Black Caribbean pupils (36 per cent), but they have

### Figure **A.5**

**Attainment of five or more GCSE grades A* to C or equivalent: by ethnic group, 2004**

England
Percentages

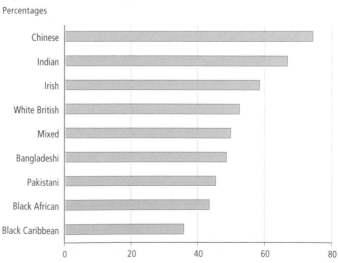

Source: *Department for Education and Skills*

made significant gains in educational attainment over the last decade. The socio-economic position of many Black children accounts in part for their relatively low attainment levels. Overall, pupils from a mixed ethnic group gained similar grades to White British pupils (50 per cent and 52 per cent respectively). There were however variations between the individual mixed groups, reflecting in part their respective parentage. Pupils from the Mixed White and Asian group achieved the highest grades, two thirds (66 per cent) achieving five or more A* to C grades (or equivalent) in 2004. Attainment levels were lower among Mixed White and Black African pupils (47 per cent) and lowest among Mixed White and Black Caribbean pupils (40 per cent), these being similar to the grades among the Black African (43 per cent) and Black Caribbean (36 per cent) groups. (See also Table 3.13).

For all ethnic groups, the attainment of higher qualifications increases employment rates, offering greater economic security. People with degree level qualifications were over 30 percentage points more likely than those with no qualifications to be in employment in 2004. Among Pakistanis, whose employment rates were generally among the lowest, there was a difference of 47 percentage points in the employment rates of those with degree level qualifications (75 per cent) and those with no qualifications (28 per cent) (Figure A.6). There were also large differences in the employment rates of those with degree level qualifications and those with no qualifications among people from a Mixed group (56 percentage points) and Black Africans (47 percentage points).

Young British-born ethnic minority populations face fewer barriers to economic success than were faced by their parents, particularly

## Figure **A.6**

**Employment rates:[1] by ethnic group[2] and highest qualification, 2004[3]**

Great Britain

Percentages

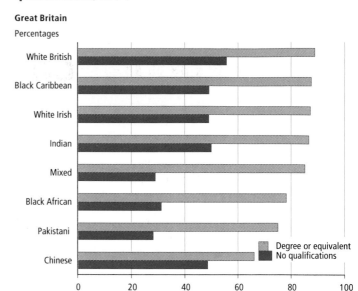

1 All people of working age.
2 The Bangladeshi group are excluded due to a small number of respondents.
3 January to December. See Appendix, Part 4: Annual Population Survey.

*Source: Annual Population Survey, Office for National Statistics*

with regard to language and educational barriers. The extent to which they are successful will reflect their socio-economic diversity, and the constraints of the wider society in which they are working, as well as their ethnic and religious diversity.

## References

1   Owen D, (1996) Size, structure and growth of the ethnic minority populations, in Coleman D and Salt J (eds), *Ethnicity in the 1991 Census,* Volume one, London, HMSO, pp 80-123.

2   The 'Other' ethnic categories are not discussed here, being far from recognisable ethnic groups in themselves and actually containing a number of distinct ethnic groups. An analysis of their heterogeneity has been published previously in Gardener, D. and Connolly, H. (2005), *Who are the 'Other' ethnic groups?* Office for National Statistics http://www.statistics.gov.uk/cci/article.asp?id=1291

3   Office for National Statistics (2003) *Ethnic group statistics: A guide for the collection and classification of ethnicity data,* London: HMSO.

4   Peach, C. (1996) *Black-Caribbeans: Class, gender and geography.* In Peach, C. (Ed): *Ethnicity in the 1991 Census: Volume Two: The ethnic minority populations of Great Britain,* London: HMSO, pp 25-43

5   Robinson, V. (1996) *The Indians: onward and upward.* In Peach, C. (Ed): *Ethnicity in the 1991 Census: Volume Two: The ethnic minority populations of Great Britain,* London: HMSO, pp 95-120

6   Ballard, R. (1996) *The Pakistanis: stability and introspection.* In Peach, C. (Ed): *Ethnicity in the 1991 Census: Volume Two: The ethnic minority populations of Great Britain,* London: HMSO, pp121-149

7   Eade, J., Vamplew, T., and Peach, C. (1986) *The Bangladeshis: the encapsulated community.* In Peach, C. (Ed): *Ethnicity in the 1991 Census: Volume Two: The ethnic minority populations of Great Britain,* London: HMSO, pp150-160

8   Daley, P. (1996) *Black Africans: students who stayed.* In Peach, C. (Ed): *Ethnicity in the 1991 Census: Volume Two: The ethnic minority populations of Great Britain,* London: HMSO, pp 44-65

9   Focus on Ethnicity and Identity, web report 2004. Office for National Statistics. http//www.statistics.gov.uk/focuson

10  Smallwood, S. and Jeffries, J. (2003) *Family building intentions in England and Wales: trends, outcomes and interpretations,* Population Trends 112, p.24.

11  Heath, A.F. and Yu, S. (2005) *The puzzle of ethnic minority disadvantage.* In Heath, A.F., Ermisch, J. and Gallie, D. (Eds.): *Understanding Social Change: Proceedings of the British Academy,* Oxford: Oxford University Press, pp.187-224.

12  Smith, D. (1977) *Racial Disadvantage in Britain,* Penguin: London; Brown, C and Gay, P (1985) *Racial Discrimination 17 Years After the Act,* Policy Studies Institute: London.; Modood, T. , Berthoud, R. et al (1997) Ethnic Minorities in Britain: diversity and disadvantage, Policy Studies Institute: London cited in Heath, A.F. and Yu, S. (2005) *The puzzle of ethnic minority disadvantage* in Heath, A.F., Ermisch, J. and Gallie, D. (Eds.) *Understanding Social Change: Proceedings of the British Academy,* Oxford: Oxford University Press, pp.187-224.

13  Home Office Research Study 289, 2003 *Home Office Citizenship Survey: People, Families and Communities,* Crown Copyright 2004.

# Population

- The population of the United Kingdom has grown steadily between 1971 and 2001 to reach 59.8 million people in 2004, an increase of 3.9 million. (Table 1.1)

- In 2004 there were 11.6 million people aged under 16 in the United Kingdom, a decline of 2.6 million since 1971, and 9.6 million people aged over 65, an increase of 2.2 million. (Table 1.2)

- In 2001, 38 million people (nearly seven in ten) in Great Britain described their ethnicity as White British and their religion as Christian. Other large faith groups were Pakistani Muslims (686,000), Indian Hindus (471,000), Black Caribbean Christians (417,000), Black African Christians (334,000) and Indian Sikhs (307,000). (Page 13)

- There were 716,000 live births in the United Kingdom in 2004 – an increase of 20,500 compared with 2003. (Figure 1.9)

- In 2004 nearly 222,600 more people migrated to the United Kingdom than left it. This was 71,600 greater than in 2003 and the highest net inflow since the present method of estimation began in 1991. (Page 17)

- The United Kingdom had a rate of 0.7 asylum seekers per 1,000 population in 2004, higher than the EU-25 average of 0.6 per 1,000 population. (Table 1.14)

The number of births and deaths, and the number of people entering and leaving the country all affect the size, sex and age structure and the geography of the population. Changes in demographic patterns not only influence social structures, but also the demand for services. Information on the size and structure of the population by other factors, such as marital and partnership status, ethnicity, and social class are essential in understanding aspects of society, such as the labour market and household composition.

## Population profile

The population of the United Kingdom has grown steadily between 1971 and 2001 to reach 59.8 million people in 2004, an increase of 3.9 million (Table 1.1). During this period the populations of England, Wales and Northern Ireland all grew but the population of Scotland declined by 0.1 million people. The 2004 based population projections suggest that the population of the United Kingdom will still be rising in 2031.

## Table **1.1**

### Population[1] of the United Kingdom

Millions

|  | 1971 | 1981 | 1991 | 2001 | 2004 | 2011 | 2021 |
|---|---|---|---|---|---|---|---|
| United Kingdom | 55.9 | 56.4 | 57.4 | 59.1 | 59.8 | 61.9 | 64.7 |
| England | 46.4 | 46.8 | 47.9 | 49.4 | 50.1 | 52.0 | 54.6 |
| Wales | 2.7 | 2.8 | 2.9 | 2.9 | 3.0 | 3.0 | 3.2 |
| Scotland | 5.2 | 5.2 | 5.1 | 5.1 | 5.1 | 5.1 | 5.1 |
| Northern Ireland | 1.5 | 1.5 | 1.6 | 1.7 | 1.7 | 1.8 | 1.8 |

1 Mid-year estimates for 1971 to 2004; 2004-based projections for 2011 and 2021. See Appendix, Part 1: Population estimates and projections.

**Source: Office for National Statistics; Government Actuary's Department; General Register Office for Scotland; Northern Ireland Statistics and Research Agency**

## Table **1.2**

### Population:[1] by sex and age

United Kingdom

Thousands

|  | Under 16 | 16–24 | 25–34 | 35–44 | 45–54 | 55–64 | 65–74 | 75 and over | All ages |
|---|---|---|---|---|---|---|---|---|---|
| **Males** | | | | | | | | | |
| 1971 | 7,318 | 3,730 | 3,530 | 3,271 | 3,354 | 3,123 | 1,999 | 842 | 27,167 |
| 1981 | 6,439 | 4,114 | 4,036 | 3,409 | 3,121 | 2,967 | 2,264 | 1,063 | 27,412 |
| 1991 | 5,976 | 3,800 | 4,432 | 3,950 | 3,287 | 2,835 | 2,272 | 1,358 | 27,909 |
| 2001 | 6,077 | 3,284 | 4,215 | 4,382 | 3,856 | 3,090 | 2,308 | 1,621 | 28,832 |
| 2004 | 5,970 | 3,533 | 3,954 | 4,553 | 3,780 | 3,391 | 2,374 | 1,717 | 29,271 |
| 2011 | 5,744 | 3,768 | 4,074 | 4,293 | 4,301 | 3,598 | 2,652 | 2,008 | 30,438 |
| 2021 | 5,821 | 3,436 | 4,487 | 4,133 | 4,201 | 4,042 | 3,158 | 2,664 | 31,943 |
| **Females** | | | | | | | | | |
| 1971 | 6,938 | 3,626 | 3,441 | 3,241 | 3,482 | 3,465 | 2,765 | 1,802 | 28,761 |
| 1981 | 6,104 | 3,966 | 3,975 | 3,365 | 3,148 | 3,240 | 2,931 | 2,218 | 28,946 |
| 1991 | 5,709 | 3,691 | 4,466 | 3,968 | 3,296 | 2,971 | 2,795 | 2,634 | 29,530 |
| 2001 | 5,786 | 3,220 | 4,260 | 4,465 | 3,920 | 3,186 | 2,640 | 2,805 | 30,281 |
| 2004 | 5,676 | 3,408 | 3,983 | 4,640 | 3,859 | 3,509 | 2,659 | 2,830 | 30,564 |
| 2011 | 5,487 | 3,563 | 4,050 | 4,358 | 4,412 | 3,755 | 2,898 | 2,931 | 31,454 |
| 2021 | 5,578 | 3,257 | 4,347 | 4,146 | 4,295 | 4,244 | 3,452 | 3,465 | 32,784 |

1 Mid-year estimates for 1971 to 2004; 2004-based projections for 2011 and 2021. See Appendix, Part 1: Population estimates and projections.

**Source: Office for National Statistics; Government Actuary's Department; General Register Office for Scotland; Northern Ireland Statistics and Research Agency**

The population is expected to pass 60 million in 2005, 65 million in 2023 and reach 67 million by 2031. This is a projected increase of 7.2 million people between 2004 and 2031: 43 per cent of this increase is attributed to natural increase (the difference between births and deaths) and 57 per cent is projected to be net migration. Projected trends differ for the four parts of the United Kingdom. The population of Scotland is expected to increase slightly until 2019 and then start to fall, while the Northern Ireland population is projected to grow until the early 2030s and then decline. The Welsh population projections suggest the population will increase beyond 2031 but at a low rate of growth, while the English population is also projected to continue rising but at a higher rate.

The populations of England, Northern Ireland, Scotland and Wales as proportions of the UK population varied little from 1971 to 2004. In 2004 England represented approximately 84 per cent of the population, Scotland 8 per cent, Wales 5 per cent and Northern Ireland 3 per cent. Similar values are shown in the projections to 2021.

More boys than girls are born each year; nearly 368,000 boys were born in the United Kingdom in 2004 compared with 348,000 girls. However, overall there were more women than men in the UK – 30.6 million and 29.3 million respectively (Table 1.2). In 2004 the numbers of men and women were similar from age 22, but by age 30 women outnumbered men. This is partly because of higher net in-migration among young women (aged 15 to 24) than men in recent years and higher death rates from accidents and suicide for young men than young women. Although at birth there were 105 boys for every 100 girls, by age 65 there were 94 men for every 100 women. The difference was most pronounced in the very elderly as women tend to live longer than men. The Second World War has also had an impact on the number of men aged over 80: at age 89 there were 40 men per 100 women in 2004.

The age structure of the population reflects past trends in births, deaths and migration. The number of people in any age group within the population depends on how many people are born in a particular period and how long they live. It is also affected by the numbers and ages of migrants moving to and from the country.

The population of the United Kingdom is ageing. There are increasing numbers of people aged 65 and over and decreasing numbers of children under 16. This is illustrated by the differences between the population pyramids for 1821 (when age was first collected in the census) and 2004 (Figure 1.3). In 1821 the population pyramid was much larger at the bottom than at the top showing large numbers of young people but

### Figure **1.3**

**Population: by sex and age, 1821 and 2004**

Great Britain

Millions

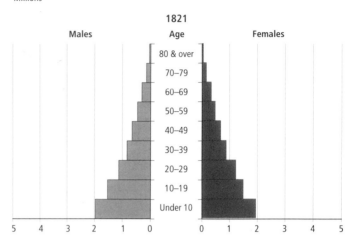

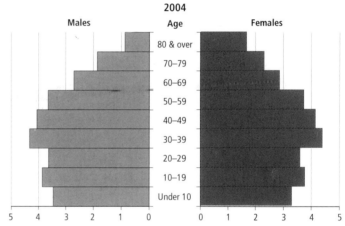

*Source: Office for National Statistics; General Register Office for Scotland*

few surviving to older ages. By 2004 the pyramid had become more uniform with similar numbers of people at all ages, except in the oldest age groups. The peaks of the 1960s 'baby boom' can be seen in the 30 to 39 age group. Those aged under 10 fell from 27 per cent of the population in 1821 to 12 per cent in 2004 while those aged 80 and over rose from 1 to 4 per cent.

Historically the ageing of the population was largely the result of a fall in fertility that began towards the end of the 19th century. Early in the 20th century the number of people surviving to adulthood increased due to lower infant mortality. In the last three decades of the 20th century population ageing has been due to both lower fertility and falling mortality rates at older ages.

The change in the population structure of Great Britain over time is also true for the United Kingdom with a decline in the younger population and an increase in those aged 65 and over.

## Table 1.4

### Population: by age, EU comparison, 2004

Percentages

| | Under 15 | 15–64 | 65 and over | All people (=100%) (thousands) | | Under 15 | 15–64 | 65 and over | All people (=100%) (thousands) |
|---|---|---|---|---|---|---|---|---|---|
| Austria | 16.3 | 68.1 | 15.5 | 8,140 | Luxembourg | 18.8 | 67.1 | 14.1 | 452 |
| Belgium | 17.3 | 65.6 | 17.1 | 10,396 | Malta | 18.2 | 68.7 | 13.0 | 400 |
| Cyprus | 20.0 | 68.1 | 11.9 | 730 | Netherlands | 18.5 | 67.6 | 13.8 | 16,258 |
| Czech Republic | 15.2 | 70.8 | 13.9 | 10,211 | Poland | 17.2 | 69.8 | 13.0 | 38,191 |
| Denmark | 18.9 | 66.2 | 14.9 | 5,398 | Portugal | 15.7 | 67.4 | 16.8 | 10,475 |
| Estonia[1] | 16.0 | 67.8 | 16.2 | 1,351 | Slovakia | 17.6 | 70.9 | 11.5 | 5,380 |
| Finland | 17.6 | 66.8 | 15.6 | 5,220 | Slovenia | 14.6 | 70.4 | 15.0 | 1,996 |
| France | 18.6 | 65.1 | 16.4 | 59,901 | Spain | 14.5 | 68.6 | 16.9 | 42,345 |
| Germany | 14.7 | 67.3 | 18.0 | 82,532 | Sweden | 17.8 | 65.0 | 17.2 | 8,976 |
| Greece | 14.5 | 67.7 | 17.8 | 11,041 | United Kingdom | 18.2 | 65.8 | 16.0 | 59,700 |
| Hungary | 15.9 | 68.6 | 15.5 | 10,117 | EU-25 | 16.4 | 67.2 | 16.5 | 456,890 |
| Ireland | 20.9 | 68.0 | 11.1 | 4,028 | | | | | |
| Italy | 14.2 | 66.6 | 19.2 | 57,888 | | | | | |
| Latvia | 15.4 | 68.4 | 16.2 | 2,319 | | | | | |
| Lithuania | 17.7 | 67.3 | 15.0 | 3,446 | | | | | |

1 'All people' includes data for individuals where age was not defined.

*Source: Eurostat*

In 1971 there were 14.3 million people aged under 16 and 7.4 million aged 65 and over. By 2004 there were 11.6 million people under 16, a decline of 2.6 million (18 per cent) and 9.6 million people over 65, an increase of 2.2 million (29 per cent). By 2014 projections suggest that the number of people over 65 will exceed those under 16 for the first time and then the gap will widen. By 2021 it is projected that 17.6 per cent of the population will be under 16 and 19.7 per cent will be aged 65 and over.

Population ageing is not just a characteristic of the United Kingdom but is happening throughout the European Union (Table 1.4). In 2004 Italy had the largest percentage of people aged 65 and over (19.2 per cent), followed by Germany (18.0 per cent) and Greece (17.8 per cent). Ireland had the lowest proportion, at 11.1 per cent. The United Kingdom had 16.0 per cent of the population aged 65 and over, just under the EU-25 average of 16.5 per cent. The United Kingdom also had a larger proportion of children under 15 than the EU-25 average – 18.2 per cent compared with 16.4 per cent. This was the same proportion as Malta and similar to France (18.6 per cent), the Netherlands (18.5 per cent) and Sweden (17.8 per cent). Ireland, which had the highest birth rate in Europe, has the largest percentage of the population aged under 15 at

20.9 per cent, nearly twice that of older people, followed by Cyprus (20.0 per cent). In seventeen of the EU-25 countries the young dependant population is larger than the older dependant population. As well as Ireland where the young dependant population is 9.7 percentage points greater than the older dependant population, these include Cyprus (8.1 percentage points) and the United Kingdom (2.2 percentage points). Conversely, Italy, Greece and Germany have an older population. Those countries with an older population structure have the combination of both a high chance of survival to old age and have experienced low fertility over the last decade. There were seven countries with less than a one percentage point difference between the younger and older population; Estonia and Belgium were the countries closest to zero.

Historically the population of Great Britain is made up of people from a White British ethnic background. The pattern of migration since the 1950s has produced a number of distinct ethnic minority groups within the general population. In 2001 the majority of the population in Great Britain were White British (88 per cent). The remaining 6.7 million people (or 11.8 per cent of the population) belonged to other ethnic groups. Of these smaller ethnic populations, White Other were the largest group (2.5 per cent), followed by Indians

## Figure **1.5**

### Population: by ethnic group[1] and age, 2001

**Great Britain**
Percentages

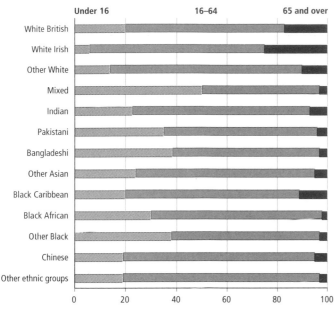

1  See Appendix, Part 1: Classification of ethnic groups.

**Source: Census 2001, Office for National Statistics; Census 2001, General Register Office for Scotland**

(1.8 per cent), Pakistanis (1.3 per cent), White Irish (1.2 per cent), those of Mixed ethnic backgrounds (1.2 per cent), Black Caribbeans (1.0 per cent), Black Africans (0.8 per cent) and Bangladeshis (0.5 per cent). The remaining ethnic minority groups each accounted for less than 0.5 per cent of the Great Britain population and together accounted for a further 1.4 per cent.

White ethnic groups have an older age structure than other ethnic groups, reflecting past immigration and fertility patterns. Among the White British population in Great Britain 17 per cent were aged 65 and over in 2001. The White Irish group however had the oldest age structure, with 25 per cent aged 65 and over (Figure 1.5). Among the non-White groups, Black Caribbeans had the largest proportion of people aged 65 and over (11 per cent), partly reflecting their earlier migration to Britain. Large scale migration from South Asia began in the 1960s so these groups have the next oldest population structures – between 4 and 7 per cent were aged 65 and over. Only 2 per cent of Black Africans were 65 and over, large scale migration to Britain having only begun since the 1980s. The Mixed group had the youngest age profile, with a very small proportion of people aged 65 and over (3 per cent). The majority of the Mixed group were born in the UK,

### Classification of ethnic groups

Membership of an ethnic group is something that is subjectively meaningful to the person concerned. Ethnic group questions are designed to ask people which group they see themselves belonging to.  This means the information collected is not based on objective, quantifiable information like age or gender.

There are two levels to the National Statistics classification of ethnic groups. Level 1 has five main ethnic groups: White, Mixed, Asian or Asian British, Black or Black British, Chinese or other ethnic group.  Level 2, the preferred approach, provides a finer breakdown than level 1 and is used here.

For more details see Appendix, Part 1: Classification of ethnic groups.

predominantly the children of partnerships between first or second generation migrants and White British people.

Besides ethnic diversity, migration during the latter part of the 20th century has also led to religious diversity in Great Britain (see article on ethnic and religious populations page 1).

Christianity was the main religion in Great Britain; 41 million people identified as Christians in 2001, making up 72 per cent of the population. People with no religion formed the second largest group, comprising 15 per cent of the population, and 8 per cent of the Great Britain population chose not to state their religion as the question was voluntary (see Appendix, Part 1: Religion). Muslims formed the largest non-Christian religious group, comprising 3 per cent of the total population. Hindus were the next largest group (1 per cent of the total population), followed by Sikhs (0.6 per cent), Jews (0.5 per cent) and Buddhists (0.3 per cent).

Ethnicity and religion tend to be closely linked. In 2001, 38 million people (nearly seven in ten) described their ethnicity as White British and their religion as Christian. Other large faith groups were Pakistani Muslims (686,000), Indian Hindus (471,000), Black Caribbean Christians (417,000), Black African Christians (334,000) and Indian Sikhs (307,000). The Indian group was the most religiously diverse of all ethnic groups; 45 per cent of Indians were Hindu, 29 per cent were Sikh, 13 per cent were Muslim and 5 per cent were Christian. In contrast, Pakistani and Bangladeshi groups tended to share the same faith, Muslims accounting for 92 per cent in both groups.

## Table **1.6**

### Main ethnic group: by religion, 2001

Great Britain

Percentages

| | White British | White Irish | Mixed | Indian | Pakistani | Bangladeshi | Black Caribbean | Black African | Chinese |
|---|---|---|---|---|---|---|---|---|---|
| Christian | 75.7 | 85.7 | 52.3 | 5.0 | 1.1 | 0.5 | 73.7 | 68.8 | 21.1 |
| Buddhist | 0.1 | 0.2 | 0.7 | 0.2 | - | 0.1 | 0.2 | 0.1 | 15.1 |
| Hindu | - | - | 0.9 | 44.8 | 0.1 | 0.6 | 0.3 | 0.2 | 0.1 |
| Jewish | 0.5 | 0.2 | 0.5 | 0.1 | 0.1 | - | 0.1 | 0.1 | 0.1 |
| Muslim | 0.1 | 0.1 | 9.7 | 12.6 | 91.9 | 92.4 | 0.8 | 20.0 | 0.3 |
| Sikh | - | - | 0.4 | 29.2 | 0.1 | - | - | 0.1 | - |
| Any other religion | 0.2 | 0.3 | 0.6 | 1.7 | 0.1 | - | 0.6 | 0.2 | 0.5 |
| No religion | 15.7 | 6.2 | 23.3 | 1.8 | 0.6 | 0.5 | 11.3 | 2.4 | 53.0 |
| Not stated | 7.7 | 7.4 | 11.6 | 4.7 | 6.2 | 5.8 | 13.0 | 8.2 | 9.8 |
| Total (=100%) (thousands) | 50,366 | 691 | 674 | 1,052 | 747 | 283 | 566 | 485 | 243 |

Source: Census 2001, Office for National Statistics; Census 2001, General Register Office for Scotland

Among Black Africans seven out of ten were Christian and two out of ten were Muslim (Table 1.6).

In the Labour Force Survey (LFS) information on socio-economic classification based on occupation is available for those of working age (16 to 59 for women and 16 to 64 for men). Students and those whose occupation was not stated or who were not classifiable for other reasons are excluded. The largest group in spring 2005 was the lower managerial and professional

occupational group both in total (22 per cent), and for men and women separately (20 and 24 per cent respectively) (Figure 1.7). The second largest group was those who had never worked or were long-term unemployed (18 per cent). The largest sex differences were in the higher managerial and professional occupational group where the proportion of men was 8 percentage points higher than women and in the intermediate occupational group where the proportion of women was 10 percentage points higher than men. Most men and women in

## Figure **1.7**

### Socio-economic classification: by sex, 2005[1]

United Kingdom

Percentages

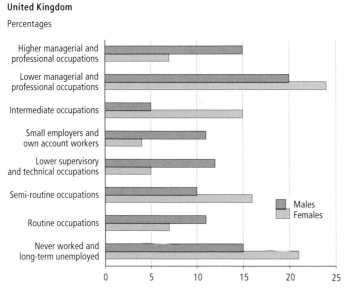

1 At spring. Males aged 16 to 64, females aged 16 to 59.

Source: Labour Force Survey, Office for National Statistics

### National Statistics Socio-economic Classification (NS-SEC)

NS-SEC was launched in 2001 to replace the Registrar Generals Social Class measure based on occupation. The NS-SEC is an occupationally based classification but has rules to provide coverage of the whole adult population. The information required to create the NS-SEC is occupation coded to the unit groups (OUG) of the Standard Occupational Classification 2000 (SOC2000) and details of employment status (whether an employer, self-employed or employee; whether a supervisor; number of employees at the workplace).

See Appendix, Part 1: National Statistics Socio-economic Classification (NS-SEC).

## Table **1.8**

### Population change[1]

United Kingdom

Thousands

| | Population at start of period | Annual averages | | | | |
|---|---|---|---|---|---|---|
| | | Live births | Deaths | Net natural change | Net migration & other | Overall change |
| 1951–1961 | 50,287 | 839 | 593 | 246 | 6 | 252 |
| 1961–1971 | 52,807 | 962 | 638 | 324 | -12 | 312 |
| 1971–1981 | 55,928 | 736 | 666 | 69 | -27 | 42 |
| 1981–1991 | 56,357 | 757 | 655 | 103 | 5 | 108 |
| 1991–2001 | 57,439 | 731 | 631 | 100 | 68 | 167 |
| 2001–2004 | 59,113 | 684 | 603 | 81 | 160 | 240 |
| 2004–2011 | 59,835 | 704 | 582 | 122 | 171 | 294 |
| 2011–2021 | 61,892 | 716 | 578 | 139 | 145 | 284 |

1 Mid-year estimates for 1951–1961 to 2001–2004; 2004-based projections for 2004–2011 and 2011–2021. See Appendix, Part 1: Population estimates and projections.

**Source: Office for National Statistics; Government Actuary's Department; General Register Office for Scotland; Northern Ireland Statistics and Research Agency**

the 16 to 19 age group (excluding students), had either never worked or were unemployed. For other age groups the lower managerial and professional group was the largest.

## Population change

The rate of population change over time depends upon the net natural change – the difference between numbers of births and deaths – and the net effect of people migrating to and from the country. In the 1950s and 1960s natural change was an important factor in population growth in the United Kingdom, although from the 1980s onwards net migration has had a growing influence (Table 1.8). Between 2001 and 2004 net migration accounted for two thirds of the population change resulting in an increase of 160,000 people, compared with an increase of 81,000 people due to natural change. This contrasts with the 1950s when net natural change accounted for 98 per cent of population change and net migration for only 2 per cent. In the 1960s and 1970s net out-migration was more than compensated for by natural increases and so the total population increased. Between 2011 and 2021, net migration is projected to result in an increase in the population of 145,000, and natural change an increase of 139,000, accounting for 51 per cent and 49 per cent of the total change respectively. These projections are dependent on net migration to the United Kingdom, as this influences the number of births and deaths.

There were 716,000 live births in the United Kingdom in 2004, an increase of 20,500 compared with 2003 (Figure 1.9). However, this was 34 per cent fewer births than in 1901 and 20 per cent fewer than 1971. The two World Wars had a major

impact on births. There was a fall in births during the First World War followed by a post war 'baby boom', with births peaking at 1.1 million in 1920. The number of births then fell and remained low during the inter-war period and the Second World War. Births increased again after the Second World War with another

## Figure **1.9**

### Births[1,2] and deaths[1]

United Kingdom

Millions

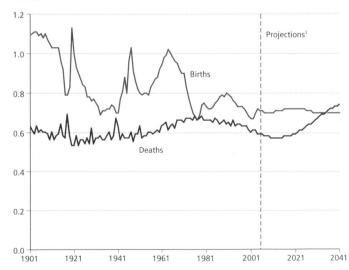

1 Data for 1901 to 1921 exclude Ireland which was constitutionally a part of the United Kingdom during this period.
2 Data from 1981 exclude the non-residents of Northern Ireland.
3 2004-based projections for 2005 to 2041.

**Source: Office for National Statistics; Government Actuary's Department; General Register Office for Scotland; Northern Ireland Statistics and Research Agency**

# Map **1.10**

## Population density: by area, 1901[1] and 2004[2]

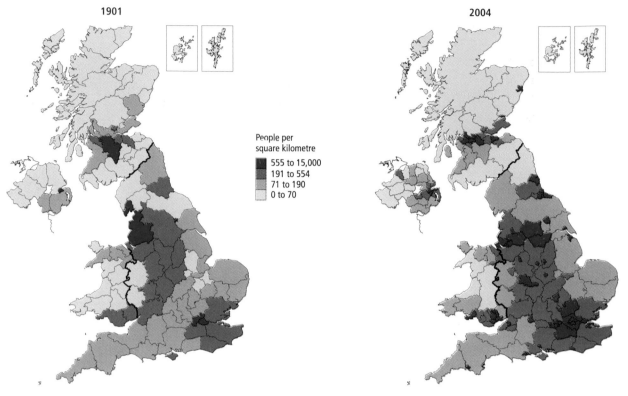

1901                                    2004

People per
square kilometre

■ 555 to 15,000
■ 191 to 554
□ 71 to 190
□ 0 to 70

1  Administrative boundaries for 1901 use some information from www.en.wikipedia.org.
2  Counties, unitary authorities, Inner and Outer London in England, unitary authorities in Wales, council areas in Scotland and district council areas in
   Northern Ireland for 2004.

**Source: Census 1901, 2004-based population estimates, Office for National Statistics; General Register Office for Scotland; Northern Ireland
Statistics and Research Agency**

'baby-boom'. There was an increase in births in the late 1980s
and early 1990s, the result of the larger cohorts of women born
in the 1960s entering their child-bearing years, before numbers
began falling again. The larger cohort of women having children
combined with increased numbers of births meant that birth
rates were only slightly changed. Projections to 2041 suggest
that the number of births will remain relatively stable ranging
from 700,000 to 720,000 each year.

The annual number of deaths has remained relatively steady
since 1901. However, as the population has increased death
rates have fallen; between 1971 and 2004 the death rate for all
males fell by 21 per cent, while the death rate for all females fell
by 9 per cent. There were peaks in the number of deaths during
both the First and Second World Wars. The peak of 690,000 in
1918 represented the highest annual number of deaths ever
recorded; these were due both to losses during the First World
War and the influenza epidemic which followed it. Population
projections suggest that the annual number of deaths will
decline to a low of around 570,000 between 2010 and 2015
and will then gradually rise to reach around 740,000 in 2041.

The steady increase in the population through both natural
change and net migration (Table 1.8) means that there is
now a larger population living in the same geographic space.
The measure of the number of people living in a country or
region relative to its land area is known as population density.
The population density of the four parts of the UK varies
considerably. In 2004 England had approximately 385 people
per square kilometre compared with 65 people resident per
square kilometre in Scotland. Wales had 142 people per
square kilometre and Northern Ireland had 126.

Due to boundary and classification changes it is difficult to
trace regional population densities over time. However, it is
still possible to see that London had the highest concentration
of people in both 1901 and 2004 (Map 1.10). This was also
true in 1801 when London was part of the county of Middlesex.
In 2004 Kensington and Chelsea in West London was the most
densely populated area, and Highland in Scotland had the
fewest people per square kilometre. The Belfast region was
the most densely populated area in Northern Ireland in both
1901 and 2004.

Regional changes in population in the United Kingdom are caused not just by births and deaths and by international migration, but also by people moving within the country. In 2004 England recorded a net loss of 25,000 people to other parts of the United Kingdom while other countries experienced a net inflow; Wales (10,900), Scotland (11,700) and Northern Ireland (2,300) (Table 1.11). Within England, London experienced the largest net loss of 105,100 people moving to elsewhere in the United Kingdom. The only other region in England to experience a net loss of people to other areas of the country was the West Midlands. The North East and North West regions of the UK both had little change in their populations due to internal migration. The remaining areas had a net inflow of people; in the case of the East Midlands, East, South East and South West regions there was a greater net inflow than experienced by Wales, Scotland or Northern Ireland. The majority of people leaving Scotland, Northern Ireland and Wales came to England, though there was no dominant place within England to which migrants moved. UK Census data for 2001 showed that while workers tended to move south to find employment, students were more likely to move to northern areas to study.

## International migration

The pattern of people entering and leaving the United Kingdom changed over the 20th century. During the first four decades there was a net loss due to international migration, but since 1983 there has generally been net migration into the United Kingdom. In 2004 nearly 222,600 more people migrated to the United Kingdom than left it. This estimated net inflow is 71,600 people higher than in 2003 and is the highest since the present method of estimation began in 1991 (see Appendix, Part 1: International migration estimates).

Since 1991 there has been an increase in international migration both in and out of the United Kingdom (Figure 1.12). In 1991 the estimated numbers of males and females migrating in and out of the country were very similar. In-migration for males was 157,200 and 171,200 for females. Out-migration for males was 145,600 and 139,300 for females. However from 1994 onwards the number of both males and females arriving to live in the United Kingdom exceeded the numbers leaving to live elsewhere; in 2003 the differences were 67,900 for males and 83,200 for females. The inflow of females has always been higher than the outflow. In 2003 single males were the group

## Table **1.11**

### Inter-regional movements[1] within the United Kingdom, 2004

|  |  |  | Thousands |
|---|---|---|---|
|  | Inflow | Outflow | Balance |
| England | 97 | 122 | -25 |
| North East | 41 | 39 | 1 |
| North West | 105 | 104 | 1 |
| Yorkshire & the Humber | 98 | 92 | 6 |
| East Midlands | 112 | 97 | 15 |
| West Midlands | 95 | 101 | -6 |
| East | 146 | 128 | 17 |
| London | 155 | 260 | -105 |
| South East | 223 | 208 | 15 |
| South West | 139 | 108 | 30 |
| Wales | 60 | 49 | 11 |
| Scotland | 57 | 45 | 12 |
| Northern Ireland | 12 | 10 | 2 |

1 Based on patients re-registering with NHS doctors in other parts of the United Kingdom. Moves where the origin and destination lie within the same region do not appear in the table. See Appendix, Part 1: Internal migration estimates.

**Source: National Health Service Central Register; General Register Office for Scotland; Northern Ireland Statistics and Research Agency**

## Figure **1.12**

### International migration into and out of the United Kingdom: by sex[1]

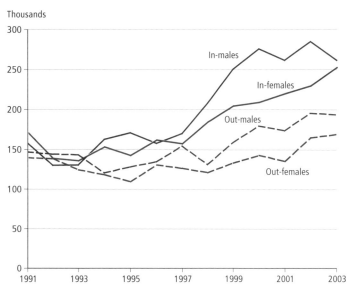

1 Estimates for Total International Migration use International Passenger Survey data adjusted for 'visitor switchers' (short term visitors granted an extension to stay a year or more), 'migrant switchers' (persons who intend to be migrants but stay in UK, or abroad for less than a year), most asylum seekers and their dependants and migration to and from Ireland.

**Source: Office for National Statistics**

# Figure **1.13**

## Grants of settlement: by region of origin

United Kingdom
Thousands

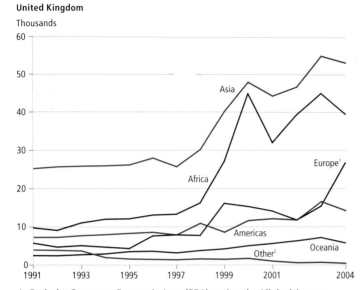

1  Excludes European Economic Area (EEA) nationals. All decisions on nationals from countries that acceded to the European Union on 1 May 2004 are included before that date but excluded after it.
2  Includes British Overseas citizens, those whose nationality was unknown and, up to 1993, acceptances where the nationality was not separately identified; from 1994 these nationalities have been included in the relevant geographical area.

**Source: Home Office**

with the highest proportion migrating both to and from the United Kingdom and widowed and divorced people were the smallest group. Out-migration for both sexes was highest in the 25 to 44 age group, while those over retirement age and children under 15 had the lowest numbers migrating in and out.

Almost half of overseas-born migrants to the United Kingdom in the 1970s, 1980s and 1990s emigrated again within five years of arrival. There were large variations by country of birth. Between half and two thirds of the migrants born in the European Union, North America and Oceania emigrated within five years compared with about a sixth of those born in the Indian subcontinent.

Nationals of the European Economic Area (EEA) (Europe plus Iceland, Liechtenstein, and Norway) have the right to reside in the United Kingdom provided they are working or are able to support themselves financially. Nearly all other overseas nationals wishing to live permanently in the United Kingdom require Home Office acceptance for settlement. Between 1991 and 2004 the number of acceptances for settlement in the United Kingdom more than doubled, rising from 53,900 to 139,260 (Figure 1.13). The largest increase in acceptances was for people from Europe (but excluding EEA nationals) which

# Table **1.14**

## Asylum applications, including dependants: EU comparison, 2004

|  | Number of asylum seekers[1] | Asylum seekers per 1,000 population |
|---|---|---|
| Austria | 24,700 | 3.0 |
| Belgium[2] | 17,500 | 1.7 |
| Cyprus[3] | 9,900 | 11.0 |
| Czech Republic[3] | 5,500 | 0.5 |
| Denmark | 3,200 | 0.6 |
| Estonia[3] | - | - |
| Finland | 3,900 | 0.7 |
| France | 65,600 | 1.1 |
| Germany | 35,600 | 0.4 |
| Greece[3] | 4,500 | 0.4 |
| Hungary[3] | 1,600 | 0.2 |
| Ireland | 4,800 | 1.2 |
| Italy[3] | 7,400 | 0.1 |
| Latvia[3] | - | - |
| Lithuania[3] | 200 | - |
| Luxembourg[3] | 1,600 | 3.2 |
| Malta[3] | 1,000 | 2.5 |
| Netherlands | 9,800 | 0.6 |
| Poland[3] | 8,100 | 0.2 |
| Portugal[3] | 100 | - |
| Slovakia[3] | 11,400 | 2.1 |
| Slovenia[3] | 1,300 | 0.6 |
| Spain | 5,600 | 0.1 |
| Sweden | 23,200 | 2.6 |
| United Kingdom | 40,600 | 0.7 |
| All applications to EU-25 | 286,800 | 0.6 |

1  Figures rounded to the nearest 100.
2  Figures based on Intergovernmental Consultations on Asylum, Refugees and Migration Policies in Europe, North America and Australia (IGC) data but adjusted to include an estimated number of dependants.
3  Figures based on United Nations High Commissioner for Refugees (UNHCR) data, including dependants.

**Source: Home Office**

nearly quadrupled, followed by those from Africa which tripled. The overall number of people accepted for settlement in the United Kingdom remained almost level between 2003 and 2004. The increase in acceptances from European countries outside the EEA, of 11,300 people, outweighted declines from all other areas leaving the total number stable. The main reason for acceptance in 2004 was for asylum, followed by employment reasons and family formation and reunion reasons.

# Table **1.15**

## World demographic indicators, 2004

| | Population (millions) | Population density (sq km) | Infant mortality rate[1,2] | Total Fertility Rate[2] | Life expectancy at birth (years)[2] | |
| --- | --- | --- | --- | --- | --- | --- |
| | | | | | Males | Females |
| Asia | 3,860 | 121 | 53.7 | 2.47 | 65.4 | 69.2 |
| Africa | 887 | 29 | 94.2 | 4.97 | 48.2 | 49.9 |
| Europe | 729 | 32 | 9.2 | 1.40 | 69.6 | 78.0 |
| Latin America & Caribbean | 554 | 27 | 26.0 | 2.55 | 68.3 | 74.9 |
| North America | 327 | 15 | 6.8 | 1.99 | 74.8 | 80.2 |
| Oceania | 33 | 4 | 28.7 | 2.32 | 71.7 | 76.2 |
| World | 6,389 | 47 | 57.0 | 2.65 | 63.2 | 67.7 |

1 Per 1,000 live births.
2 Data are for 2000-05.

**Source: United Nations**

The number of people seeking asylum in the United Kingdom varies from year to year. However the total number of asylum applications, including dependants, to EU-25 countries remained relatively steady between 1999 and 2002 but then fell in both 2003 and 2004. In 2004 the United Kingdom received 40,600 applications, a fall of 32 per cent compared with 2003 (Table 1.14). Applications to the United Kingdom peaked in 2002 at 103,100. Over a third of countries recorded a rise in applications between 2003 and 2004 (nine out of 25) although, with the exception of France, the overall numbers were still low. When the relative size of the countries' populations are taken into account, the United Kingdom ranked tenth in 2004, with a rate of 0.7 asylum seekers per 1,000 population. This was higher than the EU-25 average of 0.6 per 1,000 population. Cyprus had the highest rate at 11.0 per 1,000 population, followed by Luxembourg, Austria, Sweden, Malta and Slovakia which also had a large number of applications for asylum given the size of their population. In comparison with the EU countries, the USA received 63,000 asylum claims in 2004, 0.2 per 1,000 population and Australia received 3,300 claims, 0.2 per 1,000 population. In 2004 the majority of principal asylum applicants to the UK were aged under 35 years (82 per cent), 15 per cent were aged between 35 and 49 and only 3 per cent were aged 50 and older. Seventy per cent of principal applicants were male.

## International perspectives

In 2004 the world population was nearly 6.4 billion people (Table 1.15). Over 3.8 billion lived in Asia – 60 per cent, while 14 per cent lived in Africa and 11 per cent lived in Europe. The remaining 15 per cent lived in North America, Latin America

## Total Fertility Rate (TFR)

TFR is the average number of children a woman would have if she experienced the age-specific fertility rates of a particular year for her entire childbearing years. Changes in the number of births are in part due to changes in the population age structure. The TFR is commonly used to look at fertility because it standardises for the changing age structure of the population.

## Replacement level fertility

Replacement level fertility is the level at which a population would be exactly replacing itself in the long term, other things being equal. In developing countries this is valued at 2.1 children per woman to take account of infant mortality and those who choose not to have children.

and Oceania. Population density was also highest in Asia, with 121 people resident per square kilometre. Oceania was the least densely populated with only 4 people per square kilometre. All the areas shown in Table 1.15 are less densely populated than England, Wales and Northern Ireland, but Scotland is less densely populated than Asia (see page 16). It is estimated that the population of Africa will grow by 2.1 per cent between 2005 and 2010; while Europe will decline by 0.07 per cent. Most other areas are projected to have population growth during this period.

The Total Fertility Rate (TFR) varies widely between the different areas of the world. In Africa it was 4.97 children per woman in 2004 but in both North America and Europe the TFR

## Table **1.16**

### European demographic indicators, 2005

| | Population (millions) | Infant mortality rate[1,2] | Total Fertility Rate[2] | Life expectancy at birth (years) | | | Population (millions) | Infant mortality rate[1,2] | Total Fertility Rate[2] | Life expectancy at birth (years) | |
|---|---|---|---|---|---|---|---|---|---|---|---|
| | | | | Males | Females | | | | | Males | Females |
| Austria | 8.2 | 4.5 | 1.42 | 76.4 | 82.1 | Luxembourg[3] | 0.5 | 3.9 | 1.70 | 75.1 | 81.6 |
| Belgium[3] | 10.4 | 4.3 | 1.64 | 75.9 | 81.7 | Malta[3] | 0.4 | 5.9 | 1.37 | 76.4 | 80.4 |
| Cyprus[3] | 0.7 | 3.5 | 1.49 | 77.0 | 81.4 | Netherlands | 16.3 | 4.1 | 1.73 | 76.4 | 81.1 |
| Czech Republic | 10.2 | 3.7 | 1.23 | 72.6 | 79.0 | Poland | 38.2 | 6.8 | 1.23 | 70.0 | 79.2 |
| Denmark | 5.4 | 4.4 | 1.78 | 75.2 | 79.9 | Portugal[3] | 10.5 | 4.0 | 1.42 | 74.0 | 80.6 |
| Estonia[3] | 1.3 | 6.3 | 1.40 | 66.0 | 76.9 | Slovakia | 5.4 | 6.8 | 1.25 | 70.3 | 77.8 |
| Finland | 5.2 | 3.3 | 1.80 | 75.3 | 82.3 | Slovenia[3] | 2.0 | 3.7 | 1.22 | 73.2 | 80.7 |
| France | 60.6 | 3.9 | 1.90 | 76.7 | 83.8 | Spain | 43.0 | 3.5 | 1.32 | 77.2 | 83.8 |
| Germany | 82.5 | 4.1 | 1.37 | 75.7 | 81.4 | Sweden | 9.0 | 3.1 | 1.75 | 78.4 | 82.7 |
| Greece[3] | 11.1 | 3.9 | 1.29 | 76.6 | 81.4 | United Kingdom[3] | 60.0 | 5.1 | 1.74 | 76.2 | 80.7 |
| Hungary | 10.1 | 6.6 | 1.28 | 68.6 | 76.9 | | | | | | |
| Ireland[3] | 4.1 | 4.9 | 1.99 | 75.4 | 80.5 | | | | | | |
| Italy[3] | 58.5 | 4.1 | 1.33 | 76.8 | 82.5 | | | | | | |
| Latvia | 2.3 | 9.4 | 1.24 | 65.5 | 77.2 | | | | | | |
| Lithuania | 3.4 | 7.9 | 1.26 | 66.4 | 77.8 | | | | | | |

1  Per 1,000 live births.
2  Infant mortality rate and Total Fertility Rate data are for 2004.
3  Life expectancy data are for 2003.

*Source: Eurostat*

is below replacement level (1.99 and 1.40 children per woman respectively). This reflects the low infant mortality in these areas; in Europe and North America only 9.2 and 6.8 live births per 1,000 died before age one in 2004 respectively. However in Africa the infant mortality rate is 94.2 per 1,000, suggesting that nearly one in ten children will not survive to their first birthday. Life expectancy is also lower in Africa and is the only continent with life expectancy below the World average. In 2004 there was a difference in life expectancy of 26.6 years for males and 30.3 years for females between Africa and North America (the areas with the lowest and highest levels). For all continents female life expectancy is higher than male; the largest differences were in Europe where females could expect to live 8.4 years longer than males.

Total Fertility Rates were low throughout Europe, ranging from 1.99 children per woman in Ireland to 1.22 children per woman in Slovenia in 2004 (Table 1.16). The lowest fertility rates were found predominantly in countries which joined the EU-25 in 2004, with the lowest seven TFRs being recorded in these countries. Infant mortality rates followed a similar pattern, with the highest rates in the accession countries; though not necessarily the same accession countries as those with the lowest fertility rates. The United Kingdom had the highest infant mortality rate outside the accession countries in both 2003 and 2004.

Across Europe female life expectancy in 2004 ranged from 76.9 years in Estonia and Hungary to 83.8 years in Spain and France; a difference of 6.9 years. For males the difference in life expectancy was 12.9 years, from 65.5 years in Latvia to 78.4 years in Sweden. Within each country the difference between male and female life expectancy was highest in Latvia (11.7 years) and lowest in Malta (4.0 years), while the average differences for all EU-25 countries was 6.6 years. In the United Kingdom life expectancy was 76.2 years for men and 80.7 years for women: a difference of 4.5 years.

# Households and families

- The number of households in Great Britain increased by 30 per cent between 1971 and 2005 from 18.6 million to 24.2 million. (Table 2.1)

- The proportion of one-person households in Great Britain increased by 9 percentage points between 1971 and 1991, and a further 2 percentage points to 29 per cent in 2001 and then remained at this level to 2005. (Table 2.1)

- In England, young men were more likely than young women to live with their parents. In 2005, 57 per cent of men aged 20 to 24 did so compared with 38 per cent of women of the same age. (Table 2.5)

- In spring 2005 nearly one in four dependent children lived in a lone-parent family in Great Britain. (Page 24)

- In 2001 people from the Mixed ethnic group were the most likely to be married to someone outside their ethnic group in England and Wales. (Figure 2.10)

- In England and Wales the average age of mothers at childbirth increased by over two years from 26.6 in 1971 to 28.9 in 2004. (Table 2.17)

- There has been a rise in the proportion of births occurring outside marriage. In 1980, 12 per cent of all births in the United Kingdom were outside marriage; by 2004 this had increased to 42 per cent. (Table 2.19)

# Chapter 2

People live in a variety of household types over their lifetime. They may leave their parental home, form partnerships, marry and have children. They may also experience separation and divorce, lone-parenthood, and the formation of new partnerships, leading to new households and second families. People may also spend more time living on their own, either before forming relationships, after a relationship has broken down, or after the death of a spouse.

## Household composition

There were 24.2 million households in Great Britain in spring 2005 (Table 2.1). Although the population has been increasing, the number of households has increased faster because of the trend towards smaller household sizes. The number of households in Great Britain increased by 30 per cent between 1971 and 2005. The average household size fell over this period from 2.9 to 2.4 people. More lone-parent families, smaller family sizes, and the increase in one-person households has contributed to this decrease. The rise in one-person households has levelled off in recent years. As a proportion of all households it increased by 9 percentage points between 1971 and 1991, and a further 2 percentage points to 2001 and then remained at this level to 2005.

There has been a decrease in the proportion of households containing the 'traditional' family unit – couple families with dependent children – and an increase in the proportion of lone-parent families (Table 2.2). The proportion of households in Great Britain comprising a couple with dependent children fell from over a third in 1971 to less than a quarter in 2005. Over the same period the proportion of lone-parent

## Table **2.1**

### Households:[1] by size

| Great Britain | | | | | Percentages |
|---|---|---|---|---|---|
| | 1971 | 1981 | 1991 | 2001[2] | 2005[2] |
| One person | 18 | 22 | 27 | 29 | 29 |
| Two people | 32 | 32 | 34 | 35 | 35 |
| Three people | 19 | 17 | 16 | 16 | 16 |
| Four people | 17 | 18 | 16 | 14 | 13 |
| Five people | 8 | 7 | 5 | 5 | 5 |
| Six or more people | 6 | 4 | 2 | 2 | 2 |
| All households (=100%) (millions) | 18.6 | 20.2 | 22.4 | 24.2 | 24.2 |
| Average household size (number of people) | 2.9 | 2.7 | 2.5 | 2.4 | 2.4 |

1  See Appendix, Part 2: Households.
2  At spring. See Appendix, Part 4: LFS reweighting.

**Source: Census, Labour Force Survey, Office for National Statistics**

## Table **2.2**

### Households:[1] by type of household and family

| Great Britain | | | | | Percentages |
|---|---|---|---|---|---|
| | 1971 | 1981 | 1991 | 2001[2] | 2005[2] |
| **One person** | | | | | |
| Under state pension age | 6 | 8 | 11 | 14 | 15 |
| Over state pension age | 12 | 14 | 16 | 15 | 14 |
| **One family households** | | | | | |
| Couple[3] | | | | | |
| No children | 27 | 26 | 28 | 29 | 29 |
| 1–2 dependent children[4] | 26 | 25 | 20 | 19 | 18 |
| 3 or more dependent children[4] | 9 | 6 | 5 | 4 | 4 |
| Non-dependent children only | 8 | 8 | 8 | 6 | 6 |
| Lone parent[3] | | | | | |
| Dependent children[4] | 3 | 5 | 6 | 7 | 7 |
| Non-dependent children only | 4 | 4 | 4 | 3 | 3 |
| **Two or more unrelated adults** | 4 | 5 | 3 | 3 | 3 |
| **Multi-family households** | 1 | 1 | 1 | 1 | 1 |
| **All households (=100%) (millions)** | 18.6 | 20.2 | 22.4 | 23.8 | 24.2 |

1  See Appendix, Part 2: Households, and Families.
2  At spring. See Appendix, Part 4: LFS reweighting.
3  Other individuals who were not family members may also be included.
4  May also include non-dependent children.

**Source: Census, Labour Force Survey, Office for National Statistics**

households with dependent children doubled, to 7 per cent of households in 2005.

While Table 2.2 shows that over half of households were headed by a couple in spring 2005, Table 2.3 is based on people. It shows that over two thirds of people living in private households lived in couple family households in 2005. However, since 1971 the proportion of people living in the traditional family household of a couple with dependent children has fallen from just over a half to just over a third, while the proportion of people living in couple family households with no children has increased from almost a fifth to a quarter. One in eight people lived in a lone-parent household in spring 2005 – three times the proportion in 1971.

One of the most notable changes in household composition over the last three decades has been the increase in one-person households. In 2005 there were 7 million people living alone in Great Britain. The proportion of such households increased from 18 per cent in 1971 to 27 per cent in 1991. It then rose slightly to 29 per cent in 2001 and remained at this

## Table 2.3

### People in households:[1] by type of household and family

Great Britain · Percentages

| | 1971 | 1981 | 1991 | 2001[2] | 2005[2] |
|---|---|---|---|---|---|
| **One person** | 6 | 8 | 11 | 12 | 12 |
| **One family households** | | | | | |
| Couple | | | | | |
| No children | 19 | 20 | 23 | 25 | 25 |
| Dependent children[3] | 52 | 47 | 41 | 39 | 37 |
| Non-dependent children only | 10 | 10 | 11 | 8 | 9 |
| Lone parent | 4 | 6 | 10 | 12 | 12 |
| **Other households** | 9 | 9 | 4 | 4 | 5 |
| **All people in private households (=100%) (millions)** | 53.4 | 53.9 | 55.4 | 56.4 | 57.0 |
| **People not in private households (millions)** | 0.9 | 0.8 | 0.8 | .. | .. |
| **Total population (millions)[4]** | 54.4 | 54.8 | 56.2 | 57.4 | .. |

1 See Appendix, Part 2: Households, and Families.
2 At spring. See Appendix, Part 4: LFS reweighting.
3 May also include non-dependent children.
4 Data for 1971 to 1991 are census enumerated. Data for 2001 are 2001 mid-year estimates.

Source: Census, Labour Force Survey, Office for National Statistics

level to 2005. In the mid-1980s and 1990s these households mainly comprised older women. This was a reflection of there being fewer men than women in older age groups and, in particular, the tendency for women to outlive their partners. In 2004/05, 59 per cent of women aged 75 and over were living alone, much the same proportion as in 1986/87 (Figure 2.4). More recently there has been an increasing tendency for people to live on their own at younger ages. The largest increases over the past 20 years were among people aged 25 to 44 and men aged 45 to 64. These proportions more than doubled between 1986/87 and 2004/05.

Another notable change in family structure and relationships has been the increase in the number of adults who live with their parents (Table 2.5 overleaf). Some young people may remain at home while in education or because of economic necessity, such as difficulties entering the housing market (see Figure 10.22). Others may simply choose to continue living with their parents. Young men were more likely than young women to live with their parents. In 2005, 57 per cent of men aged 20 to 24 did so compared with 38 per cent of women of the same age. Between 1991 and 2005 the proportion of men and women in this age group who were living with their parents increased by over 6 percentage points.

There have been changes in the proportion of dependent children within different family types. There has been a fall in the percentage of children living in families headed by a couple with

## Figure 2.4

### People living alone: by sex and age[1]

Great Britain
Percentages

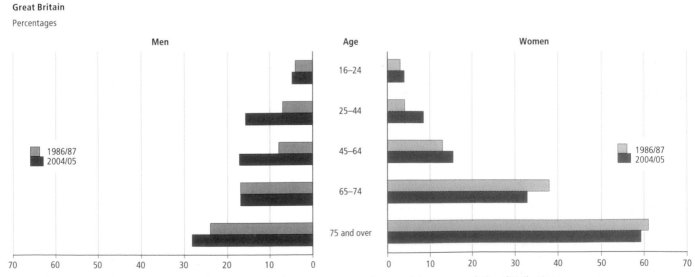

1 Data from 2001/02 onwards are weighted to compensate for nonresponse and to match known population distributions.

Source: General Household Survey, Office for National Statistics

## Table **2.5**

### Adults living with their parents: by sex and age

England

Percentages

| | 1991 | 2001[1] | 2002[1] | 2004[1] | 2005[1] |
|---|---|---|---|---|---|
| **Men** | | | | | |
| 20–24 | 50 | 57 | 56 | 59 | 57 |
| 25–29 | 19 | 22 | 19 | 23 | 23 |
| 30–34 | 9 | 8 | 8 | 8 | 8 |
| **Women** | | | | | |
| 20–24 | 32 | 36 | 37 | 38 | 38 |
| 25–29 | 9 | 11 | 10 | 11 | 11 |
| 30–34 | 5 | 3 | 2 | 4 | 3 |

1 At spring. See Appendix, Part 4: LFS reweighting.

*Source: Survey of English Housing, Office of the Deputy Prime Minister;*
*Labour Force Survey, Office for National Statistics*

three or more children since the early 1970s, and for couple families with two children since the early 1980s (Table 2.6). In spring 2005, 76 per cent of children lived in a family unit headed by a couple, compared with 92 per cent in 1972. In contrast there was an increase in the percentage of children living in lone-parent families which increased from 7 per cent in 1972 to 24 per cent in spring 2005. Lone mothers head around nine out of ten lone-parent families.

## Table **2.6**

### Dependent children:[1] by family type

Great Britain

Percentages

| | 1972 | 1981 | 1992[2] | 2001[2] | 2005[2] |
|---|---|---|---|---|---|
| **Couple families** | | | | | |
| 1 child | 16 | 18 | 17 | 17 | 18 |
| 2 children | 35 | 41 | 38 | 37 | 36 |
| 3 or more children | 41 | 29 | 28 | 24 | 23 |
| **Lone mother families** | | | | | |
| 1 child | 2 | 3 | 5 | 6 | 7 |
| 2 children | 2 | 4 | 6 | 8 | 8 |
| 3 or more children | 2 | 3 | 5 | 6 | 6 |
| **Lone father families** | | | | | |
| 1 child | .. | 1 | 1 | 1 | 1 |
| 2 or more children | 1 | 1 | 1 | 1 | 1 |
| **All children[3]** | 100 | 100 | 100 | 100 | 100 |

1 See Appendix, Part 2: Families.
2 At spring. See Appendix, Part 4: LFS reweighting.
3 Excludes cases where the dependent child is a family unit, for example, a foster child.

*Source: General Household Survey, Census, Labour Force Survey, Office for National Statistics*

### 'Reference person' definitions

Though the majority of households contain one family, some households contain multiple families, while others do not contain a family at all (for example, where the household consists of only one person or of non-related adults). This chapter mainly refers to the household reference person but some data are based on the family reference person. The UK Census 2001 defines family reference person and household reference person as follows:

### Family reference person (FRP)

In a couple family, the FRP is chosen from the two people in the couple on the basis of their economic activity. If both people have the same economic activity, the FRP is defined as the elder of the two, or if they are the same age, the first member of the couple on the form. The FRP is taken to be the lone parent in a lone-parent family.

### Household reference person (HRP)

For a person living alone, this person is the HRP. If the household contains one family the HRP is the same as the FRP. If there is more than one family in the household, the HRP is chosen from among the FRPs using the same criteria for choosing the FRP. If there is no family, the HRP is chosen from the individuals using the same criteria.

Among families with dependent children in the United Kingdom a high proportion of lone-parent families live in London and other built-up and industrial areas, such as Glasgow City and Manchester. In nine London boroughs, over 40 per cent of families with dependent children were lone-parent families in 2001; the highest were in Lambeth (48 per cent), Islington (47 per cent) and Southwark (46 per cent) (Map 2.7). Lone parenthood and cohabitation are more prevalent among the younger adults in Great Britain and this was reflected by major cities that had younger age structures (including Manchester, Glasgow City, Liverpool, Belfast and Nottingham). Across the United Kingdom the smallest proportion of lone-parent families were in the South East and East of England. Cohabiting couples with dependent children were least common in Northern Ireland. There were larger than average proportions of married couple families with dependent children in Northern Ireland, East Renfrewshire in Scotland and Hart in the South East of England.

Family type also varies by ethnic group. In the United Kingdom families of Asian and Chinese ethnic origin with dependent children were most likely to be married and least likely to be lone-parent families (Figure 2.8). In 2001, 85 per cent of Indian families with dependent children were headed by a married couple. Lone-parent families were most common among

## Map **2.7**

### Lone parent families with dependent children, 2001[1]

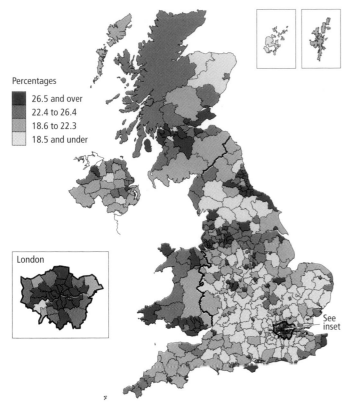

Percentages

- 26.5 and over
- 22.4 to 26.4
- 18.6 to 22.3
- 18.5 and under

London

See inset

1 Unitary and local authorities in England, unitary authorities in Wales, council areas in Scotland and district council areas in Northern Ireland.

**Source: Census 2001, Office for National Statistics; Census 2001, General Register Office for Scotland; Census 2001, Northern Ireland Statistics and Research Agency**

## Figure **2.8**

### Families with dependent children: by ethnic group and family type, 2001

United Kingdom
Percentages

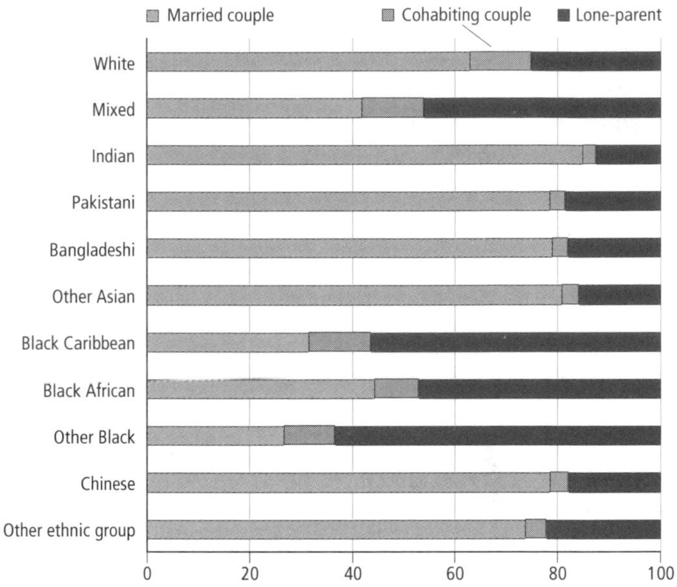

- Married couple
- Cohabiting couple
- Lone-parent

White
Mixed
Indian
Pakistani
Bangladeshi
Other Asian
Black Caribbean
Black African
Other Black
Chinese
Other ethnic group

0    20    40    60    80    100

**Source: Census 2001, Office for National Statistics; Census 2001, General Register Office for Scotland; Census 2001, Northern Ireland Statistics and Research Agency**

Other Black (64 per cent), Black Caribbean (57 per cent), Black African (47 per cent), and Mixed ethnic groups (46 per cent). Cohabiting couple families with dependent children were most common among Mixed, Black Caribbean and White families.

Among all families, those headed by a person of non-White ethnic background were more likely than White families to have dependent children living in them. In 2001 nearly four out of five Bangladeshi families in the United Kingdom contained at least one dependent child compared with over two out of five White families (the smallest for any ethnic group). Over 70 per cent of Black African, Other Black and Pakistani families had dependent children. These differences partly reflect the age structures of the non-White ethnic groups, and past immigration and fertility patterns. In 2001 Bangladeshi and Pakistani families were larger than families of all other ethnic groups, with an average household size of over four. The average family size of Indian and Other Asian families was more than three. Households headed by a person of White Irish, Black Caribbean or White British origin tend to be the smallest (2.2 to 2.3).

## Partnerships

The pattern of partnership formation has changed since the early 1970s but, despite the decrease in the overall numbers of people marrying, married couples are still the main type of partnership for men and women. In 2005 there were 17.1 million families in the United Kingdom and around seven in ten were headed by a married couple.

In 1950 there were 408,000 marriages in the United Kingdom. The number grew during the mid- to late-1960s to reach a peak of 480,300 in 1972. This growth was partly a result of the babies born in the immediate post-war boom reaching marriageable ages. Also at that time people got married at younger ages than in more recent years. The annual number of marriages then began to decline to reach a low of 286,100 in 2001 (Figure 2.9 overleaf). However there have since been indications of a slight increase. In 2003 there were 308,600 marriages, which was the second successive annual rise. It is too early to tell if this will become a longer term trend.

The age at which people get married for the first time has continued to rise. In 1971 the average age at first marriage was 25 for men and 23 for women in England and Wales; this increased to 31 for men and 29 for women in 2003. There has been a similar trend across Europe. Between 1971 and 2002 the average age at first marriage in the European Union prior

## Figure **2.9**

### Marriages and divorces

United Kingdom
Thousands

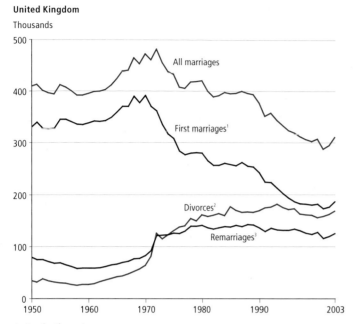

1 For both partners.
2 Includes annulments. Data for 1950 to 1970 for Great Britain only.
3 For one or both partners.

**Source: Office for National Statistics; General Register Office for Scotland; Northern Ireland Statistics and Research Agency**

to the ten accession countries joining in 2004 (the EU-15) increased from 26 to 30 for men and 23 to 28 for women. There were differences between all 25 Member States of the European Union (EU-25). In 2003 the country with the youngest newly-weds was Lithuania (27 for men and 24 for women). Sweden had the oldest (33 for men and 31 for women). Traditionally women have married men who are older than themselves. The average age difference between partners in first marriages ranged from just under two years in Ireland and in Portugal, to just under four years in Greece.

In England and Wales, three quarters of women marry men older than themselves. However an increasing proportion of women are marrying younger men. The proportion of couples where the husband was younger than the wife increased from 15 per cent for those who married in 1963 to 26 per cent for those who married in 2003. Over the same period, the proportion of couples where the man was at most five years older than the woman fell from just under two thirds to just under a half. There was only a small change in the proportion of marriages where the man was more than five years older than the woman: 21 per cent in 1963 compared with 27 per cent in 2003.

Two per cent of marriages were between people from different ethnic backgrounds in England and Wales in 2001. Proportions

of inter-ethnic marriages vary greatly between ethnic groups. People from the Mixed ethnic group were the most likely to be married to someone outside their ethnic group (78 per cent). This group is relatively small and there are limited opportunities to marry someone from the same ethnic group. White people are the least likely to be married to someone outside their ethnic group.

Black Caribbeans were more likely to be in an inter-ethnic marriage than Black Africans. Married people of Indian, Pakistani or Bangladeshi ethnicity had the lowest proportion of inter-ethnic marriages of the ethnic minority groups (Figure 2.10). Only 6 per cent of Indians, 4 per cent of Pakistanis and 3 per cent of Bangladeshis had married someone outside the South Asian group. This low inter-ethnic marriage rate may be explained by the fact that as well as cultural differences between the ethnic groups, people from South Asian backgrounds generally have different religions to people from other ethnic groups (see article on ethnic and religious populations, page 1). The most common inter-ethnic marriages were between White and Mixed ethnic groups (26 per cent). The next most common were between a White person and someone who described their ethnic group as 'Other' (15 per cent), followed by White and Black Caribbean marriages (12 per cent) and White and Indian marriages (11 per cent).

## Figure **2.10**

### Inter-ethnic marriages:[1] by ethnic group, 2001

England and Wales
Percentages

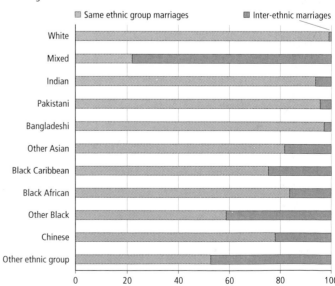

1 Defined as a marriage between people from different aggregate ethnic groups. For example, a White person married to someone from a non-White ethnic group or a Pakistani person married to someone from a non-Asian ethnic group.

**Source: Census 2001, Office for National Statistics**

## Table **2.11**

### Non-married people[1] cohabiting: by marital status and sex, 2004/05

Great Britain

Percentages

| | Men | Women |
|---|---|---|
| Single | 23 | 27 |
| Widowed | 12 | 6 |
| Divorced | 36 | 29 |
| Separated | 23 | 11 |

1 Aged 16 to 59. Includes those who described themselves as separated but were, in a legal sense, still married.

*Source: General Household Survey, Office for National Statistics*

The number of divorces taking place each year in Great Britain more than doubled between 1958 and 1969. By 1972 the number of divorces in the United Kingdom had doubled again. This latter increase was partly a result of the *Divorce Reform Act 1969* in England and Wales, which came into effect in 1971. The Act introduced a single ground for divorce – irretrievable breakdown – which could be established by proving one or more certain facts: adultery; desertion; separation either with or without consent; or unreasonable behaviour. Divorce was also permitted in Northern Ireland from 1969. Although there was a slight drop in the number of divorces in 1973, the number rose again in 1974 and peaked in 1993 at 180,000. The number of divorces then fell to 154,600 in 2000. In 2004 the number of divorces in the United Kingdom was 167,100, the fourth successive annual rise. The average age of divorce has increased over time from 39 in 1991 to 43 in 2004 for husbands and from 36 to 40 for wives for the same period.

Following divorce, people often form new relationships and may remarry. Remarriages, for one or both partners, increased by a third between 1971 and 1972 (after the introduction of the *Divorce Reform Act 1969*) in the United Kingdom, and peaked at 141,900 in 1988. In 2003 there were 123,300 remarriages, accounting for two fifths of all marriages.

The proportion of non-married people cohabiting has increased greatly since the mid-1980s among both men and women. The rise in cohabitation may in part be related to people marrying later in life. The percentage of non-married men and women under the age of 60 cohabiting in Great Britain increased between 1986 (the earliest year data are available on a consistent basis) and 2004; from 11 per cent to 24 per cent for men and from 13 per cent to 25 per cent for women.

Cohabiting men were usually divorced, whereas cohabiting women were equally likely to be divorced or single. In 2004/05,

36 per cent of divorced men and 29 per cent of divorced women aged under 60 were cohabiting; 23 per cent of cohabiting men under 60 were separated compared with 11 per cent of women (Table 2.11).

Cohabiting couple families are much younger than married couple families. In 2001, 50 per cent of cohabiting couple families in the United Kingdom were headed by a person aged under 35 compared with only 12 per cent of married couple families (Figure 2.12). A couple's age is taken from one of the adults. The difference in age between cohabiting and married couple families is mostly explained by whether they have children living with them. Cohabiting couples with no children were younger than married couples. This reflects the increase in the number of people cohabiting instead of, or before, getting married. Lone-parent families in 2001 were also younger than married couple families and lone-mother families were younger than lone-father families. Over 60 per cent of families with dependent children were headed by a person in their 30s or early 40s.

Changes in patterns of cohabitation, marriage and divorce have led to considerable changes in the family environment since the early 1970s. The number of children aged under 16 in England and Wales who experienced the divorce of their parents

## Figure **2.12**

### Age of family reference person:[1] by family type, 2001

United Kingdom

Percentages

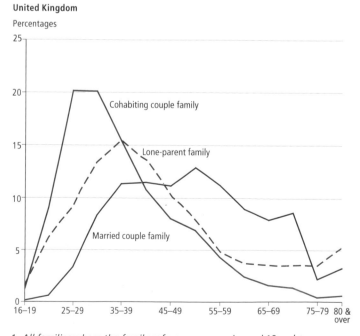

1 All families where the family reference person is aged 16 and over.

*Source: Census 2001, Office for National Statistics; Census 2001, General Register Office for Scotland; Census 2001, Northern Ireland Statistics and Research Agency*

## Figure **2.13**

### Children of divorced couples: by age of child

**England & Wales**

Thousands

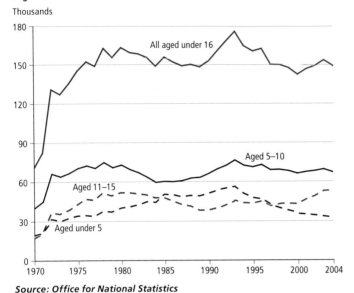

*Source: Office for National Statistics*

## Table **2.14**

### Stepfamilies[1] with dependent children:[2] by family type, 2001

**United Kingdom**

|  | Percentages | Thousands |
|---|---|---|
| Married couples with children from: |  |  |
| woman's previous marriage/cohabitation | 81 | 303.9 |
| man's previous marriage/cohabitation | 15 | 57.0 |
| both partners, previous marriage/cohabitation | 4 | 16.4 |
| **All married couple stepfamilies** | **100** | **377.3** |
| Cohabiting couples with children from: |  |  |
| woman's previous marriage/cohabitation | 85 | 265.8 |
| man's previous marriage/cohabitation | 10 | 32.4 |
| both partners, previous marriage/cohabitation | 5 | 15.1 |
| **All cohabiting couple stepfamilies** | **100** | **313.3** |
| All couples with children from: |  |  |
| woman's previous marriage/cohabitation | 82 | 569.7 |
| man's previous marriage/cohabitation | 13 | 89.4 |
| both partners, previous marriage/cohabitation | 5 | 31.5 |
| **All stepfamilies** | **100** | **690.7** |

1 All stepfamilies where the family reference person is aged 16 and over. A 'stepfamily' is one where there is a child (or children) who belongs to only one member of the married or cohabiting couple.

2 A dependent child is a person in a household aged 0 to 15 (whether or not in a family) or a person aged 16 to 18 who is a full-time student in a family with parent(s).

*Source: Census 2001, Office for National Statistics; Census 2001, General Register Office for Scotland; Census 2001, Northern Ireland Statistics and Research Agency*

peaked at 176,000 in 1993 (Figure 2.13). This fell to 142,500 in 2000, and then increased each year to reach 153,500 in 2003. This number decreased the following year by 3 per cent to 149,300 in 2004. A fifth of children affected by divorce in 2004 were under five years old and just under two thirds were aged ten or under.

Children are living in an increasing variety of different family structures during their lives. Parents separating can result in lone-parent families, and new relationships can create stepfamilies. The General Household Survey (GHS) showed that 10 per cent of all families with dependent children in Great Britain were stepfamilies in 2004/05. As children tend to stay with their mother following the break-up of a previous relationship, the vast majority (over 80 per cent) consisted of a stepfather and natural mother and 10 per cent consisted of a stepmother and natural father. In the 2001 Census, 38 per cent of cohabiting couple families with dependent children were stepfamilies compared with 8 per cent of married couple families with dependent children. Married couple stepfamilies were also more likely than cohabiting couple stepfamilies to have natural dependent children as well as stepchildren (57 per cent compared with 35 per cent) (Table 2.14).

## Family formation

Fertility patterns influence the size of households and families, and also affect the age structure of the population. The number of births fluctuated throughout the 20th century, but the overall trend was downward. There were sharp peaks in births at the end of both World Wars and a more sustained boom throughout the 1960s. Like births, fertility rates have fluctuated over this period, with similar peaks and an overall downward trend, from 115 live births per 1,000 women aged 15 to 44 at the start of the century to 57 in 1999. Fertility rates fell continually from the highs in the mid-1960s, resulting in a record low in births in 1977. Since then, fertility rates have remained at low levels. The number of births rose in the mid-1980s despite low fertility. These were sustained by the large generations of women born in the late 1950s and 1960s reaching their peak child-bearing age.

The Total Fertility Rate (TFR) is the number of children that would be born to a woman if current age patterns of fertility persisted throughout her child-bearing life. This measure summarises the fertility rates for women at each age occurring in one year. In 2004 the United Kingdom had a TFR of 1.77 children per woman. This was an increase from 1.71 in 2003 and a further increase from the record low of 1.63 in 2001. The UK rate in 2004 was higher than the average of 1.50 children per woman in the EU-25.

## Figure **2.15**

### Completed family size

United Kingdom
Average number of children per woman

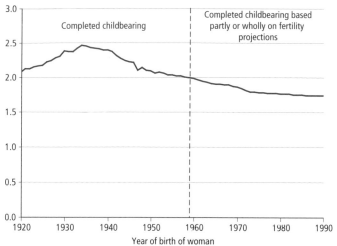

*Source: Office for National Statistics; Government Actuary's Department*

The average number of children per woman is used as an indicator of family size. In the United Kingdom this increased from 2.07 children for women born in 1920 to a peak of 2.46 children for women born in 1934 (Figure 2.15). This peak corresponds with the 1960s 'baby boom'. Family size declined for subsequent generations and is projected to decline to around 1.74 children for women born in the mid-1980s. Women born in 1959, and now at the end of their child-

bearing years, had an average of 1.99 children. Within the EU-25 countries family size for this generation of mothers was highest for Ireland (2.67 children) and lowest in Germany (1.67 children). The decline in family size among women born from the mid-1930s onwards is the result both of fewer women having large families, and more women remaining childless. In England and Wales, 31 per cent of women born in 1920 had given birth to three or more children by the end of their child-bearing years. This increased to around 40 per cent of women born in the 1930s and in 1940. It then dropped rapidly to a level of around 30 per cent and has remained at this level for women born after 1945.

Women are having children at an older age than they were 30 years ago. In general, fertility rates for women aged 30 and over have increased, while those for women in their 20s have declined (Table 2.16). However, there was an increase in fertility rates for women in their 20s from 2001 to 2004. Since 1992 the fertility rate for women aged 30 to 34 has exceeded that of women aged 20 to 24 and in 2004 it was higher than the rate for women aged 25 to 29, making this the age group with the highest fertility. This is despite the recent increase in fertility rates for women in their 20s. Changing attitudes to family sizes, delayed entry into marriage and cohabitation and increased female participation in education and the labour market are some of the factors that have encouraged the trend towards later child-bearing and smaller families.

In England and Wales the average age of mothers at childbirth increased by just over two years between 1971 and 2004, to 28.9 years (Table 2.17). Women have also been delaying starting a family, reflected by the increase in the age at which a woman has her first birth. In 2004 the average age at first birth was 27.1 years, over three years older than in 1971.

## Table **2.16**

### Fertility rates: by age of mother at childbirth

United Kingdom                                          Live births per 1,000 women

|                              | 1971  | 1981  | 1991  | 2001  | 2004  |
| ---------------------------- | ----- | ----- | ----- | ----- | ----- |
| Under 20[1]                  | 50.0  | 28.4  | 32.9  | 27.9  | 26.7  |
| 20–24                        | 154.4 | 106.6 | 88.9  | 68.0  | 71.5  |
| 25–29                        | 154.6 | 130.8 | 119.9 | 91.5  | 98.0  |
| 30–34                        | 79.4  | 69.4  | 86.5  | 88.0  | 99.1  |
| 35–39                        | 34.3  | 22.4  | 32.0  | 41.3  | 48.6  |
| 40 and over                  | 9.2   | 4.7   | 5.3   | 8.6   | 10.1  |
| Total Fertility Rate[2]      | 2.41  | 1.82  | 1.82  | 1.63  | 1.77  |
| Total births (thousands)     | 901.6 | 730.7 | 792.3 | 669.1 | 716.0 |

1  Live births per 1,000 women aged 15 to 19.
2  Number of children that would be born to a woman if current patterns of fertility persisted throughout her child-bearing life. For 1981 onwards, this is based on fertility rates for each single year of age, but for 1971 it is based on the rates for each five year age group.

*Source: Office for National Statistics*

## Table **2.17**

### Average age of mother:[1] by birth order[2]

England & Wales                                                                    Years

|                      | 1971 | 1981 | 1991 | 2001 | 2004 |
| -------------------- | ---- | ---- | ---- | ---- | ---- |
| 1st child            | 23.7 | 24.8 | 25.6 | 26.6 | 27.1 |
| 2nd child            | 26.4 | 27.3 | 28.2 | 29.2 | 29.5 |
| 3rd child            | 29.1 | 29.2 | 29.9 | 30.7 | 30.8 |
| 4th child            | 30.9 | 30.9 | 31.2 | 31.5 | 31.6 |
| 5th child and higher | 33.6 | 33.8 | 33.5 | 34.4 | 34.5 |
| All births           | 26.6 | 27.0 | 27.7 | 28.6 | 28.9 |

1  Age-standardised to take account of the changing population distribution of women.
2  See Appendix, Part 2: True birth order.

*Source: Office for National Statistics*

## Table **2.18**

### Childless women at ages 25, 35 and 45[1]: by year of birth

England & Wales

Percentages

|  | Age 25 | Age 35 | Age 45 |
|---|---|---|---|
| 1929 | 45 | 17 | 15 |
| 1939 | 35 | 13 | 12 |
| 1949 | 40 | 15 | 13 |
| 1959 | 54 | 22 | 18 |
| 1969 | 60 | 27 | . |
| 1979 | 69 | . | . |

1 Includes births at ages over 45.

**Source: Office for National Statistics**

The trend in waiting longer before starting a family is demonstrated by successive cohorts of women in England and Wales born since the Second World War who have waited longer before starting a family. Forty per cent of women born in 1949 were still childless at age 25; this increased to 69 per cent for women aged 25 who were born in 1979 (Table 2.18). There has also been a rise in childlessness at age 35 from 15 per cent of those born in 1949 to 27 per cent of those born

in 1969. The proportions of women reaching the end of the child-bearing years (age 45) who remained childless, rose from 13 per cent of women born in 1949 to 18 per cent of those born in 1959, the most recent cohort of women to have reached the end of their child-bearing years.

The average age of married women giving birth for the first time has increased by six years since 1971, to 30 in 2003. Births occurring outside marriage tend to take place at a younger age than those inside marriage. In 2001 women giving birth outside marriage were around four years younger than their married counterparts.

Although most children are born to married couples, there has been a substantial rise in the proportion of births occurring outside marriage. With the exception of the periods immediately after the two World Wars, few births occurred outside marriage during the first 60 years of the 20th century. During the 1960s and 1970s such births became more common. In 1980, 12 per cent of all births in the United Kingdom were outside marriage. By 2004 this figure was 42 per cent (Table 2.19). Most of the increase in the number of births outside marriage has been a result of the proportion of children registered by both parents rather than only one parent. This indicates an increase in cohabiting parents.

## Table **2.19**

### Births outside marriage: EU comparison

Percentages

|  | 1980 | 1990 | 2000 | 2002[1] | 2003 | 2004 |
|---|---|---|---|---|---|---|
| Austria | 18 | 24 | 31 | 33 | 35 | 36 |
| Belgium[2] | 4 | 12 | 26 | 28 | 31 | .. |
| Denmark | 33 | 46 | 45 | 45 | 45 | 45 |
| Finland | 13 | 25 | 39 | 40 | 40 | 41 |
| France | 11 | 30 | 43 | 44 | 45 | .. |
| Germany | 12 | 15 | 23 | 25 | 27 | 28 |
| Greece | 1 | 2 | 4 | 4 | 5 | 5 |
| Ireland | 5 | 15 | 32 | 31 | 31 | .. |
| Italy[3] | 4 | 7 | 10 | 11 | 14 | 15 |
| Luxembourg | 6 | 13 | 22 | 23 | 25 | 26 |
| Netherlands | 4 | 11 | 25 | 27 | 31 | 33 |
| Portugal | 9 | 15 | 22 | 24 | 27 | 29 |
| Spain[2] | 4 | 10 | 18 | 20 | 23 | .. |
| Sweden | 40 | 47 | 55 | 55 | 56 | 55 |
| United Kingdom | 12 | 28 | 39 | 40 | 42 | 42 |
| EU-15 average[2,3] | 10 | 20 | 29 | 30 | 32 | 33 |

1 Data for Belgium, Spain, Italy and EU-15 average are for 2001.
2 Data for 2003 are estimated.
3 Data for 2004 are estimated.

**Source: Eurostat**

Table **2.20**

**Teenage conceptions:[1] by age at conception and outcome, 2003**

England & Wales

| | Conceptions (numbers) | Leading to abortions (percentages) | Rates per 1,000 females[2] | | |
| --- | --- | --- | --- | --- | --- |
| | | | Leading to maternities | Leading to abortions | All conceptions |
| Under 14 | 334 | *62* | 0.4 | 0.6 | 1.0 |
| 14 | 1,888 | *64* | 2.0 | 3.6 | 5.7 |
| 15 | 5,802 | *55* | 7.7 | 9.4 | 17.2 |
| All aged under 16 | 8,024 | *57* | 3.4 | 4.6 | 8.0 |
| 16 | 13,303 | *46* | 21.7 | 18.4 | 40.1 |
| 17 | 20,835 | *41* | 37.5 | 26.1 | 63.6 |
| All aged under 18 | 42,162 | *46* | 13.7 | 11.5 | 42.3 |
| 18 | 26,610 | *38* | 50.2 | 30.4 | 80.6 |
| 19 | 29,820 | *35* | 60.4 | 32.3 | 92.7 |
| All aged under 20 | 98,592 | *40* | 35.7 | 24.1 | 59.8 |

*1 See Appendix, Part 2: Conceptions.*
*2 Rates for females aged under 14, under 16, under 18 and under 20 are based on the population of females aged 13, 13 to 15, 15 to 17 and 15 to 19 respectively.*

**Source: Office for National Statistics**

In 2004 the United Kingdom was among the EU-15 countries with the highest levels of births outside marriage, together with Sweden, Denmark, France and Finland (using 2003 data for France, which is the latest available). The highest proportion was in Sweden with 55 per cent, while the lowest proportion was in Greece, at 5 per cent.

Despite the overall trend towards later child-bearing (and the fall in fertility among the under 20s), the teenage pregnancy rate in England and Wales rose in the 1980s, but then fell slightly in the 1990s. There were 98,600 conceptions to girls aged under 20 in 2003 of which less than a tenth were to girls under the age of 16 (Table 2.20). Between 2002 and 2003 the under 20 conception rate fell by 1 per cent from 60.3 to 59.8 conceptions per thousand females aged 15 to 19. The number of conceptions to girls under 14 decreased from 390 in 2002 to 334 in 2003 and just under two fifths of these led to maternities. Between ages 16 and 19, the proportion of conceptions resulting in abortions is lower than at younger ages. Over a third of conceptions to 19 year olds resulted in an abortion, compared with under half of conceptions to 16 year olds.

In 2003 the United Kingdom had the highest rate of live births to teenagers in the EU-25, with an average of 26 live births per 1,000 females aged 15 to 19. This was 19 per cent higher than in Latvia, the country with the next highest rate. Cyprus, Slovenia, Sweden and Denmark had the lowest rates, with around 6 births per 1,000 females aged 15 to 19.

Trends in abortion rates also vary by age of women (Figure 2.21). Since 1969, following the introduction of the *Abortion Act 1967*, abortion rates have risen overall but particularly for women

Figure **2.21**

**Abortion rates:[1] by age**

England & Wales

Rates per 1,000 women

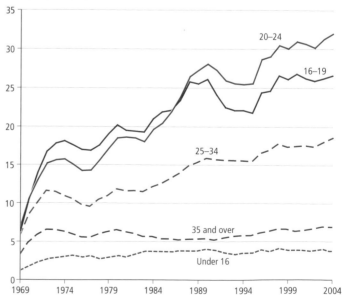

*1 The rates for girls aged under 16 are based on the population of girls aged 13–15. The rates for women aged 35 and over are based on the population of women aged 35–44.*

**Source: Office for National Statistics; Department of Health**

# Table **2.22**

## Maternities with multiple births: by age of mother at childbirth, 2004

United Kingdom

Rate per 1,000 maternities

|  | Maternities with twins only | Maternities with triplets and over |
|---|---|---|
| Under 20 | 6.7 | 0.1 |
| 20–24 | 9.1 | 0.1 |
| 25–29 | 12.8 | 0.2 |
| 30–34 | 17.5 | 0.3 |
| 35–39 | 20.9 | 0.4 |
| 40 and over | 20.9 | 0.4 |
| All mothers | 14.6 | 0.2 |

*Source: Office for National Statistics; General Register Office for Scotland; Northern Ireland Statistics and Research Agency*

# Figure **2.23**

## Adoption orders: by year of registration[1] and whether adopted child was born within or outside marriage[2]

England & Wales

Thousands

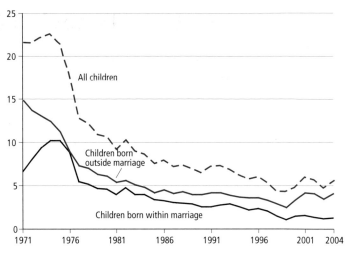

1 Year of entry into the Adopted Children Register. Data for 1990 and 2001 include cases where age of child was greater than 17 years.
2 Data for all children for 1985 to 1989 include cases where marital status was not stated. Where marital status for 1998 are missing they have been imputed.

*Source: Office for National Statistics*

aged between 16 and 34 years. In 2004 women aged between 20 and 24 years had the highest rate, at 31.9 per 1,000 women, whereas girls aged 13 to 15 had the lowest rate, at 3.7 per 1,000 girls.

During the early 1990s the abortion rate among young women aged 16 to 24 fell slightly, but then rose again – as it did for all age groups – between 1995 and 1996. This increase is thought to have been the result of a pill scare. In 1995 the Committee on Safety of Medicines warned that several brands of the contraceptive pill carried an increased risk of thrombosis. This warning is believed to have contributed to an increase in abortion rates in 1996, particularly among young women as they were more likely to have been using the pill. Since the pill scare, abortion rates have not fallen back to the 1995 level but have continued to rise for all age groups except for those aged under 16.

The rate of multiple births increased from 13.2 per 1,000 of all maternities in 1994 to 14.9 per 1,000 of all maternities in 2004. This could be a result of the increased use of IVF (in vitro fertilisation) treatment. In 2004 twins were born at a rate of 14.6 per 1,000 maternities, while 0.2 per 1,000 maternities led to triplets, quadruplets or more (Table 2.22). Multiple-birth rates are higher for women over the age of 35. Among women aged 35 to 39 years and 40 and over, twins accounted for 20.9 per 1,000 maternities, and triplets for 0.4 per 1,000

maternities. In comparison, for women aged under 20 the rates were 6.7 and 0.1 respectively.

Another way in which people may extend their families is through adoption. In 2004 there were 5,500 adoptions in England and Wales, with 47 per cent of adopted children being between one and four years old. Increased use of contraception, new abortion laws and changed attitudes towards lone motherhood have meant that 16,000 fewer children were adopted in 2004 in England and Wales than in 1971 (Figure 2.23).

There was a rapid decline in the number of children available for adoption following the introduction of legal abortion in the *Abortion Act 1967* and after the implementation of the *Children Act 1975*. This latter Act required courts dealing with adoption applications for children of divorced parents to dismiss applications for adoption where a legal custody order was in the child's best interests. Despite these changes, one quarter of the children adopted in England and Wales in 2004 were born inside marriage.

# Education and training

- The proportion of three and four year olds enrolled in all schools in the United Kingdom rose from 21 per cent in 1970/71 to 65 per cent in 2004/05. (Figure 3.1)

- In 2004 persistent truants in year 11 in England and Wales were around six times less likely than those who did not truant to gain five or more GCSEs grades A* to C (or the equivalent). (Figure 3.14)

- In England and Wales 76 per cent of pupils whose parents were in higher professional occupations achieved five or more GCSEs grades A* to C (or the equivalent) in 2004 compared with 33 per cent of those whose parents were in routine occupations. (Page 41)

- In spring 2005, 22 per cent of employees qualified to degree level in the United Kingdom received job-related training in the four weeks prior to interview, compared with 5 per cent of those with no qualifications. (Page 44)

- In 2003/04 there were around 32,400 entrants into teaching in maintained schools in England; 64 per cent of these were new to teaching. (Figure 3.23)

- In 2004/05, 81 per cent of eligible students in the United Kingdom took out a loan to support them through higher education, the average amount being £3,390. (Page 47)

# Chapter 3

For increasing numbers of people, experience of education is no longer confined to compulsory schooling. Early learning and participation in pre-school education is seen as being important for building a foundation for future learning, and most people continue in full-time education beyond school-leaving age. Qualifications attained at school are increasingly supplemented by further education and training to equip people with the skills required by a modern labour market.

## Pre-school education

There has been a major expansion in pre-school education over the last 30 or so years with the aim of ensuring that all children begin their compulsory education with key skills such as listening, concentration and learning to work with others, as well as a basic foundation in literacy and numeracy. The proportion of three and four year olds enrolled in all schools in the United Kingdom rose from 21 per cent in 1970/71 to 65 per cent in 2004/05 (Figure 3.1). This reflects both the growth in the number of places – there were over 3,400 state nursery schools in 2004/05, two and a half times the number in 1990/91 – and a fall in the three and four year old population in recent years. In 2004/05, 35 per cent of three and four year olds were enrolled in other non-school settings offering early education such as playgroups in the private and voluntary sectors, either instead of, or in addition to, their school place.

The pattern of participation varies regionally. The proportion of three and four year olds in maintained nursery and primary schools is generally higher in Wales and the north of England

### Figure **3.1**

#### Children under five[1] in schools as a percentage of all three and four year olds

**United Kingdom**
Percentages

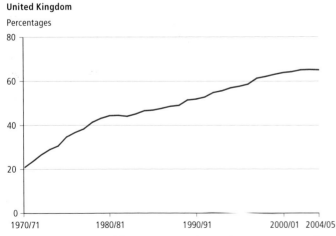

1 Pupils aged three and four at 31 December each year. See Appendix, Part 3: Stages of education.

*Source: Department for Education and Skills; National Assembly for Wales; Scottish Executive; Northern Ireland Department of Education*

than in the south of England. In January 2005 around twice the proportion of three and four year olds attended maintained nursery and primary schools in the North East (84 per cent) and Wales (80 per cent) compared with the South East (42 per cent) and South West (43 per cent) of England. However, more children were enrolled with private and voluntary providers in the south than in other parts of the country.

In 2004 over a quarter of adults aged 18 and over questioned in the British Social Attitudes survey thought that cheaper nursery education and childcare would be the most important improvement for improving nursery education and childcare for children under five years of age, while over a fifth of respondents said an increase in the number of nursery and childcare places would be the most important improvement (Table 3.2).

Respondents were also asked about funding childcare. When asked who should be responsible for paying for the cost of childcare for a couple on a relatively high income (whose child goes to nursery while they both work), 82 per cent of

### Table **3.2**

#### Attitudes to improving nursery education and childcare:[1] by sex, 2004

**Great Britain**                                           Percentages

|  | Men | Women | All |
| --- | --- | --- | --- |
| Cheaper nursery education and childcare | 23 | 28 | 26 |
| Increase number of nursery and childcare places | 22 | 22 | 22 |
| More choice for parents in the sorts of nursery and childcare available locally | 15 | 14 | 14 |
| Better quality nursery and childcare staff | 15 | 13 | 14 |
| More flexible opening hours or term times | 12 | 10 | 11 |
| More places for very young children | 6 | 6 | 6 |
| More information about the nursery education and childcare available locally | 4 | 4 | 4 |
| None of the above | 2 | 1 | 2 |
| Other | 2 | 2 | 2 |
| All | 100 | 100 | 100 |

1 Adults aged 18 and over were shown the above list and asked 'This card shows a number of things that some people think would improve the nursery education and childcare outside the family, available for children under 5. From what you have heard, which, if any, would be the most important improvement?' Excludes those who answered 'Don't know' or did not answer.

*Source: British Social Attitudes Survey, National Centre for Social Research*

respondents said that responsibility should rest mainly with the couple themselves. In contrast, 10 per cent said responsibility should lie mainly with the Government, through taxation. When asked the same question regarding a couple on a relatively low income, 16 per cent of respondents said the couple themselves should be mainly responsible for paying for the childcare, while 66 per cent said the Government should be responsible. In both cases only small proportions suggested their employers should be mainly responsible, 5 per cent and 11 per cent respectively.

## Compulsory education

In 2004/05 there were around 34,400 schools in the United Kingdom, accommodating just under 10 million pupils (Table 3.3). Public sector schools (not including special schools) were attended by 9.2 million pupils (92 per cent), while 7 per cent of pupils attended one of the 2,500 non-maintained mainstream schools. These proportions have remained around this level since the 1970s. One per cent of pupils attended one of the 1,400 special schools in 2004/05, and there were almost 480 pupil referral units (PRUs), catering for 15,000 pupils. PRUs provide suitable alternative education on a temporary basis for pupils who may not be able to attend a mainstream school.

The Government expects that over 80 per cent of all secondary schools in England will become specialist schools by September 2006. Specialist schools receive extra funding to establish curriculum centres of excellence and although they focus on one or two chosen specialisms, these schools must still meet national curriculum requirements and deliver a broad and balanced education to all pupils. Any maintained secondary school in England can apply to be designated as a specialist school. In September 2005 there were 2,380 schools in the specialist schools programme.

In England and Wales parents have the right to express a preference for a maintained school at all stages of their child's education. If their choice is not met, they may appeal against the decision to a panel made up of representatives that are independent of the school's governing body and the local authority that maintains the school. Not all appeals are heard by an appeal panel, as parents may be offered places that become available either at the school they have appealed for, or at another suitable school, before their appeal can be heard. As parents may lodge multiple appeals, they may withdraw other appeals if an earlier one has been successful.

The number of admission appeals to secondary schools in England increased by over two and a half times between

## Table 3.3

### School pupils:[1] by type of school[2]

United Kingdom

Thousands

|  | 1970/71 | 1980/81 | 1990/91 | 2000/01 | 2003/04 | 2004/05 |
|---|---|---|---|---|---|---|
| **Public sector schools** | | | | | | |
| Nursery | 50 | 89 | 105 | 152 | 150 | 142 |
| Primary | 5,902 | 5,171 | 4,955 | 5,298 | 5,107 | 5,045 |
| Secondary | | | | | | |
| Comprehensive | 1,313 | 3,730 | 2,925 | 3,340 | 3,456 | 3,457 |
| Grammar | 673 | 149 | 156 | 205 | 216 | 217 |
| Modern | 1,164 | 233 | 94 | 112 | 107 | 107 |
| Other | 403 | 434 | 298 | 260 | 235 | 220 |
| **All public sector schools** | 9,507 | 9,806 | 8,533 | 9,367 | 9,271 | 9,189 |
| **Non-maintained schools** | 621 | 619 | 613 | 626 | 654 | 652 |
| **Special schools** | 103 | 148 | 114 | 113 | 109 | 107 |
| **Pupil referral units** | . | . | . | 10 | 13 | 15 |
| **All schools** | 10,230 | 10,572 | 9,260 | 10,116 | 10,048 | 9,963 |

1 Headcounts.
2 See Appendix, Part 3: Stages of education, and Main categories of educational establishments.

**Source: Department for Education and Skills; National Assembly for Wales; Scottish Executive; Northern Ireland Department of Education**

## Figure **3.4**

### Appeals by parents against non-admission of their children to maintained schools decided in parents' favour[1]

England

Percentages

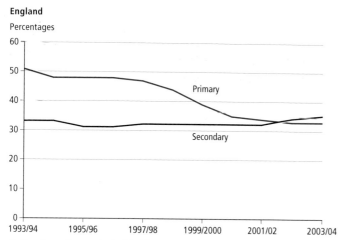

1  Number of appeals decided in favour of the parents expressed as a percentage of the number of appeals heard by panels.

**Source: Department for Education and Skills**

## Figure **3.5**

### School classes[1] with 31 or more pupils

England

Percentages

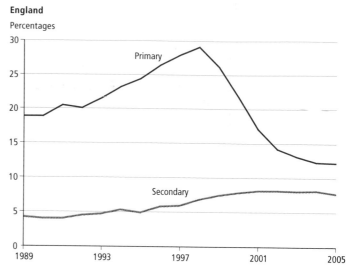

1  Classes taught by one teacher, in maintained schools. Data are at January each year.

**Source: Department for Education and Skills**

1993/94 and 2003/04 from 24,600 to 65,200, as have the number of appeals decided in the parents' favour, rising from 5,900 to 16,300. Around a third of appeals lodged to secondary schools and heard by the appeals panel in England were decided in favour of the parents each year since 1993/94 (Figure 3.4). The number of admission appeals both lodged to primary schools and heard by panels increased after 1993/94 to peak in 1996/97 and after another peak in 1998/99 the number of appeals lodged and heard by panels fell. In 2003/04, 20,800 appeals were lodged and 13,200 heard – slightly fewer than in 1993/94. However the success rate for decisions in the parents' favour in primary schools declined from 51 per cent of appeals heard by appeal panels in 1993/94 to 33 per cent in 2003/04.

For several years reductions have been made in class sizes, particularly in the size of primary classes. In January 1989, 19 per cent of classes taught by one teacher in primary schools in England had 31 or more pupils; this proportion increased to 29 per cent in January 1998 (Figure 3.5). Since January 1998, the proportion of primary school classes in England with 31 or more pupils has fallen to 12 per cent in January 2005. There is a marked difference in class sizes between Key Stage 1 (5 to 7 year olds) and Key Stage 2 (7 to 11 year olds). In January 2005 around 2 per cent of classes at Key Stage 1 had 31 or more pupils, whereas at Key Stage 2 the proportion was 21 per cent.

In 2004/05, the average class size in Great Britain (based on all classes – not just those taught by one teacher) was 25 pupils for Key Stage 1, and 27 pupils for Key Stage 2. Key Stage 2

pupils were far more likely than Key Stage 1 pupils to be in classes of 31 or more pupils (20 per cent and 2 per cent, respectively). At least one in four Key Stage 2 classes in the East Midlands, South West and North West had 31 or more pupils in 2004/05 compared with around one in ten classes in London and even fewer in Northern Ireland and Wales.

Average class size in Key Stages 3 and 4 (11 to 16 year olds) in England was around 22 pupils, despite secondary schools being larger than primary schools. This small average class size is in part because students choose different subjects in preparation for formal exams at the end of their compulsory secondary schooling.

Some pupils have special educational needs (SEN), this means they have significantly greater difficulty in learning than other children of the same age, or have a disability that makes it difficult for them to use normal educational facilities. When a school identifies a child with SEN it must try and meet the child's needs, having regard to provisions outlined in the SEN Code of Practice (or in Scotland, the Code of Practice on supporting children's learning). If the initial attempts do not meet the child's needs then an education authority or board may determine the education for a child with SEN, and if so can draw up a formal statement of those needs and the action it intends to take to meet them. Over 286,000 pupils in the United Kingdom had these statements (called a Co-ordinated Support Plan in Scotland from late 2005 but previously known as a Record of Needs) in 2004/05 compared with 273,000 in 1996/97.

## Figure **3.6**

### Pupils with statements of Special Educational Needs (SEN):[1] by type of need, 2005[2]

**England**
Percentages

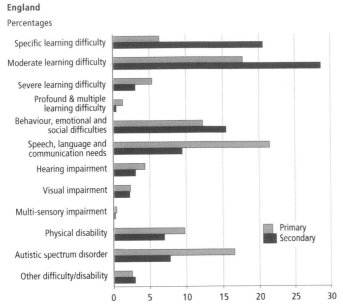

Specific learning difficulty
Moderate learning difficulty
Severe learning difficulty
Profound & multiple learning difficulty
Behaviour, emotional and social difficulties
Speech, language and communication needs
Hearing impairment
Visual impairment
Multi-sensory impairment
Physical disability
Autistic spectrum disorder
Other difficulty/disability

Primary
Secondary

0  5  10  15  20  25  30

1 As a proportion of all children with statements of SEN in maintained primary and secondary schools.
2 Data are at January.

*Source: Department for Education and Skills*

In England the number of pupils with statements of SEN increased from 195,000 in January 1994 to peak at an estimated 258,000 in 2001. Numbers have since declined to around 243,000 in January 2005. In Scotland there were 16,200 pupils with a Record of Needs in 2004/05, and in Wales and Northern Ireland, there were 15,900 and 11,500 pupils with statements respectively.

Figure 3.6 shows the most prevalent types of special educational need among pupils in England with statements of SEN. In January 2005 the most prevalent need of pupils in primary schools was speech, language and communication (21 per cent). A slightly smaller proportion (18 per cent) had moderate learning difficulties. Children with moderate learning difficulties have much greater difficulty than their peers in acquiring basic literacy and numeracy skills and in understanding concepts. They may also have low levels of concentration and under-developed social skills. This type of need was the most prevalent among secondary school pupils with statements of SEN (29 per cent), followed by specific learning difficulty (21 per cent). Children with a specific learning difficulty have particular trouble in learning to read, write, spell or manipulate numbers, so their performance in these areas is below their performance in other areas.

In 2003/04, there were 10,500 permanent exclusions of children from schools in Great Britain, that is they were

## Table **3.7**

### Permanent and fixed period exclusions from schools:[1] by reason, 2003/04

**England**

Percentages[2]

| | Permanent exclusions | Fixed period exclusions[3] |
|---|---|---|
| Persistent disruptive behaviour | 31 | 26 |
| Physical assault against a pupil | 17 | 20 |
| Physical assault against an adult | 12 | 5 |
| Verbal abuse/threatening behaviour against an adult | 11 | 22 |
| Verbal abuse/threatening behaviour against a pupil | 4 | 4 |
| Drug and alcohol related | 6 | 4 |
| Damage | 3 | 3 |
| Theft | 2 | 2 |
| Bullying | 2 | 2 |
| Sexual misconduct | 1 | 1 |
| Racist abuse | - | 1 |
| Other | 9 | 11 |
| All exclusions (=100%) (thousands) | 9.9 | 344.5 |

1 Maintained primary, secondary and special schools. Excludes non-maintained special schools. Includes middle schools as deemed.
2 The number of exclusions by reason expressed as a percentage of the total number of exclusions.
3 There were 50 fixed period exclusions for which circumstance was not known; these are included in the total.

*Source: Department for Education and Skills*

excluded from the school and their name removed from the school register. These pupils would then be educated at another school or through some other form of provision. This figure was around 5 per cent higher than the previous year, but considerably lower than 1996/97, when there were over 13,000 permanent exclusions. The number of permanent exclusions of boys in 2003/04 outnumbered girls by four to one.

In 2003/04 around 25 in every 10,000 pupils of Mixed ethnic origin were permanently excluded from schools in England. Although this was similar to the rate for Black pupils (29 in every 10,000), there was variation within the Black group. Black African pupils were far less likely to be excluded (16 in every 10,000) than Black Caribbean pupils (41 in every 10,000) or those from any other Black background (42 in every 10,000). White pupils and Asian pupils had rates of 14 exclusions and 6 exclusions for every 10,000 pupils respectively.

The most common reason in 2003/04 for exclusion in England was persistent disruptive behaviour, which accounted for 31 per cent of all permanent exclusions and 26 per cent of all fixed period exclusions (Table 3.7). The second most common reason for permanent exclusion was physical assault against a pupil (17 per cent). Although comprising a smaller proportion of the total number of exclusions, around 1 in 8 (12 per cent) permanent exclusions and 1 in 20 (5 per cent) fixed period exclusions in 2003/04 were for physical assault against an adult. Sexual misconduct and racist abuse were the least common reasons for both permanent and fixed period exclusion in England. In 2003/04 there were 38,900 exclusions from local authority schools in Scotland, an increase of 7 per cent from 2002/03. Nearly all (99 per cent) of these were temporary. The most common reason for exclusion was general or persistent disobedience (25 per cent) followed by verbal abuse of members of staff (22 per cent) and physical abuse of fellow pupils (14 per cent).

## Post compulsory participation

Following compulsory education, young people at the age of 16 can choose to continue in further education and in 2003/04 there were 4.9 million further education students in the United Kingdom. In 2003/04 there were four times as many female further education students as in 1970/71, but only twice as many male students. In 1970/71 the majority (58 per cent) of further education students in the United Kingdom were men, 1 million compared with 725,000 women (Table 3.8). However by 2003/04 the majority (59 per cent) of further education students were women – 2.9 million compared with 2.0 million men.

Part-time study dominates the further education sector with 78 per cent of students studying part time in 2003/04. Similar numbers of men and women study full time, but women are more likely than men to study part time, 81 per cent and 73 per cent respectively of further education students. This contrasts to 1970/71 when a similar proportion of women (87 per cent) and men (88 per cent) studied part time.

There have also been substantial increases in the number of students in higher education in the United Kingdom. In 1970/71 there were 0.6 million students in higher education, 33 per cent of whom were women. In 2003/04 there were 2.4 million students in higher education and the proportion who were women had increased to 57 per cent. The number of enrolments has increased for both sexes over the last 30 years. For women, there were almost seven times as many enrolments in higher education in 2003/04 than in 1970/71. For men, enrolments increased by two and a half times over the same period.

Not everyone working towards a qualification beyond the age of 16 has worked their way continuously through the various levels of education. Just under half of working-age people who were studying towards a qualification in the United Kingdom in spring 2005 were aged 25 or over and a fifth were aged 40 or over (Table 3.9). The age distribution varies according to the qualification being undertaken. Adults aged 25 and over

## Table **3.8**

### Students in further and higher education:[1] by type of course and sex

United Kingdom

Thousands

| | Men | | | | Women | | | |
|---|---|---|---|---|---|---|---|---|
| | 1970/71 | 1980/81 | 1990/91 | 2003/04 | 1970/71 | 1980/81 | 1990/91 | 2003/04 |
| **Further education[2]** | | | | | | | | |
| Full-time | 116 | 154 | 219 | 532 | 95 | 196 | 261 | 548 |
| Part-time | 891 | 697 | 768 | 1,434 | 630 | 624 | 986 | 2,336 |
| All further education | 1,007 | 851 | 987 | 1,966 | 725 | 820 | 1,247 | 2,884 |
| **Higher education** | | | | | | | | |
| Undergraduate | | | | | | | | |
| Full-time | 241 | 277 | 345 | 543 | 173 | 196 | 319 | 664 |
| Part-time | 127 | 176 | 193 | 261 | 19 | 71 | 148 | 445 |
| Postgraduate | | | | | | | | |
| Full-time | 33 | 41 | 50 | 110 | 10 | 21 | 34 | 111 |
| Part-time | 15 | 32 | 50 | 138 | 3 | 13 | 36 | 170 |
| All higher education[3] | 416 | 526 | 638 | 1,054 | 205 | 301 | 537 | 1,392 |

1 Home and overseas students. See Appendix, Part 3: Stages of education.
2 2003/04 includes 2002/03 data for further education institutions in Wales.
3 Figures for 2003/04 include a small number of higher education students for whom details are not available by level.

Source: Department for Education and Skills; National Assembly for Wales; Scottish Executive; Northern Ireland Department for Employment and Learning; Higher Education Statistics Agency

## Table **3.9**

### People working towards a qualification:[1] by age, 2005[2]

United Kingdom

Percentages

| | Degree or higher or equivalent | Higher education[3] | GCE A level or equivalent | GCSE or equivalent | Other qualification[4] | All studying |
|---|---|---|---|---|---|---|
| 16–19 | 16 | 17 | 71 | 63 | 13 | 33 |
| 20–24 | 43 | 16 | 9 | 7 | 11 | 20 |
| 25–29 | 13 | 12 | 4 | 6 | 13 | 10 |
| 30–39 | 15 | 26 | 6 | 10 | 27 | 17 |
| 40–49 | 10 | 19 | 6 | 9 | 22 | 13 |
| 50–59/64[5] | 4 | 9 | 3 | 5 | 14 | 7 |
| All aged 16–59/64[5] (=100%) (millions) | 1.9 | 0.5 | 1.5 | 0.8 | 1.8 | 6.5 |

1  For those working towards more than one qualification, the highest is recorded. See Appendix, Part 3: Qualifications. Excludes those who did not answer.
2  At spring. Data are not seasonally adjusted and have been adjusted in line with population estimates published in spring 2003. See Appendix, Part 4: LFS reweighting.
3  Below degree level but including NVQ level 4.
4  Includes those who did not know the qualification they were working towards.
5  Males aged 16 to 64 and females aged 16 to 59.

**Source: Labour Force Survey, Office for National Statistics**

comprised 20 per cent of people of working age studying towards a GCE A level or equivalent and 30 per cent of those studying towards a GCSE or equivalent. In contrast, 67 per cent of working-age people taking higher education qualifications below degree level, and 41 per cent of those studying at degree level or higher, were in this age group.

Participation rates by 16 year olds in post compulsory education varies by socio-economic status (see Appendix, Part 1: National Statistics Socio-economic Classification). According to the Youth Cohort Study (YCS), young people aged 16 in England and Wales whose parents were in higher professional occupations in 2004 were more likely to be in full-time education than young people whose parents were in routine occupations (85 per cent

and 57 per cent respectively). Around a tenth of 16 year olds whose parents were in higher professional socio-economic occupations were in a full or part-time job, or in government-supported training. This compares with around a quarter of those with parents in routine occupations.

There was also variation by socio-economic status in the qualifications 16 year olds in full-time education studied. This was particularly the case for those studying for GCE A level or equivalent – 74 per cent of 16 year olds whose parents were in higher professional occupations were studying for this level of qualification compared with 31 per cent of 16 year olds whose parents were in routine occupations (Table 3.10).

## Table **3.10**

### Main study aim at 16:[1] by parents' socio-economic classification,[2] 2004

England & Wales

Percentages

| | GCE A level or equivalent | GCSE | Intermediate or foundation GNVQ | NVQ 1 or 2, or equivalent | Level unclear or not stated | Any qualification |
|---|---|---|---|---|---|---|
| Higher professional | 74 | 2 | 3 | 6 | 2 | 86 |
| Lower professional | 62 | 3 | 5 | 8 | 3 | 81 |
| Intermediate | 51 | 3 | 7 | 11 | 4 | 76 |
| Lower supervisory | 40 | 3 | 6 | 15 | 3 | 67 |
| Routine | 31 | 3 | 8 | 15 | 3 | 61 |
| Other[3] | 33 | 3 | 11 | 12 | 3 | 63 |

1  Pupils in Year 11. Includes equivalent GNVQ qualifications in Year 11.
2  See Appendix, Part 1: National Statistics Socio-economic Classification.
3  Includes respondents for whom neither parent had an occupation.

**Source: Youth Cohort Study, Department for Education and Skills**

## Table 3.11

### Destinations of UK graduates:[1] by type of degree, 2003/04

United Kingdom                                                    Percentages

|  | First degree | Other undergraduate[2] | Postgraduate |
|---|---|---|---|
| Full-time paid work only[3] | 55 | 49 | 70 |
| Part-time paid work only | 8 | 8 | 7 |
| Voluntary/unpaid work only | 1 | - | 1 |
| Work and further study | 10 | 18 | 10 |
| Further study only | 14 | 19 | 5 |
| Assumed to be unemployed | 6 | 3 | 3 |
| Not available for employment | 5 | 3 | 3 |
| Other | 1 | 1 | 1 |
| All (=100%) (thousands) | 201 | 31 | 68 |

1 Destination of UK domiciled full- and part-time graduates about six months after completion of their degree.
2 Other undergraduate includes foundation degrees and all other higher education qualifications not included as first degree or postgraduate.
3 Including self-employed.

**Source: Department for Education and Skills; Higher Education Statistics Agency**

The pattern of participation in full-time education by socio-economic status continued into higher education – 44 per cent of 18 year olds in England and Wales whose parents were in higher professional occupations in 2004 were studying for a degree or equivalent compared with 13 per cent whose parents were in routine occupations.

In 2003/04 there were 300,000 home and EU domiciled students who left UK higher education institutions in the United Kingdom. Of these 67 per cent were first degree graduates, 23 per cent were postgraduates and 10 per cent were other undergraduates. Women comprised 59 per cent of all leavers in 2003/04. Destinations of graduates in the United Kingdom include continuing in education, as well as moving into employment. Around two thirds (63 per cent) of first degree graduates, and over three quarters (77 per cent) of postgraduates, went into full- or part-time paid work after they graduated (Table 3.11). Around a quarter of first degree graduates combined work with further study or continued with further study only, compared with around one in seven postgraduates. The proportion of other undergraduates who combined work with further study or continued in further study only, was higher at 37 per cent.

Of those first degree graduates in 2003/04 whose first destination after graduation was known to be employment, 29 per cent were employed in the associate professional and

technical occupations (such as nurses, financial and business analysts, and sales representatives) and 25 per cent were in professional occupations (such as medical and dental practitioners, accountants and teachers). A higher proportion of female than male graduates gained posts in the associate professional and technical occupations (31 per cent compared with 26 per cent), whereas a higher proportion of male than female graduates gained employment in professional occupations (29 per cent compared with 23 per cent). Around 2 per cent of first degree graduates went into skilled trades and process, plant and machine operation occupations.

## Educational attainment

The Key Stages form part of the National Curriculum in England and Wales, more details of which can be found in Appendix, Part 3: The National Curriculum. Scotland and Northern Ireland have their own schemes. In 2005 the proportion of boys in England reaching the required standard for reading and writing at Key Stage 1 and English at Key Stages 2 and 3 was lower than that for girls (Table 3.12). The difference between the proportions of boys and girls reaching the expected level in tests and teacher assessments for mathematics and science

## Table 3.12

### Pupils reaching or exceeding expected standards:[1] by Key Stage and sex, 2005

England                                                          Percentages

|  | Teacher assessment | | Tests | |
|---|---|---|---|---|
|  | Boys | Girls | Boys | Girls |
| **Key Stage 1[2]** | | | | |
| English | | | | |
| Reading | 81 | 89 | . | . |
| Writing | 77 | 88 | . | . |
| Mathematics | 90 | 92 | . | . |
| Science | 88 | 91 | . | . |
| **Key Stage 2[3]** | | | | |
| English | 70 | 81 | 74 | 84 |
| Mathematics | 76 | 76 | 76 | 75 |
| Science | 82 | 84 | 86 | 87 |
| **Key Stage 3[4]** | | | | |
| English | 64 | 78 | 67 | 80 |
| Mathematics | 74 | 77 | 73 | 74 |
| Science | 70 | 73 | 69 | 70 |

1 See Appendix, Part 3: The National Curriculum.
2 Pupils achieving level 2 or above at Key Stage 1.
3 Pupils achieving level 4 or above at Key Stage 2.
4 Pupils achieving level 5 or above at Key Stage 3.

**Source: Department for Education and Skills**

# Table **3.13**

## Attainment of five or more GCSE grades A* to C:[1] by ethnic group

England & Wales

Percentages

|  | 1992 | 1996 | 2000 | 2004 |
|---|---|---|---|---|
| White | 37 | 45 | 50 | 54 |
| Indian | 38 | 48 | 60 | 72 |
| Pakistani | 26 | 23 | 29 | 37 |
| Bangladeshi | 14 | 25 | 29 | 46 |
| Other Asian[2] | 46 | 61 | 72 | 66 |
| Black | 23 | 23 | 39 | 35 |
| Other ethnic group[3] | .. | 46 | 43 | 59 |

1 Attainment in Year 11.
2 Includes the Chinese group.
3 Data for 1992 are not available due to small sample size.

**Source: Youth Cohort Study, Department for Education and Skills**

was less pronounced. However for Key Stage 2 mathematics, boys performed as well as girls in teacher assessments and slightly better in tests.

The proportion of pupils achieving the expected level in English and science declined for both boys and girls between Key Stages 2 and 3. Seventy per cent of boys reached the expected standard in English teacher assessments at Key Stage 2 compared with 81 per cent of girls, whereas at Key Stage 3 these proportions had fallen to 64 per cent and 78 per cent respectively. Similarly in science teacher assessments, 82 per cent of boys and 84 per cent of girls at Key Stage 2 reached the expected level, compared with 70 per cent and 73 per cent, respectively, at Key Stage 3.

The attainment levels of pupils from all ethnic groups have improved over time. However some ethnic groups have improved much more than others. According to data from the Youth Cohort Study (YCS) Indian pupils, as well as being the most likely to achieve five or more GCSE grades A* to C (or equivalent) in 2004, also showed the largest improvements over the last 12 years (Table 3.13). The proportion who achieved these grades increased by 34 percentage points from 38 per cent in 1992 to 72 per cent in 2004. Although less than half of Bangladeshi pupils achieved GCSE grades at this level in 2004, they have also shown large improvements. In 2004, 46 per cent of Bangladeshi pupils achieved five or more GCSE grades A* to C compared with 14 per cent in 1992 – an increase of 32 percentage points. Two thirds of pupils from the Other Asian group, and over half from the White group achieved five or more GCSE grades A* to C. Pupils from the Black and Pakistani ethnic groups were least likely to achieve these grades.

# Figure **3.14**

## Academic attainment:[1] by truancy, 2004[2]

England & Wales

Percentages

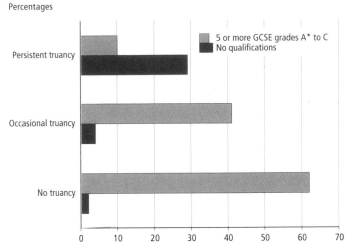

1 GCSE and GNVQ qualifications in Year 11.
2 Truancy in Year 11.

**Source: Youth Cohort Study, Department for Education and Skills**

Figures from the Pupil Level Annual Schools Census by the Department for Education and Skills (DfES), and attainment data collected in England showed that in 2004, around three quarters (74 per cent) of Chinese pupils achieved five or more GCSE grades A* to C (or equivalent). This ethnic group had the highest proportion of both boys and girls who achieved this level; 69 per cent and 79 per cent respectively (see Figure A.5). It should be noted that the sample size for the Chinese group is too small for the data to be presented separately in the YCS (Table 3.13) where these data are included in the Other Asian category.

Absence from school through truancy has a serious impact upon the likelihood of gaining qualifications. In 2004 persistent truants in year 11 in England and Wales were around six times less likely than those who did not truant to gain five or more GCSEs grades A* to C (Figure 3.14). Around 1 in 3 pupils who were persistent truants gained no qualifications compared with 1 in 50 who did not truant.

The socio-economic status of parents can have a significant impact on the GCSE attainment of their children. In England and Wales 76 per cent of pupils whose parents were in higher professional occupations achieved higher grade GCSEs (or the equivalent) in 2004, compared with 33 per cent of those whose parents were in routine occupations. The educational attainment of parents can also influence the attainment of their children; 73 per cent of young people who had at least one parent qualified to degree level and 64 per cent who had at least one parent whose highest qualification was a GCE A level achieved five or more GCSEs at grades A* to C. This

## Figure **3.15**

### Achievement of two or more GCE A levels[1] or equivalent: by sex

**United Kingdom**

Percentages

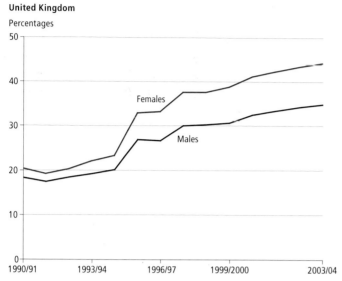

1 Two A levels are equivalent to three or more Highers. Data are for pupils in schools and further education institutions. Data prior to 1995/96, and for Wales and Northern Ireland from 2002/03, relate to schools only. Data for Scottish Qualifications from 2000/01 are not on the same basis as earlier years. See Appendix, Part 3: Qualifications.

**Source: Department for Education and Skills; National Assembly for Wales; Scottish Executive; Northern Ireland Department of Education**

## Figure **3.16**

### Graduation rates[1] from first university degrees: EU comparison,[2] 2003

Percentages

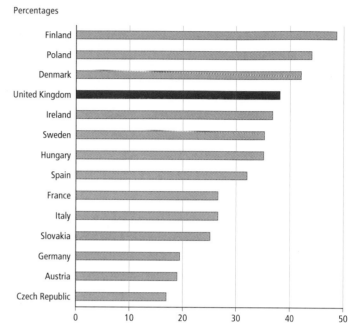

1 Graduation rates at typical age of graduation.
2 Data are not available for other EU-25 countries.

**Source: Organisation for Economic Co-operation and Development**

compares with 41 per cent of young people with parents whose highest qualification was below GCE A level.

The proportion of pupils in the United Kingdom gaining two or more GCE A levels (or equivalent) increased from 19 per cent in 1990/91 to 39 per cent in 2003/04, although the performance gap between the sexes has widened. The proportion of young women who achieved two or more GCE A levels (or equivalent) increased from 20 per cent in 1990/91 to 44 per cent in 2003/04 (Figure 3.15). For young men the proportion increased from 18 per cent to 35 per cent over the same period. Thus the performance gap between the sexes has increased from 2 percentage points in 1990/91 to 9 percentage points in 2003/04.

There is a wide variety of subjects available in schools and further education institutions to study at GCE A level, and there are differences in subject choice between males and females. In 2003/04, 76 per cent of young people aged around 16 to 18 who entered for GCE A level (or equivalent) physics and 73 per cent of those entered for computer studies in the United Kingdom were male. Other male-dominated subjects included economics (70 per cent) and design and technology (65 per cent). In comparison, most young people who entered for home economics were female (94 per cent). In addition, females made up around 70 per cent of those entered for religious studies, social studies, English literature, modern languages, drama, and art and design.

In 2003/04 there were around 364,000 qualifications obtained by full-time UK and European Union (EU) domiciled students at higher education institutions in the United Kingdom, of which two thirds were first degrees. Of those first degrees 11 per cent were graded first class, 46 per cent were upper second class and 31 per cent were graded lower second. Similar proportions were graded third class/pass or were unclassified (each around 6 per cent).

Graduation rates from university vary across the EU. In 2003 the United Kingdom had the fourth highest graduation rate from first university degrees at 38 per cent, behind Finland, Poland and Denmark (Figure 3.16). The graduation rate in the Czech Republic, at 17 per cent, was lower than in any other EU country for which data were available. A possible explanation for the difference in graduation rates across the countries is the variation in provision of non-university education. Alternative vocational education and apprenticeships, for example, may reduce the perceived need of some students to enrol in formal university-level studies as preparation for work.

The highest qualification held varies between the different ethnic groups. The ethnic group with the largest proportion of men holding a qualification equal to or above GCE A level (or equivalent) in 2004 was White British (56 per cent), whereas for women it was White Irish (53 per cent) (Table 3.17).

Table **3.17**

**Highest qualification held:[1] by sex and main ethnic group, 2004[2]**

Great Britain

Percentages

| | Degree or equivalent | Higher education qualification[3] | GCE A level or equivalent | GCSE grades A* to C or equivalent | Other qualification | No qualification | All |
|---|---|---|---|---|---|---|---|
| **Males** | | | | | | | |
| White British | 18 | 8 | 30 | 19 | 10 | 14 | 100 |
| White Irish | 23 | 6 | 24 | 12 | 17 | 18 | 100 |
| Mixed | 22 | 6 | 24 | 20 | 13 | 15 | 100 |
| Indian | 30 | 6 | 17 | 11 | 22 | 15 | 100 |
| Pakistani | 15 | 4 | 15 | 16 | 22 | 29 | 100 |
| Bangladeshi | 11 | 2 | 10 | 12 | 25 | 40 | 100 |
| Black Caribbean | 11 | 6 | 26 | 24 | 15 | 18 | 100 |
| Black African | 24 | 9 | 18 | 14 | 25 | 12 | 100 |
| Chinese | 33 | 4 | 13 | 10 | 21 | 19 | 100 |
| **Females** | | | | | | | |
| White British | 16 | 10 | 19 | 29 | 10 | 16 | 100 |
| White Irish | 25 | 13 | 15 | 15 | 16 | 16 | 100 |
| Mixed | 20 | 7 | 22 | 27 | 13 | 11 | 100 |
| Indian | 21 | 6 | 16 | 16 | 24 | 18 | 100 |
| Pakistani | 10 | 4 | 14 | 20 | 18 | 35 | 100 |
| Bangladeshi | 5 | 2 | 12 | 17 | 15 | 49 | 100 |
| Black Caribbean | 15 | 13 | 16 | 33 | 14 | 10 | 100 |
| Black African | 17 | 9 | 15 | 15 | 26 | 18 | 100 |
| Chinese | 29 | 6 | 10 | 8 | 26 | 21 | 100 |

1 Males aged 16 to 64, females aged 16 to 59.
2 January to December. See Appendix: Part 4, Annual Population Survey.
3 Below degree level.

**Source: Annual Population Survey, Office for National Statistics**

Although Table 3.13 showed the improvement in performance of Bangladeshi students in recent years, people from this ethnic group, along with Pakistanis, are more likely than other groups to hold no qualifications. One reason is that these data are for people of working age and the Bangladeshi and Pakistani working-age population includes migrants who came to live in the United Kingdom as adults with no qualifications.

There are also variations in highest qualification by religious identity. For example although over half of working-age Indian men had a highest qualification equal to or above GCE A level (or equivalent), data from the Labour Force Survey showed there was a difference in the proportions of Hindus and Sikhs (both are generally from the Indian ethnic group) who achieved a highest qualification to at least this level. In 2003–04, 56 per cent of working-age Hindu men had a highest qualification equal to or above GCE A level compared with 42 per cent of Sikh men. This pattern was similar for working-age Hindu and Sikh women. Almost a third (31 per cent) of Muslims of working

age in Great Britain in 2003–04 had no qualifications – the highest proportion for any religious group. They were also the least likely to have degrees (or equivalent qualifications). Jews and Buddhists, followed by Hindus, were the least likely to have no qualifications and the most likely to have degrees. A third of Jews and Buddhists (37 and 33 per cent respectively), and a quarter (26 per cent) of Hindus, had a degree in 2003–04.

An alternative to the more traditional and academic qualifications are National Vocational Qualifications (NVQs) and Scottish Vocational Qualifications (SVQs), which were introduced in 1987 (see Appendix, Part 3: Qualifications). There has been an increase in the take up of these qualifications as shown by the numbers awarded. In 2003/04 around 491,000 NVQs and SVQs were awarded in the United Kingdom whereas in 1991/92 around 153,000 were awarded (Figure 3.18 overleaf). Awards at level 2 have been the most common over the period, accounting for 285,000 (58 per cent) awards in 2003/04, while awards at level 1 have declined over

## Figure **3.18**

### NVQ/SVQs awarded:[1] by level of qualification

**United Kingdom**
Thousands

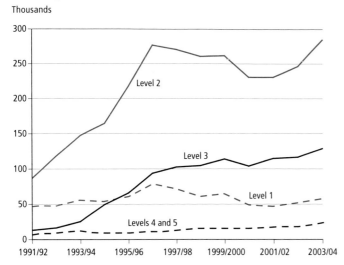

1 Data for 2000/01 are NVQ awards only.
**Source: Department for Education and Skills**

the period from 31 per cent to 12 per cent. In 1991/92, 8 per cent of all awards were at level 3 compared with 26 per cent in 2003/04.

In 2003/04, 24 per cent of NVQs and SVQs awarded in the United Kingdom were in areas providing goods and services (such as catering and tourism). A further 21 per cent were in areas providing health, social and protective services (such as health care and health and safety) and 20 per cent were in areas providing business services (such as management studies).

## Adult training and learning

Learning throughout working life is becoming increasingly necessary because of the pace of change within the labour market, and many people receive training in the workplace. In spring 2005, 16 per cent of employees of working age in the United Kingdom had received some job-related training in the four weeks prior to interview, this was a similar proportion to each of the spring quarters since 1995. In general, greater proportions of women than men received job-related training, and the proportion was higher for younger than for older employees. Compared with other age groups, men aged 16 to 17 (23 per cent) and women aged 18 to 24 (23 per cent) were the most likely to have received job-related training in spring 2005 (Figure 3.19).

Employees with higher qualifications were more likely to receive job-related training than those with lower or no qualifications in spring 2005. Those with higher qualifications were therefore more likely to gain more work-related skills and

## Figure **3.19**

### Employees receiving job-related training:[1] by age and sex, 2005[2]

**United Kingdom**
Percentages

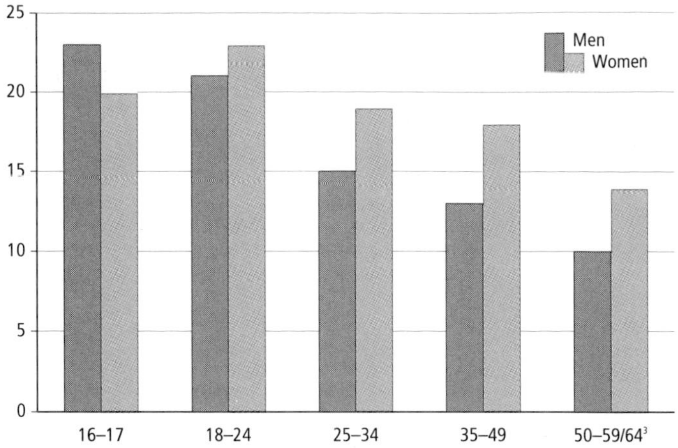

1 Employees (those in employment excluding the self-employed, unpaid family workers and those on government programmes) who received job-related training in the four weeks before interview.
2 At spring. Data are not seasonally adjusted and have been adjusted in line with population estimates published in spring 2003. See Appendix, Part 4: LFS reweighting.
3 Men aged 50 to 64, women aged 50 to 59.
**Source: Department for Education and Skills from the Labour Force Survey**

experiences that could benefit them in their career progression, compared with those with lower or no qualifications. In spring 2005, 22 per cent of employees qualified to degree level in the United Kingdom received job-related training in the four weeks prior to interview, compared with 5 per cent of those with no qualifications.

There are various education and training options available to young people who decide not to continue in full-time education, including a number of government-supported training initiatives. In England and Wales Work-Based Learning for Young People aims to ensure that all young people have access to post-compulsory education or training. Included in this initiative are apprenticeships that provide structured learning programmes for young people aged 16 to 24 and combine work-based training with off-the-job learning. Apprenticeships offer training to NVQ level 2. Advanced Apprenticeships offer training to level 3, and are aimed at developing technical, supervisory and craft-level skills.

In 2004/05 there were 518,500 young people (aged 16 to 24) on Work Based Learning Schemes in England. The most common area of learning was engineering, technology and manufacturing in which 101,100 young people were training – 97 per cent of whom were men (Table 3.20). Men also dominated in the area of construction (99 per cent).

## Table **3.20**

### Young people[1] in Work Based Learning:[2] by sex and area of learning, 2004/05

England

Thousands

| | Men | Women | All |
|---|---|---|---|
| Engineering, technology & manufacturing | 98.3 | 2.8 | 101.1 |
| Retailing, customer service & transportation | 25.4 | 34.3 | 59.8 |
| Construction | 55.2 | 0.5 | 55.7 |
| Health, social care & public services | 6.1 | 49.3 | 55.4 |
| Business administration, management & professional | 14.2 | 38.1 | 52.3 |
| Hospitality, sports, leisure & travel | 23.5 | 22.4 | 45.9 |
| Hairdressing & beauty therapy | 2.9 | 33.2 | 36.1 |
| Land-based provision | 6.0 | 5.1 | 11.1 |
| Information & communications technology | 8.6 | 1.8 | 10.4 |
| Visual and performing arts & media | 1.0 | 0.1 | 1.1 |
| Area unknown | 55.7 | 33.4 | 89.1 |
| All areas of learning[3] | 297.1 | 221.3 | 518.5 |

1 People aged 16 to 24.
2 Work Based Learning for young people comprises Advanced Apprenticeships at NVQ level 3, Apprenticeships at NVQ level 2, NVQ Learning, and Entry to Employment (E2E).
3 Includes English, languages and communications, foundation programmes, humanities, and science and mathematics.

**Source: Learning and Skills Council; Department for Education and Skills**

In contrast, women greatly outnumbered men in hairdressing and beauty therapy (92 per cent) and in health, social care and public services (89 per cent).

In 2004/05 there were 915,000 people on adult and community learning courses in England. Adult and community learning includes a wide range of community-based learning opportunities, primarily taking place through local education authorities (see Appendix, Part 3: Adult education). The majority were in either visual and performing arts and media (28 per cent) or hospitality, sports, leisure and travel (22 per cent).

The modern working environment demands a broad range of skills such as computer literacy, communication, problem solving and customer handling skills. The National Employers Skills Survey in 2003 looked at the extent of deficiencies in these areas among employees in England, as reported by employers. It was estimated that around 2.4 million employees in 2003 (11 per cent of employees) were considered by their employers to be less than fully proficient in their job.

## Figure **3.21**

### Skills characteristics of skills gaps,[1] 2003

England
Percentages

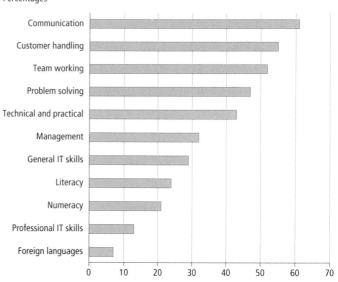

1 Employers who had experienced skills gaps were asked to define what skills they felt needed improving for an occupation where staff were considered not fully proficient. Percentages do not sum to 100 as employers could give more than one answer. See Appendix, Part 3: National Employers Skills Survey.

**Source: Learning and Skills Council**

Employers were asked to define what skills they felt needed improving in jobs where their staff were not fully proficient. Employers thought that, of their employees who they identified as having a skills gap, 61 per cent lacked adequate communication skills for their job and over 50 per cent lacked customer handling or team working skills (Figure 3.21). Although lower proportions of employees were considered to lack the required numeracy and literacy skills for their job, over 20 per cent were considered to be not fully proficient in these areas. Employers were also asked what the causes of skills gaps were (they could provide more than one answer). The majority (73 per cent) said lack of experience was the main reason, while 34 per cent said their staff lacked motivation. Other reasons given by employers were a failure to train and develop staff (29 per cent), staff not being good at keeping up with change (27 per cent), recruitment problems (25 per cent) and a high staff turnover (25 per cent).

## Educational resources

The United Kingdom spent 5.3 per cent of gross domestic product (GDP) on education in 2002, ranking towards the middle of the EU-15 countries for such expenditure. Denmark spent the most on education as a proportion of GDP (8.5 per cent) and Greece the least (4.0 per cent).

## Figure **3.22**

### Full-time teachers:[1] by sex and type of school

United Kingdom
Thousands

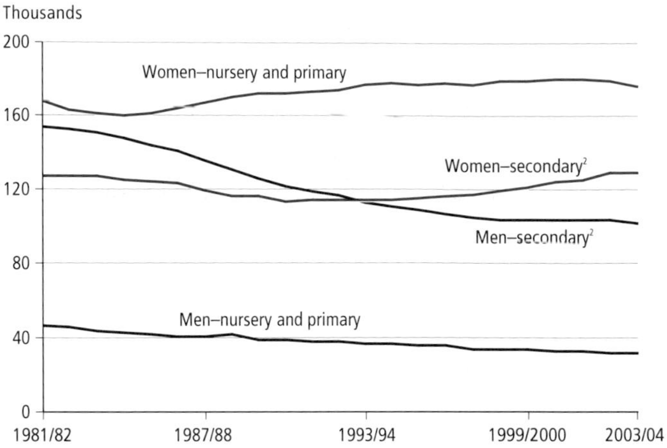

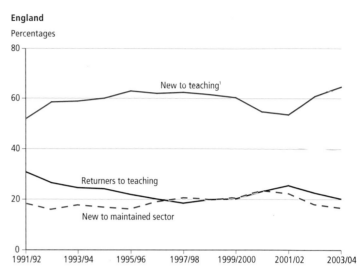

1 Qualified teachers only.
2 From 1993/94 data exclude sixth-form colleges in England and Wales which were reclassified as further education colleges on 1 April 1993.

*Source: Department for Education and Skills; Scottish Executive; Northern Ireland Department of Education*

## Figure **3.23**

### New entrants and re-entrants to full-time teaching in maintained schools

England
Percentages

1 Excluding transfers from outside the maintained sector.

*Source: Department for Education and Skills*

The number of full-time qualified teachers in public sector mainstream schools in the United Kingdom, decreased by around 57,000 between 1981/82 and 2003/04 to 436,000, although it has been rising since 1997/98. The number of full-time female teachers in these schools increased by 4 per cent to 304,000 over the period 1981/82 to 2003/04, while the number of male teachers fell by 33 per cent to 132,000 (Figure 3.22). The majority of full-time teachers in both nursery and primary, and secondary schools were female. In nursery and primary schools 85 per cent of full-time teachers were female in 2003/04, whereas in secondary schools the difference between the sexes was less marked, with females comprising 56 per cent of full-time teachers. In 2003 around two thirds of head teachers in maintained nursery and primary schools in England were female, compared with around one third of head teachers in maintained secondary schools.

In 2004/05, 36,800 students were enrolled on teacher training courses in England and Wales – just under 17,700 were enrolled in primary education training and over 18,700 were training for secondary education. There were fluctuations in the number of enrolments during the 1990s followed by a steady increase in recent years, and by 2004/05 there were 55 per cent more enrolments on teacher training courses than in 1990/91. Between one in six and one in seven enrolments at secondary level were for courses in science, English or technology (which included design and technology, computer studies and business studies). This was followed by around one in nine enrolments

for mathematics courses. Although the majority of those who enter teaching are new to the profession, others return to teaching following a period away from it. In 2003/04 there were around 32,400 entrants into teaching in maintained schools in England and 64 per cent were new to teaching. A further 20 per cent (6,500) were entrants who were returning to the profession, while 16 per cent (5,200) were teachers who transferred to jobs in maintained schools from outside the maintained sector (Figure 3.23).

The number of support staff in maintained schools in England who provide additional learning resources within the classroom increased by almost two and a half times between 1996 and 2005, to 210,000 (Figure 3.24). There was an increase in the number of support staff in all types of school, but the largest increase (over two and a half times) was in secondary schools. Most support staff are in primary schools, accounting for 55 per cent of these staff in 2005. In January 2005, around a quarter of primary level teaching assistants were employed as special needs support staff, whereas at secondary level the proportion was around a half.

Total expenditure on school staff by local authorities in England was £3,184 per pupil in 2003/04. The proportion spent on teaching staff has gradually gone down over recent years, from 77 per cent in 1994/95 to 70 per cent in 2003/04 to £2,218 per pupil. There has been a rise in spending on support staff over the same period, from £143 per pupil (equivalent to 8 per cent

# Figure **3.24**

## Support staff:[1] by type of school

England

Thousands

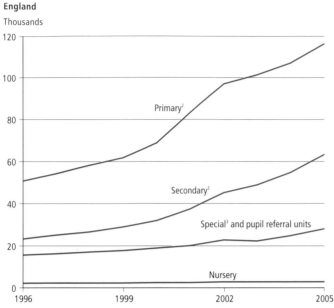

1 In maintained schools. Includes teaching assistants, technicians and
  other support staff but excludes administrative staff. Includes both
  full-time and the full-time equivalent of part-time support staff.
2 Includes middle schools as deemed.
3 Includes non-maintained special schools.

*Source: Department for Education and Skills*

# Figure **3.25**

## Use of information and communications technology:[1] by type of school

England

Percentages

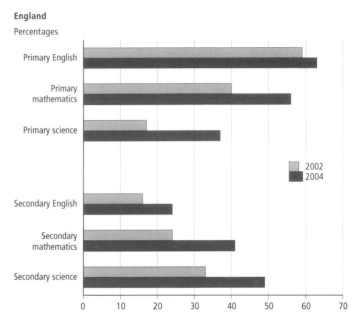

1 Schools reporting a substantial use of information and communications
  technology (ICT) in areas of the national curriculum by pupils. Computers
  used mainly for teaching and learning by pupils in maintained schools.

*Source: Department for Education and Skills*

of all spending on school staff) to £419 per school pupil (13 per cent). Spending per pupil on other staff (such as premises related, administrative and clerical, and catering) has changed little, ranging between 16 and 18 per cent of total staff expenditure each year.

In 2004 most school teachers reported regular use of ICT (information and communications technology) for teaching and learning. This varied by type of school – primary and special school teachers (92 and 91 per cent respectively) were more likely to use it than secondary school teachers (70 per cent). Use levels varied across the curriculum, with ICT, not surprisingly, being the subject that showed the highest proportions of staff making substantial use of ICT in 2004 (84 per cent of primary schools and 99 per cent of secondary schools). Even when ICT as a subject is excluded, use levels have grown in all areas of the national curriculum since 2002 (Figure 3.25). In primary schools in 2004, ICT was most likely to be used substantially in English (63 per cent) and mathematics (56 per cent). In secondary schools, less use appeared to be made of ICT in these subject areas (24 per cent and 41 per cent respectively reported substantial use). Science was more likely to make a substantial use of ICT than both English and mathematics at secondary level.

Schools were also asked for the main ways in which they disposed of obsolete or broken ICT equipment (they could give more than one answer). Among primary schools, the most common responses in 2004 were that old equipment was disposed of as refuse (56 per cent), or sold or given away (43 per cent). Secondary schools were most likely to cascade old equipment within the school (64 per cent), with nearly as many saying that equipment was disposed of as refuse (60 per cent).

Financial support for students in higher education has changed considerably in recent years. Since 1991/92, when student loans were first introduced, the average loan has steadily increased in real terms while the average maintenance grant has decreased. The two sources of funding reached broad parity in 1996/97, from when most student support has been paid in the form of loans. In 2004/05, 81 per cent of eligible students in the United Kingdom took out a loan to support them through higher education, the average amount being £3,390.

According to the Student Income and Expenditure Survey, students graduating in 2002/03 could expect to finish university with debts two and half times greater than students who graduated in 1998/99. Between 1998/99 and 2002/03 the average anticipated level of student debt on graduation rose from £3,465 in real terms to £8,666 – an increase of 150 per cent above the underlying rate of inflation, and 135 per cent above real rises in average earnings (Figure 3.26). The average amount of money final year students borrowed from commercial sources (for example, through credit cards, bank loans and higher purchase agreements) rose in real terms from £106 in the academic year 1998/99 to £350 in 2002/03. The average value of final year students' overdraft at graduation increased by £15 in real terms between 1998/99 (£982) and 2002/03 (£997).

## Figure **3.26**

### Borrowings, savings and debt of students[1]

**England & Wales**

£ (at 2002/03 prices)

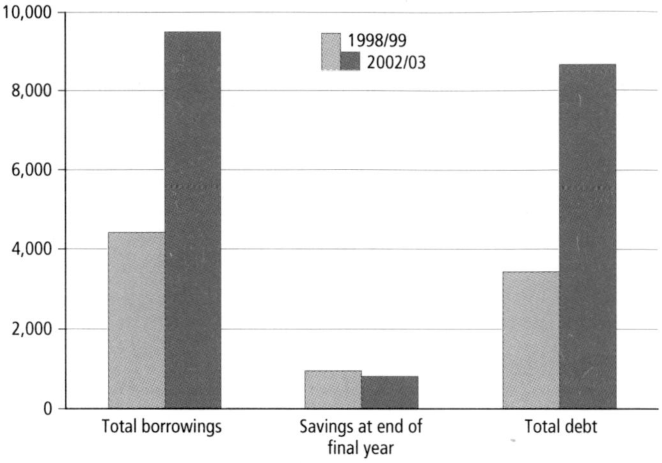

1  Final year full-time, single, childless undergraduate students who were aged under 25 at the start of their course.

**Source: Department for Education and Skills**

# Labour market

- Between spring 1971 and spring 2005, the number of economically active people in the United Kingdom increased by around 4.5 million to over 30 million. (Figure 4.1)

- In spring 2005, around 16 per cent of working-age households in the United Kingdom were workless – where no one of working age is in employment. (Figure 4.2)

- The UK employment rate of working-age men fell from 92 per cent in 1971, to 79 per cent in spring 2005, having reached a low of 75 per cent in 1993, while the rate for working-age women rose from 56 per cent to 70 per cent. (Figure 4.3)

- In spring 2005, 88 per cent of working-age people with a degree or equivalent in the United Kingdom were in employment compared with only 48 per cent of those with no qualification. (Table 4.5)

- Between spring 1994 and spring 2004, employment rates for lone parents in the United Kingdom increased by 12 percentage points from 42 per cent to 54 per cent. (Figure 4.7)

- In spring 2005, nearly one in five full-time employees in the United Kingdom usually worked over 48 hours a week, with a higher proportion of male employees (23 per cent) than female (11 per cent) usually working these longer hours. (Table 4.16)

- The UK male working-age inactivity rate rose from 5 per cent in spring 1971 to 17 per cent in spring 2005; although the female rate is higher, it fell from 41 per cent to 27 per cent. (Figure 4.24)

# Chapter 4

Most people spend a large proportion of their lives in the labour force, and so their experience of the world of work has an important impact on their lives and attitudes. However this proportion has been falling. Young people are remaining longer in education and older people, due to the increase in longevity, are spending more years in retirement. More women than ever before are in paid employment, and employment in service industries continues to increase while employment in manufacturing continues to fall.

## Labour market profile

People are considered to be economically active, or in the labour force, if they are aged 16 and over and are either in work or actively looking for work. Between spring 1971 and spring 2005 the number of economically active people in the United Kingdom increased by around 4.5 million to over 30 million, whereas over the same period the number economically inactive (aged 16 and over and neither in work nor looking for work) increased by 2.7 million to 17.6 million (Figure 4.1). Since the early 1990s there has been a general increase in economic activity levels in the United Kingdom. This is because the increase in employment levels over the period has been steeper than the decrease in unemployment levels.

While there are overall increases in the numbers of economically active and inactive, there have been different trends between men and women. The increase in economic activity levels have largely been driven by women – between spring 1971 and spring 2005 the number of economically active women increased by around 4.3 million compared with an increase of 0.2 million men. Conversely the number of economically inactive women decreased by around 1.0 million over the period compared with an increase of 3.6 million men. In spring 2005 there were 28.7 million people in employment in the United Kingdom. This is the highest number of people in employment in spring recorded by the Labour Force Survey (LFS) since it began in 1971. Comparing the labour market in spring 2005 with spring 1971, the number of people in employment has risen by 4.1 million.

Over a quarter of employees were working part time in spring 2005 and around four in five part-time employees were women. However, more than two and a half times as many men as women were self-employed.

One of the consequences of the increasing levels of employment in the United Kingdom is a rise in the number of working-age households that are working – that is, households that include at least one person of working age and where all the people of working age are in employment. There were 10.8 million working households in spring 2005 out of a total

## Figure **4.1**

### Economic activity levels[1]

United Kingdom
Millions

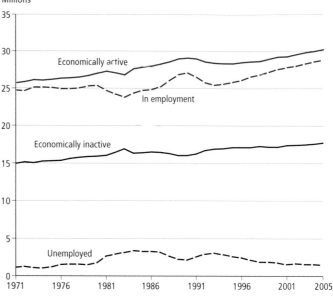

1 At spring each year. People aged 16 and over. Data are seasonally adjusted and have been adjusted in line with population estimates published in autumn 2005. See Appendix, Part 4: LFS reweighting, and Historical LFS-consistent time series.

**Source: Labour Force Survey, Office for National Statistics**

of 18.8 million working-age households, an increase of almost 2 million working households since spring 1992. Working households as a proportion of all working-age households rose

## Labour Force Survey (LFS) data

Since October 2002, the Office for National Statistics (ONS) has published aggregate LFS estimates consistent with the population estimates derived from the 2001 Census. In March 2004 the ONS also published reweighted LFS microdata consistent with the post-2001 Census population estimates (published in February and March 2003). Since then the population estimates have been further revised as a result of methodological improvements and population studies. The aggregate LFS estimates continue to be adjusted to stay in line with the latest population estimates. They were most recently updated in September 2005. Analysis by the ONS has shown that the effect of the adjustments has a greater impact on levels data than on rates. Generally, revisions to rates are within sampling variability, while those for levels are not. This chapter uses the latest interim adjusted data where possible. However, where adjusted data are not available, only rates have been used.

See Appendix, Part 4: LFS reweighting.

# Figure **4.2**

## Working-age households:[1] by household economic status

**United Kingdom**
Percentages

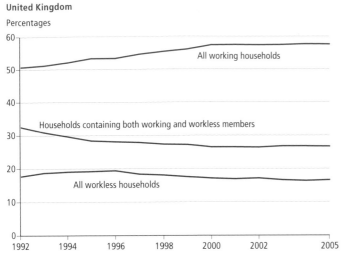

1 Percentages have been adjusted to include estimates for households with unknown economic activity and are for spring each year. Data are as a percentage of working-age households. A working-age household is a household that includes at least one woman aged between 16 and 59 or a man aged between 16 and 64. Data are not seasonally adjusted and have been adjusted in line with population estimates published in spring 2003. See Appendix, Part 4: LFS reweighting.

**Source: Labour Force Survey, Office for National Statistics**

from 50 per cent in spring 1992 to 57 per cent in 2000 – and remained at this level to spring 2005 (Figure 4.2). In spring 2005, around 16 per cent of working-age households were workless – that is, households where at least one person is of working age but no one is in employment.

The distribution of working and workless households varies considerably by household type. Working-age couple households with dependent children were the least likely to be workless in spring 2005 (5 per cent), whereas lone parents with dependent children were most likely (41 per cent). There is also variation in the distribution by region. Households in the South East were most likely to be working (64 per cent), while households in Inner London and Northern Ireland were least likely (48 per cent).

## Employment

Although Figure 4.1 showed an increase in the levels of employment in the United Kingdom, it is also important to consider these changes in relation to changes in the size of the population. The proportion of the working-age population in the United Kingdom who were in employment (the employment rate) decreased from the mid-1970s to a low of 68 per cent in spring 1983 (Figure 4.3 overleaf). Since then employment rates have generally risen. Although there was

## Glossary

**Employees** – a measure, obtained from household surveys of people aged 16 and over who regard themselves as paid employees. People with two or more jobs are counted only once.

**Self-employed** – a measure obtained from household surveys of people aged 16 and over who regard themselves as self-employed, that is, who in their main employment work on their own account, whether or not they have employees.

**In employment** – a measure obtained from household surveys and censuses of employees, self-employed people, participants in government employment and training programmes, and people doing unpaid family work.

**Government employment and training programmes** – a measure obtained from household surveys of those who said they were participants on Youth Training, Training for Work, Employment Action or Community Industry, or a programme organised by the Learning and Skills Council (LSC) in England, the National Council for Education and Training for Wales (ELWa), or Local Enterprise Companies in Scotland.

**Unemployment** – the measure based on International Labour Organisation (ILO) guidelines, and used in the Labour Force Survey, which counts as unemployed those aged 16 and over who are without a job, are available to start work in the next two weeks, who have been seeking a job in the last four weeks or are out of work and waiting to start a job already obtained in the next two weeks.

**Economically active** (or **the labour force**) – those aged 16 and over who are in employment or unemployed.

**Unemployment rate** – the percentage of the economically active who are unemployed.

**Economically inactive** – people who are neither in employment nor unemployment. For example, those looking after a home or retired, or those unable to work due to long term sickness or disability.

**Economic activity rate** – the percentage of the population, for example in a given age group, which is economically active.

**Working age household** – a household that includes at least one person of working age (16 to 64 for men and 16 to 59 for women).

**Working household** – a household that includes at least one person of working age and where all the people of working age are in employment.

**Workless household** – a household that includes at least one person of working age where no one aged 16 and over is in employment.

## Figure **4.3**

### Employment rates:[1] by sex

United Kingdom

Percentages

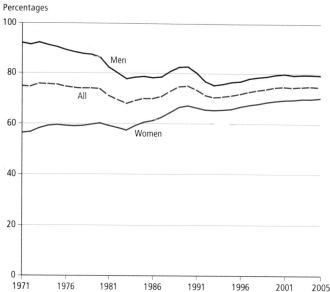

1 At spring each year. Men aged 16 to 64, women aged 16 to 59. The percentage of the population that is in employment. Data are seasonally adjusted and have been adjusted in line with population estimates published in autumn 2005. See Appendix, Part 4: LFS reweighting, and Historical LFS-consistent time series.

**Source: Labour Force Survey, Office for National Statistics**

a slight fall following the recession of 1990 and 1991, the employment rate was 75 per cent in spring 2005, the same as in spring 1971.

However, this overall picture conceals large and very different changes for men and women. The employment rate for men fell from 92 per cent in 1971 to 79 per cent in spring 2005 – though it reached a low of 75 per cent in 1993 – while the rate for women rose from 56 per cent to 70 per cent. The gap between men's and women's employment rates fell by a factor of nearly four, from 35 to 9 percentage points.

Employment rates also differ between the English regions and devolved administrations. In 2004 the highest working-age employment rate in England was in the South East (79 per cent) and the lowest was in London (69 per cent). Rates in Scotland, Wales and Northern Ireland were: 75 per cent, 71 per cent and 68 per cent, respectively.

Differences in employment rates within regions are often greater than differences between regions. In 2004 the greatest contrast between local authorities was in London (see Appendix, Part 4: Annual Population Survey). The region contains Tower Hamlets, with the lowest working-age employment rate in Great Britain (54 per cent). The difference between the highest and lowest working-age employment rates in London was 25 percentage points (excluding the City

of London as the data are based on a very small sample). The London borough with the highest working-age employment rate was Bromley, at 79 per cent.

The local authority with the highest employment rate in Great Britain outside London was South Northamptonshire in the East Midlands with a rate of 86 per cent. Just over a fifth of local authorities in Great Britain had an employment rate of over 80 per cent in 2004.

In March 2000, the Lisbon European Council agreed an aim to achieve an overall European Union (EU) working-age employment rate as close as possible to 70 per cent by 2010 and, for women, an employment rate of more than 60 per cent. In 2004 the overall employment rate in the EU-25 was 63 per cent (Table 4.4). The United Kingdom had one of the highest employment rates after Denmark, the Netherlands and Sweden and was one of only four out of the EU-25 with an employment rate above the 2010 overall target.

The average employment rate in the EU-25 was 71 per cent for men and 56 per cent for women – the United Kingdom had the fourth highest male rate (78 per cent) and, together with Finland, the fourth highest female rate (66 per cent). The lowest employment rates for women were in the southern European countries of Greece, Italy and Malta. In contrast, the north European countries of Denmark, Sweden and the Netherlands had the highest rates. Among men the rates in 2004 varied from 57 per cent in Poland to 80 per cent in the Netherlands.

There is a range of factors underlying these comparisons. As well as economic cycle effects, which will vary across countries in a given year, they will also be affected by population structures and differing cultures, retirement ages and participation in post-compulsory full-time education across countries.

One of the factors that can affect employment rates is educational attainment: for both sexes, employment rates generally increase with the level of qualifications in the United Kingdom (Table 4.5). In spring 2005, 88 per cent of working-age people in the United Kingdom with a degree or equivalent were in employment compared with only 48 per cent of those with no qualification. This relationship was more marked for women than for men – 89 per cent of men who had a degree were in employment compared with 87 per cent of women, whereas 54 per cent of men and 42 per cent of women who did not have any qualifications were in employment. This means that the difference in employment rates between men and women generally decreases as the level of qualification increases. For those with a degree or equivalent there was a

## Table **4.4**

**Employment rates:[1] by sex, EU comparison, 2004**

Percentages

| | Men | Women | All | | Men | Women | All |
|---|---|---|---|---|---|---|---|
| Denmark | 79.7 | 71.6 | 75.7 | Luxembourg | 72.4 | 50.6 | 61.6 |
| Netherlands | 80.2 | 65.8 | 73.1 | Lithuania | 64.7 | 57.8 | 61.2 |
| Sweden | 73.6 | 70.5 | 72.1 | Spain | 73.8 | 48.3 | 61.1 |
| United Kingdom | 77.8 | 65.6 | 71.6 | Belgium | 67.9 | 52.6 | 60.3 |
| Cyprus | 79.8 | 58.7 | 68.9 | Greece | 73.7 | 45.2 | 59.4 |
| Austria | 74.9 | 60.7 | 67.8 | Italy | 70.1 | 45.2 | 57.6 |
| Portugal | 74.2 | 61.7 | 67.8 | Slovakia | 63.2 | 50.9 | 57.0 |
| Finland | 69.7 | 65.6 | 67.6 | Hungary | 63.1 | 50.7 | 56.8 |
| Ireland | 75.9 | 56.5 | 66.3 | Malta | 75.2 | 32.8 | 54.1 |
| Slovenia | 70.0 | 60.5 | 65.3 | Poland | 57.2 | 46.2 | 51.7 |
| Germany | 70.8 | 59.2 | 65.0 | EU-25 average | 70.9 | 55.7 | 63.3 |
| Czech Republic | 72.3 | 56.0 | 64.2 | | | | |
| France | 69.0 | 57.4 | 63.1 | | | | |
| Estonia | 66.4 | 60.0 | 63.0 | | | | |
| Latvia | 66.4 | 58.5 | 62.3 | | | | |

1 See Appendix, Part 4: Eurostat rates.

**Source: Labour Force Survey, Eurostat**

## Table **4.5**

**Employment rate:[1] by sex and highest qualification, 2005[2]**

**United Kingdom**      Percentages

| | Men | Women | All |
|---|---|---|---|
| Degree or equivalent | 89 | 87 | 88 |
| Higher education | 87 | 84 | 85 |
| GCE A level or equivalent | 81 | 73 | 77 |
| Trade apprenticeship | 83 | 73 | 81 |
| GCSE grades A* to C or equivalent | 79 | 71 | 75 |
| Qualifications at NVQ level 1 and below | 75 | 63 | 69 |
| Other qualifications – level unknown | 78 | 64 | 72 |
| No qualifications | 54 | 42 | 48 |
| All[3] | 79 | 70 | 74 |

1 The percentage of the working-age population in employment. Men
  aged 16 to 64, women aged 16 to 59.
2 At spring. Data are not seasonally adjusted and have been adjusted in
  line with population estimates published in spring 2003. See
  Appendix, Part 4: LFS reweighting.
3 Includes those who did not state their highest qualification.

**Source: Labour Force Survey, Office for National Statistics**

gap of 3 percentage points in employment rates between men and women, compared with 12 percentage points for those with qualifications at NVQ level 1 and below.

There are clear differences in employment rates between parents and non-parents, between mothers and fathers, and between couple parents and lone parents. Table 4.6 overleaf shows that in spring 2004 in the United Kingdom, working-age mothers with dependent children were less likely to be in employment than working-age women without dependent children (67 per cent compared with 73 per cent). For men, the opposite was true – fathers were more likely to be in employment than working-age men without dependent children (90 per cent and 74 per cent). There is also an employment hierarchy evident between the different subgroups of parents. Fathers as a whole had higher employment rates than mothers (90 per cent compared with 67 per cent); couple parents had higher employment rates than lone parents (81 per cent and 54 per cent); and lone fathers had higher employment rates than lone mothers (67 per cent and 53 per cent). There were differences in employment rates between parents and non-parents, and between different types of parent, across all age groups.

In spring 2005, the employment rate for lone parents in the United Kingdom was 56 per cent, up 2 percentage points from

Table **4.6**

**Employment rates of people[1] with and without dependent children:[2] by age and sex, 2004[3]**

United Kingdom

Percentages

| | 16–24 | 25–34 | 35–49 | 50–59/64 | All |
|---|---|---|---|---|---|
| Mothers with dependent children | 35 | 59 | 73 | 68 | 67 |
| Married/cohabiting mothers | 45 | 63 | 76 | 72 | 71 |
| Lone mothers | 25 | 46 | 62 | 55 | 53 |
| Women without dependent children | 62 | 90 | 81 | 68 | 73 |
| Fathers with dependent children | 81 | 89 | 92 | 84 | 90 |
| Married/cohabiting fathers | 82 | 89 | 93 | 85 | 91 |
| Lone fathers | 26 | 55 | 72 | 61 | 67 |
| Men without dependent children | 61 | 87 | 85 | 69 | 74 |
| All parents with dependent children | 45 | 70 | 82 | 78 | 77 |
| Married/cohabiting parents | 57 | 75 | 84 | 80 | 81 |
| Lone parents | 25 | 47 | 64 | 56 | 54 |
| All people without dependent children | 61 | 88 | 83 | 69 | 74 |

1 Men aged 16 to 64 and women aged 16 to 59. Excludes people with unknown employment status.
2 Children under 16 and those aged 16 to 18 who are never-married and in full-time education.
3 At spring. Data are not seasonally adjusted and have been adjusted in line with population estimates published in spring 2003. See Appendix, Part 4: LFS reweighting.

*Source: Labour Force Survey, Office for National Statistics*

the previous year. In comparison, the employment rate for married or cohabiting mothers in spring 2005 was 72 per cent, up 1 percentage point from the previous year.

Between spring 1994 and spring 2004 the employment rate for couple mothers and couple fathers increased by 7 percentage points and 5 percentage points respectively. However employment rates for lone parents increased by 12 percentage points from 42 per cent to 54 per cent (Figure 4.7). These upward trends reflect increases in both full-time and part-time employment.

Couple mothers and lone parents tend to have lower qualification levels than couple fathers. In spring 2004, 17 per cent of couple mothers and only 9 per cent of lone parents had a degree or equivalent qualification, compared with 21 per cent of couple fathers. Over a fifth (22 per cent) of lone parents and 12 per cent of couple mothers had no qualifications compared with 10 per cent of couple fathers. Not surprisingly, employment rates were highest among graduates and lowest among those with no qualifications – couple mothers and lone parents with a degree or equivalent qualification each had an employment rate of 81 per cent, while couple mothers and lone parents with no qualifications had employment rates of 44 per cent and 29 per cent respectively.

Since October 1998 the Government's New Deal for Lone Parents (NDLP) has aimed at helping lone parents in Great

Figure **4.7**

**Employment rates of working-age lone parents:[1] by type of employment**

United Kingdom

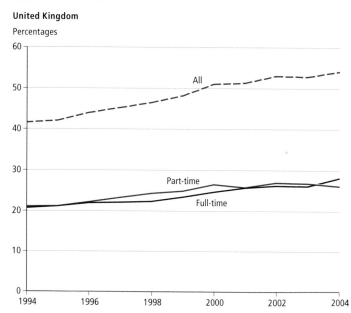

Percentages

1 Lone parents in employment as a percentage of all lone parents. At spring each year. Data are not seasonally adjusted and have been adjusted in line with population estimates published in spring 2003. See Appendix, Part 4: LFS reweighting.

*Source: Labour Force Survey, Office for National Statistics*

## Figure **4.8**

**Parents leaving the New Deal for Lone Parents[1] to enter employment:[2] by age of youngest child[3]**

**Great Britain**
Percentages

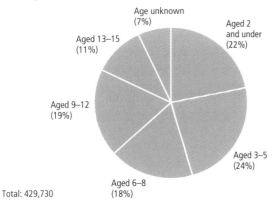

Total: 429,730

1  The New Deal for Lone Parents programme started in October 1998. Data are as a proportion of cases where the destination was known to be employment and are for October 1998 to May 2005.
2  Those who are recorded by Jobcentre Plus as having been placed into unsubsidised employment, those who are recorded on HM Revenue and Customs records as having obtained a job, and those who have evidence of both employment and benefit spells immediately after leaving the programme.
3  Age of youngest child when the lone parent attended the programme's initial interview.

*Source: Department for Work and Pensions*

## Figure **4.9**

**Employment rates[1] of older people[2]**

**United Kingdom**
Percentages

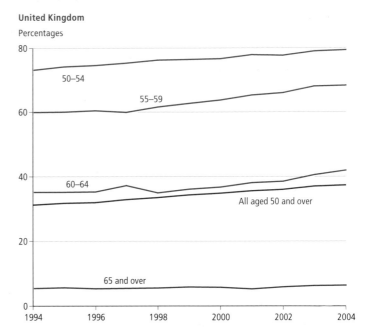

1  At spring each year. Data are not seasonally adjusted and have been adjusted in line with population estimates published in spring 2003. See Appendix, Part 4: LFS reweighting.
2  State pension age for men is currently 65 and 60 for women.

*Source: Labour Force Survey, Office for National Statistics*

Britain into work. The programme involves an initial interview with an advisor to discuss work issues and advice on in-work benefits – further participation is voluntary. Main features of the programme include work trials, help with costs of approved training or education courses, and help with costs incurred while training, such as travel expenses and registered childcare costs. Between October 1998 and the end of May 2005, 429,700 lone parents left NDLP and moved directly into employment. Of these, 46 per cent had a youngest child aged five or under at the initial New Deal interview (Figure 4.8).

Other New Deal programmes aimed at helping particular groups of people into work include New Deal for Young People (NDYP) and New Deal 25 plus (ND25+). During the period April 1998 to the end of May 2005, 567,900 (46 per cent) of those leaving NDYP left the programme to enter employment. Among those aged 25 and over leaving the enhanced ND25+ programme between April 2001 and the end of May 2005, 126,600 (32 per cent) also left directly to enter employment. In addition there is a New Deal programme for those aged over 50 (ND50+). Between April 2000 and the end of August 2005, 146,000 people gained employment through ND50+.

Although the employment rate of older people declined markedly between the late 1970s and mid-1990s, employment rates of older workers have increased in recent years from

31 per cent in spring 1994 for those aged 50 and over to 37 per cent in spring 2004 (Figure 4.9). The main increase occurred among those aged 50 to state pension age (65 for men, 60 for women). Between spring 1994 and 2004 the employment rate among this group increased by 7 percentage points to 70 per cent. This compares with an increase of 1 percentage point to reach 6 per cent among those aged 65 and over. The increase in employment was experienced by both men and women. The proportion of men aged 50 and over in employment rose from 39 per cent to 44 per cent over the ten years to spring 2004, while the employment rate for women aged 50 and over rose from 25 per cent to 31 per cent.

Those with formal qualifications were more likely to stay in work than the unqualified. Of those aged 50 to state pension age in spring 2004, 81 per cent with a degree or equivalent were in employment, compared with 74 per cent of people with the equivalent of at least one GCSE and 52 per cent of people with no qualifications. However, over a fifth (22 per cent) of economically inactive people (those neither in work nor looking for work – see also page 63) aged 50 and over in 2002–04 had left their last job because of health reasons. The proportion was highest among those who were previously in process, plant and machine occupations (30 per cent) and lowest among those who were in administrative and secretarial (14 per cent).

## Figure **4.10**

### Sickness absence:[1] by occupation, 2004[2]

**United Kingdom**
Percentages

1 Employees who were absent from work for at least one day in the reference week.
2 At spring. People aged 16 and over. Data are not seasonally adjusted and have been adjusted in line with population estimates published in spring 2003. See Appendix, Part 4: LFS reweighting.

**Source: Labour Force Survey, Office for National Statistics**

In spring 2004 in the United Kingdom, some 1.7 million scheduled working days were lost to sickness absence among employees and around 3 per cent of employees took at least one day off work (in the survey reference week) because of sickness or injury. Sickness absence rates were generally higher for female employees (3.3 per cent) than male (2.4 per cent). They were also higher for younger employees than older employees – 3.2 per cent of 16 to 24 year olds took at least one day off sick in the reference week compared with 2.8 per cent of employees aged 50 to 59/64. Days lost to sickness were fairly evenly spread across the weekdays. This is counter to the common perception that sickness absence is higher on Mondays and Fridays as a result of non-genuine absence.

Sickness absence in spring 2004 also varied between occupations from 2.0 per cent for managers and senior officials to 3.6 per cent for employees in personal service occupations (Figure 4.10). As well as employees in personal service occupations, those who were process, plant and machine operatives, employees in administrative and secretarial, elementary, and sales and customer service occupations were more likely to take sickness absence than the average for employees in all occupations (2.9 per cent).

The Workplace Employment Relations Survey 2004 collected information about employees' job-related well-being via a six

item measure. Employees were asked how often their job made them feel tense, worried, uneasy, calm, relaxed and content. Almost one fifth (19 per cent) of employees in Great Britain said that their job made them feel tense all or most of the time, 42 per cent said they felt tense some of the time and 39 per cent said that they felt job-related tension only occasionally or never. The survey also asked employees how satisfied or dissatisfied they were with the following eight aspects of their job: sense of achievement; scope for using initiative; influence over job; training; pay; job security; the work itself; and involvement in decision making. The survey found that employees were most likely to say that they were very satisfied or satisfied with the scope they had for using their initiative in their work, closely followed by satisfaction with their sense of achievement and the work itself. Employees were least likely to be satisfied with their pay (35 per cent) and with their involvement in decision making (38 per cent).

According to the British Social Attitudes survey most people do not think that pay should be the most important consideration in making career choices. In 2004 around one in ten people in Great Britain thought that good pay was the most important consideration, whereas one in three thought job security was the most important consideration, one in four thought interesting work was most important and one in five favoured a good work-life balance (Table 4.11).

## Table **4.11**

### Most important factors influencing career choices:[1] by sex, 2004

**Great Britain**

Percentages

| | Men | Women | All |
|---|---|---|---|
| Secure job | 36 | 35 | 36 |
| Interesting work | 26 | 24 | 25 |
| Good work-life balance | 21 | 21 | 21 |
| Good pay | 9 | 11 | 10 |
| Opportunities for promotion | 7 | 8 | 8 |
| Chance to help other people | 1 | 1 | 1 |

1 Respondents were shown the above options and asked 'Suppose you were thinking about a person's career in general and the choices that they have to make. Which one of these would you say is the most important for them to think about?' Excludes those who responded 'Don't know' or did not answer.

**Source: British Social Attitudes Survey, National Centre for Social Research**

## Table **4.12**

### All in employment: by sex and occupation, 2005[1]

| United Kingdom | | Percentages |
| --- | --- | --- |
| | Men | Women |
| Managers and senior officials | 18 | 11 |
| Professional | 14 | 12 |
| Associate professional and technical | 13 | 15 |
| Administrative and secretarial | 4 | 22 |
| Skilled trades | 20 | 2 |
| Personal service | 2 | 14 |
| Sales and customer service | 5 | 12 |
| Process, plant and machine operatives | 12 | 2 |
| Elementary | 12 | 11 |
| All occupations | 100 | 100 |

1 At spring. People aged 16 and over. Data are not seasonally adjusted and have been adjusted in line with population estimates published in spring 2003. See Appendix, Part 4: LFS reweighting.

*Source: Labour Force Survey, Office for National Statistics*

## Patterns of employment

The pattern of occupations followed by men and women is quite different (Table 4.12). In spring 2005, just over a fifth of women in employment were employed in administrative and secretarial work, while men were most likely to be employed in skilled trade occupations or as managers and senior officials. These occupations were among the ones least likely to be followed by women. Conversely women were more likely than men to be in employment in the personal services (for example hairdressers and child care assistants) and in sales and customer services. Only the professional, associate professional and technical, and the elementary occupations (such as farm workers, labourers and catering assistants) were almost equally likely to be followed by both men and women: between around one in seven and one in nine were employed in each of these occupations.

It is well-known that the UK economy has experienced structural change since the end of World War Two with a decline in the manufacturing sector and an increase in service industries (Figure 4.13). Jobs in the service industries have increased by 45 per cent, from 14.8 million in 1978 (when the series began) to 21.5 million in 2005, while those in manufacturing have fallen by 54 per cent from 6.9 million to 3.2 million over the same period. Virtually all the increase in women's labour market participation has been through taking up jobs in the service sector. In 1978 there were fewer jobs done by women (10.2 million) than by men (13.9 million). However, by 2005 the number of jobs done by women and men were very similar (13.0 million and 13.4 million, respectively).

## Figure **4.13**

### Employee jobs:[1] by sex and industry

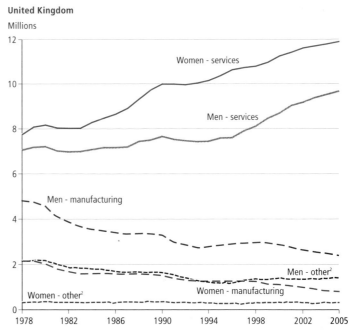

United Kingdom

Millions

1 At June each year.
2 Includes agriculture, construction, energy and water.

*Source: Short-term Turnover and Employment Survey, Office for National Statistics*

The largest increase in both male and female employee jobs has been in financial and business services which accounted for about one in ten employee jobs in 1978 compared with one in five employee jobs in 2005. Note that these data are based on jobs rather than people – one person may have more than one job, and jobs may vary in the number of hours' work they involve.

Not all people in employment work as employees. In spring 2005 there were 3.6 million self-employed people in the United Kingdom, accounting for 13 per cent of all those in employment. Self-employment is dominated by men – in spring 2005, 74 per cent of self-employed people were men.

Men and women also vary considerably in the type of self-employed work they undertake. Almost a third of self-employed men worked in the construction industry in spring 2005 but very few women worked in this sector (Figure 4.14 overleaf). On the other hand, 23 per cent of self-employed women worked in other services – for example community, social and personal services (such as textile washing and dry cleaning, hairdressing and other beauty treatments) – and 22 per cent worked in public administration, education and health. Fewer than one in twelve self-employed men worked in each of these industries.

# Figure **4.14**

## Self-employment: by industry and sex, 2005[1]

**United Kingdom**

Percentages

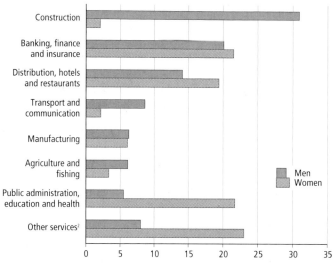

1 At spring. People aged 16 and over. Data are not seasonally adjusted and have been adjusted in line with population estimates published in autumn 2005. See Appendix, Part 4: LFS reweighting.
2 Community, social and personal services including sanitation, dry cleaning, personal care, and recreational, cultural and sporting activities.

**Source: Labour Force Survey, Office for National Statistics**

Homeworkers are people who work mainly in their home, or in different places using home as a base, in their main job (see Appendix, Part 4: Homeworkers and teleworkers). In spring 1997, there were 2.3 million homeworkers in the United Kingdom but by spring 2005 the number had increased to around 3.1 million. Of these almost two thirds were self-employed. Most of these homeworkers (2.4 million) were teleworkers – people who used a telephone and computer to carry out their work. The number of teleworkers has increased by more than 150 per cent (1.5 million) since spring 1997, the earliest year for which data are available. In spring 1997 teleworkers represented 40 per cent of homeworkers but by spring 2005 this had risen to 77 per cent. Although teleworkers only represent a small proportion of the workforce, this proportion increased from 4 per cent in spring 1997 to 8 per cent in spring 2005 (Figure 4.15).

Sixty five per cent of teleworkers were men in spring 2005. This partly reflects the fact that men accounted for the larger share of the workforce overall but teleworking (and homeworking in general) was more prevalent among male workers than among female workers. In spring 2005, the teleworking rate for men was 11 per cent, compared with 6 per cent for women. Men are more likely than women to telework in different places using their home as a base, and it is in this style of work that the greatest increase in teleworking rates has taken place.

# Figure **4.15**

## Homeworkers[1] and teleworkers[2] as a percentage of people in employment[3]

**United Kingdom**

Percentages

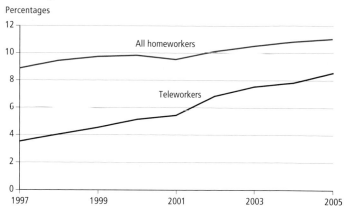

1 Homeworkers are people who mainly work in their home, or in different places using home as a base, in their main job.
2 Teleworkers are a subgroup of homeworkers, who use both a telephone and a computer to work at home, or in different places using home as a base. See Appendix, Part 4: Homeworkers and teleworkers.
3 At spring each year. Data are for people aged 16 and over and excludes people on government employment and training schemes. Data are not seasonally adjusted and have been adjusted in line with population estimates published in spring 2003. See Appendix, Part 4: LFS reweighting. Estimates have been adjusted for nonresponse to the homeworking and teleworking questions.

**Source: Labour Force Survey, Office for National Statistics**

There were 18.4 million full-time and 6.4 million part-time employees in spring 2005. However, to distinguish only between full time and part time masks differences in usual working hours. The 1998 Working Time Regulations implemented an EC Directive on working time in the United Kingdom. The regulations apply to full-time, part-time and temporary workers and provide for a maximum working week of 48 hours (on average), although individual workers can choose to work longer hours. In spring 2005, around a fifth (18 per cent) of full-time employees in the United Kingdom usually worked over 48 hours a week (Table 4.16). However, a higher proportion of male employees (23 per cent) than female (11 per cent) usually worked these longer hours. Those who worked as managers and senior officials were most likely to work over 48 hours a week (30 per cent), whereas those who worked in administrative and secretarial jobs were least likely (4 per cent). Although men were more likely than women usually to work over 48 hours in most occupational groups, the exception were professionals – in spring 2005 a similar proportion of professional women (28 per cent) usually worked longer hours as professional men (26 per cent).

In 2004 the British Social Attitudes survey asked working adults in Great Britain to consider the number of hours they worked (including regular overtime) and to say whether they would prefer more hours per week, fewer hours per week or whether

## Table **4.16**

**Employees[1] who usually worked over 48 hours a week: by sex and occupation, 2005[2]**

United Kingdom                                              Percentages

| | Men | Women | All employees |
|---|---|---|---|
| Managers and senior officials | 36 | 18 | 30 |
| Professional | 26 | 28 | 27 |
| Associate professional and technical | 18 | 7 | 13 |
| Administrative and secretarial | 8 | 2 | 4 |
| Skilled trades | 19 | 7 | 19 |
| Personal service | 13 | 7 | 9 |
| Sales and customer service | 11 | 3 | 6 |
| Process, plant and machine operatives | 28 | 8 | 25 |
| Elementary | 18 | 8 | 16 |
| All occupations | 23 | 11 | 18 |

1 Full-time employees aged 16 and over. Time rounded to the nearest hour respondents worked on their main job. Includes regular paid and unpaid overtime. Excludes employees who did not state their usual hours.
2 At spring. Data are not seasonally adjusted and have been adjusted in line with population estimates published in spring 2003. See Appendix, Part 4: LFS reweighting.

**Source: Labour Force Survey, Office for National Statistics**

## Table **4.17**

**Employees with flexible working patterns:[1] by sex, 2005[2]**

United Kingdom                                              Percentages

| | Men | Women | All employees |
|---|---|---|---|
| **Full-time employees** | | | |
| Flexible working hours | 10.2 | 16.1 | 12.5 |
| Annualised working hours | 4.9 | 5.1 | 5.0 |
| Four and a half day week | 1.4 | 0.9 | 1.2 |
| Term-time working | 1.2 | 5.9 | 3.0 |
| Nine day fortnight | 0.3 | 0.3 | 0.3 |
| Any flexible working pattern[3] | 18.2 | 28.5 | 22.1 |
| **Part-time employees** | | | |
| Flexible working hours | 6.8 | 9.3 | 8.9 |
| Annualised working hours | 3.0 | 4.1 | 3.9 |
| Term-time working | 4.2 | 10.9 | 9.6 |
| Job sharing | 0.8 | 2.2 | 1.9 |
| Any flexible working pattern[3] | 15.8 | 27.3 | 25.0 |

1 Percentages are based on totals which exclude people who did not state whether or not they had a flexible working arrangement. Respondents could give more than one answer.
2 At spring. People aged 16 and over. Data are not seasonally adjusted and have been adjusted in line with population estimates published in spring 2003. See Appendix, Part 4: LFS reweighting.
3 Includes other categories of flexible working not separately identified.

**Source: Labour Force Survey, Office for National Statistics**

they were happy with their weekly hours. Over a third of men said that they would prefer to work fewer hours, as did over a quarter of women. The majority of both men and women were happy with their current working hours. Those who answered they would prefer to work fewer hours per week were then asked 'Would you still prefer to work fewer hours, if it meant earning less money as a result?' Twenty two per cent of these men and 30 per cent of these women said they would still prefer to work fewer hours.

Government policy over recent years has stressed the importance of maintaining a healthy work-life balance. One factor seen as important is the availability of flexible working. Over a fifth of full-time employees and a quarter of part-time employees had some form of flexible working arrangement in spring 2005 (Table 4.17). Flexible working hours was the most common form of flexible working for full-time employees of both sexes. It was the most common arrangement among men who worked part time and second most common for women – exceeded only by term-time working.

Regulations introduced across the United Kingdom in April 2003 give parents of children under 6, or parents of disabled children under 18, the right to request a flexible work pattern. This could be either a change to the hours they work; a change to the times when they are required to work; or the opportunity to work from home. Employers have a statutory

duty to consider such requests seriously and may only refuse on business grounds. According to the Second Flexible Working Employee Survey, female employees in Great Britain in 2005 were more likely to have requested to work flexibly than males (19 per cent and 10 per cent respectively) in the previous two years. Requests were higher among employees with dependent children under the age of 6 (22 per cent), aged between 6 and 12 (18 per cent) or aged between 12 and 16 (15 per cent) than those employees without dependent children (10 per cent).

Temporary work increased during the early to mid-1990s but has declined in recent years. In spring 1992, 6 per cent of employees in the United Kingdom worked on a temporary basis and by spring 1997 this had increased to 8 per cent (Figure 4.18 overleaf). However by spring 2005 the proportion of employees who were in temporary work had fallen and was again 6 per cent which represented 1.5 million employees. Throughout the period a slightly higher proportion of female employees than male worked on a temporary contract.

Employees on fixed-period contracts accounted for about half of all temporary employees between spring 1992 and spring 2005. Other types of temporary work such as casual or seasonal work have declined slightly as a proportion of all

## Figure **4.18**

### Temporary workers:[1] by sex

United Kingdom
Percentages

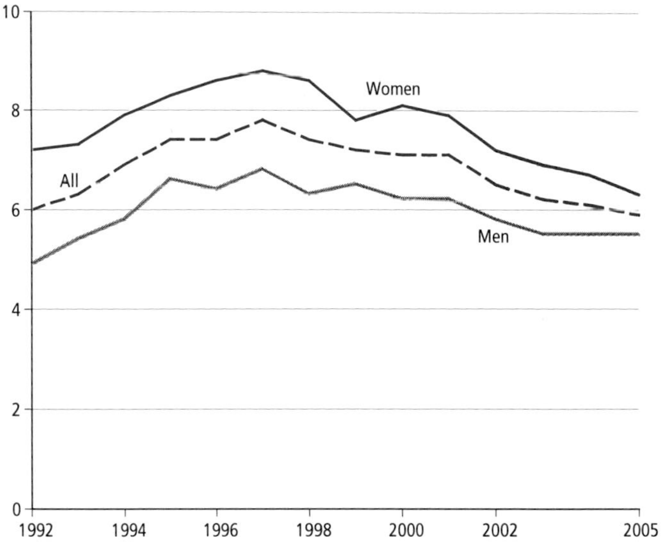

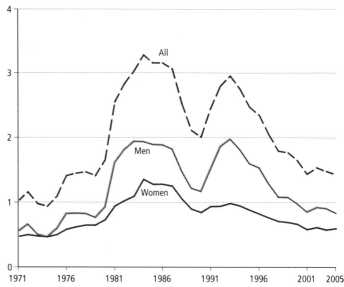

1 As a percentage of all employees. Employees who said that their main
  job was non-permanent. At spring each year. People aged 16 and
  over. Data are seasonally adjusted and have been adjusted in line with
  population estimates published in autumn 2005. See Appendix,
  Part 4: LFS reweighting.

**Source: Labour Force Survey, Office for National Statistics**

## Figure **4.19**

### Unemployment:[1] by sex

United Kingdom
Millions

1 At spring each year. People aged 16 and over. Data are seasonally
  adjusted and have been adjusted in line with population estimates
  published in autumn 2005. See Appendix, Part 4: Unemployment, and
  LFS reweighting, and Historical LFS-consistent time series.

**Source: Labour Force Survey, Office for National Statistics**

temporary work. However, agency temping increased from
7 per cent of all temporary work in spring 1992 to 19 per cent
in spring 2005. Just over a quarter of employees who worked
in a temporary job did so because they did not want
a permanent one. This proportion was higher for women than
men (29 per cent compared with 24 per cent). A slightly lower
proportion of employees were in a temporary job because they
could not find a permanent job (24 per cent overall).

## Unemployment

The number of unemployed people is linked to the economic
cycle, albeit with a time lag. Broadly speaking, as the country
experiences economic growth so the number of jobs grows
and unemployment falls, though any mismatches between
the skill needs of the new jobs and the skills of those available
for work may slow this process. Conversely as the economy
slows and goes into recession so unemployment tends to rise.
Since spring 1971 there have been two main peaks in
unemployment. The first was in spring 1984 when
unemployment reached 3.3 million, and the latest peak
occurred in spring 1993 when it reached nearly 3 million
(Figure 4.19). In spring 2001 the number of people
unemployed fell to 1.4 million. Unemployment then increased
slightly before falling back to 1.4 million again in spring 2005.

The peak for female unemployment was in spring 1984 when
1.3 million women were unemployed. The recession in the
early 1990s had a much greater effect on unemployment
among men than among women, as the peak for male
unemployment was in 1993 when just under 2 million men
were unemployed.

The unemployment rate in the United Kingdom was 4.7 per
cent in spring 2005 but unemployment rates varied across the
Government Office Regions and devolved administrations, with
the highest rate in London (7.2 per cent) and the lowest rate in
the South West (3.4 per cent). In Scotland, Northern Ireland
and Wales unemployment rates in spring 2005 were 5.7 per
cent, 4.9 per cent and 4.5 per cent respectively.

In 2004 the unemployment rate in the EU-25 was 9.0 per cent,
ranging from 4.5 per cent in Ireland to 18.8 per cent in Poland
(Table 4.20). The United Kingdom (4.7 per cent) had the third
lowest overall unemployment rate of all the EU-25, although it
had the sixth lowest rate for men (5.0 per cent) and the second
lowest rate for women (4.2 per cent). The differences in rates
between men and women were greatest in the southern
European countries of Greece and Spain where rates for
women were between 7 and 10 percentage points higher than
for men. For the majority of the other EU countries, including

**Table 4.20**

**Unemployment rates:[1] by sex, EU comparison, 2004**

Percentages

| | Men | Women | All | | Men | Women | All |
|---|---|---|---|---|---|---|---|
| Ireland | 4.9 | 4.0 | 4.5 | Finland | 8.7 | 8.9 | 8.8 |
| Netherlands | 4.3 | 4.8 | 4.6 | Estonia | 10.4 | 8.0 | 9.2 |
| United Kingdom | 5.0 | 4.2 | 4.7 | Germany | 8.7 | 10.5 | 9.5 |
| Luxembourg | 3.3 | 6.8 | 4.8 | France | 8.7 | 10.5 | 9.6 |
| Austria | 4.4 | 5.3 | 4.8 | Latvia | 9.4 | 10.1 | 9.8 |
| Cyprus | 4.1 | 6.5 | 5.2 | Greece | 6.6 | 16.2 | 10.5 |
| Denmark | 5.1 | 5.7 | 5.4 | Lithuania | 10.5 | 11.2 | 10.9 |
| Slovenia | 5.6 | 6.4 | 6.0 | Spain | 8.1 | 15.0 | 11.0 |
| Hungary | 5.9 | 6.1 | 6.0 | Slovakia | 17.3 | 19.3 | 18.2 |
| Sweden | 6.5 | 6.1 | 6.3 | Poland | 18.0 | 19.8 | 18.8 |
| Portugal | 5.9 | 7.6 | 6.7 | EU-25 average | 8.1 | 10.2 | 9.0 |
| Malta | 7.1 | 8.7 | 7.6 | | | | |
| Belgium | 7.1 | 8.9 | 7.9 | | | | |
| Italy | 6.4 | 10.5 | 8.0 | | | | |
| Czech Republic | 7.1 | 9.9 | 8.3 | | | | |

1 See Appendix, Part 4: Eurostat rates.

*Source: Labour Force Survey, Eurostat*

the United Kingdom, the differences in rates were no more than 2 percentage points.

Unemployment rates in Great Britain for people from non-White ethnic groups were generally higher than those from White ethnic groups in 2004 (Figure 4.21). Male unemployment rates were highest among Black Caribbeans (15 per cent). Rates among men from the Black African, Bangladeshi and Mixed ethnic groups were each around 13 per cent – almost three times the rate for White British and White Irish men (each 5 per cent). Of the men from non-White ethnic groups, Indians had the lowest unemployment rates in 2004.

Among women, Pakistanis had the highest unemployment rates (20 per cent). Unemployment rates for women from the Black African (13 per cent) and Mixed ethnic groups (12 per cent) were also relatively high and around three times the rate for White Irish and White British women (each 4 per cent) (see article on ethnic and religious populations page 1).

Age and sex also influence the length of time that people spend unemployed. Younger unemployed people are less likely than older people to have been so for a long period, and women are less likely than men to have been unemployed for a long period (Table 4.22 overleaf). In spring 2005, over half of unemployed women aged between 16 and 19 had been out of work for less than three months, and less than one in fourteen

**Figure 4.21**

**Unemployment rates: by ethnic group[1] and sex, 2004[2]**

**Great Britain**

Percentages

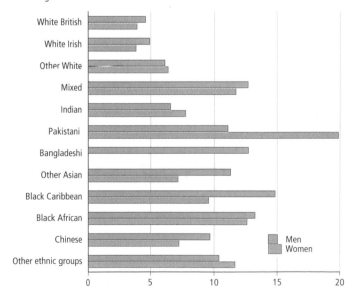

1 The estimates for the Other Black group and Bangladeshi women are excluded due to a small number of respondents.

2 January to December. See Appendix, Part 4: Annual Population Survey.

*Source: Annual Population Survey, Office for National Statistics*

Table **4.22**

**Duration of unemployment:[1] by sex and age, 2005[2]**

United Kingdom

Percentages

| | Less than 3 months | 3 months but less than 6 months | 6 months but less than 1 year | 1 year but less than 2 years | 2 years or more | All durations |
|---|---|---|---|---|---|---|
| **Men** | | | | | | |
| 16–19 | 38 | 27 | 20 | 11 | 5 | 100 |
| 20–29 | 43 | 22 | 18 | 10 | 8 | 100 |
| 30–39 | 32 | 17 | 17 | 19 | 16 | 100 |
| 40–49 | 36 | 24 | 11 | 13 | 16 | 100 |
| 50–64 | 27 | 16 | 18 | 16 | 23 | 100 |
| All aged 16 and over[3] | 36 | 21 | 17 | 13 | 13 | 100 |
| **Women** | | | | | | |
| 16–19 | 57 | 16 | 20 | 7 | - | 100 |
| 20–29 | 55 | 21 | 14 | 6 | 4 | 100 |
| 30–39 | 50 | 18 | 13 | 12 | 7 | 100 |
| 40–49 | 38 | 25 | 13 | 13 | 11 | 100 |
| 50–59 | 41 | 14 | 8 | 19 | 18 | 100 |
| All aged 16 and over[3] | 50 | 19 | 14 | 10 | 6 | 100 |

1 Excludes those who did not state their duration of unemployment. See Appendix, Part 4: Unemployment.
2 At spring. Data are not seasonally adjusted and have been adjusted in line with population estimates published in spring 2003. See Appendix, Part 4: LFS reweighting.
3 Includes men aged 65 and over and women aged 60 and over.

Shaded cell indicates the estimate is unreliable and any analysis using this figure may be invalid. Any use of this shaded figure must be accompanied by this disclaimer.

Source: Labour Force Survey, Office for National Statistics

had been unemployed for a year or more. However, around one in six unemployed men in their 30s and 40s had been unemployed for two years or more and this rose to nearly one in four among those aged 50 to 64.

In the LFS people are defined as long-term unemployed if they have been unemployed for one year or more. In spring 2005, 0.3 million people in the United Kingdom had been unemployed for this length of time and of this group around 1 in 3 worked in an elementary occupation in their previous job. Those who were employed in associate, professional and technical occupations in their previous job were among the least likely to be long-term unemployed (around 1 in 15).

Job separations occur when an employee leaves a paid job of their own accord – a voluntary separation – or when the employer initiates the separation – an involuntary separation (see Appendix, Part 4: Job separations). In 2004 more people in the United Kingdom left their job voluntarily than involuntarily (3.3 per cent and 1.2 per cent respectively of those in employment in 2004). Men were also more likely than women to separate involuntarily, whereas women were more likely than men to separate from their job voluntarily.

It is possible in the LFS to determine the current economic activity status of people who separated from a job in the three months before they were interviewed. In winter 2004, the

Table **4.23**

**Economic activity status:[1] by sex and job separation type, 2004**

United Kingdom

Percentages

| | Involuntary job separation | Voluntary job separation | All job separations |
|---|---|---|---|
| **Men** | | | |
| In employment | 45 | 68 | 60 |
| Unemployed | 40 | 17 | 25 |
| Economically inactive | 15 | 16 | 16 |
| All men | 100 | 100 | 100 |
| **Women** | | | |
| In employment | 47 | 62 | 58 |
| Unemployed | 33 | 13 | 18 |
| Economically inactive | 20 | 25 | 24 |
| All women | 100 | 100 | 100 |
| **All** | | | |
| In employment | 46 | 65 | 59 |
| Unemployed | 37 | 15 | 22 |
| Economically inactive | 17 | 20 | 19 |
| All people | 100 | 100 | 100 |

1 The current economic activity status of people who separated from paid jobs in the three months before their Labour Force Survey interview in Winter 2004. See Appendix, Part 4: Job separations. Men aged 16 to 64, women aged 16 to 59. Data are not seasonally adjusted and have been adjusted in line with population estimates published in spring 2003. See Appendix, Part 4: LFS reweighting.

Source: Labour Force Survey, Office for National Statistics

majority of people (59 per cent) who had separated from a job were back in paid employment within three months, although this proportion was higher for those who left voluntarily (65 per cent) than for those who left involuntarily (46 per cent) (Table 4.23). Women were more likely to find employment following an involuntary separation than men, while men were more likely to find employment after a voluntary separation than women. Women were more likely than men to become economically inactive following a voluntary separation.

## Economic inactivity

In spring 2005, 7.9 million people of working age in the United Kingdom were economically inactive, of whom 60 per cent were women. If those over state pension age (65 for men and 60 for women) are included this number rises to 17.6 million.

The inactivity rate among people of working age in the United Kingdom was 21 per cent in spring 2005 and has been stable since 1971 (Figure 4.24). However this masks quite marked differences in the trends for men and women. The inactivity rate among men rose from 5 per cent in spring 1971 to 17 per cent in spring 2005. In comparison although the rate for women is still higher than that for men, it fell from 41 per cent to 27 per cent over the same period.

Between spring 1995 and spring 2005 the total number of working-age economically inactive people in the United Kingdom increased by 0.3 million. The number of inactive men over the period increased by 0.5 million, whereas the number of women decreased by 0.2 million. Conversely the total number of economically active increased by 1.6 million which was the result of an increase of 1.1 million economically active women and an increase of 0.5 million men.

Economic inactivity rates of young people in the United Kingdom (aged 16 to 24) are affected by whether or not they are in full-time education. Inactivity rates of those in full-time education fell between spring 1992 and spring 2005, although throughout the period the rate for males was consistently around 3 to 8 percentage points higher than for females (Figure 4.25). Among those who were not in full-time education young women were more likely than young men to be economically inactive.

The proportion of people aged 50 and over who were economically inactive fell over the 10 years to spring 2004 from 66 per cent to 62 per cent. For men of this age the rate decreased only slightly from 57 per cent to 54 per cent, whereas the rate for older women fell from 74 per cent to 69 per cent over the decade. Despite the overall decline in the

## Figure **4.24**

**Economic inactivity rates:[1] by sex**

United Kingdom

Percentages

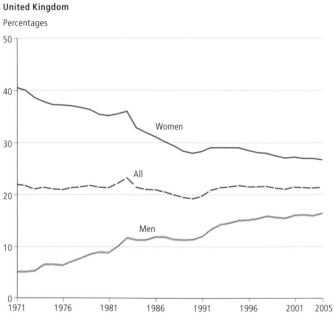

1 At spring each year. Men aged 16 to 64, women aged 16 to 59. Data are seasonally adjusted and have been adjusted in line with population estimates published in autumn 2005. See Appendix, Part 4: LFS reweighting, and Historical LFS-consistent time series.

**Source: Labour Force Survey, Office for National Statistics**

## Figure **4.25**

**Economic inactivity rates of young people:[1] by whether in full-time education**

United Kingdom

Percentages

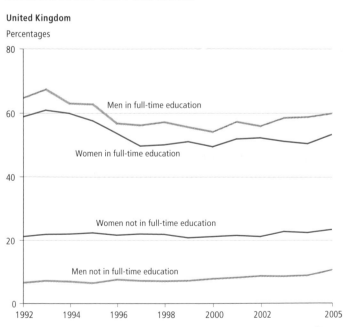

1 At spring each year. Young people aged 16 to 24. Data are seasonally adjusted and have been adjusted in line with population estimates published in autumn 2005. See Appendix, Part 4: LFS reweighting.

**Source: Labour Force Survey, Office for National Statistics**

## Table **4.26**

### Reasons for economic inactivity: by sex and age, 2005[1]

United Kingdom

Percentages

| | 16–24 | 25–34 | 35–49 | 50–59/64 | All aged 16–59/64 |
|---|---|---|---|---|---|
| **Men** | | | | | |
| Long-term sick or disabled | 5 | 40 | 61 | 52 | 37 |
| Looking after family or home | 1 | 12 | 15 | 4 | 6 |
| Student | 83 | 24 | 5 | - | 30 |
| Retired | 0 | 0 | - | 30 | 13 |
| Other | 11 | 24 | 18 | 13 | 14 |
| All men | 100 | 100 | 100 | 100 | 100 |
| **Women** | | | | | |
| Long-term sick or disabled | 4 | 9 | 25 | 40 | 20 |
| Looking after family or home | 22 | 71 | 60 | 28 | 44 |
| Student | 66 | 10 | 4 | 1 | 21 |
| Retired | 0 | 0 | - | 15 | 4 |
| Other | 8 | 10 | 11 | 16 | 11 |
| All women | 100 | 100 | 100 | 100 | 100 |

1 At spring. Data are not seasonally adjusted and have been adjusted in line with population estimates published in spring 2003. See Appendix, Part 4: LFS reweighting.

**Source: Labour Force Survey, Office for National Statistics**

rate of inactivity of older people, they still constituted the largest inactive group in spring 2004 compared with younger age groups.

Reasons for inactivity also vary by age. Long-term sickness or disability was the main reason for economic inactivity among working-age men, particularly for 35 to 49 year olds (61 per cent) (Table 4.26). Looking after the family or home was the most common reason for inactivity among working-age women; 44 per cent said this was their main reason for not seeking work but this rose to 71 per cent of 25 to 34 year olds.

There were over 7 million people in the United Kingdom who were disabled or had a work-limiting disability in spring 2005. Of these just under half (46 per cent) were economically inactive. However 50 per cent were in employment and 4 per cent were unemployed.

### Industrial relations at work

Total UK trade union membership was 6.8 million in autumn 2004, a decrease of 36,000 (0.5 per cent) since the previous year. Between 1995 and 2004 the number of male union members fell by 13 per cent, whereas over the same period female union membership rose by 7 per cent. Trade union density – membership as a proportion of all employees – fell

over this period for both men and women. However, the fall for men was faster so that in autumn 2004 the proportion of male employees belonging to a union (28.5 per cent) fell below that for females (29.1 per cent) for the first time. The widest gender gap was among the 25 to 34 age group, where membership among women employees was 4.1 percentage points higher than among men (Figure 4.27). Between 1995 and 1999 the proportion of women aged 25 to 34 who were members fell from 31 per cent to 27 per cent and remained at around this level to 2004. For men of the same age the proportion fell from 31 per cent in 1995 to 23 per cent in 2002 and remained at around this level to 2004. The only group among whom union membership increased between 1995 and 2004 was women aged 50 and over, from 31 to 34 per cent. However, men in this age group were still marginally more likely to be union members than women.

Employment Tribunals are judicial bodies which resolve disputes between employers and employees over employment rights. Their aim is to provide speedy, accessible and relatively informal justice. Employment Tribunals have powers to determine over 70 different types (or jurisdiction) of complaint including unfair dismissal, payment related complaints and discrimination. A claim to an Employment Tribunal can cover more than one type of complaint and in 2004/05 just over 86,000 claims were

# Figure **4.27**

## Trade union membership[1] of employees: by sex and age

United Kingdom

Percentages

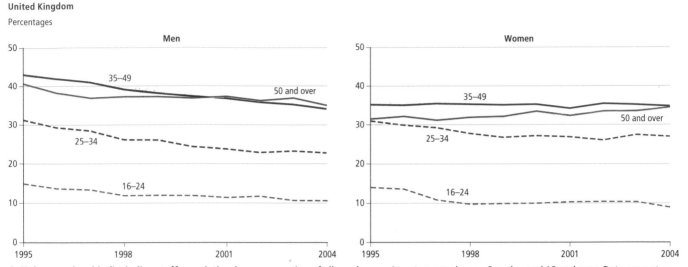

1  Union membership (including staff associations) as a proportion of all employees. At autumn each year. People aged 16 and over. Data are not
   seasonally adjusted and have been adjusted in line with population estimates published in spring 2003. See Appendix, Part 4: LFS reweighting.

*Source: Labour Force Survey, Office for National Statistics*

registered with Employment Tribunals, which covered
156,000 types of complaint. Since 2000/01 there has been a
general decrease in the number of claims – 130,000 claims were
made in 2000/01 covering 218,000 types of complaint.

Complaints made to Employment Tribunals regarding unfair
dismissal (25 per cent of all complaints) were the most
common type registered in 2004/05, closely followed by
claims for unauthorised deduction of wages (24 per cent)

(Table 4.28). These reasons for complaint have been the most
common registered since 2000/01; on average they comprised
just under half of all complaints each year. Complaints
concerning the Working Time Directive were usually the least
common registered during this period, with the exception of
2003/04. During that year there were a large number of cases
where more than one claimant brought a complaint against an
employer. This resulted in this category accounting for 9 per cent
of all types of complaints in 2003/04.

# Table **4.28**

## Employment tribunal claims:[1] by jurisdiction of complaint

Great Britain

Percentages

|  | 2000/01 | 2001/02 | 2002/03 | 2003/04 | 2004/05 |
|---|---|---|---|---|---|
| Unfair dismissal | 23 | 27 | 27 | 23 | 25 |
| Unauthorised deduction of wages[2] | 19 | 22 | 23 | 22 | 24 |
| Breach of contract | 14 | 16 | 17 | 15 | 15 |
| Sex, race and disability | 16 | 13 | 12 | 14 | 13 |
| Equal pay | 8 | 5 | 3 | 2 | 5 |
| Redundancy pay | 4 | 5 | 5 | 5 | 5 |
| Working Time Directive | 3 | 3 | 4 | 9 | 2 |
| Others | 12 | 10 | 10 | 11 | 11 |
| All jurisdictions (=100%) (thousands) | 218 | 194 | 172 | 197 | 156 |

1  A claim may have been brought under more than one jurisdiction or may have been subsequently amended or clarified in the course of
   proceedings. Prior to October 2004 claims were called 'applications'.
2  Prior to 2002/03 this jurisdiction was known as the Wages Act.

*Source: Employment Tribunals Service, Department of Trade and Industry*

Table **4.29**

**Stoppages in progress: by size of dispute,[1] 2004**

United Kingdom

| | Stoppages in progress (numbers) | Percentage of all stoppages | Working days lost (thousands) | Percentage of all working days lost |
|---|---|---|---|---|
| **Working days lost in each dispute** | | | | |
| Under 250 days | 62 | 47.7 | 6.9 | 0.8 |
| 250 and under 500 | 16 | 12.3 | 5.4 | 0.6 |
| 500 and under 1,000 | 20 | 15.4 | 12.3 | 1.4 |
| 1,000 and under 5,000 | 22 | 16.9 | 51.4 | 5.7 |
| 5,000 and under 25,000 | 5 | 3.8 | 59.3 | 6.6 |
| 25,000 and under 50,000 | 0 | 0.0 | 0.0 | 0.0 |
| 50,000 days and over | 5 | 3.8 | 769.5 | 85.0 |
| All stoppages | 130 | 100.0 | 904.9 | 100.0 |

1 See Appendix, Part 4: Labour disputes.

*Source: Office for National Statistics*

In 2004 there were 905,000 working days lost in the United Kingdom through labour disputes, almost twice the number lost in 2003 (499,000). The 2004 total is higher than the average number of working days lost per year in the 1990s (660,000), but considerably lower than the average for both the 1980s (7.2 million) and the 1970s (12.9 million).

The majority of working days lost resulted from large stoppages – 92 per cent of working days lost in 2004 resulted from stoppages where more than 5,000 days were lost in total – but only 8 per cent of stoppages were that large (Table 4.29).

By contrast 48 per cent of stoppages involved the loss of less than 250 days, but only 1 per cent of all working days lost came from stoppages of this size. Ninety six per cent of all working days lost in 2004 were as a result of 101 stoppages in the service sector. Nearly half of all working days lost (48 per cent) were through stoppages in the public administration and defence and compulsory social security sector, followed by education with 42 per cent. The industries with the fewest working days lost were construction which accounted for 0.01 per cent of all working days lost and electricity, gas and water supply which accounted for 0.03 per cent.

# Income and wealth

- Between 2003 and 2004, UK real household disposable income per head rose by 2.1 per cent, compared with growth in GDP per head of 3.1 per cent. (Figure 5.1)

- Although the gap between men's and women's incomes is still substantial in Great Britain, it narrowed between 1996/97 and 2003/04. Median net income of women increased by 29 per cent in real terms compared with an increase of 13 per cent for men. (Table 5.4)

- In spring 2005, average gross weekly earnings in the United Kingdom for both men and women with a degree or equivalent were double those of men and women with no qualifications. (Table 5.8)

- A relatively small proportion of deaths in the United Kingdom result in the payment of inheritance tax – only 6 per cent of deaths in 2004/05, or 34,000 estates. (Table 5.11)

- The proportion of people living in households below 60 per cent of median disposable income in Great Britain has been stable between 2000/01 and 2003/04, at 17 per cent. (Figure 5.17)

- Around three in five men aged between 35 and 54 in the United Kingdom were contributing to a non-state pension in 2003/04, compared with less than half of women of the same age. (Table 5.23)

# Chapter 5

People's income plays an important role in their social well-being, because it determines how much they have to spend on the goods and services that together make up their material standard of living. Household income depends on the level of activity within the economy as a whole each year – the national income – and on the way in which national income is distributed. Income represents a flow of money over a period of time, whereas wealth describes the ownership of assets, such as housing or pension rights, valued at a point in time.

## Household income

Gross domestic product (GDP) is the most commonly used measure of overall economic activity. The total income generated is shared between individuals, companies and other organisations (for example in the form of profits retained for investment), and government (in the form of taxes on production). If GDP is growing in real terms (in other words, after taking out the effect of inflation) this means that the economy is expanding and there is more 'cake' available for distribution. Household disposable income per head represents the amount of this 'cake' that ends up in people's pockets – in other words it is the amount they have available to spend or save. Analysis of the trends in UK GDP may be found in the final section of this chapter.

Household income is derived directly from economic activity in the form of wages and salaries and self-employment income, and through transfers such as social security benefits. It is then subject to a number of deductions such as income tax, council tax (domestic rates in Northern Ireland), and contributions towards pensions and national insurance. The amount of income remaining is referred to as household disposable income – the amount people actually have available to spend or save – and it is this measure that is commonly used to describe people's 'economic well-being'.

Household disposable income per head, adjusted for inflation, increased more than one and a third times between 1971 and 2004 (Figure 5.1). During the 1970s and early 1980s growth fluctuated, and in some years there were small year on year falls, such as in 1974, 1976, 1977, 1981 and 1982. Since 1982 there has been growth each year. Over the period as a whole since 1971, growth in household disposable income per head has been stronger than that in GDP per head, indicating that there has been a small shift between the shares of households and organisations in GDP in favour of households. However, between 2003 and 2004, real household disposable income per head grew by 2.1 per cent compared with growth in GDP per head of 3.1 per cent.

### Figure **5.1**

**Real household disposable income per head[1] and gross domestic product per head[2]**

**United Kingdom**
Indices (1971=100)

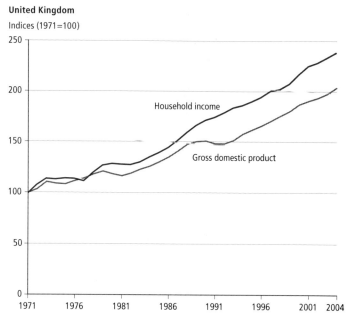

1  Adjusted to real terms using the expenditure deflator for the household sector. See Appendix, Part 5: Household income data sources.
2  Adjusted to real terms using the GDP deflator.

*Source: Office for National Statistics*

Household disposable income differs considerably across the United Kingdom. In 2003, the London region had disposable income per head that was 21 per cent above the UK average in current prices, while in Northern Ireland and the North East it was only 86 per cent of the UK average. However, there are often greater income differences between the local areas within regions than between regions (Map 5.2). For example, within the London region, Inner London-West had household disposable income per head that was 78 per cent above the UK average in 2003 – the highest of all the areas shown on the map. Inner London-East was only 3 per cent above the UK average. In general, the highest household incomes were recorded in and around London, the South East and East of England, though values of 10 per cent or more above the UK average were also recorded in the City of Edinburgh and in Solihull in the West Midlands.

Blackburn with Darwen had the lowest household disposable income per head of all the areas shown, at 73 per cent of the UK average. There were 55 areas out of 133 with disposable income per head lower than 90 per cent of the UK average, spread across virtually all regions within the United Kingdom though with concentrations in Wales, Northern Ireland, Scotland and the major conurbations of England outside London.

## Map **5.2**

### Household disposable income per head, 2003[1,2]

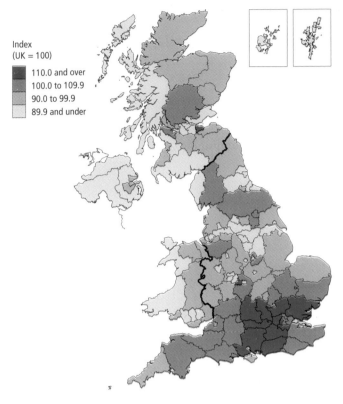

Index
(UK = 100)

■ 110.0 and over
■ 100.0 to 109.9
■ 90.0 to 99.9
□ 89.9 and under

1  NUTS (Nomenclature of Territorial Statistics) level 3. NUTS is a
   hierarchical classification developed to allow comparisons between
   economic territories of the European Union.
2  Excludes Extra-regio: parts of UK economic territory that cannot be
   attached to any particular region.

**Source: Office for National Statistics**

Despite strong growth in household disposable income since 1987, there has been considerable stability in its composition. Although there was a fall in the proportion derived from wages and salaries, from 52 per cent in 1987 to 48 per cent in 1996, this has since risen to remain at around 51 per cent between 1999 and 2004. In addition, the proportion of income derived from social benefits has remained at around 19 per cent over the last decade. Taxes on income as a proportion of household income have also remained stable since 1987, at around 11 per cent, as have social contributions (that is, employees' national insurance and pension contributions) at around 7 per cent of household income.

The data in Figure 5.1, Map 5.2 and in the previous paragraph are derived from the UK National and Regional Accounts. In these statistics, households are combined with the non-profit making institutions serving households such as universities, charities and clubs, and it is not presently possible to separate the two sectors. Non-profit making bodies receive income mainly in the form of property income (that is, investment

income) and of other current receipts. The household sector includes people living in institutions such as nursing homes, as well as people living in private households. In most of the remainder of this chapter, the tables and figures are derived directly from surveys of households (such as the Family Resources Survey, the Expenditure and Food Survey and the British Household Panel Survey) and surveys of businesses (such as the Annual Survey of Hours and Earnings). Data from these surveys cover the population living in households and some cover certain parts of the population living in institutions, but all exclude non-profit making institutions. They can be used to analyse the distribution of household income between different sub-groups of the population, such as pensioners. Appendix, Part 5: Household income data sources, describes the main differences between household income as defined in the National Accounts and as defined in most survey sources.

The composition of household income varies between different types of households. Among households where the household reference person is of working age, wages and salaries are by far the most important component of gross (before any deductions) household income in the United Kingdom, followed by self-employment income (Table 5.3 overleaf). Income from employment (wages, salaries and self-employment income) was the most important element of income for all socio-economic groups in 2003/04, with the exception of households headed by someone who has never worked or is long-term unemployed. Benefits and pensions were the most important sources of income for this latter group, making up nearly four fifths of their total income.

Pensions are also the major component of the incomes of pensioner households in Great Britain. The Pensioners' Income Series produced by the Department for Work and Pensions (DWP) shows that in 2003/04, just over half the average gross income of pensioner units (pensioner couples where the man is over 65, or single pensioners over state pension age) came from state benefits, including the State Retirement Pension, and a further quarter came from occupational pensions (see also Table 8.8). Pensioner units have experienced strong income growth over the last nine years. Their gross income rose by 29 per cent in real terms between 1994/95 and 2003/04, compared with an increase of about 15 per cent in real average earnings. The fastest growing sources of income over this period were occupational pensions, which grew by over two fifths in real terms; personal pensions, which more than doubled, though still only a small minority of pensioners receive them; and earnings, which have also increased by nearly a half, though again this type of income is concentrated among a small group of pensioners. It should be noted that changes in

## Table 5.3

### Sources of gross weekly income: by socio-economic classification,[1] 2003/04

United Kingdom
Percentages

| | Wages & salaries | Self-employment | Investment income | Tax credits | Retirement pensions[2] | Private pensions | Disability benefits | Other benefits | Other income | All income |
|---|---|---|---|---|---|---|---|---|---|---|
| Higher managerial and professional occupations | 84 | 8 | 2 | - | - | 2 | - | 1 | 1 | 100 |
| Lower managerial and professional occupations[3] | 87 | 5 | 1 | 1 | - | 2 | - | 2 | 2 | 100 |
| Intermediate occupations | 85 | 2 | 1 | 2 | 1 | 3 | 1 | 3 | 2 | 100 |
| Small employers and own account workers | 23 | 66 | 2 | 2 | 1 | 2 | 1 | 2 | 3 | 100 |
| Lower supervisory and technical occupations | 89 | 2 | 1 | 2 | 1 | 1 | 1 | 3 | 1 | 100 |
| Semi-routine occupations | 79 | 2 | 1 | 5 | 1 | 2 | 2 | 6 | 3 | 100 |
| Routine occupations | 82 | 1 | 1 | 4 | 1 | 2 | 2 | 6 | 1 | 100 |
| Never worked and long-term unemployed | 11 | 3 | 1 | 1 | 1 | 5 | 10 | 61 | 6 | 100 |
| All households[4] | 74 | 10 | 2 | 1 | - | 3 | 2 | 5 | 3 | 100 |

1 Of the household reference person. Males aged 20 to 64, females aged 20 to 59. See Appendix, Part 1: National Statistics Socio-economic Classification.
2 Includes any payments from minimum income guarantee or pension credit.
3 Includes those who are in a 'Higher supervisory occupation'.
4 Includes households where the reference person is a full-time student, and those whose occupation was inadequately stated or not classifiable.

Source: Family Resources Survey, Department for Work and Pensions

average income do not simply reflect changes experienced by individual pensioners, but also reflect changes in the composition of the group, for example as new retirees with greater entitlement to occupational pensions join the group.

Most of the information presented so far has been in terms of household income. This is generally considered to be the unit across which resources are shared, so that total household income can be taken as representing the (potential) standard of living of each of its members. The assumption of equal sharing of resources between each member of the household is difficult to test. Using certain assumptions it is possible to use household survey data to derive estimates of the income accruing to individuals, but it is not possible to infer their living standards from these.

The results of such an exercise are shown in Table 5.4, which compares the median net incomes of men and women by family type. See Appendix, Part 5: Individual income, for details of how these estimates were derived, and the analysing income distribution box on page 76 for explanation of median. Note also that, as explained further in the Appendix, the term net income is used in place of disposable income because the term disposable income for this series has a different definition from elsewhere in this chapter.

On average, men's incomes exceed women's irrespective of the type of family that they live in. Overall the median net income of women was 60 per cent of that of men in 2003/04 in Great Britain. However, the difference between men's and women's

## Table 5.4

### Median net individual income:[1] by sex and family type, 2003/04

Great Britain

| | £ per week | | Percentage change in income, 1996/97 to 2003/04[2] | |
|---|---|---|---|---|
| | Men | Women | Men | Women |
| Single without children | 188 | 180 | 18 | 28 |
| Single pensioner | 164 | 141 | 26 | 27 |
| Single with children | 248 | 203 | 26 | 48 |
| Couple without children | 306 | 185 | 13 | 21 |
| Pensioner couple | 199 | 77 | 18 | 29 |
| Couple with children | 333 | 160 | 11 | 38 |
| All individuals | 250 | 151 | 13 | 29 |

1 See Appendix, Part 5: Individual income.
2 Change in real terms, deflated using the retail prices index less council tax.

Source: Individual Incomes, Department for Work and Pensions

net incomes was narrowest for single people under pension age without children, for whom women's incomes were very nearly equal to those of men, at 96 per cent. The gap was largest for pensioner couples, where women's median net income was 39 per cent that of men. This arises as a result of historic factors leading to lower entitlements among wives for both state and occupational pensions while their husbands are alive, but higher incomes in their own right when they are widowed because of entitlements to widows' pensions.

Although the gap between men's and women's incomes is still substantial, Table 5.4 shows that it has narrowed between 1996/97 and 2003/04. Over this period median net income of women has increased by 29 per cent in real terms, whereas that of men has increased by 13 per cent. The difference is most marked for single women with children, whose incomes have increased by nearly 50 per cent. A major factor behind this is increased labour market participation and reduced reliance on benefits for this group of women.

## Earnings

Income from employment is the most important component of household income overall. The average earnings index (AEI), a monthly measure of the pay of a representative sample of all employees across all sectors of the economy, is one of the indicators used to judge the state of the UK economy. If the index rises rapidly, this may indicate that the labour market is under-supplied with employees in the right numbers and with the right skills to meet the level of demand within the economy. In addition, a rapid rise may indicate that wage settlements are higher than the rate of economic growth can sustain and thus create inflationary pressures. A fall in the index may be a reflection of reduced demand within the economy and may be a warning that GDP is about to fall and unemployment is about to increase. The relationship between the AEI and the retail prices index (RPI) is also of importance. If the AEI rises faster than the RPI, this means that employees' pay is increasing faster than the prices they have to pay for goods and services and that therefore, all things being equal, their purchasing power will rise and they will feel 'better off'.

During the two decades from 1971, the AEI and RPI showed similar patterns of change, but with the RPI generally showing slower growth (Figure 5.5). For example, the peak in earnings growth over this period occurred in February 1975 when it reached an annual rate of 32 per cent. The peak in the RPI occurred in August that year at 27 per cent. During most of the 1990s, the AEI outpaced the RPI. This was made possible mainly through increases in productivity, enabling employers to pay higher wages while not increasing their prices to the same extent to finance their wage bill. The periods during which prices have risen faster than earnings – for example in the latter

### Figure **5.5**

**Retail prices index and average earnings index[1]**

United Kingdom/Great Britain[2]
Percentage change over 12 months

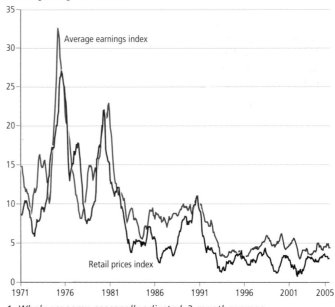

1  Whole economy, seasonally adjusted, 3-month average.
2  Data for the retail prices index are for United Kingdom and the average earnings index data are for Great Britain.

**Source: Office for National Statistics**

half of 1995 – have been times of economic downturn, when a fall in demand for labour depressed earnings growth. Although the RPI did not overtake the AEI in the period February to July 2003, the gap between the two narrowed appreciably, with the indices being less than 0.5 percentage points apart. Since August 2003, they have moved further apart, so that in August 2005 the annual increase in the AEI stood at 4.2 per cent compared with 2.8 per cent for the RPI.

A variety of factors influence the level of earnings that an employee receives, such as their skills and experience, their occupation, the economic sector in which they work and the hours they work. The area of the United Kingdom where they work and their sex may also have an impact. The remainder of this section explores some of these factors. However, it should be noted that all factors are interlinked, and no attempt is made here to disentangle the effect that any single factor may have.

Government legislation can affect wages. The *Equal Pay Act 1970* and subsequent revisions, together with the *Sex Discrimination Act 1975*, established the principle of equal pay for work that can be established to be of equal value to that done by a member of the opposite sex, employed by the same employer, under common terms and conditions of employment. The impact of this legislation, together with other factors such as the opening up of higher paid work to women, has been to narrow the differential between the hourly earnings of men and women (Figure 5.6). In 2004, the hourly earnings of women working full time in Great Britain were 82 per cent of those of men, a rise from 74 per cent in 1986. On average, part-time employees receive lower hourly earnings than full-time employees, and the differential between men and women working part time is smaller. For example part-time women's hourly earnings were 89 per cent those of men in 2004. However this proportion fluctuates from year to year and shows no clear trend over the 19 years shown in the chart. It should be noted that coverage of part-time employees by the New Earnings Survey (NES) was not comprehensive because many employees with earnings below the income tax threshold were excluded, and the extent to which they are included or excluded in each survey contributes to the volatility of the data.

In 2004, the Office for National Statistics (ONS) replaced the New Earnings Survey (NES) with the Annual Survey of Hours and Earnings (ASHE) – see Appendix Part 5: Earnings surveys, for a summary of the differences between the two. In Figure 5.6 the NES has been used for data from 1986 to 1996 inclusive, and for 1998 to 2003 a series has been used that applies ASHE methodology to NES data. Data for 1997 are presented on both bases, and data for 2004 are from the ASHE but excluding supplementary information that was not available in the NES (for example on employees in businesses outside the PAYE system).

## Figure **5.6**

### Gross hourly earnings:[1] by sex and whether working full time or part time

**Great Britain**

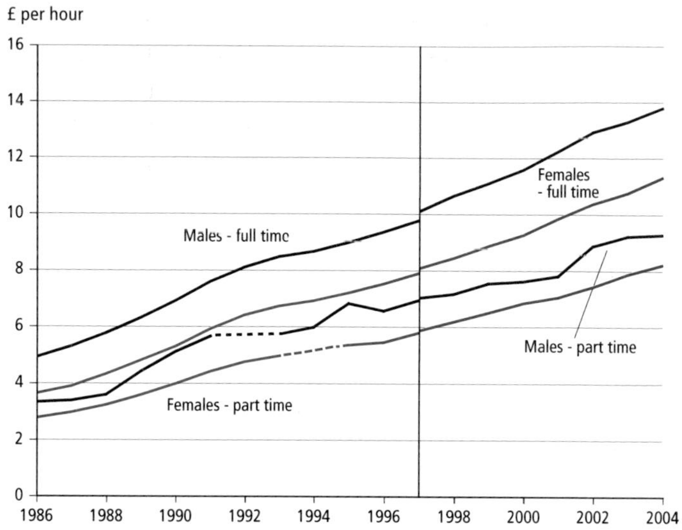

£ per hour

1  Average gross hourly earnings for employees on adult rates at April each year. Data are not available for male part-time earnings for 1992, or for female part-time earnings for 1994.

**Source: New Earnings Survey (1986–1997) and Annual Survey of Hours and Earnings (1997–2004), Office for National Statistics**

## Table **5.7**

### Median hourly earnings:[1] by industry

**United Kingdom**                                                                 Median hourly earnings excluding overtime (£)

|  | 1997 | 1998 | 1999 | 2000 | 2001 | 2002 | 2003 | 2004 |
|---|---|---|---|---|---|---|---|---|
| Financial intermediation | 10.50 | 11.02 | 11.52 | 11.86 | 12.65 | 13.13 | 13.28 | 14.04 |
| Electricity, gas and water supply | 9.76 | 9.99 | 10.25 | 11.00 | 11.00 | 11.29 | 11.97 | 13.02 |
| Education | 10.94 | 11.04 | 11.36 | 11.53 | 11.65 | 12.01 | 12.57 | 12.94 |
| Real estate, renting and business activities | 8.51 | 8.96 | 9.32 | 9.65 | 10.51 | 11.12 | 11.34 | 12.19 |
| Public administration and defence, and compulsory social security | 9.63 | 9.67 | 10.06 | 10.31 | 10.62 | 11.02 | 11.00 | 11.70 |
| Mining and quarrying | 8.86 | 9.35 | 9.06 | 9.53 | 10.20 | 10.31 | 11.19 | 10.63 |
| Health and social work | 7.60 | 7.88 | 8.21 | 8.70 | 9.11 | 9.62 | 9.90 | 10.40 |
| Construction | 7.19 | 7.39 | 7.75 | 8.10 | 8.68 | 9.21 | 9.75 | 10.20 |
| Manufacturing | 7.56 | 7.95 | 8.26 | 8.46 | 8.88 | 9.21 | 9.61 | 10.03 |
| Transport, storage and communication | 7.29 | 7.60 | 8.00 | 8.15 | 8.59 | 8.95 | 9.22 | 9.93 |
| Other community, social and personal service activities | 6.76 | 7.25 | 7.61 | 7.79 | 8.11 | 8.79 | 8.92 | 9.22 |
| Wholesale and retail trade, and repair of motor vehicles, motorcycles and personal and household goods | 6.21 | 6.50 | 6.76 | 6.99 | 7.34 | 7.68 | 7.81 | 8.18 |
| Agriculture, hunting, forestry | 4.95 | 5.16 | 5.32 | 5.56 | 5.90 | 6.16 | 6.30 | 6.70 |
| Hotels and restaurants | 4.62 | 4.98 | 5.09 | 5.25 | 5.49 | 5.75 | 6.03 | 6.34 |
| All industries and services | 7.83 | 8.16 | 8.50 | 8.76 | 9.21 | 9.64 | 9.96 | 10.47 |

1  Full-time employees on adult rates, whose pay for the survey period was unaffected by absence.

**Source: Annual Survey of Hours and Earnings, Office for National Statistics**

Wage rates can vary considerably between industrial sectors. The hotel and restaurant sector is the lowest paid industry in the United Kingdom, with median hourly earnings of £6.34 in April 2004, followed by agriculture with median hourly earnings of £6.70 per hour (Table 5.7). The wholesale and retail trade is also relatively low paid with median earnings of £8.18 per hour. At the other end of the scale, median earnings of those in financial intermediation were just over £14 per hour. Averaged over all industries and services, hourly earnings increased by 34 per cent between 1997 and 2004, but the increase was highest in the construction industry at 42 per cent and lowest in education, at 18 per cent. However, these data are affected by changes over time in the mix of lower and higher paid workers within a sector and so do not necessarily indicate changes in wage rates for particular employees or jobs.

The broad industrial groupings in Table 5.7 can hide substantial variation within sectors. Analysis of the ASHE at a more detailed level indicates that in addition to those employees in the electricity, gas and water supply sector and the financial intermediation sector shown already in Table 5.7, full-time employees involved in the extraction of crude petroleum and natural gas, and computer and related activities were among the highest paid per week in April 2004. Various branches of the manufacturing, hotel and restaurant, and agriculture and

fisheries sectors make up much of the ten lowest paid industries, though people employed in private households were the lowest paid of all.

Although average hourly pay provides a useful comparison between the earnings of men and women, it does not reveal differences in rates of pay for comparable jobs. This is because these averages do not reflect the different employment characteristics of men and women, such as the proportions in different occupations and their length of time in jobs. Also, for many employees, overtime and other additions can supplement basic weekly pay. Overtime, bonuses and commissions and shift payments accounted for 8 per cent of average (mean) weekly earnings of adults working full time in Great Britain in April 2004, but they were a larger component of men's than women's pay: 10 per cent compared with 5 per cent.

A person's qualifications can have a substantial impact on their earning power. In spring 2005, average gross weekly earnings for male employees with a degree were £726 per week (Table 5.8). These fell as educational attainment fell, so that male employees with no qualifications had earnings of £342 per week. There was a large increase in earnings for men aged 25 to 34 compared with those aged 16 to 24, across all attainment levels. Among female employees, the relationship

## Table **5.8**

### Average gross weekly earnings: by sex, highest qualification attained and age, 2005[1]

United Kingdom                                                                                                          £ per week

|  | 16–24 | 25–34 | 35–44 | 45–54 | 55–59/64 | All working age |
|---|---|---|---|---|---|---|
| **Men** | | | | | | |
| Degree or equivalent | 356 | 619 | 810 | 862 | 732 | 726 |
| Higher education below degree level | 366 | 501 | 588 | 619 | 583 | 554 |
| GCE A level or equivalent | 290 | 446 | 545 | 536 | 436 | 470 |
| GCSE grades A* to C or equivalent | 253 | 410 | 469 | 463 | 503 | 410 |
| Other (including GCSE below grade C) | 253 | 389 | 453 | 435 | 417 | 407 |
| No qualifications | 250 | 325 | 359 | 366 | 335 | 342 |
| All men[2] | 283 | 483 | 574 | 575 | 487 | 506 |
| **Women** | | | | | | |
| Degree or equivalent | 319 | 528 | 627 | 679 | 651 | 561 |
| Higher education below degree level | 267 | 384 | 464 | 491 | 488 | 440 |
| GCE A level or equivalent | 250 | 353 | 421 | 364 | 390 | 347 |
| GCSE grades A* to C or equivalent | 227 | 330 | 331 | 329 | 309 | 308 |
| Other (including GCSE below grade C) | 187 | 378 | 299 | 315 | 302 | 313 |
| No qualifications | 182 | 300 | 235 | 262 | 259 | 251 |
| All women[2] | 253 | 425 | 433 | 424 | 381 | 397 |
| **All working age[2]** | 270 | 459 | 524 | 515 | 457 | 464 |

1 At spring. Data are not seasonally adjusted and have been adjusted in line with population estimates published in spring 2003. See Appendix, Part 4: LFS reweighting. Males aged 16 to 64, females aged 16 to 59.
2 Includes people who did not state their highest qualification.

**Source: Labour Force Survey, Office for National Statistics**

between earnings and qualifications was similar; those with a degree had average earnings over twice as much as those with no qualifications, £561 compared with £251 per week. However, for both men and women there was little difference in the earnings between those whose highest qualification was GCSE grades A* to C or equivalent and those with other qualifications including GCSE below grade C.

## Taxes

Taxation is the main means by which governments raise revenue. There are a wide variety of taxes levied on both individuals and institutions. The major taxes paid by individuals are income tax and taxes on expenditure. However, every individual is entitled to a personal allowance and those with income below this do not pay any income tax. In 2005/06 the personal allowance was set at £4,895 for those aged under 65, with further allowances for people aged over 65. The income tax regime on earnings for 2005/06 includes three different rates of tax. Taxable income of up to £2,090 (that is, after the deduction of allowances and any other tax relief to which the individual may be entitled) is charged at 10 per cent. Taxable income above £2,090 but less than £32,400 is charged at 22 per cent, while income above this level is charged at 40 per cent. Special rates apply to savings and dividend income.

HM Revenue and Customs estimates that in 2005/06 there will be around 30.5 million taxpayers in the United Kingdom (Table 5.9). Given the progressive nature of the income tax system, the amount of tax payable increases both as a proportion of income and in cash terms as income increases, averaging £126 per year for taxpayers with taxable incomes between £5,000 and £7,499 and £71,100 for those with incomes of £100,000 and over.

National insurance contributions are paid according to an individual's earnings rather than their total income, and for employees, payments are made both by the individual and by their employer. In 2005/06, employees with earnings less than £94 per week pay no contributions, and neither do their employers. Employees pay contributions equal to 11.0 per cent of their earnings between £94 and £630 per week, and an additional 1.0 per cent on earnings above £630 per week. Employers pay contributions equal to 12.8 per cent of earnings above £94 per week.

In addition to direct taxes such as income tax, households pay indirect taxes through their expenditure. Indirect taxes include value added tax (VAT), customs duties and excise duties and are included in the prices of consumer goods and services. These taxes are specific to particular commodities: for example, in 2003/04 VAT was payable on most consumer goods at

## Table 5.9

### Income tax payable: by annual income,[1] 2005/06[2]

United Kingdom

| | Number of taxpayers (millions) | Total tax liability after tax reductions[3] (£ million) | Average rate of tax (percentages) | Average amount of tax (£) |
|---|---|---|---|---|
| £4,895–£4,999 | 0.1 | 1 | 0.1 | 5 |
| £5,000–£7,499 | 2.9 | 369 | 2.0 | 126 |
| £7,500–£9,999 | 3.5 | 1,580 | 5.1 | 445 |
| £10,000–£14,999 | 6.1 | 7,560 | 9.8 | 1,220 |
| £15,000–£19,999 | 5.1 | 11,500 | 13.0 | 2,260 |
| £20,000–£29,999 | 6.4 | 24,000 | 15.4 | 3,760 |
| £30,000–£49,999 | 4.3 | 28,900 | 17.9 | 6,690 |
| £50,000–£99,999 | 1.5 | 25,900 | 25.7 | 17,000 |
| £100,000 and over | 0.5 | 34,200 | 33.4 | 71,100 |
| All incomes | 30.5 | 134,000 | 18.2 | 4,390 |

1 Total income of the individual for income tax purposes including earned and investment income. Figures relate to taxpayers only.
2 Based on projections in line with the March 2005 Budget.
3 In this context tax reductions refer to allowances given at a fixed rate, for example the Married Couple's Allowance.

**Source: HM Revenue and Customs**

17.5 per cent of their value, though not on most foods, books and newspapers, and children's clothing, and was payable at a reduced rate on heating and lighting. Customs and excise duties on the other hand tend to vary by the volume rather than value of goods purchased.

High income households are more likely to devote a larger proportion of their income to investments or repaying loans, and low income households may be funding their expenditure through taking out loans or drawing down savings. As a result, the proportion of income paid in indirect taxes tends to be higher for those on low incomes than for those on high incomes. In 2003/04, households in the top fifth of the income distribution were paying 14 per cent of their disposable income in indirect taxes, compared with 31 per cent for those in the bottom fifth of the distribution.

A further means of raising revenue from households is through council tax (domestic rates in Northern Ireland). These taxes are raised by local authorities to part-fund the services they provide. For both council tax and domestic rates, the amount payable by a household depends on the value of the property they occupy. For those on low incomes, assistance is available in the form of council tax benefits (rates rebates in Northern Ireland). In 2003/04, the average council tax/rates payable (excluding payments for water and sewerage) in the United Kingdom was

## Table **5.10**

### Net council tax[1] paid by households: by region, 2003/04

| | Net council tax[1] (£ per year) | Net council tax[1] as a percentage of gross household income |
|---|---|---|
| United Kingdom | 760 | 2.5 |
| England | 780 | 2.5 |
| North East | 620 | 2.8 |
| North West | 720 | 2.6 |
| Yorkshire & the Humber | 660 | 2.5 |
| East Midlands | 740 | 2.6 |
| West Midlands | 730 | 2.6 |
| East | 830 | 2.5 |
| London | 840 | 2.1 |
| South East | 900 | 2.6 |
| South West | 810 | 2.9 |
| Wales | 600 | 2.3 |
| Scotland | 810 | 2.9 |
| Northern Ireland | 460 | 1.8 |

1  Council tax net of council tax benefit in Great Britain; domestic rates net of rates rebate in Northern Ireland.

**Source: Office for National Statistics**

£760 per household, after taking into account the relevant benefit payments (Table 5.10). Net council tax varied from £900 per year in the South East to £600 in Wales. Net domestic rates in Northern Ireland, which are based on a quite different valuation system, averaged £460, representing 1.8 per cent of gross income. Within Great Britain, council tax as a percentage of gross household income varied from 2.1 per cent in London to 2.9 per cent in the South West and in Scotland.

Taxes are also paid on certain forms of wealth, generally when assets are realised. For example, capital gains tax is payable when the difference between the proceeds from the sale of shares and the cost of purchasing them exceeds a certain level. When a person dies and someone inherits their assets – generally known as their estate – inheritance tax may be payable. In 2004/05 inheritance tax was payable on estates valued at more than £263,000. Table 5.11 shows that a relatively low proportion of deaths result in the payment of inheritance tax – only 6 per cent in 2004/05, or 34,000 estates. However, both the number of estates paying inheritance tax and the proportion of deaths where tax was paid have risen considerably between 1996/97 and 2004/05, and have now reached similar levels to those of 1971/72 – though the relevant tax then was estate duty rather than inheritance tax.

## Table **5.11**

### Estates passing on death and paying inheritance tax[1]

United Kingdom

| | Proportion of deaths where tax paid (percentages) | Estates which paid inheritance tax (thousands) |
|---|---|---|
| 1971/72[2] | 6 | 38 |
| 1981/82 | 4 | 24 |
| 1991/92 | 3 | 19 |
| 1996/97 | 2 | 15 |
| 2001/02 | 4 | 23 |
| 2004/05 | 6 | 34 |

1  By year that tax was paid. The tax payable in 1971/72 was estate duty. The tax payable in 1981/82 was capital transfer tax.
2  Figures for 1971/72 are for Great Britain only.

**Source: HM Revenue and Customs**

Research from the Joseph Rowntree Foundation has investigated people's attitudes to inheritance. People like the idea of being able to leave a bequest, but most do not think that older people should be careful with their money just so that they have something to bequeath. People's knowledge of inheritance law and taxation is poor. The research found that most people either had no idea how the inheritance tax system worked or thought that more people pay it, and pay more, than actually do – only 6 per cent of respondents to the survey knew that fewer than one in ten estates pay inheritance tax.

## Income distribution

The first two sections of this chapter demonstrated how the various components of income differ in importance for different household types and how the levels of earnings vary between individuals. The result is an uneven distribution of total income between households, though the inequality is reduced to some extent by the deduction of taxes and social contributions and their redistribution to households in the form of social security benefits. The analysis of income distribution is therefore usually based on household disposable income, that is total income less payments of taxes and social contributions. In the analysis of Households Below Average Income (HBAI) carried out by the Department for Work and Pensions (DWP), on which most of the tables and figures in this and the next section are based, payments of income tax, council tax (domestic rates in Northern Ireland) and employee national insurance contributions are deducted to obtain disposable income. For more details see Appendix, Part 5: Households Below Average Income.

In the HBAI analysis, disposable income is also presented both before and after the further deduction of housing costs.

It can be argued that the costs of housing at a given time may or may not reflect the true value of the housing that different households actually enjoy. For example, the housing costs of someone renting a property from a private landlord may be much higher than those for a local authority property of similar quality for which the rent may be set without reference to a market rent. Equally, a retired person living in a property that they own outright will enjoy the same level of housing as their younger neighbour in an identical property owned with a mortgage, though their housing costs will be very different. Thus estimates are presented on both bases to take into account variations in housing costs that do not correspond to comparable variations in the quality of housing. Neither is given pre-eminence over the other. For more details, see Appendix, Part 5: Households Below Average Income.

The picture of the income distribution in Great Britain in 2003/04, summarised in Figure 5.12, shows considerable inequality. Each bar represents the number of people living in households with equivalised weekly disposable income in a particular £10 band. There is a greater concentration of people at the lower levels of weekly income and the distribution has a long tail at the upper end. The upper tail is in fact longer than shown: there are estimated to be an additional 1.8 million individuals living in households with disposable income greater than £1,000 per week who are not shown on the chart. The highest bar represents nearly 1.6 million people with incomes between £260 and £270 per week. If housing costs are deducted, the concentration of incomes towards the lower end of the distribution is even greater, because housing costs for low income households form on average a higher proportion of their income.

The shape of the income distribution and the extent of inequality have changed considerably over the last three decades. In Figure 5.13, the closer the percentiles are to the median line, the greater the equality within the distribution. During the early 1970s the distribution of disposable income among households was broadly stable. During the mid to late 1970s there was a gradual decrease in inequality, but this was reversed during the early 1980s and the extent of inequality in the distribution continued to grow throughout the 1980s. During the first half of the 1990s the income distribution appeared to be stable again, albeit at a much higher level of income dispersion than in the 1970s. The early 1990s were a period of economic downturn when there was little real growth in incomes anywhere in the distribution. Between 1994/95 and 2002/03, income at the 90th and 10th percentiles and at the median all grew by around 23 per cent in real terms. The Gini coefficient – a widely used measure of inequality – increased between 1994/95 and 2000/01 (implying an increase

## Figure **5.12**

### Distribution of weekly household disposable income,[1] 2003/04

Great Britain

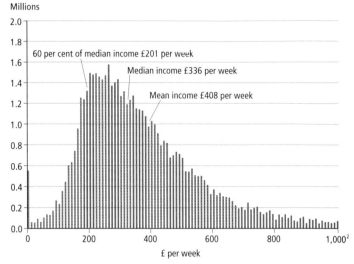

1 Equivalised household disposable income before deduction of household costs (in £10 bands). See Appendix, Part 5: Households Below Average Income, and Equivalisation scales.
2 There were also 1.8 million individuals with income above £1,000 per week.

Source: Households Below Average Income, Department for Work and Pensions

## Analysing income distribution

Equivalisation – in analysing the distribution of income, household disposable income is usually adjusted to take account of the size and composition of the household. This is in recognition of the fact that, for example, to achieve the same standard of living a household of five would require a higher income than would a single person. This process is known as equivalisation (see Appendix, Part 5: Equivalisation scales).

Quintile and decile groups – the main method of analysing income distribution used in this chapter is to rank units (households, individuals or adults) by a given income measure, and then to divide the ranked units into groups of equal size. Groups containing 20 per cent of units are referred to as 'quintile groups' or 'fifths'. Thus the 'bottom quintile group' is the 20 per cent of units with the lowest incomes. Similarly, groups containing 10 per cent of units are referred to as 'decile groups' or tenths.

Percentiles – an alternative method also used in the chapter is to present the income level above or below which a certain proportion of units fall. Thus the 90th percentile is the income level above which only 10 per cent of units fall when ranked by a given income measure. The *median* is then the midpoint of the distribution above and below which 50 per cent of units fall.

## Figure **5.13**

### Distribution of real[1] disposable household income[2]

**United Kingdom/Great Britain[3]**

£ per week at 2003/04 prices

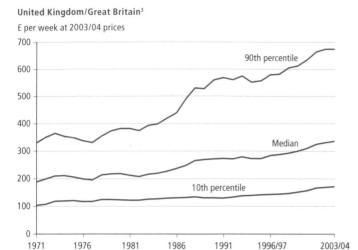

1 Adjusted to 2003/04 prices using the retail prices index less local taxes.
2 Equivalised household disposable income before deduction of housing costs. See Appendix, Part 5: Households Below Average Income, and Equivalisation scales.
3 Data from 1993/94 onwards are for financial years. Source of data changed in 1994/95, definition of income changed slightly and geographic coverage changed from United Kingdom to Great Britain.

**Source: Institute for Fiscal Studies from Family Expenditure Survey, Office for National Statistics (1971 to 1993/94); Households Below Average Income, Department for Work and Pensions (1994/95 onwards)**

in inequality) with indications of a slight fall (implying an increase in equality) between 2000/01 and 2003/04. (See Appendix, Part 5: Gini coefficient.)

The Institute for Fiscal Studies (IFS) has investigated some of the possible explanations for these changes in inequality. They found that changes to the labour market have played an important role. In particular inequality rose during the 1980s when the incomes of the higher paid grew much more rapidly than those of the lower paid or of households where no one was working. Growth in self-employment income and in unemployment were also found to be associated with periods of increased inequality. It would appear that demographic factors such as the growth in one person households make a relatively unimportant contribution compared with labour market changes. However, the IFS has found that changes in the tax and benefit system have had an impact. The income tax cuts of the 1970s and late 1980s worked to increase income inequality while direct tax rises in the early 1980s and 1990s – together with the increases in means-tested benefits in the late 1990s – produced the opposite effect.

During the 1980s the higher the income the greater was income growth, and it was this that drove the increase in inequality. Between 1996/97 and 2003/04, income growth has been much more evenly spread across the whole of the income distribution, with exceptions only at the very top and

## Table **5.14**

### Individuals in the top and bottom quintile groups of household disposable income:[1] by selected risk factors,[2] 2003/04

| Great Britain | | Percentages |
| --- | --- | --- |
| | Bottom quintile | Top quintile |
| **Economic status of adults in the family** | | |
| Single or couple, all in full-time work | 3 | 38 |
| Couple, one full-time work, one part-time work | 4 | 23 |
| Workless, head or spouse aged 60 or over | 29 | 7 |
| Workless, head or spouse unemployed | 70 | 2 |
| Workless, other inactive | 52 | 4 |
| **Family type** | | |
| Single pensioner, female | 28 | 6 |
| Couple without children | 11 | 38 |
| Single with children | 38 | 5 |
| **Ethnic group of head of household** | | |
| Asian or Asian British | 42 | 14 |
| Black or Black British | 32 | 12 |
| Chinese or Other ethnic groups | 32 | 22 |
| **Disability** | | |
| One or more disabled children and one or more disabled adults in family | 32 | 8 |
| **All individuals** | 20 | 20 |

1 Equivalised household disposable income before deduction of housing costs has been used to rank individuals. See Appendix, Part 5: Households Below Average Income, and Equivalisation scales.
2 Where the proportion of individuals in the top or bottom quintile groups are more than 10 percentage points either side of the expected 20 per cent threshold for these groups were there to be an even distribution.

**Source: Households Below Average Income, Department for Work and Pensions**

bottom of the distribution. Changes at the very bottom of the distribution are difficult to disentangle from measurement error. There is evidence from these data, based on the Family Resources Survey (FRS) and also from data from tax returns, that there has been much more rapid growth in the top 1 per cent of incomes than for the rest of the distribution. The reasons for this growth are not yet well understood, but possible explanations include changes in the nature of executive remuneration and the dynamic effects of the cut in top rates of tax over the 1980s on capital accumulation.

There are a variety of factors that influence an individual's position in the income distribution. For example, single person and couple families all in full-time work had nearly twice the expected likelihood of being in the top quintile group in 2003/04 (Table 5.14). Being unemployed increased the risk of being in the bottom quintile group more than threefold

## Table **5.15**

### People's perceptions of the adequacy of their income[1]

Great Britain

Percentages

| | 1986 | 1994 | 2002 | 2003 | 2004 |
|---|---|---|---|---|---|
| Living comfortably | 24 | 29 | 39 | 44 | 40 |
| Coping | 50 | 49 | 45 | 43 | 46 |
| Finding it difficult to manage | 18 | 15 | 13 | 10 | 11 |
| Finding it very difficult to manage | 8 | 6 | 3 | 3 | 3 |
| Other answer | - | - | - | - | - |

1 Respondents were asked, 'Which of these phrases would you say comes closest to your feelings about your household's income these days? Living comfortably, coping, finding it difficult to manage, or finding it very difficult to manage on present income'. Excludes those who responded 'Don't know' or did not answer.

**Source: British Social Attitudes Survey, National Centre for Social Research**

and being economically inactive but under pension age increased the risk by two and a half times compared with the average. All ethnic minority groups had greater than average likelihood of being in the bottom quintile group, with the Pakistani/Bangladeshi group being particularly at risk. Other groups with greater than average risks of being in the bottom quintile group were single parents and families containing both disabled adults and one or more disabled children. Couples without children had a greater than average likelihood of being in the top quintile group.

Income is important to people's overall well-being in terms of the access that it provides to goods and services. People's satisfaction with their income will depend on their material needs and expectations, and the extent to which the income available to them enables these to be met. It is therefore possible that individuals with the same income but different needs, real or perceived, may differ in how they think about their income. The same may be true of those who are faced with different prices for the same level and quality of goods or services, for example housing. Table 5.15 explores trends in people's perception of economic hardship or lack of it. The proportion of respondents who said that they were 'living comfortably' rose from 24 per cent in 1986 to a peak of 44 per cent in 2003, but fell back to 40 per cent in 2004. In contrast, the proportion who were finding it difficult or very difficult to manage fell from 26 per cent in 1986 to 14 per cent in 2004. This is of course not necessarily inconsistent with a widening of the distribution – as Figure 5.13 showed, the 90th, 50th (median) and 10th percentiles have moved apart, but each has increased in real terms.

The DWP's Households Below Average Income analysis from which Figures 5.12, 5.13 and Table 5.14 are derived, provides an annual cross-sectional snapshot of the distribution of income based on the Family Resources Survey. The British Household Panel Survey (BHPS) complements this by providing longitudinal information about how the incomes of a fixed sample of individuals change from year to year. This enables people to be tracked as they move through the income distribution over time, and to identify the factors associated with changes in their position in the distribution.

## Table **5.16**

### Position of individuals in the income distribution[1] in 2003 in relation to their position in 1991

Great Britain

Percentages

| | 1991 income grouping | | | | | |
|---|---|---|---|---|---|---|
| | Bottom fifth | Next fifth | Middle fifth | Next fifth | Top fifth | All individuals |
| **2003 income grouping** | | | | | | |
| Bottom fifth | 37 | 24 | 17 | 11 | 11 | 100 |
| Next fifth | 28 | 27 | 22 | 14 | 10 | 100 |
| Middle fifth | 17 | 19 | 25 | 25 | 15 | 100 |
| Next fifth | 11 | 18 | 19 | 26 | 26 | 100 |
| Top fifth | 7 | 12 | 18 | 25 | 38 | 100 |
| All individuals | 100 | 100 | 100 | 100 | 100 | |

1 Equivalised household disposable income before deduction of housing costs has been used for ranking the individuals. See Appendix, Part 5: Households Below Average Income, and Equivalisation scales.

**Source: Department for Work and Pensions from British Household Panel Survey, Institute for Social and Economic Research**

Around 38 per cent of those adults in the top quintile group of net equivalised household income in 1991 were also in that group in 2003, and a very similar proportion were in the lowest quintile group in both years (Table 5.16). By the end of the 13-year period, over the whole of the distribution individuals were more likely to end up in the quintile group they started in than any other quintile group. There is more movement in and out of the three middle quintile groups, simply because it is possible to move out of these groups through either an increase or a decrease in income. Movement out of the top group generally only occurs if income falls – an individual will remain in the group however great the increase in their income. The converse is true at the bottom of the distribution. About one in ten of those in the bottom quintile group in 2003 had been in the top group in 1991, whereas a slightly smaller proportion moved from the bottom group to the top quintile group. This does not necessarily mean that the individual's income has changed to this extent, but that the total income of the household in which they live has changed. This can happen in a wide variety of ways – for example, a young person living with their parents in 1991 then setting up their own household might move from the top to the bottom quintile group. While the picture painted of income mobility is a complicated one, for the majority of individuals their position in 2003 in relation to 1991 – that is whether it was lower, higher or the same – was generally indicative of where they had spent the majority of the 13-year period.

## Low incomes

Low income could be defined as being in the bottom quintile or decile group, but these definitions are not generally used because of their relative nature. It would mean that 20 or 10 per cent of the population would always be defined as poor. Other approaches generally involve fixing a threshold in monetary terms, below which a household is considered to be 'poor'. This threshold may be calculated in variety of ways. In countries at a very low level of development it may be useful to cost the bare essentials to maintain human life and use this as the yardstick against which to measure income. This 'basic needs' measure is of limited usefulness for a developed country such as the United Kingdom.

The approach generally used in more developed countries is to fix a low income threshold in terms of a fraction of population median income. This threshold may then be fixed in real terms for a number of years, or it may be calculated in respect of the distribution for each successive year. The Government's Opportunity for All (OfA) indicators use both approaches. The proportions of people living in households with incomes below various fractions of contemporary median income are

monitored, referred to as those with relative low income. In addition, the proportions with incomes below various fractions of median income in 1996/97, known as those with absolute low income, are also monitored. A third OfA indicator measures the number of people with persistent low income, defined as being in a low income household in three out of the last four years. In addition, the Government has announced that to monitor progress against its child poverty target, it will add to these measures one that combines material deprivation and relative low income. There is a strong relationship between material deprivation and persistent low income. This is explored in Table 5.21 later on.

In this section, the low income threshold generally adopted is 60 per cent of contemporary equivalised median household disposable income before the deduction of housing costs. In 2003/04, this represented an income of £201 per week, just below the lowest quintile (£214 per week). As well as being one of the OfA indicators, this definition was adopted by the Laeken European Council in December 2001 as one of a set of 18 statistical indicators for social inclusion. Using this threshold, the Institute for Fiscal Studies calculates that the proportion of the population living in low income households rose from 11 per cent in 1982 and 1983 to reach a peak of 21 per cent in 1992 (Figure 5.17). Official estimates made by DWP indicate

## Figure **5.17**

### Proportion of people whose income is below various fractions of median household disposable income[1]

United Kingdom/Great Britain[2]

Percentages[3]

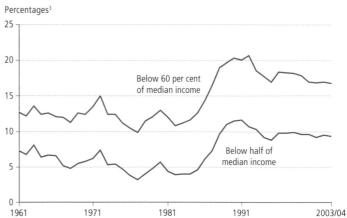

1  Equivalised contemporary household disposable income before deduction of housing costs. See Appendix, Part 5: Households Below Average Income, and Equivalisation scales.
2  Data from 1993/94 onwards are for financial years. Source of data changed in 1994/95, definition of income changed slightly and geographic coverage changed from United Kingdom to Great Britain.
3  Figures for 1994/95 to 2002/03 have been subject to minor revisions due to the new grossing regime which was introduced in 2003/04.

**Source: Institute for Fiscal Studies from Family Expenditure Survey, Office for National Statistics (1961 to 1993/94); Households Below Average Income, Department for Work and Pensions (1994/95 onwards)**

that it has since fallen back to 17 per cent in each of the four years 2000/01 to 2003/04. This pattern is also reflected in the proportion of people with incomes less than 50 per cent of the median. Note that from 1994/95 onwards these figures exclude Northern Ireland. However, the proportion of individuals living in low income households in Northern Ireland in 2003/04, at 18 per cent, was very similar to that in Great Britain.

Children are disproportionately present in low-income households: 21 per cent of children (2.6 million) were living in households with below 60 per cent of median income (before deduction of housing costs) in Great Britain in 2003/04 (Figure 5.18). This compares with 17 per cent of all individuals. The proportion of children in low income households rose steeply between 1979 and 1981 from 12 per cent to 18 per cent and continued to rise to reach a peak of 27 per cent in 1991–92 and 1992–93. It fell back during the first half of the 1990s but then rose again to 25 per cent in 1996/97 and 1997/98, since when there was again a gradual fall to 21 per cent in 2000/01, a level that has been unchanged since. If housing costs are deducted from income, the pattern of annual change during the 1990s is much the same, but at a level around 10 percentage points higher, resulting in 3.5 million children living in low-income households in 2003/04 on this basis. This is principally because housing costs for low income households are large in relation to their income as a whole. This relationship applies to the results in Table 5.19 as well as to Figure 5.18.

Children are at greater than average risk of living in a low income family if they are part of a large family, have one or more disabled adults in the family, or are in a family where the head of household comes from a ethnic minority group, particularly if of Pakistani or Bangladeshi origin. However, the greatest risk factor is being in a workless family. Around half of children in workless lone-parent families and just under two thirds of children in workless couple families in 2003/04 were living in households with below 60 per cent of median income (before deduction of housing costs). If housing costs are deducted, these proportions rise to around three quarters for children in both workless couples and lone-parent families.

People living in workless households are over-represented among low income households in Great Britain whatever their age (Table 5.19). Overall, 17 per cent of the population were living in low-income households in 2003/04, compared with 3 per cent of those living in families where two adults were in full-time work or one was in full-time work and one was working part-time (income measured before deducting housing costs). In contrast, 63 per cent of people in families where the head or spouse were unemployed had low incomes.

## Figure **5.18**

### Children living in households below 60 per cent of median household disposable income[1]

United Kingdom/Great Britain[2]

Percentages[3]

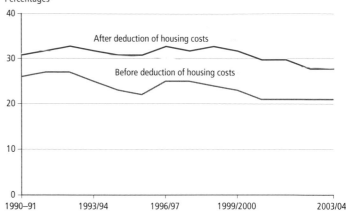

1 Equivalised contemporary household disposable income before and after deduction of housing costs. See Appendix, Part 5: Households Below Average Income, and Equivalisation scales.
2 Data from 1993/94 onwards are for financial years. Source of data changed in 1994/95, definition of income changed slightly and geographic coverage changed from United Kingdom to Great Britain.
3 Figures for 1994/95 to 2002/03 have been subject to minor revisions due to the new grossing regime which was introduced in 2003/04.

**Source: Institute for Fiscal Studies from Family Expenditure Survey, Office for National Statistics (1990–91 to 1993/94); Households Below Average Income, Department for Work and Pensions (1994/95 onwards)**

This proportion has fallen since the 1991/92 estimate of 71 per cent. About a quarter of people in families where the head or spouse were aged 60 or over had low incomes in 2003/04. The relationship between income and economic status was similar in 1981, though as Figure 5.17 showed, the overall risk of low income was lower at that time.

When income is measured after the deduction of housing costs, the proportions of individuals with low incomes are generally higher than before the deduction of housing costs, whatever their economic status.

The existence of income from employment is not always sufficient to lift a household out of low income. The national minimum wage, which came into force in April 1999, aims to combat the phenomenon of the 'working poor'. As of 1 October 2005 the minimum wage rates were set at £3.00 for 16 to 17 year olds (for whom special conditions apply), £4.25 per hour for 18 to 21 year olds and £5.05 for those aged 22 and over.

For some people, such as students and those unemployed for only a brief period, the experience of low income may be a relatively transient one, but for others it may be more permanent. The British Household Panel Survey (BHPS) provides longitudinal data that allow income mobility and the persistence of low income to be analysed. The definition of

Table **5.19**

**Individuals in households with incomes below 60 per cent of median disposable income:[1] by economic activity status**

United Kingdom/Great Britain[2]

Percentages[3]

| | 1981 | 1991/92 | 1996/97 | 2001/02 | 2003/04 |
|---|---|---|---|---|---|
| **Before deduction of housing costs** | | | | | |
| Workless, head or spouse unemployed | 52 | 71 | 62 | 64 | 63 |
| Workless, head or spouse aged 60 or over | 19 | 31 | 25 | 26 | 24 |
| One or more in part-time work | 24 | 26 | 25 | 25 | 23 |
| Self-employed[4] | 13 | 19 | 18 | 19 | 19 |
| One in full-time work, one not working | 8 | 12 | 16 | 12 | 13 |
| One in full-time work, one in part-time work | 2 | 3 | 3 | 4 | 3 |
| Single or couple, all in full-time work | 1 | 2 | 2 | 2 | 3 |
| Workless, other inactive[5] | 36 | 51 | 42 | 42 | 44 |
| All individuals | 13 | 21 | 18 | 17 | 17 |
| **After deduction of housing costs** | | | | | |
| Workless, head or spouse unemployed | 57 | 76 | 79 | 75 | 78 |
| Workless, head or spouse aged 60 or over | 23 | 36 | 31 | 27 | 23 |
| One or more in part-time work | 27 | 32 | 33 | 33 | 29 |
| Self-employed[4] | 15 | 24 | 22 | 22 | 23 |
| One in full-time work, one not working | 9 | 17 | 21 | 18 | 18 |
| One in full-time work, one in part-time work | 3 | 5 | 5 | 6 | 5 |
| Single or couple, all in full-time work | 1 | 2 | 3 | 3 | 4 |
| Workless, other inactive[5] | 45 | 62 | 64 | 64 | 62 |
| All individuals | 15 | 25 | 25 | 22 | 21 |

1 Equivalised contemporary household disposable income before and after deduction of housing costs. See Appendix, Part 5: Households Below Average Income, and Equivalisation scales.
2 Data for 1981 and 1991/92 are based on the Family Expenditure Survey, which covers the United Kingdom. Data for 1996/97 onwards are based on the Family Resources Survey, which covers Great Britain only.
3 Figures for 1994/95 to 2002/03 have been subject to minor revisions due to the new grossing regime that was introduced in 2003/04.
4 Those in benefit units that contain one or more adults who are normally self-employed for 31 or more hours a week.
5 Includes long-term sick and disabled people and non-working single parents.

*Source: Households Below Average Income, Department for Work and Pensions*

the Government's Opportunity for All indicator for persistent low income is 'at least three years out of four below thresholds of 60 or 70 per cent of median income'. Between 2000 and 2003, around 11 per cent of individuals experienced persistent low income and this figure has changed little since 1991 to 1994 (Table 5.20 overleaf). However, the risk of different family types experiencing persistent low income has changed over the last decade. In particular, the proportion of single people with children experiencing persistent low income has fallen substantially, from 40 per cent during 1991 to 1994 to 23 per cent during 2000 to 2003. Those living in couple households without children – at least in the first year of each four year period – were at least risk of persistent low income. Pensioner families, whether single or couples, were at greater than average risk of persistent low income, and the risk for pensioner couples seems to have risen slightly over the period,

despite the overall growth in income for pensioners as discussed in the Household Income section at the beginning of this chapter.

Table 5.20 shows entry rates into and exit rates from low income over the period 1991 to 2003. For the purposes of this analysis, persistent low income for an individual is defined as having lived in a household with equivalised income below 60 per cent of contemporary median income for at least three consecutive years. An entry into persistent low income is defined as where an individual spent two consecutive years above the threshold followed by three further consecutive years below the threshold. An exit from persistent low income is defined as where an individual spent three consecutive years below the low income threshold followed by two further consecutive years above the threshold.

## Table **5.20**

### Persistent low income: by family type,[1] 1991–2003

Great Britain                                                                                                Percentages

| | 3 out of 4 years below 60 per cent of median income[2] | | | Entry rate into persistent low income[3] | Exit rate from persistent low income[3] |
|---|---|---|---|---|---|
| | 1991–94 | 1996–99 | 2000–03 | 1991–2003 | 1991–2003 |
| Pensioner couple | 13 | 17 | 17 | 2 | 9 |
| Single pensioner | 21 | 23 | 21 | 3 | 10 |
| Couple with children | 13 | 11 | 10 | 1 | 17 |
| Couple without children | 3 | 3 | 4 | 1 | 21 |
| Single with children | 40 | 27 | 23 | 3 | 16 |
| Single without children | 5 | 7 | 7 | 1 | 34 |
| All individuals | 12 | 11 | 11 | 1 | 16 |

1 Families are classified according to their type in the first year of the relevant period.
2 Equivalised contemporary household disposable income before housing costs. See Appendix, Part 5: Households Below Average Income, and Equivalisation scales.
3 Persistent low income is defined as experiencing low income for at least three consecutive years. An entry occurs during the first year of a persistent low income period, following a period of two years not in low income. An exit occurs as the first year of two not in low income, following a persistent low income period.

**Source: Department for Work and Pensions from the British Household Panel Survey, Institute for Social and Economic Research**

The exit rate from persistent low income, at 16 per cent, was considerably greater than the entry rate of 1 per cent. Single people with children and single pensioners had the highest entry rates into persistent low income, at 3 per cent, whereas single people without children were the most likely to exit. Couples without children also had a relatively high exit rate. Pensioners were less likely to exit persistent low income than all other family types. Overall, the events most frequently associated with an exit from persistent low income were a rise in the earnings of the head of household and a rise in benefit income. Conversely an entry into persistent low income was most often associated with a fall in the head of household's earnings.

Although low income is an important measure of poverty, it does not present the whole picture. Material hardship provides a wider measure of people's living standards, reflecting the inability of families to afford to buy essential goods or to participate in leisure activities. The DWP's Families and Children Study (FACS) analyses the affordability of 34 'deprivation items', covering four dimensions of material deprivation: food and meals; clothing and shoes; consumer durables; and leisure activities. For more details see Appendix, Part 5: Material hardship. The data can be used to calculate the total number of all deprivation items a family would like but could not afford. The survey also provides data on income that allow the same definition of low income to be applied as for the Households Below Average Income series used above, and since it is a longitudinal survey incomes can also be tracked over time. It is thus possible using this data source to explore the relationship between income and material hardship over time.

Table 5.21 shows that being in material hardship is related to poverty, though the relationship is not altogether straightforward. Being in severe hardship increases as the number of years spent in poverty increases. A quarter of families who spent all the years between 1999 and 2002 in a low income household were in severe hardship compared with virtually none of those who had not spent any years in poverty. However, not all families who had spent four years in a low income household experienced severe or even moderate hardship at the end of that period. Although 85 per cent of families who had not spent any years in poverty were not in

## Table **5.21**

### Relationship between material hardship[1] and years spent in poverty,[2] 2002

Great Britain                                                     Percentages

| | Number of years between 1999 and 2002 spent in poverty | | | | |
|---|---|---|---|---|---|
| | None | One | Two | Three | Four |
| Not in hardship | 85 | 68 | 42 | 38 | 31 |
| Moderate hardship | 14 | 25 | 42 | 42 | 45 |
| Severe hardship | 1 | 7 | 16 | 21 | 25 |
| All families | 100 | 100 | 100 | 100 | 100 |

1 See Appendix, Part 5: Material hardship.
2 Families are classified as being in poverty if their income is below 60 per cent of median equivalised disposable income before housing costs.

**Source: Families and Children Study, Department for Work and Pensions**

hardship in 2002, 31 per cent of families who had spent all four years in a low income household were also not in hardship.

This analysis of the FACS also studied how movements in and out of both low income and material hardship are related to each other. Among families who had moved in and out of poverty, the risk of hardship at the end of the period varied according to the number of years poor, but it hardly mattered whether the experience of low income was recent or some time ago. Only a small proportion of families who moved out of low income between one year and the next, also moved out of hardship at the same time. On the other hand there was a general drift out of hardship over the four year period, as levels of hardship seem to decline even among low income families.

## Wealth

Although the terms 'wealthy' and 'high income' are often used interchangeably, they relate to quite distinct concepts. 'Income' represents a flow of resources over a period, received either in cash or in kind, while 'wealth' describes the ownership of assets valued at a particular point in time. Wealth can be held in the form of financial assets, such as savings accounts or shares, which provide a flow of current income, or pension rights that provide entitlement to a future income flow. These types of asset form financial wealth. Ownership of non-financial wealth may provide financial security even if it does not provide a current

income flow; a house or a work of art, for example, could be sold to provide income if necessary. In this section the term 'wealth' includes both financial and non-financial assets. There is a further distinction sometimes made between marketable and non-marketable wealth. Marketable wealth comprises assets that can be sold and their value realised, whereas non-marketable wealth comprises mainly pension rights that often cannot be 'cashed in'. Wealth may be accumulated either by the acquisition of new assets, through saving or by inheritance, or by the increase in value of existing assets.

Aggregate data on the wealth of the household sector compiled in the UK National Accounts indicate that of total assets of over £7,000 billion in 2004, nearly 55 per cent were held in the form of non-financial assets, primarily housing (Table 5.22). Even when account is taken of the loans outstanding on the purchase of housing, this form of wealth has shown strong growth between 1991 and 2004. This reflects the buoyant state of the housing market, as well as the continued growth in the number of owner-occupied dwellings. Note that in Table 5.22, as in Figure 5.1, households are combined with the non-profit making institutions serving households.

The second most important element of household wealth is financial assets held in life assurance and pension funds,

## Table 5.22

### Composition of the net wealth[1] of the household sector

United Kingdom                                                                 £ billion at 2004 prices[2]

|  | 1991 | 1996 | 2001 | 2002 | 2003 | 2004 |
|---|---|---|---|---|---|---|
| **Non-financial assets** | 1,958 | 1,718 | 2,666 | 3,163 | 3,468 | 3,829 |
| **Financial assets** | | | | | | |
| Life assurance and pension funds | 822 | 1,212 | 1,601 | 1,423 | 1,520 | 1,625 |
| Securities and shares | 351 | 515 | 610 | 453 | 503 | 553 |
| Currency and deposits | 528 | 575 | 712 | 753 | 803 | 858 |
| Other assets | 110 | 118 | 132 | 133 | 142 | 143 |
| Total assets | 3,769 | 4,138 | 5,721 | 5,924 | 6,436 | 7,008 |
| **Financial liabilities** | | | | | | |
| Loans secured on dwellings | 438 | 476 | 617 | 689 | 783 | 875 |
| Other loans | 117 | 106 | 166 | 184 | 188 | 208 |
| Other liabilities | 62 | 59 | 64 | 77 | 90 | 111 |
| Total liabilities | 617 | 640 | 847 | 951 | 1,061 | 1,194 |
| **Total net wealth** | 3,152 | 3,498 | 4,874 | 4,974 | 5,375 | 5,814 |

1 See Appendix, Part 5: Net wealth of the household sector.
2 Adjusted to 2004 prices using the expenditure deflator for the household sector.

*Source: Office for National Statistics*

# Expenditure

- Between 1996 and 2004 the volume of expenditure by UK households on goods grew at an average rate of 5.0 per cent per year. This was nearly three times the rate for expenditure on services, which grew at 1.8 per cent per year. (Figure 6.1)

- The greatest increase in the volume of spending between 1971 and 2004 has been on communications, with a ninefold rise. (Table 6.2)

- In September 2005 annual growth in the volume of retail sales in Great Britain, measured using the seasonally adjusted index was 0.7 per cent, the lowest figure for almost ten years. (Figure 6.7)

- In 2004 the number of debit card transactions in the United Kingdom was ten times higher than it had been in 1991. Over the same period credit card usage increased by a factor of almost three. (Figure 6.8)

- Individual borrowing rose considerably between the second quarter of 1993 and the second quarter of 2005, increasing by £550 billion to over £1 trillion in 2004 prices. (Figure 6.10)

- The number of individual insolvencies in England and Wales rose to 46,700 in 2004, an increase of 31 per cent over the previous year. (Figure 6.11)

- In July 2005 the CPI went above the 2.0 per cent target set by the Chancellor for the first time since it has been the official measure of inflation. By September 2005 it had reached 2.5 per cent. (Figure 6.12)

# Chapter 6

The types of goods and services on which people choose to spend their income have changed considerably over the past 30 years. Personal spending patterns provide insights into people and society. They provide an indication of a household's standard of living and material well being, as well as being a reflection of changes in society, consumer preference, and the growth in choices available to the consumer.

## Household and personal expenditure

The volume of spending by households on goods and services has increased steadily within the United Kingdom since 1971, at an average rate of 2.7 per cent a year after allowing for the effects of inflation (Figure 6.1). However, there were years when it fell – 1974, 1980, 1981 and 1991. These falls coincided with general downturns within the UK economy (see Figure 5.25). From 1996, spending on goods has grown at a faster rate than spending on services, by an average of 5.0 per cent a year compared with 1.8 per cent.

### Figure 6.1

**Volume of domestic household expenditure[1] on goods and services**

United Kingdom

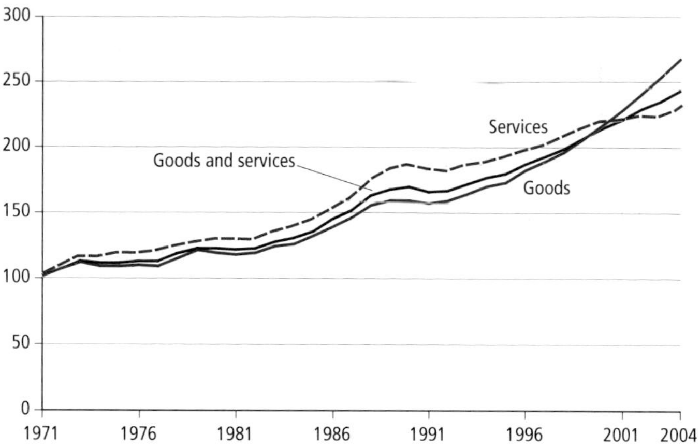

Indices (1971=100)

1 Chained volume measures. See Appendix, Part 6: Household expenditure.

Source: Office for National Statistics

### Table 6.2

**Volume of household expenditure[1]**

United Kingdom

Indices (1971=100)

| | 1971 | 1981 | 1991 | 2001 | 2004 | £ billion (current prices) 2004 |
|---|---|---|---|---|---|---|
| Food and non-alcoholic drink | 100 | 105 | 117 | 137 | 143 | 64.4 |
| Alcohol and tobacco | 100 | 99 | 92 | 88 | 92 | 27.8 |
| Clothing and footwear | 100 | 120 | 187 | 345 | 451 | 43.9 |
| Housing, water and fuel | 100 | 117 | 139 | 152 | 159 | 134.8 |
| Household goods and services | 100 | 117 | 160 | 262 | 310 | 45.9 |
| Health | 100 | 125 | 182 | 188 | 212 | 12.8 |
| Transport | 100 | 128 | 181 | 246 | 263 | 108.0 |
| Communication | 100 | 190 | 306 | 789 | 899 | 16.6 |
| Recreation and culture | 100 | 161 | 283 | 548 | 683 | 91.5 |
| Education | 100 | 160 | 199 | 258 | 229 | 10.0 |
| Restaurants and hotels[2] | 100 | 126 | 167 | 193 | 202 | 81.9 |
| Miscellaneous goods and services | 100 | 121 | 230 | 282 | 300 | 82.3 |
| Total domestic household expenditure | 100 | 121 | 165 | 220 | 242 | 719.7 |
|    of which goods | 100 | 117 | 156 | 227 | 266 | 358.4 |
|    of which services | 100 | 129 | 182 | 220 | 227 | 361.3 |
| Less expenditure by foreign tourists, etc | 100 | 152 | 187 | 210 | 227 | -15.7 |
| Household expenditure abroad | 100 | 193 | 298 | 669 | 753 | 27.7 |
| All household expenditure[3] | 100 | 122 | 167 | 227 | 250 | 731.8 |

1 Chained volume measures. See Appendix, Part 6: Household expenditure. Classified to COICOP ESA95. See Appendix, Part 6: Classification of Individual Consumption by Purpose.
2 Includes purchases of alcoholic drinks.
3 Includes expenditure by UK households in the United Kingdom and abroad.

Source: Office for National Statistics

## Table 6.3

**Household expenditure:[1] by socio-economic classification,[2] 2004/05**

United Kingdom

£ per week

| | Occupations | | | Never worked[3] and long-term unemployed | All households[4] |
|---|---|---|---|---|---|
| | Managerial and professional | Intermediate | Routine and manual | | |
| Food and non-alcoholic drink | 53.80 | 49.60 | 45.90 | 34.40 | 44.70 |
| Alcohol and tobacco | 13.80 | 13.00 | 13.40 | 10.60 | 11.30 |
| Clothing and footwear | 35.30 | 27.70 | 25.50 | 23.30 | 23.90 |
| Housing, fuel and power[5] | 49.40 | 42.30 | 43.70 | 57.20 | 40.40 |
| Household goods and services | 46.10 | 34.70 | 28.80 | 15.40 | 31.60 |
| Health | 7.60 | 4.50 | 3.70 | 1.60 | 4.90 |
| Transport | 95.60 | 71.00 | 61.30 | 27.10 | 59.60 |
| Communication | 15.00 | 13.60 | 13.70 | 10.80 | 11.70 |
| Recreation and culture | 84.60 | 60.10 | 63.30 | 31.10 | 59.00 |
| Education | 14.00 | 5.20 | 1.70 | 33.40 | 6.50 |
| Restaurants and hotels | 55.70 | 42.60 | 37.30 | 28.40 | 36.10 |
| Miscellaneous goods and services | 53.80 | 37.70 | 33.00 | 15.00 | 34.90 |
| Other expenditure items | 121.80 | 82.20 | 64.80 | 19.80 | 69.70 |
| All household expenditure | 646.40 | 484.30 | 436.00 | 308.20 | 434.40 |
| Average household size (number of people) | 2.7 | 2.7 | 2.8 | 2.6 | 2.4 |

1  See Appendix, Part 6: Household expenditure. Expenditure rounded to the nearest 10 pence.
2  Of the household reference person. Excludes retired households. See Appendix, Part 1: National Statistics Socio-economic Classification, and Appendix, Part 6: Retired households.
3  Includes households where the reference person is a student.
4  Includes retired households and others that are not classified.
5  Excludes mortgage interest payments, water charges, council tax and Northern Ireland domestic rates. These are included in 'Other expenditure items'.

**Source: Expenditure and Food Survey, Office for National Statistics**

Between 1971 and 2004, spending by households increased in volume terms for all the broad categories of expenditure, with the exception of alcohol (bought from off-licences) and tobacco, which fell (Table 6.2). This was due to the fall in the volume of household expenditure on tobacco which halved over this period. This reflects the decline in smoking, as described in the Health chapter (see Figure 7.14).

The greatest increases in spending since 1971 have been on communication, household expenditure abroad, and recreation and culture. There have been rises in household expenditure on non-essential items while proportionally less was spent on essentials such as food or housing. This reflects increases in household disposable income (see Figure 5.1). Spending on communication has almost trebled since 1991 due to mass ownership of mobile phones.

Levels of expenditure vary among different groups in the population. In Table 6.3 average UK household expenditure is analysed by the socio-economic classification (NS-SEC) of the household reference person (see Appendix, Part 1: National Statistics Socio-economic Classification). Total expenditure in 2004/05 was highest for those households where the household reference person was in the managerial and professional group (£646.40 per week), more than double that of households in the never worked and long-term unemployed group. The managerial and professional group had the highest level of spending on most expenditure categories. However the never worked and long-term unemployed group had higher expenditure on housing, fuel and power (which includes rent but excludes mortgage interest payments) and on education. This reflects the inclusion of student households in this group.

Over the last eight years, the expenditure gap between those at the top and bottom of the income distribution has narrowed. In 2004/05 average expenditure per week by households in

# Figure **6.4**

## Household expenditure:[1] by income quintile group[2]

United Kingdom

£ per week

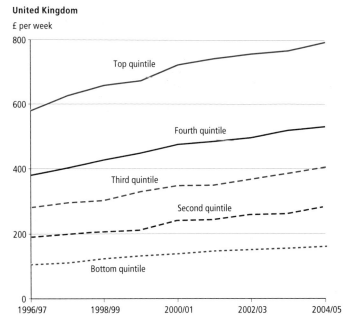

1  See Appendix, Part 6: Household expenditure.
2  See Chapter 5: Analysing income distribution box for an explanation
   of quintile groups.

**Source: Family Expenditure Survey and Expenditure and Food Survey,
Office for National Statistics**

# Table **6.5**

## Household expenditure[1] per head: by region

Indices (UK=100)

|  | 1997–2000[2] | 2002–05[3] |
|---|---|---|
| United Kingdom | 100 | 100 |
| England | 102 | 102 |
| North East | 86 | 83 |
| North West | 94 | 96 |
| Yorkshire and the Humber | 93 | 96 |
| East Midlands | 95 | 95 |
| West Midlands | 92 | 90 |
| East | 104 | 108 |
| London | 117 | 110 |
| South East | 116 | 116 |
| South West | 98 | 105 |
| Wales | 89 | 87 |
| Scotland | 94 | 92 |
| Northern Ireland | 79 | 85 |

1  See Appendix, Part 6: Household expenditure.
2  Combined data from 1997/98, 1998/99 and 1999/2000.
3  Combined data from 2002/03, 2003/04 and 2004/05.

**Source: Family Expenditure Survey and Expenditure and Food Survey,
Office for National Statistics**

the bottom disposable income quintile group was £163, while those in the top quintile group spent £795 per week (Figure 6.4). Since 1996/97 average expenditure by households in the bottom income quintile group had risen by 53 per cent compared with a rise of 35 per cent for households in the top quintile group.

In 2004/05 there were some notable differences between the expenditure patterns of households with different levels of income. Households in the top quintile group spent relatively small proportions of their total expenditure on essential items such as food and non-alcoholic drink, and housing, fuel and power (8 per cent and 7 per cent respectively). In contrast, households in the bottom quintile group spent about 16 per cent of their total expenditure on each of these. Also, on average, households with lower incomes spent larger proportions of their total expenditure on alcohol and tobacco.

Total household expenditure varies across the United Kingdom. For the period 2002/03 to 2004/05 households in Scotland, on average, spent 10 per cent less per person than those in England, while those in Wales spent 15 per cent less, and those in Northern Ireland 17 per cent less (Table 6.5). However, average household expenditure also varied across England, with the highest spending per person in the South East, and the lowest spending in the North East.

Spending on most categories of goods and services was highest per person for households in the South East and London, reflecting the high overall levels of spending by these households. Households in the South East consistently spent more than the UK average per person on all categories except alcohol and tobacco, on which spending was very similar to the UK average. Households in London also spent more than average on most categories, but 6 per cent less than average on recreation and culture and 5 per cent less on transport, two large components of total household expenditure.

Recreation and culture is one of the areas where spending has increased most rapidly – by a factor of nearly seven between 1971 and 2004 (see Table 6.2). Only spending abroad and spending on communication increased by more over this period. Spending on recreation and culture is an important part of total household expenditure, accounting for 14 per cent of all household expenditure in 2004/05. For the period 2002/03 to 2004/05, an average household spent £57.60 per week on recreation and culture, of which almost two thirds was spent on package holidays and holiday accommodation, restaurant and café meals, and alcoholic drinks (not consumed at home) (Table 6.6). Although households in the North East spent least overall (see Table 6.5), they spent on average £5.50 per week on gambling payments, 49 per cent above the UK average.

**Table 6.6**

**Household expenditure[1] on selected leisure items and activities: by region, 2002–05[2]**

£ per week

| | Alcoholic drinks (away from home) | Games, toys and hobbies[3] | Gambling payments | Package holidays[4] | Sports admissions, subscriptions and leisure class fees | Restaurant and café meals | Holiday accommo- dation[4] | Total recreation and culture |
|---|---|---|---|---|---|---|---|---|
| United Kingdom | 8.60 | 3.50 | 3.70 | 12.70 | 5.10 | 11.60 | 4.90 | 57.60 |
| England | 8.80 | 3.50 | 3.70 | 13.00 | 5.30 | 11.90 | 5.10 | 58.70 |
| North East | 9.10 | 3.10 | 5.50 | 10.80 | 3.90 | 8.80 | 3.00 | 54.20 |
| North West | 10.10 | 3.40 | 4.40 | 14.00 | 5.10 | 11.00 | 4.10 | 58.70 |
| Yorkshire and the Humber | 9.80 | 3.40 | 5.50 | 14.30 | 3.90 | 10.60 | 4.40 | 58.80 |
| East Midlands | 8.60 | 3.40 | 3.60 | 11.90 | 4.70 | 11.80 | 5.40 | 58.00 |
| West Midlands | 8.00 | 3.40 | 3.60 | 13.70 | 4.10 | 9.80 | 4.90 | 55.60 |
| East | 7.40 | 3.60 | 3.60 | 12.60 | 5.90 | 11.90 | 5.40 | 61.60 |
| London | 9.80 | 3.60 | 2.90 | 11.90 | 7.20 | 15.70 | 5.90 | 56.90 |
| South East | 8.40 | 3.70 | 2.80 | 13.70 | 5.90 | 13.10 | 6.20 | 62.20 |
| South West | 8.10 | 3.30 | 3.00 | 12.50 | 5.10 | 11.50 | 5.30 | 58.60 |
| Wales | 7.80 | 3.40 | 3.40 | 11.20 | 3.10 | 9.30 | 3.80 | 52.50 |
| Scotland | 7.00 | 3.30 | 4.10 | 11.30 | 4.60 | 9.70 | 4.30 | 53.00 |
| Northern Ireland | 8.50 | 4.00 | 3.20 | 9.50 | 3.90 | 12.00 | 2.40 | 46.30 |

1 See Appendix, Part 6: Household expenditure. Expenditure rounded to the nearest 10 pence.
2 Combined data from 2002/03, 2003/04 and 2004/05.
3 Includes computer software and games.
4 In the United Kingdom and abroad.

*Source: Expenditure and Food Survey, Office for National Statistics*

## Transactions and credit

In all years, retail sales follow a strong seasonal pattern. Sales increase sharply in the build up to Christmas. On average the volume of sales in November is about 10 per cent above trend, and in December about 30 per cent above trend. For the rest of the year sales are a few per cent below trend.

Apart from seasonal or other short term effects, the volume of retail sales in Great Britain has grown continuously since 1992, although there have been periods of relatively faster and slower growth (Figure 6.7). Since late 2004, growth in retail sales has been slow. The rate of annual growth in the seasonally adjusted retail sales index in September 2005 was 0.7 per cent, the lowest for almost ten years.

This slow down in the rate of growth affected some retail sectors more than others. In September 2005 the annual change in the volume of sales in stores selling household goods was -2.5 per cent. For all stores selling predominantly non-food items there was no change. This was in contrast to sales in stores selling predominantly food items, which increased by 2.1 per cent over the same period.

**Figure 6.7**

**Annual growth in the volume of retail sales[1]**

**Great Britain**

Percentage change over 12 months[2]

1 See Appendix, Part 6: Retail sales index.
2 In the seasonally adjusted index.

*Source: Office for National Statistics*

## Figure **6.8**

### Non-cash transactions:[1] by method of payment

**United Kingdom**

Billions

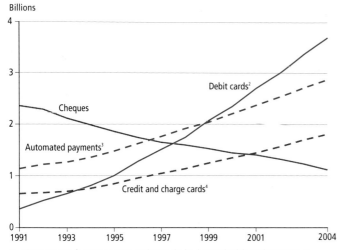

1  Figures are for payments only made by households or businesses. Cheque encashments and cash withdrawals from ATMs and branch counters using credit/charge and debit cards are not included. Based on data supplied by UK card issuers.
2  Visa Debit and Switch cards in all years; includes Electron cards from 1996 and Solo cards from 1997.
3  Includes direct debits, standing orders, direct credits, inter-branch automated items.
4  Visa, MasterCard, travel/entertainment cards and store cards.

**Source: APACS – Association for Payment Clearing Services**

The way in which spending transactions are undertaken in the United Kingdom changed dramatically between 1991 and 2004. During this period the number of transactions using plastic cards increased from 1.0 billion to 5.5 billion, while the number of transactions using cheques fell from 2.4 billion to 1.1 billion (Figure 6.8). According to the Association for Payment Clearing Services (APACS), 94 per cent of men and 91 per cent of women in Great Britain had at least one plastic card in 2004. This compares with 80 per cent of men and 73 per cent of women in 1993.

Between 1991 and 2004, growth in debit card use in the United Kingdom was greater than that of credit cards. There were ten times more debit card transactions in 2004 than there were in 1991. Credit card transactions increased by a factor of almost three. It is not only individuals who are using plastic cards more regularly. Credit cards are now the most widely used method of finance for small and medium sized companies – 55 per cent used credit cards in 2004.

The growth in the use of plastic cards has been accompanied by a rise in card fraud. This can involve criminals 'skimming' cards to copy the information from the magnetic strips. In October 2003 card companies began issuing 'chip and PIN' cards in an attempt to combat this. At the end of June 2005, there were more than 107 million 'chip and PIN' cards in circulation out of a total of 135 million. These cards help combat fraud in two ways. First, cardholders' account details are stored on a microchip, which is far safer than a magnetic

## Table **6.9**

### Debit and credit card spending[1,2]

**United Kingdom**

Percentages

| | Debit cards | | | Credit cards | | |
|---|---|---|---|---|---|---|
| | 1996 | 2001 | 2004 | 1996 | 2001 | 2004 |
| Food and drink | 43 | 29 | 25 | 13 | 11 | 11 |
| Motoring | 12 | 13 | 14 | 13 | 13 | 11 |
| Household | 6 | 9 | 8 | 10 | 12 | 12 |
| Mixed business | 10 | 7 | 7 | 7 | 6 | 8 |
| Clothing | 6 | 6 | 5 | 6 | 5 | 5 |
| Travel | 5 | 7 | 6 | 14 | 12 | 11 |
| Entertainment | 3 | 5 | 5 | 7 | 7 | 6 |
| Hotels | 1 | 1 | 1 | 6 | 5 | 4 |
| Other retail | 9 | 10 | 11 | 14 | 16 | 16 |
| Other services | 4 | 12 | 18 | 10 | 14 | 17 |
|   of which financial | .. | .. | 10 | .. | .. | 8 |
| Total (=100%) (£ billions) | 37.0 | 93.3 | 147.1 | 47.7 | 91.5 | 122.1 |

1  By principal business activity of where the purchase was made. Excludes spending outside the United Kingdom by UK cardholders.
2  Based on data reported by the largest UK merchant acquirers, who process plastic card transactions for retailers and other service providers.

**Source: APACS – Association for Payment Clearing Services**

strip. Second, the Personal Identification Number (PIN), known only to the cardholder, is used to verify a transaction rather than the cardholder's signature, which could be forged.

According to APACS, spending patterns differ between credit and debit cards (Table 6.9). The rapid increase in spending on debit cards, which has now overtaken spending on credit cards, has been accompanied by a change in the pattern of debit card usage. In 1996 spending on debit cards was concentrated in certain types of outlets, such as food and drink and motoring, whereas spending on credit cards was spread among a wider variety of outlets. In 2004 this was still true but to a much lesser extent, and spending on debit cards was spread across a wider variety of outlets. Between 1996 and 2004, purchases from food and drink outlets have fallen from 43 to 25 per cent of the total while spending on other services, including financial services, has increased from 4 to 18 per cent. In contrast, the distribution of spending on credit cards has changed less over time. In 2004 the amount spent on credit cards in motoring outlets, travel agents and household goods stores each accounted for between 11 and 12 per cent of total credit card expenditure. Use of credit cards for goods from 'other retailers', which include book shops, record stores, pharmacies, jewellers and computer shops, accounted for 16 per cent of the total.

Individuals in the United Kingdom can borrow money from five main sources – banks, building societies, other specialist lenders, retailers, and other organisations, such as government and pension funds. Borrowing rose considerably between the second quarter of 1993 and the second quarter of 2005, increasing by £550 billion to over £1 trillion (one thousand billion) in 2004 prices (Figure 6.10). During the first six months of 2005, 83 per cent of total borrowing was secured on dwellings, a percentage that had changed little from 1993. The remaining 17 per cent consisted of consumer credit. The ways in which consumer credit is financed have changed over the past 12 years. In 1993, 81 per cent was financed by overdrafts and loans – only 19 per cent was borrowed on credit cards. By 2005, 29 per cent of consumer credit was borrowed on credit cards.

High and continuous levels of borrowing can lead to debts that people cannot afford to pay. In some cases, the courts encourage a voluntary arrangement to be agreed between the debtor and the creditors. However, individuals are said to be insolvent and may be officially declared bankrupt if a court is satisfied that there is no prospect of the debt being paid. In 2004 the number of individual insolvencies in England and Wales rose by 11,100 to reach 46,700, an increase of 31 per cent over the previous year (Figure 6.11). This is the largest increase since the recession of the early 1990s when individual insolvencies increased by 44 per cent between 1991 and 1992. Bank of England figures show that the value of bad debts

## Figure **6.10**

### Total lending to individuals[1]

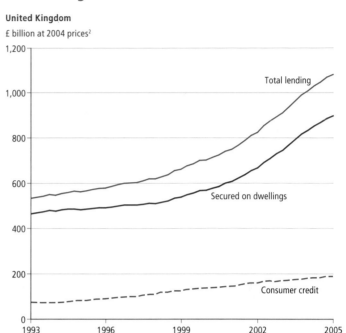

**United Kingdom**
£ billion at 2004 prices[2]

1  Lending secured on dwellings and consumer credit, both to individuals and to housing associations. Seasonally adjusted.
2  Adjusted to 2004 prices using the retail prices index.

***Source: Bank of England***

## Figure **6.11**

### Number of individual insolvencies

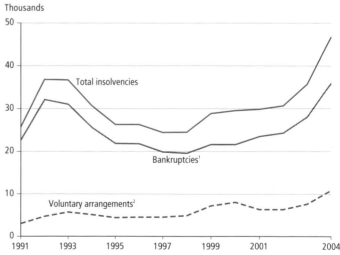

**England & Wales**
Thousands

1  Individuals declared bankrupt by a court.
2  Individuals who make a voluntary agreement with their creditors.

***Source: Department of Trade and Industry***

written-off by banks for insolvent individuals increased from £1.9 billion in 2000 to £4.2 billion in 2004. In line with the increase in borrowing on credit cards, write-offs of credit card debt rose from 19 per cent of total write-offs (£0.28 billion) in 1993 to 38 per cent (£1.60 billion) in 2004.

## Prices

The way people choose to spend their money is affected by the prices of goods and services. An index of prices for a 'shopping basket', containing the goods and services on which people typically spend their money, can be used to measure the 'cost of living'. As the prices of the various items change over time, so does the total cost of the basket. Since 10 December 2003, the consumer prices index (CPI) has been used as the main domestic measure of UK inflation for macroeconomic purposes. It measures the average change, from month to month, in the prices of goods and services purchased by most households in the United Kingdom.

Before December 2003 the retail prices index (RPI), which was introduced in 1947, was the most familiar UK index. Both indices are broadly similar, but there are several differences – the main one being that the CPI does not take account of changes in the price of certain housing costs such as house depreciation, council tax, and buildings insurance, as well as mortgage interest payments. The CPI covers spending by all private households, foreign visitors to the United Kingdom and residents in institutions; the RPI covers spending by private households only, and excludes the spending of the highest income households

and pensioner households mainly dependent on state benefits. There are also some methodological differences in how the two indices combine individual prices. These differences mean that most of the time the CPI inflation rate is lower than the RPI inflation rate (Figure 6.12). As a result of the change in December 2003, the Chancellor of the Exchequer announced a new inflation target of 2.0 per cent measured by the 12-month change in the CPI. It was previously 2.5 per cent measured by RPIX (RPI excluding mortgage interest payments).

Levels of UK inflation have varied considerably over the past 30 or so years. Inflation (measured by the RPI) exceeded 20 per cent during some periods in the 1970s and 1980, and was above 10 per cent again in 1990, but since August 1991 it has remained below 5 per cent. Between June 1998 and May 2005, the CPI was consistently below the 2.0 per cent target. However, in June 2005 inflation (measured by the CPI) reached 2.0 per cent, and from July to September 2005 it was slightly above the target.

Figure 6.13 shows the percentage change in price of components of the UK CPI between 2003 and 2004. Price increases in housing and household services, miscellaneous goods and services (which includes household insurance,

### Figure **6.12**

**Consumer prices index[1] and retail prices index[2]**

**United Kingdom**
Percentage change over 12 months

1  Data prior to 1997 are estimates. See Appendix, Part 6: Harmonised index of consumer prices.
2  See Appendix, Part 6: Retail prices index, and Consumer prices index.

**Source: Office for National Statistics**

### Figure **6.13**

**Percentage change in consumer prices index, 2004[1]**

**United Kingdom**
Percentages

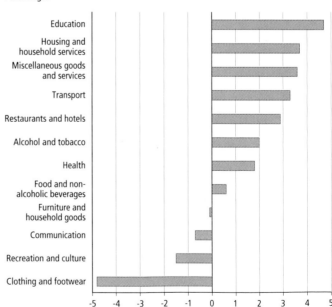

1  Percentage change on the previous year. See Appendix, Part 6: Consumer prices index.

**Source: Office for National Statistics**

## Table **6.14**

### Cost of selected items

United Kingdom

Pence

| | 1971 | 1981 | 1991 | 1996 | 2001 | 2004 |
|---|---|---|---|---|---|---|
| 500g back bacon[1] | 37 | 142 | 235 | 293 | 343 | 356 |
| 250g cheddar cheese | 13 | 58 | 86 | 115 | 128 | 142 |
| Eggs (size 2), per dozen | 26 | 78 | 118 | 158 | 172 | 169 |
| 800g white sliced bread | 10 | 37 | 53 | 55 | 51 | 65 |
| 1 pint pasteurised milk[2] | 5 | 19 | 32 | 36 | 36 | 35 |
| 1 kg granulated sugar | 9 | 39 | 66 | 76 | 57 | 74 |
| 100g instant coffee | 25 | 95 | 130 | 189 | 181 | 175 |
| 250g tea bags | .. | .. | 150 | 134 | 146 | 139 |
| Packet of 20 cigarettes (filter tip)[3] | 27 | 97 | 186 | 273 | 412 | 439 |
| Pint of beer[4] | 15 | 65 | 137 | 173 | 203 | 233 |
| Whisky (per nip) | .. | .. | 95 | 123 | 148 | 171 |
| Litre of unleaded petrol | .. | .. | 45 | 57 | 76 | 80 |

1 In 1971 and 1981 the price is for unsmoked. In 1991 the price is an average of vacuum and not vacuum-packed.
2 Delivered milk included from 1996.
3 Change from standard to king size in 1991.
4 Bottled until 1981 and draught lager after.

**Source: Office for National Statistics**

professional fees and credit card charges, among other things) and transport all contributed to growth in the overall index. This is because these component groups had increases in price of over 3.0 per cent and CPI weightings greater than 10.0 per cent. Prices fell for four components – clothing and footwear, recreation and culture, communication, and household goods. Of these, the largest decrease was for clothing and footwear (4.8 per cent), larger than the 3.8 per cent fall during 2003. Education prices, which include university tuition fees and private school fees, increased by 4.7 per cent, more than any other component. However the weight for education is less than 2 per cent, so it has relatively little effect on the overall CPI.

The goods and services in the basket, and their corresponding weights, are changed slightly each year to reflect shifting consumer spending patterns. For instance, lard, bottled pale lager and vinyl records were in the basket in 1970 but have since been removed. In contrast, caffè latte, DVD players, Internet subscription, and digital cameras are some of the items in the basket in 2005, that have been introduced since 1970. Some items such as cigarettes, sliced white bread and granulated sugar have been included for a considerable period. This allows price comparisons to be made over time. In 2004 the price of cheddar cheese was £1.42 for 250 grams, over ten times the price in 1971 (Table 6.14). Prices for other

goods rose even more. The price of cigarettes in 2004 was more than 16 times the price in 1971 and has more than doubled since 1991. Similarly the price of beer had risen considerably since 1971, and the prices of beer, whisky and unleaded petrol had all nearly doubled since 1991. This partly reflects the large increases in duties imposed on them over these periods.

Prices vary across the United Kingdom, which may partly explain some of the differences in regional spending patterns (see Table 6.5). In 2004 London prices were nearly 10 per cent higher than the UK average, while prices in Wales were nearly 7 per cent below average (Table 6.15 overleaf). The price of housing and household expenditure showed the most variation. This is largely due to variation in housing costs which include rent, mortgage interest payments, and council tax. Housing costs on their own are highest in London (29 per cent above the UK average) and the South East (22 per cent above the UK average). They are lowest in Northern Ireland (32 per cent below the UK average), Wales and Scotland (both 23 per cent below the UK average). In Northern Ireland, the price of travel and leisure was 11 per cent above average, despite prices overall being over 4 per cent lower than the UK average, a result of higher motoring costs in Northern Ireland.

## Table **6.15**

### Relative prices: by region,[1] 2004

Indices (UK=100)

| | Food and catering | Alcohol and tobacco | Housing and household expenditure | Personal expenditure | Travel and leisure | All items |
|---|---|---|---|---|---|---|
| United Kingdom | 100.0 | 100.0 | 100.0 | 100.0 | 100.0 | 100.0 |
| England | | | | | | |
| North East | 97.1 | 97.3 | 88.4 | 97.8 | 97.8 | 94.2 |
| North West | 98.8 | 97.6 | 92.9 | 100.1 | 99.8 | 96.9 |
| Yorkshire and the Humber | 96.9 | 96.6 | 90.1 | 96.3 | 96.6 | 94.2 |
| East Midlands | 100.3 | 98.5 | 95.2 | 97.3 | 98.4 | 97.4 |
| West Midlands | 99.2 | 98.2 | 94.9 | 99.7 | 99.9 | 97.8 |
| East | 100.8 | 100.6 | 104.3 | 100.1 | 97.7 | 101.1 |
| London | 103.1 | 105.3 | 120.1 | 106.7 | 102.5 | 109.7 |
| South East | 101.7 | 103.0 | 114.0 | 100.7 | 98.4 | 105.3 |
| South West | 100.9 | 101.5 | 103.5 | 100.5 | 99.0 | 101.3 |
| Wales | 96.8 | 97.1 | 85.3 | 97.7 | 98.2 | 93.1 |
| Scotland | 101.0 | 99.4 | 85.5 | 100.1 | 99.0 | 94.5 |
| Northern Ireland | 102.0 | 98.4 | 80.1 | 97.0 | 111.3 | 95.8 |

1 Regional price indices are based mainly on a survey of regional price levels as well as some prices collected for the retail prices index and consumer prices index.

**Source: Office for National Statistics**

The CPI is used for inflation comparisons between the United Kingdom and other European Union (EU) countries. The United Kingdom still experiences a low inflation rate compared with the majority of EU countries. It was 0.7 percentage points below the EU-25 average in 2004 (Table 6.16). Only Finland, Denmark, Sweden and Lithuania had lower inflation rates. Within the EU, the accession states generally had the highest rates of inflation – Slovakia having the highest at 7.5 per cent.

The worldwide spending power of sterling depends on the relative prices of goods and services and the exchange rates between countries. Comparative price levels are used to indicate whether other countries appear cheaper or more expensive to UK residents. In April 2005, six of the EU-15 countries (Denmark, Ireland, Finland, Sweden, France and Germany) would have appeared more expensive. The Netherlands and Austria would have appeared similar in price, while Belgium, Italy, Greece, Spain, and Portugal would have appeared cheaper. Figures were also available for four of the new Member States (Hungary, Slovakia, the Czech Republic and Poland). A UK visitor to any of these countries would have found prices just over half those in the United Kingdom.

## Table **6.16**

### Percentage change in consumer prices:[1] EU comparison, 2004

| | Percentage change over 12 months | | Percentage change over 12 months |
|---|---|---|---|
| Austria | 2.0 | Luxembourg | 3.2 |
| Belgium | 1.9 | Malta | 2.7 |
| Cyprus | 1.9 | Netherlands | 1.4 |
| Czech Republic | 2.6 | Poland | 3.6 |
| Denmark | 0.9 | Portugal | 2.5 |
| Estonia | 3.0 | Slovakia | 7.5 |
| Finland | 0.1 | Slovenia | 3.6 |
| France | 2.3 | Spain | 3.1 |
| Germany | 1.8 | Sweden | 1.0 |
| Greece | 3.0 | United Kingdom | 1.3 |
| Hungary | 6.8 | EU-25 average | 2.0 |
| Ireland | 2.3 | | |
| Italy | 2.3 | | |
| Latvia | 6.2 | | |
| Lithuania | 1.1 | | |

1 As measured by the harmonised index of consumer prices. See Appendix, Part 6: Harmonised index of consumer prices.

**Source: Office for National Statistics; Eurostat**

# Health

- In 2004 life expectancy at birth in the United Kingdom was 77 years for males and 81 years for females. (Figure 7.1)

- The number of cases of mumps recorded in the United Kingdom in 2004 was almost 21,000 – four and a half times the number recorded in 2003. (Figure 7.6)

- In 2003, 40 per cent of women and 27 per cent of men in the highest fifth of the income distribution in England ate five or more portions of fruit and vegetables a day compared with 17 per cent of women and 14 per cent of men in the lowest fifth. (Figure 7.8)

- In 2004/05, 39 per cent of men and 22 per cent of women in Great Britain exceeded the recommended daily benchmarks for sensible drinking at least one day in the previous week. (Table 7.11)

- In 2004/05 smoking was most common among adults in routine and manual households (33 per cent of men and 30 per cent of women) and least prevalent among those in managerial and professional households (20 per cent of men and 17 per cent of women). (Page 107)

- In 2004/05 more than a third of men aged under 25 in Great Britain reported having more than one sexual partner in the previous year compared with a fifth of women aged 16 to 19 and a quarter aged 20 to 24. (Table 7.22)

Over the past century improved nutrition, advances in medical science and technology, and the development of health services that are freely available to all have led to notable improvements in health in the United Kingdom. Many of the most common causes of morbidity and premature mortality are linked to a range of behaviours such as diet, sedentary lifestyles, smoking and drinking. Healthier lifestyles may reduce avoidable ill health, and so in recent years government health strategies throughout the United Kingdom have placed an increasing emphasis on promoting these.

## Key health indicators

Life expectancy is a widely used indicator of the state of the nation's health. Large improvements in expectation of life at birth have taken place over the past century for both males and females. In 1901 males born in the United Kingdom could expect to live around 45 years and females to around 49 (Figure 7.1). By 2004 life expectancy at birth had risen to almost 77 years for males and to just over 81 years for females. Life expectancy at birth is projected to continue rising, to reach 80 years for males and 84 years for females by 2021.

Life expectancy has increased at all ages over the past century, not just at birth. However, for those aged 65 there have been different patterns for men and women. Men aged 65 in 2004 could expect to live a further 16.7 years, an increase of

### Figure **7.1**

### Expectation of life[1] at birth: by sex

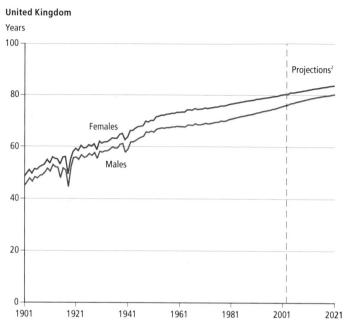

United Kingdom

Years

1 See Appendix, Part 7: Expectation of life. The average number of years a new-born baby would survive if he or she experienced age-specific mortality rates for that time period thoughout his or her life.
2 2004-based projections for 2005 to 2021.

**Source: Government Actuary's Department**

### Figure **7.2**

### Life expectancy at birth:[1] by deprivation group[2] and sex, 1994–99

England
Years

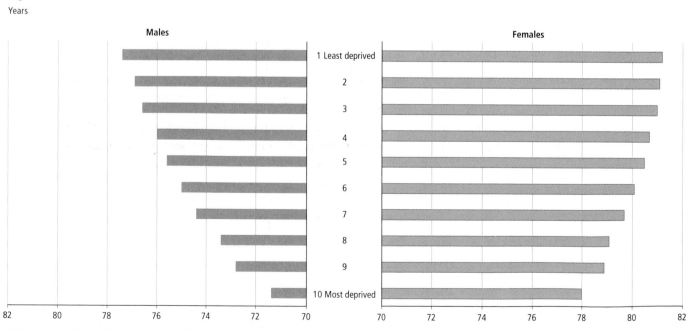

1 See Appendix, Part 7: Expectation of life.
2 See Appendix, Part 7: Area deprivation.

**Source: Health Survey for England, Department of Health; Census 1991, Office for National Statistics; Small Area Health Statistics Unit, Imperial College**

4.4 years since 1971. This compared with an increase of 1.7 years between 1901 and 1971. In contrast, there has been a more steady increase in life expectancy from the 1920s onwards for women aged 65. In 2004 they could expect to live for a further 19.6 years compared with 16.3 years in 1971, an increase of 3.3 years over this period.

The association between health inequalities and socio-economic status is well established. Differences in life expectancy are often used to make comparisons of the health status of people living in advantaged and disadvantaged neighbourhoods and to track changes over time.

Results from a study of over 8,500 electoral wards in England revealed that averaged over the period 1994 to 1999, males living in the most deprived wards had a life expectancy at birth of 71.4 years, six years less than those living in the least deprived wards (Figure 7.2). Among females life expectancy at birth was also lowest among those living in the most deprived wards, at 78.0 years. The deprivation gap was not as great among females, with females in the least deprived wards having an extra three years of life expectancy compared with those living in the most deprived wards. Females in each deprivation group could expect to live longer than their male counterparts. This gap between the sexes widens with increasing levels of deprivation, from nearly four years in the least deprived wards to almost seven years in the most deprived wards.

Recent shifts in public policy have led to increased interest in the whole-life health experience, including longevity and health-related quality of life (see Appendix, Part 7: Healthy life expectancy). Although females can expect to live longer, they are also more likely to spend more years in poor health than males. Estimates for the period 1994 to 1999 show that at birth males and females living in the most deprived wards in England could expect to spend 22.0 years and 26.3 years respectively in poor health, around twice the number of years compared with those in the least deprived wards. The gap between the sexes in the number of years spent in poor health generally widened with levels of deprivation, from only 1.5 years between males and females in the least deprived wards to 4.3 years between those in the most deprived wards.

Cardiovascular disease (CVD), a generic term covering diseases of the heart or blood vessels, is a major cause of morbidity and mortality. The major types of CVD are angina and heart attack, known as coronary heart diseases, and stroke. These diseases are at least partially preventable, being associated with risk factors such as smoking, sedentary lifestyles, and diets that contain high levels of cholesterol, saturated fat and salt, and low levels of fresh fruit and vegetables.

### Figure **7.3**

**Prevalence[1] of cardiovascular disease: by quintile group of household income[2] and sex, 2003**

England

Percentages

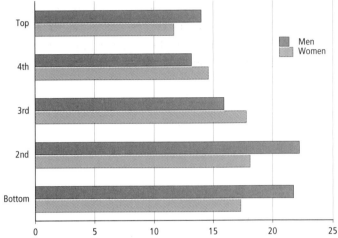

1 Data are for those aged 35 and over and are age-standardised. See Appendix, Part 7: Standardised rates.
2 Equivalised household income is a measure of household income that takes account of the number of persons in the household. Equivalised gross income has been used for ranking the households. See Appendix, Part 5: Equivalisation scales.

**Source: Health Survey for England, Department of Health**

The prevalence of CVD is related to income. In 2003, the prevalence of CVD for those aged 35 and over in England tended to increase as equivalised household income decreased, having taken account of the size of households (see Appendix, Part 5: Equivalisation scales). This trend was more apparent among men (Figure 7.3). Prevalence of CVD was between 13 and 14 per cent for men in the two highest income quintile groups, compared with 22 per cent in each of the two lowest quintile groups. Among women prevalence of CVD rose from 12 per cent in the highest income group to around 17 to 18 per cent in the three lowest income groups.

While circulatory diseases (which include CVD) have remained the most common cause of death in the United Kingdom over the past 30 years, they have also shown by far the greatest decline, particularly among males (Figure 7.4 overleaf). In 1971 age-standardised death rates were 6,900 per million males and 4,300 per million females. By 2004 these rates had fallen to 2,800 per million males and 1,800 per million females.

Cancers are the second most common cause of death among both sexes, but over the past 30 years have shown different trends for males and females. Death rates from cancer peaked in the mid 1980s for males at 2,900 per million, and by 2004 had fallen to 2,300 per million. Death rates from cancer for females did not reach a peak until the late 1980s since when

## Figure **7.4**

### Mortality:[1] by sex and leading cause groups

**United Kingdom**[2]

Rates per million population

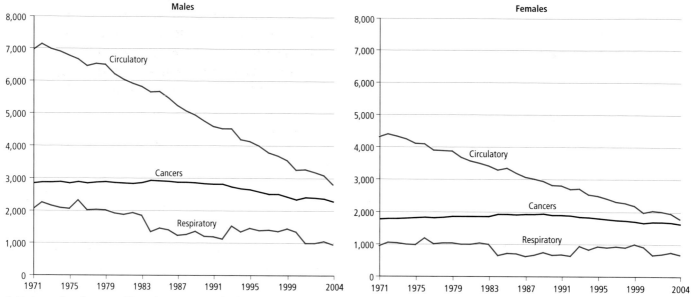

1 Data are for all ages and have been age-standardised using the European standard population. See Appendix, Part 7: Standardised rates, and International Classification of Diseases.
2 Data for 2000 are for England and Wales only.

**Source: Office for National Statistics**

they have fallen gradually from 1,900 per million in 1989 to 1,600 per million in 2004. These variations in mortality trends partly reflect differences in the types of cancer men and women are likely to experience, the risk factors associated with them and the relative survival rates of different cancers. Cancer is a more common cause of death for women aged under 65 than it is for men. This is mainly because of breast cancer, which is the most common cause of cancer death among women aged under 65, and also because the cancers that are most likely to be diagnosed among men (lung and prostate) usually cause death at a later age.

The reduction in the infant mortality rate has been one of the major factors contributing to an overall increase in life expectancy over the past century (see Figure 7.1). In 1921, 84.0 children per 1,000 live births in the United Kingdom died before the age of one; by 2004 the rate was 5.0 per 1,000 live births. Projections suggest this rate will continue falling to 4.5 per 1,000 live births in 2021.

The development of vaccines and immunisation programmes have played an important part in reducing infant mortality rates. Nearly all children in the United Kingdom are now immunised against tetanus, diphtheria, poliomyelitis, whooping cough, haemophilus influenzae b, meningitis C and measles, mumps and rubella. Current government immunisation targets

are for 95 per cent of children to be immunised against these diseases by the age of two.

The measles/mumps/rubella (MMR) vaccine was introduced in the United Kingdom in 1988 and coverage levels of 90 per cent and over were achieved by the early 1990s (Table 7.5). However, in recent years, concerns over the safety of the MMR vaccine have led to a fall in the proportion of children

## Table **7.5**

### Immunisation of children by their second birthday[1]

**United Kingdom**

Percentages

| | 1981[2] | 1991/92 | 1994/95 | 1999/2000 | 2004/05 |
|---|---|---|---|---|---|
| Tetanus | 83 | 94 | 93 | 95 | 94 |
| Diphtheria | 83 | 94 | 95 | 95 | 94 |
| Poliomyelitis | 82 | 94 | 95 | 94 | 94 |
| Whooping cough | 45 | 88 | 95 | 94 | 94 |
| Measles, mumps rubella[3] | 54 | 90 | 91 | 88 | 82 |

1 Children reaching and immunised by their second birthday.
2 Data exclude Scotland.
3 Includes measles-only vaccine for 1981. Combined vaccine was not available prior to 1988.

**Source: Department of Health; National Assembly for Wales; National Health Service in Scotland; Department of Health, Social Services and Public Safety, Northern Ireland**

## Figure **7.6**

### Notifications of measles, mumps and rubella

**United Kingdom**

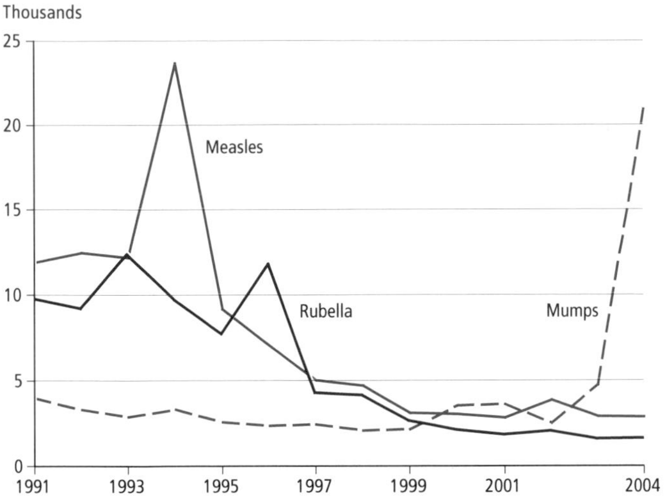

Thousands

[Line chart showing notifications of measles, mumps and rubella in thousands from 1991 to 2004. Y-axis ranges from 0 to 25. Measles peaks at about 23.5 in 1994, with Rubella and Mumps lines. Mumps rises sharply to about 21 by 2004.]

*Source: Health Protection Agency, Centre for Infections; National Health Service in Scotland; Communicable Disease Surveillance Centre (Northern Ireland)*

immunised against MMR. In 2004/05, 82 per cent of children had received the vaccine by their second birthday compared with 91 per cent in 1994/95. The regional variations in uptake were generally small, ranging from 81 to 88 per cent in most regions. However uptake in London was much lower, at only 71 per cent.

Over the past ten years there have been contrasting trends in the occurrence of the most commonly diagnosed childhood infections. A measles epidemic in 1994 in the United Kingdom had 23,500 notifications, twice the level of 1993. Since then, the underlying downward trend resumed (Figure 7.6).

In 2004 the number of cases of mumps notified in the United Kingdom was almost 21,000 – four and a half times the number recorded in 2003 and almost five times the combined 2004 total of measles and rubella notifications. Although mumps has historically been a disease most commonly experienced in early childhood, in 2004 over 80 per cent of cases were diagnosed among those aged 15 and over.

Rubella (also referred to as German measles), like measles, often occurs in epidemics in populations where vaccination has not been in use. The last epidemic occurred in 1996 when there were just under 12,000 notifications in the United Kingdom. Since 2000 the annual number of notifications has been between 1,500 and 2,100. The disease is rarely serious except in pregnant women, where it may lead to abnormalities in unborn babies.

## Obesity, diet and physical activity

Obesity is linked to heart disease, diabetes and premature death. The increase in the proportion of adults who are overweight, obese or morbidly obese (when a person's weight reaches life threatening levels) has been well documented. In recent years the same trends have become apparent among children. Between 1995 and 2003 levels of obesity among children aged two to ten in England increased from around 10 per cent to 14 per cent (see Appendix, Part 7: Body mass index). Overall, levels of obesity were similar for both boys and girls. For boys aged two to ten, obesity rose from 10 per cent in 1995 to 15 per cent in 2003, while for girls in this age group the proportion classified as obese increased from 10 per cent to 16 per cent in 2002, before falling to 13 per cent in 2003 (Figure 7.7). Increases in obesity prevalence were most marked for children aged eight to ten, rising from 11 per cent in 1995 to 20 per cent in 2002, before falling to 17 per cent in 2003.

Levels of childhood obesity differ between income groups (see Appendix, Part 5: Equivalisation scales). In 2001–02, children aged two to ten living in households in the lowest two quintile groups had higher rates of obesity (16 per cent) than children from households in the top two income quintile groups (13 per cent). There was also an association between children's obesity and that of their parents. Around 20 per cent of children living in households where both parents were either overweight or obese were themselves obese compared with 7 per cent of children living in households where neither parent was overweight or obese.

## Figure **7.7**

### Proportion of children[1] who are obese:[2] by sex

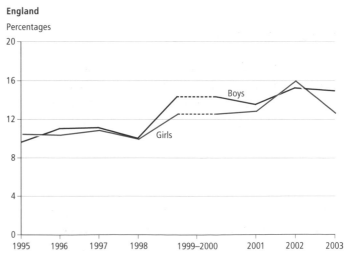

**England**

Percentages

[Line chart showing the proportion of children who are obese by sex from 1995 to 2003. Y-axis ranges from 0 to 20 per cent. Boys and Girls lines both start around 10-11 in 1995, rise, with Boys reaching about 15 and Girls peaking at about 16 in 2002 before falling to about 13 in 2003.]

1  *Children aged two to ten years.*
2  *Using the UK national Body mass index percentile classification. See Appendix, Part 7: Body mass index.*

*Source: Health Survey for England, Department of Health*

Diet has an important influence on weight and general health. A diet that is rich in complex carbohydrates (such as bread, cereals and potatoes), wholegrain cereals, fruit and vegetables, and low in total fat and salt can help to reduce the risk of obesity, diabetes, cardiovascular disease and some cancers. The Department of Health recommends that a healthy diet should include at least five portions a day of a variety of fruit and vegetables (excluding potatoes). In 2003, 22 per cent of men and 26 per cent of women in England consumed five or more portions a day, while 9 per cent of men and 6 per cent of women consumed no fruit and vegetables.

Household income may affect the affordability of a healthy diet. In 2003 consumption of the recommended five daily portions of fruit and vegetables in households in England decreased among both sexes as household income fell (Figure 7.8). Women consumed more fruit and vegetables than men at all income levels, though the gap decreased as income went down. Of women in the highest income quintile group, 40 per cent ate five or more portions a day compared with 17 per cent in the lowest income group. Among men, 27 per cent in the highest income group consumed at least five portions a day compared with 14 per cent in the lowest income group.

High salt intake has been linked to high blood pressure, which is a risk factor for cardiovascular disease. In the United Kingdom the Scientific Advisory Committee on Nutrition recommended in 2003 a reduction in salt intake among adults from 9 grams to 6 grams per day, with lower levels set for children. On this advice, the Government has set a target for adult salt intake to be reduced to 6 grams a day by 2010. Around three quarters of salt intake comes from processed foods. The other sources are salt used in cooking and salt added at the table. In 2003 over half of men and women in England used salt in cooking (Table 7.9). This practice was most common among men and women aged 75 and over, two thirds of whom added salt during cooking. A higher proportion of men (24 per cent) than women (15 per cent) added salt to food at the table without tasting it first, while a greater proportion of women (46 per cent) than men (38 per cent) reported that they never or rarely used salt at the table.

The use of salt in cooking increased as household income decreased, even when the age distribution of the population is adjusted for; 53 per cent of men in the highest income quintile group used salt to cook compared with 64 per cent of men in the lowest income group. For women the proportions were 52 per cent and 59 per cent respectively.

Evidence suggests that regular physical activity is related to reduced incidence of many chronic conditions, particularly cardiovascular disease, obesity, type 2 diabetes, some types of cancer and osteoporosis. The Chief Medical Officer recommends that adults should do moderately intense physical activity for at least 30 minutes a day on five or more days a week. This target can be accumulated in short periods of ten minutes to reach the daily target.

## Figure **7.8**

### Consumption of five or more portions of fruit and vegetables a day: by sex and income group,[1] 2003

England

Percentages

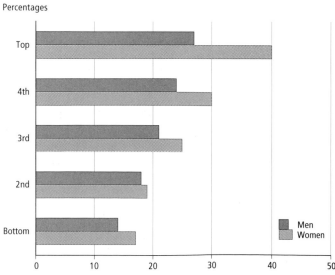

1  Equivalised household income is a measure of household income that takes account of the number of persons in the household. Equivalised gross income has been used for ranking the households. See Appendix, Part 5: Equivalisation scales. Data are age standardised. See Appendix, Part 7: Standardised rates.

**Source: Health Survey for England, Department of Health**

## Table **7.9**

### Use of salt in cooking and at the table:[1] by sex, 2003

England

Percentages

|  | Men | Women |
|---|---|---|
| **During cooking** | | |
| Adds salt | 56 | 53 |
| **After cooking** | | |
| Generally adds salt, without tasting | 24 | 15 |
| Tastes, generally adds salt | 14 | 13 |
| Tastes, occasionally adds salt | 24 | 26 |
| Rarely, or never, adds salt | 38 | 46 |
| Total (after cooking) | 100 | 100 |

1  Data are age-standardised. See Appendix, Part 7: Standardised rates.

**Source: Health Survey for England, Department of Health**

## Figure **7.10**

### Proportions achieving recommended levels of physical activity:[1] by sex and age, 2003

England
Percentages

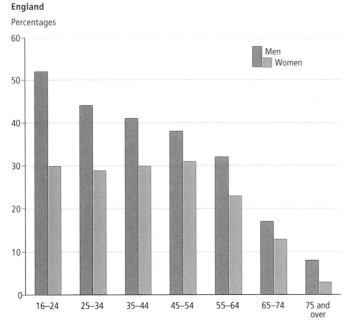

1  Participation in moderately intense activity for at least 30 minutes on five or more occasions a week.

**Source: Health Survey for England, Department of Health**

In 2003, 36 per cent of men aged 16 and over in England achieved the recommended levels of physical activity compared with 24 per cent of women. For men who had achieved this level in the four weeks before interview, the most common activities were sports and exercise (40 per cent), heavy housework (38 per cent) and walking (32 per cent). For women heavy housework was the most commonly reported activity (53 per cent) followed by sports and exercise (34 per cent) and walking (25 per cent).

The proportion of men achieving the recommended level of physical activity declined with age, from 52 per cent of men aged 16 to 24 to 8 per cent of those aged 75 and over (Figure 7.10). In contrast, the proportion of women achieving the recommended levels of physical activity remained stable at around 30 per cent of all those aged 16 to 54, and decreased thereafter to 3 per cent for women aged 75 and over. These differences largely reflect the greater participation in sports activities by men at younger ages.

Physical activity levels are related to a person's body mass index (BMI) (see Appendix, Part 7: Body mass index). The age-standardised proportion of men achieving the recommended weekly level of physical activity in 2003 was around 40 per cent for those who were underweight, normal weight and overweight. However this fell to 33 per cent for those who

were obese and 21 per cent for those who were morbidly obese. Around 30 per cent of women who were underweight and normal weight achieved the recommended weekly activity target compared with 19 per cent of those who were obese and 16 per cent who were morbidly obese.

## Alcohol, drugs and smoking

The consumption of alcohol in excessive amounts can lead to ill health, with an increased likelihood of problems such as high blood pressure, cancer and cirrhosis of the liver. The Department of Health advises that consumption of three to four units of alcohol a day for men and two to three units a day for women should not lead to significant health risks. Consistently drinking more than these levels is not advised because of the associated health risks.

In 2004/05, two fifths of men and a fifth of women in Great Britain exceeded the recommended amount of alcohol on at least one day during the week before interview (Table 7.11). Men in all age groups were more likely than women to have exceeded these levels, but the difference between the sexes was smallest in the 16 to 24 age group. Young people were also more likely than older people to have exceeded the recommended daily units, though the relationship between age and excess consumption was stronger for women than for men. The proportion of women aged 16 to 24 who had

## Table **7.11**

### Adults exceeding specified levels of alcohol:[1] by sex and age, 2004/05

Great Britain
Percentages

| | 16–24 | 25–44 | 45–64 | 65 and over | All aged 16 and over |
|---|---|---|---|---|---|
| **Men** | | | | | |
| More than 4 units and up to 8 units | 15 | 17 | 19 | 13 | 16 |
| More than 8 units | 32 | 31 | 18 | 7 | 22 |
| More than 4 units | 47 | 48 | 37 | 20 | 39 |
| **Women** | | | | | |
| More than 3 units and up to 6 units | 15 | 16 | 15 | 4 | 13 |
| More than 6 units | 24 | 13 | 6 | 1 | 9 |
| More than 3 units | 39 | 28 | 20 | 5 | 22 |

1  On at least one day in the previous week. Current Department of Health advice is that consumption of between three and four units a day for men and two to three units for women should not lead to significant health risks.

**Source: General Household Survey, Office for National Statistics**

exceeded recommended levels of alcohol on at least one day during the previous week was twice that of those aged 45 to 64 and eight times that of those aged 65 and over. The proportion for men remained relatively similar up to age 44, after which it fell sharply.

Drinking moderate amounts regularly is considered to be better for a person's health than drinking to excess occasionally. 'Binge' drinking is defined as consuming twice the recommended daily limits. Men aged 16 to 24 are the most likely to binge drink, 32 per cent having done so in the previous week in 2004/05, although this proportion was 5 percentage points lower than in 2003/04. Since 1998/99 the gap between the proportion of men and women in this age group who binge drink has narrowed from 15 percentage points to 8 percentage points.

The proportion of women consuming more than the recommended daily units of alcohol is considerably higher among those in managerial and professional occupational groups than those in routine and manual groups. In 2004/05, 28 per cent of women in the large employer and higher managerial group had exceeded the daily limit in the previous week compared with 19 per cent of women in the routine group. Higher proportions of men exceeded the recommended levels in each group, although the relationship with socio-economic classification was not so apparent (see Appendix, Part 1: National Statistics Socio-economic Classification).

There is growing concern about the amount of alcohol consumed by children. Although the prevalence of drinking has remained at similar levels since 1990, between 1990 and 2000 the amount consumed per week almost doubled and has remained at around this level. In 2004 the mean weekly consumption of boys and girls aged 11 to 15 in England who had drunk alcohol in the previous week was around ten units, compared with around five units in 1990. Between 1990 and 2004 there was an increase in the proportion of boys who had never had a drink, rising from 35 per cent to 41 per cent. The proportion of girls who had never had a drink in 2004 was also 41 per cent, a similar level to 1990.

The number of alcohol-related deaths in England and Wales, which rose throughout the 1980s and 1990s, has continued to rise in more recent years, from 5,970 in 2001 to 6,580 in 2003. The death rate for alcohol-related deaths also increased, from 10.7 per 100,000 population in 2001 to 11.6 per 100,000 in 2003.

Alcohol-related deaths are more common for males than females. In 2003 males accounted for almost two thirds of the total number of alcohol-related deaths. Between 1980 and

## Figure **7.12**

### Death rates[1] from alcohol-related causes:[2] by sex

**England & Wales**

Rates per 100,000 population

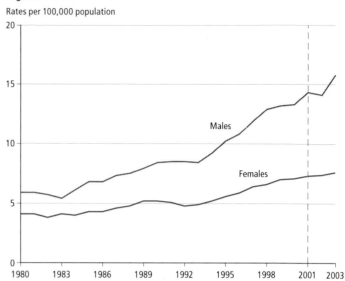

1 Age-standardised to the European standard population. See Appendix, Part 7: Standardised rates. Rates from 2001 are not directly comparable with those for earlier years because of the change from ICD-9 to ICD-10. See Appendix, Part 7: International Classification of Diseases.
2 See Appendix, Part 7: Alcohol-related causes of death.

**Source: Office for National Statistics**

2003 the death rate among males rose by over two and a half times to reach 15.8 per 100,000 (Figure 7.12). During the same period the death rate for females almost doubled to reach 7.6 per 100,000.

During the period 2001–03 there were considerable regional variations in alcohol-related deaths in England and Wales. The highest rates were found in the North West and North East while the lowest were in the East of England, South West and South East. The rate for the North West was almost double that for the East of England (15.1 and 7.7 deaths per 100,000 respectively). The West Midlands, London and Wales also had rates that were above the average for England and Wales.

The misuse of drugs is both a serious social and health problem. Results from the 2004/05 British Crime Survey indicate that 16 per cent of men and 9 per cent of women aged 16 to 59 in England and Wales had taken an illicit drug in the previous year. Young people were more likely than older people to misuse drugs; 33 per cent of men and 21 per cent of women aged 16 to 24 had done so in the previous year (Table 7.13). Cannabis remained the most commonly used drug among young people, used by 30 per cent of men and 18 per cent of women in the previous year. Ecstasy and cocaine were the most commonly used Class A drugs for this age group, each taken by 7 per cent of men and 3 per cent of women. Between 1996 and 2004/05

## Table **7.13**

**Prevalence of drug misuse by young adults[1] in the previous year: by drug category and sex, 1996 and 2004/05**

England & Wales                                              Percentages

|  | Men | | Women | |
| --- | --- | --- | --- | --- |
|  | 1996 | 2004/05 | 1996 | 2004/05 |
| Cannabis | 30 | 30 | 22 | 18 |
| Ecstasy | 9 | 7 | 4 | 3 |
| Cocaine | 2 | 7 | - | 3 |
| Amphetamines | 15 | 4 | 9 | 3 |
| Magic mushrooms or LSD | 9 | 5 | 2 | 2 |
| All Class A drugs[2] | 13 | 11 | 6 | 5 |
| Any drug[3] | 34 | 33 | 25 | 21 |

1 Those aged 16 to 24 years.
2 Includes heroin, cocaine (both cocaine powder and 'crack'), ecstasy, magic mushrooms, LSD and unprescribed use of methadone.
3 Includes less commonly used drugs not listed in the table.

**Source: British Crime Survey, Home Office**

## Figure **7.14**

**Prevalence of adult[1] cigarette smoking:[2] by sex**

Great Britain

Percentages

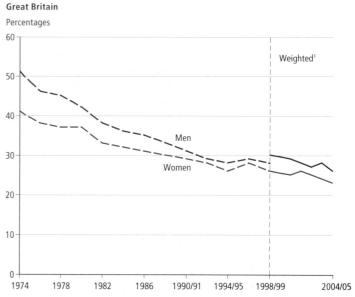

1 People aged 16 and over.
2 From 1988 data are for financial years. Between 1974 and 2000/01 the surveys were run every two years.
3 From 1998/99 data are weighted to compensate for nonresponse and to match known population distributions. Weighted and unweighted data for 1998/99 are shown for comparison.

**Source: General Household Survey, Office for National Statistics**

there was a decline in the proportions of young people using amphetamines. However, cocaine use during this period increased among both sexes (see also Table 9.8).

Drug misuse also occurs among those under the age of 16. In a survey of schoolchildren in England in 2004, almost a fifth of boys and girls aged 11 to 15 reported that they had taken illicit drugs in the last year. The proportion of those taking drugs increased with age, from 1 in 20 of all 11 year olds to 1 in 3 of all 15 year olds. Cannabis was the most common drug, used by 11 per cent of pupils aged 11 to 15 in the previous year. Six per cent reported using volatile substances such as gas, glue, aerosols or solvents in the last year.

Over the past 30 years there has been a substantial decline in the proportion of adults aged 16 and over in Great Britain who smoke cigarettes. The reduction has been greater among men, though from a higher initial level, so that the difference in prevalence between men and women has narrowed considerably. In 1974, 51 per cent of men aged 16 and over smoked compared with 41 per cent of women. By 2004/05, 26 per cent of men and 23 per cent of women were smokers (Figure 7.14). Much of the decline occurred in the 1970s and early 1980s, after which the rate of decline slowed.

The trends show different patterns for smoking. Among men the greatest fall in smoking prevalence has been in the oldest age group. Between 1974 and 2004/05 the proportion of men aged 60 and over who smoked fell by 29 percentage points from 44 per cent to 15 per cent. In contrast, for women the greatest

decline in smoking over this period was among those aged 50 to 59. In 1974, 48 per cent of this age group smoked; by 2004/05 the proportion had fallen to 22 per cent. In 2004/05 a similar proportion of men and women smoked in the youngest (16 to 19) and oldest (60 and over) age groups. In all other age groups smoking prevalence was higher among men.

Smoking is strongly associated with socio-economic classification, being far more common among those in routine and manual occupational groups than those in managerial and professional groups. In 2004/05, 33 per cent of men and 30 per cent of women living in routine or manual households were smokers compared with 20 per cent of men and 17 per cent of women in managerial and professional households (Table 7.15 overleaf). The Government has set a target for England to reduce the proportion of smokers in households headed by someone in a manual occupation from 32 per cent in 1998 to 26 per cent by 2010.

Quitting smoking can lead to better health and extended life expectancy. In 2004, 73 per cent of smokers in Great Britain said they wanted to give up. Older smokers were the least likely to want to stop smoking (43 per cent of smokers aged 65 and over compared with 80 per cent of smokers aged 25 to 44). As smoking prevalence is lower among older age groups, this suggests that smokers in these age groups who may have

## Table **7.15**

### Prevalence of cigarette smoking: by sex and socio-economic classification[1]

Great Britain                                                      Percentages

| | Men | | Women | |
|---|---|---|---|---|
| | 2001/02 | 2004/05 | 2001/02 | 2004/05 |
| **Managerial and professional** | | | | |
| Large employers and higher managerial occupations | 16 | 19 | 15 | 13 |
| Higher professional occupations | 17 | 16 | 13 | 11 |
| Lower managerial and professional occupations | 24 | 22 | 20 | 20 |
| **Intermediate** | | | | |
| Intermediate occupations | 28 | 26 | 26 | 22 |
| Small employers/ own account workers | 30 | 25 | 26 | 20 |
| **Routine and manual** | | | | |
| Lower supervisory and technical occupations | 33 | 30 | 29 | 26 |
| Semi-routine occupations | 33 | 34 | 32 | 30 |
| Routine occupations | 38 | 33 | 33 | 33 |
| **All people[2]** | 28 | 26 | 26 | 23 |

1 Of the household reference person. See Appendix, Part 1: National Statistics Socio-economic Classification.
2 Where the household reference person was a full-time student, had an inadequately described occupation, had never worked or was long-term unemployed these are not shown as separate categories, but are included in the figure for all people aged 16 and over.

**Source: General Household Survey, Office for National Statistics**

## Table **7.16**

### Main reasons for wanting to stop smoking:[1] by sex and presence of children in the household, 2004

Great Britain                                                      Percentages[2]

| | Children under 16 in household | No children in household | All |
|---|---|---|---|
| **Men** | | | |
| Better for health in general | 76 | 70 | 72 |
| Less risk of getting smoking-related illness | 32 | 25 | 27 |
| Present health problems | 10 | 16 | 14 |
| Financial reasons | 14 | 24 | 21 |
| Family pressure | 21 | 14 | 16 |
| Harms children | 39 | 5 | 15 |
| Doctor's advice | 1 | 6 | 5 |
| Pregnancy of partner | 1 | 1 | 1 |
| Other | 1 | - | 1 |
| **Women** | | | |
| Better for health in general | 60 | 69 | 66 |
| Less risk of getting smoking-related illness | 29 | 27 | 28 |
| Present health problems | 16 | 17 | 17 |
| Financial reasons | 28 | 33 | 31 |
| Family pressure | 21 | 20 | 20 |
| Harms children | 37 | 4 | 16 |
| Doctor's advice | 7 | 6 | 6 |
| Pregnancy | 1 | 1 | 1 |
| Other | 2 | 3 | 3 |

1 Smokers who want to stop smoking.
2 Percentages do not add up to 100 per cent as respondents could give more than one answer.

**Source: Omnibus Survey, Office for National Statistics**

wanted to give up smoking are likely to have already done so by the age of 65, or to have died.

Although smokers may have many different reasons for wishing to stop, the main reasons given for both sexes were health related. In 2004, 91 per cent of men and 85 per cent of women who wanted to quit mentioned at least one health reason for doing so. Smokers with children under 16 years of age in the household were more likely to want to quit than those without children (78 per cent and 71 per cent respectively). For those with children in the household, the belief that second-hand smoking could have a damaging effect on children's health was a major motivation to stop, given by almost 40 per cent of both men and women (Table 7.16).

Trends in lung cancer incidence and mortality are strongly linked to those of cigarette smoking, which is by far the greatest single risk factor for the disease, being the cause of 90 per cent of cases

among men and 80 per cent of cases among women in 2004. The incidence of lung cancer has fallen sharply in males since the early 1980s, mainly as a result of the decline in cigarette smoking (see Figure 7.14). In 1981 the age-standardised incidence rate in Great Britain was 112 per 100,000 male population. By 2002 the rate had fallen by 43 per cent to 64 per 100,000 (Figure 7.17). Lung cancer incidence rates among females were lower, largely as a consequence of lower levels of smoking in earlier years. Although similar proportions of men and women smoke, this has not always been the case. Larger proportions of men than women smoked during the 1970s and 1980s, becoming more equal in the 1990s (see Figure 7.14). This has resulted in a lower incidence of lung cancer among females and has also contributed to a different trend. The age-standardised incidence rate of lung cancer in females rose gradually to reach a plateau of around 35 per 100,000 population from 1993.

## Figure **7.17**

### Standardised incidence rates[1] of lung cancer: by sex

**Great Britain**
Rates per 100,000 population

Males

Females

1981   1984   1987   1990   1993   1996   1999   2002

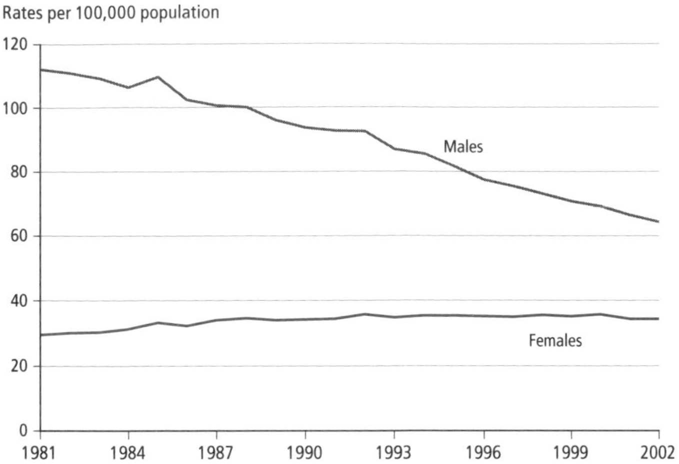

1  Age standardised using the European standard population. See
   Appendix, Part 7: Standardised rates.

**Source: Office for National Statistics; Welsh Cancer Intelligence Centre
and Surveillance Unit; Scottish Cancer Registry**

Research has shown that there are distinct regional variations
in the incidence of lung cancer across the United Kingdom.
Between 1991 and 1999 the highest incidence rates were in
Scotland, where the rates were 108 per 100,000 males and
52 per 100,000 females. Compared with the overall UK and
Ireland average these rates were 34 per cent higher for males
and 48 per cent higher for females (Map 7.18). Within England
there were further regional variations, with incidence rates for
lung cancer being higher than average in the North West, and
Northern and Yorkshire regions, and below average in the
South West, South East and Eastern regions. Many of the areas
with the highest levels of deprivation corresponded to areas
with high incidence of, and mortality from, lung cancer:
Greater Glasgow; Gateshead and South Tyneside; Liverpool;
Manchester; and East London and the City of London.

Lung cancer has one of the lowest survival rates of any cancer,
with little variation by region or deprivation area. This is
because of the frequently advanced stage of the disease at
diagnosis, the aggressiveness of the disease, and the small
number of patients for whom surgery is appropriate.

## Map **7.18**

### Incidence of lung cancer:[1] by sex, 1991–1999[2]

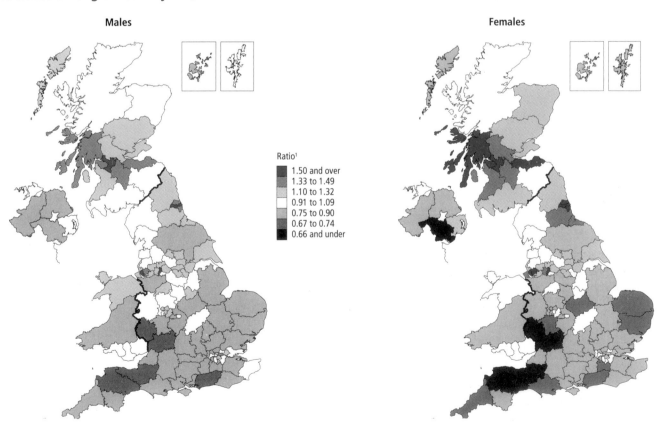

**Males**

**Females**

Ratio[1]
- 1.50 and over
- 1.33 to 1.49
- 1.10 to 1.32
- 0.91 to 1.09
- 0.75 to 0.90
- 0.67 to 0.74
- 0.66 and under

1  Ratio of directly age-standardised rate in health authority to UK and Ireland average. Data originally published in the Cancer Atlas of the
   United Kingdom and Ireland 1991–2000.
2  Health authorities in England and Wales, health boards in Scotland and health and social services boards in Northern Ireland. All boundaries are as at 2001.

**Source: National Cancer Intelligence Centre; Welsh Cancer Intelligence and Surveillance Unit; Scottish Cancer Registry; Northern Ireland Cancer
Registry; National Cancer Registry of Ireland**

## Mental health

Mental health problems may result in poorer social functioning and physical health, and higher rates of mortality. In 2000 about one in six people aged 16 to 74 living in private households in Great Britain had a neurotic disorder in the seven days prior to interview, such as depression, anxiety or a phobia.

In recent years there has been a growing awareness of the mental health problems experienced by children and young people. In 2004, 10 per cent of 5 to 16 year olds living in private households in Great Britain had a clinically recognised mental disorder. Overall, boys were more likely to have a mental disorder than girls. While boys were more likely than girls to have a conduct or hyperkinetic disorder, they were slightly less likely than girls to have an emotional disorder (Table 7.19). The prevalence of mental disorder was higher among older children of both sexes. Among five to ten year olds, 10 per cent of boys and 5 per cent of girls had a mental disorder. The proportions were larger for 11 to 16 year olds, at 13 and 10 per cent respectively.

There are socio-demographic variations in the prevalence of mental disorders in children. Children who lived in a lone-parent family in Great Britain were twice as likely to experience a mental disorder as those living with married parents in 2004. Prevalence was highest for boys who lived with a lone parent who was widowed, divorced or separated (20 per cent) (Figure 7.20). Among children who lived with married parents the proportions were lower, 8 per cent for boys and 6 per cent for girls. There was also a higher prevalence of mental disorder in children who lived in reconstituted families (14 per cent) compared with those containing no stepchildren (9 per cent).

The type of area in which children lived was also related to the likelihood of experiencing a childhood mental disorder. A higher proportion of those living in areas classed as 'hard pressed' had a mental disorder (15 per cent) compared with those living in areas classed as 'wealthy achievers' or 'urban prosperity' (6 per cent and 7 per cent respectively).

Children with mental disorders are more likely than other children to have time off school. In 2004, 17 per cent of those with an emotional disorder, 14 per cent with conduct disorders and 11 per cent with hyperkinetic disorders had been absent from school for over 15 days in the previous term. This compared with 4 per cent for other children. Around a third of children with a conduct disorder had been excluded from school and nearly a quarter had been excluded more than once (see also Table 3.7).

Mental illness is a risk factor for suicide. Trends in suicide rates have varied by age group and sex in the United Kingdom over

### Table **7.19**

**Prevalence of mental disorders[1] among children:[2] by type of disorder, sex and age, 2004**

Great Britain

Percentages

|  | Boys | | Girls | |
|---|---|---|---|---|
|  | 5–10 | 11–16 | 5–10 | 11–16 |
| Emotional disorder[3] | 2.2 | 4.0 | 2.5 | 6.1 |
| Conduct disorder | 6.9 | 8.1 | 2.8 | 5.1 |
| Hyperkinetic disorder[4] | 2.7 | 2.4 | 0.4 | 0.4 |
| Less common disorder[5] | 2.2 | 1.6 | 0.4 | 1.1 |
| Any disorder[6] | 10.2 | 12.6 | 5.1 | 10.3 |

1  See Appendix, Part 7: Mental disorders.
2  Aged 5 to 16 years and living in private households.
3  Includes separation anxiety, specific phobia, social phobia, panic disorder, agoraphobia, post traumatic stress disorder, obsessive-compulsive disorder and depression.
4  Characterised by behaviour that is hyperactive, impulsive or inattentive.
5  Includes autism, tics, eating disorders and selective mutism.
6  Individual disorder categories may sum to more than the total as more than one disorder may be reported.

**Source: Mental Health of Children and Young People Survey, Office for National Statistics**

### Figure **7.20**

**Prevalence of mental disorders[1] among children:[2] by sex and family type, 2004**

Great Britain

Percentages

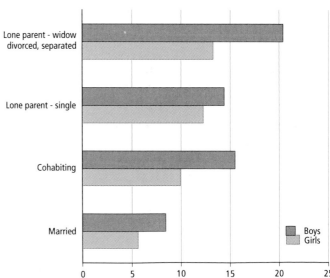

1  See Appendix, Part 7: Mental disorders.
2  Aged 5 to 16 years and living in private households.

**Source: Mental Health of Children and Young People Survey, Office for National Statistics**

## Figure **7.21**

### Suicide rates:[1] by sex and age

**United Kingdom**

Rates per 100,000 population

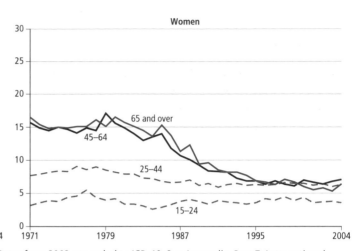

1  Includes deaths with a verdict of undetermined intent (open verdicts). Rates from 2002 are coded to ICD-10. See Appendix, Part 7: International Classification of Diseases. Rates are age standardised to the European standard population. See Appendix, Part 7: Standardised rates.

**Source: Office for National Statistics; General Register Office for Scotland; Northern Ireland Statistics and Research Agency**

the last 30 years (Figure 7.21). Until the end of the 1980s older men aged 65 and over had the highest suicide rates. In 1986 the suicide rate among men aged 65 and over peaked at 26 per 100,000 population and then fell to 15 per 100,000 in 2004. In contrast suicide rates for younger men rose, in particular for those aged 25 to 44, for whom the suicide rate almost doubled from 14 per 100,000 in 1971 to a peak of 27 per 100,000 in 1998. The suicide rate among men in this age group has since declined, but in 2004 remained the highest, at 23 per 100,000.

There is a distinct difference in suicide rates between men and women. In 2004 the age-standardised rate for all men aged 15 and over was 18 per 100,000, three times that of women at 6 per 100,000. This gap has widened considerably since 1973, when the suicide rate among all men aged 15 and over was around one and a half times that of all women. Among women aged 45 and over, suicide rates have fallen since the early 1980s. However for younger women the rates have remained fairly stable since the mid-1980s.

The likelihood of a person committing suicide depends in part on the ease of access to, and knowledge of, effective means of doing so. In 2003 the main methods of suicide for men in England and Wales were: hanging and suffocation (47 per cent); drug-related poisoning (18 per cent); and 'other poisoning' (8 per cent), which mainly comprised poisoning by motor vehicle exhaust gas. Among women the most common methods of suicide were: drug-related poisoning (44 per cent); hanging and suffocation (26 per cent); and drowning (7 per cent).

## Sexual health

Since the late 1990s the increase in the prevalence of sexually transmitted diseases, especially among young people, has become a major public health concern across the United Kingdom. Those who have unprotected sex and multiple sexual partners are at the greatest risk of contracting a sexually transmitted infection. During 2004/05 men were more likely than women in Great Britain to have had more than one sexual partner in the previous year for all age groups aged under 50 (Table 7.22).

## Table **7.22**

### Number of sexual partners[1] in the previous year: by sex and age, 2004/05

**Great Britain**                                                         Percentages

|  | 16–19 | 20–24 | 25–34 | 35–44 | 45–49 |
|---|---|---|---|---|---|
| **Men** | | | | | |
| No partners | 34 | 13 | 7 | 6 | 7 |
| 1 partner | 28 | 53 | 71 | 85 | 88 |
| 2 or 3 partners | 29 | 24 | 14 | 6 | 4 |
| 4 or more partners | 9 | 10 | 8 | 3 | 2 |
| All aged 16–49 | 100 | 100 | 100 | 100 | 100 |
| **Women** | | | | | |
| No partners | 28 | 9 | 7 | 9 | 13 |
| 1 partner | 50 | 62 | 85 | 87 | 84 |
| 2 or 3 partners | 16 | 22 | 6 | 4 | 2 |
| 4 or more partners | 6 | 7 | 2 | – | – |
| All aged 16–49 | 100 | 100 | 100 | 100 | 100 |

1  Self-reported in the 12 months prior to interview.

**Source: Omnibus Survey, Office for National Statistics**

## Figure **7.23**

### Sexually transmitted HIV infections:[1] by sex and year of diagnosis

United Kingdom

Thousands

1  Numbers of diagnoses recorded, particularly for recent years, will rise as further reports are received. Those where the probable route of infection was not known, particularly for recent years, will fall as follow-up continues.

**Source: Health Protection Agency**

For both sexes, multiple sexual partnerships were most common among those below the age of 25. Over a third of men aged under 25, a fifth of women aged 16 to 19 and a quarter of women aged 20 to 24 reported having more than one sexual partner in the previous year. Men and women aged 25 to 49 were most likely to have only one sexual partner and also least likely to have none.

An estimated 58,300 adults aged 15 to 59 were living with HIV in the United Kingdom at the end of 2004. In the early stages of the disease in 1991, infections were predominantly diagnosed among men who had sex with men (Figure 7.23). However, since 1999 there have been increasing numbers of diagnoses of HIV infections acquired through heterosexual contact. By 2004, 42 per cent of the 6,500 sexually transmitted infections were among women.

In 2004 over 2,700 women diagnosed with HIV in the United Kingdom had been infected through heterosexual contact, eight times the number who had been infected in this way in 1991. Over half as many men (1,600) were infected through heterosexual sex in 2004, five times the number in 1991. In 2004 nearly 80 per cent of infections in heterosexual men and women were acquired in high prevalence areas of the world, particularly Africa.

## Figure **7.24**

### Diagnoses[1] of genital herpes simplex virus (type 2): by sex

England & Wales

Thousands

1  First and recurrent episodes.

**Source: Health Protection Agency**

The trends in HIV diagnoses among men who have sex with men have been different to those for heterosexual men and women. Between 1991 and 1999 the number in the United Kingdom remained relatively stable. However, since 2000 the annual number of diagnoses has been rising, reaching almost 2,200 in 2004. This increase probably reflects increasing HIV testing among men who have sex with men, as well as continuing, and possibly increasing, HIV transmission.

HIV can also be acquired through injecting drug use. The number of this type of diagnoses has remained relatively low in recent years, with 128 diagnoses in 2004. A small number of infections were acquired through blood transfusions, although almost all of these individuals received transfusions in countries outside the United Kingdom, where exclusion or screening procedures for donors are less rigorous.

Genital herpes simplex virus (HSV) infection is the most common sexually transmitted disease of an ulcerative form in the United Kingdom. The infection may be painful, disabling and recurrent and is associated with considerable physical and psychological ill-health. The genital HSV infection may also facilitate HIV transmission. Type 1 HSV causes oral herpes (or cold sores) but has increasingly been implicated in genital infections. Type 2 HSV is almost exclusively associated with genital infection. During the 1970s and 1980s the rate of increase in the number of diagnoses of HSV (type 2) in England and Wales was similar for men and women (Figure 7.24). However, since the early 1990s the increase in the number of diagnoses has been much greater for women than for men. In 2004 there were almost 18,700 diagnoses among women, 76 per cent more than in 1990. Among men the number of cases diagnosed increased by 25 per cent over the same period to reach just over 12,700 in 2004. Genital herpes is most commonly diagnosed in men and women aged 25 to 34. In 2004, 38 per cent of first attack cases among men and 30 per cent among women in England and Wales were diagnosed in this age group.

In recent years the incidence of other sexually transmitted infections has been increasing. In 2004 genital chlamydia was the most common sexually transmitted infection diagnosed in genito-urinary medicine clinics in England and Wales. Almost 96,000 cases were diagnosed, 8 per cent more than in 2003 and over 200 per cent more than in 1995. Between 1995 and 2003 the increase was greatest among those aged under 25. Uncomplicated gonorrhoea was the second most common infection with over 21,000 cases diagnosed in 2004, 11 per cent lower than the number recorded in 2003.

For people who have multiple sexual partnerships, condom use can help reduce the risk of contracting sexually transmitted diseases. In 2004/05, 80 per cent of men aged 16 to 69 and 75 per cent of women aged 16 to 49 who had more than one sexual partner in the previous year used a condom in Great Britain. This compared with 33 per cent of men and 44 per cent of women who had one partner.

People's reasons for using a condom vary by age and whether or not they have multiple partners. In 2004/05, 71 per cent of men

### Table **7.25**

**Reasons for using a condom: by sex and age, 2004/05**

| Great Britain | | | | | Percentages |
|---|---|---|---|---|---|
| | 16–19 | 20–24 | 25–34 | 35–44 | 45–49 |
| **Men** | | | | | |
| Prevent pregnancy | 25 | 39 | 44 | 70 | 73 |
| Prevent infection | 8 | 4 | 9 | 5 | 6 |
| Both reasons | 63 | 57 | 44 | 23 | 19 |
| Other reason | 4 | - | 3 | 2 | 1 |
| All aged 16–49 | 100 | 100 | 100 | 100 | 100 |
| **Women** | | | | | |
| Prevent pregnancy | 29 | 31 | 59 | 65 | 60 |
| Prevent infection | 2 | 6 | 7 | 6 | 12 |
| Both reasons | 68 | 62 | 33 | 25 | 22 |
| Other reason | - | - | 1 | 4 | 5 |
| All aged 16–49 | 100 | 100 | 100 | 100 | 100 |

*Source: Omnibus Survey, Office for National Statistics*

and 70 per cent of women aged 16 to 19 reported using a condom either solely as a means of preventing infection or both to prevent infection and for contraceptive purposes (Table 7.25). Most people aged 25 and over used condoms only as a form of contraceptive, which reflects the likelihood that older people are in a monogamous relationship (see Table 7.22).

# Social protection

- In real terms, social security benefit expenditure in the United Kingdom has risen from £57 billion in 1977/78 to £125 billion in 2004/05. (Figure 8.1)

- In 2003/04, 55 per cent of single female pensioners in Great Britain had an occupational or personal pension in addition to the state pension, compared with 70 per cent of single male pensioners and 82 per cent of couples. (Table 8.8)

- Single pensioners are more likely than couples to receive any type of income-related benefits – in 2003/04, 33 per cent of single male and 43 per cent of single female pensioners in the UK received income-related benefits compared with 17 per cent of pensioner couples. (Table 8.10)

- In 2004/05, 68 per cent of females and 65 per cent of males in Great Britain who had consulted their GP in the previous two weeks had obtained a prescription. (Page 123)

- In 2004/05 the average number of visits per month to the NHS Direct Online website was 774,000, compared with 169,000 visits in 2001/02. (Page 124)

- In 2003 the majority of families where the mother was working were using some form of childcare. Around two thirds of children up to the age of ten received informal childcare in Great Britain. (Table 8.19)

# Chapter 8

# Figure **8.5**

## Charitable expenditure on social protection by the top 500 charities:[1] by function, 2003/04

United Kingdom

£ million

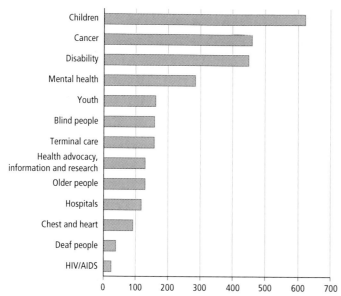

1 Charities Aid Foundation top 500 fundraising charities. Excludes administrative expenditure.

**Source: Charities Aid Foundation**

# Figure **8.6**

## Number of contact hours of home help and home care:[1] by sector

England

Millions

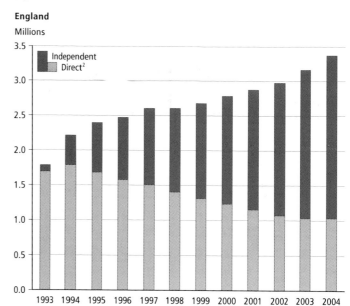

1 During a survey week in September. Contact hours provided or purchased by local authorities. Households receiving home care purchased with a direct payment are excluded.
2 Directly provided by local authorities.

**Source: Department of Health**

37,000 general medical practitioners and 23,000 general dental practitioners. In total these figures showed a 4 per cent increase between 2003 and 2004.

## Carers and caring

Local authority home care services assist people, principally those with physical disabilities (including frailty associated with ageing), dementia, mental health problems and learning difficulties to continue living in their own home, and to function as independently as possible. The number of home help hours purchased or provided by councils in England has increased over the past decade (Figure 8.6). In September 2004, local authorities provided or purchased 3.4 million hours of home care services during the survey week, compared with 2.2 million hours in September 1994. There has also been a change in the type of provider. In 1994 the majority of home help contact hours were directly provided by local authorities (81 per cent); this had fallen to 31 per cent in 2004. Instead, the number of hours of care that have been purchased by local authorities from the independent sector (both private and voluntary) has increased year on year, from 0.43 million in 1994 to 2.34 million in 2004 and has become the main type of provision.

The proportion of households receiving more than five hours of home help or home care contact and six or more visits per

week has increased steadily, from 16 per cent in 1994 to 46 per cent in 2004. This reflects an increased focus by councils with social services responsibilities on increasing the number and intensity of home care visits. For those receiving low intensity care (two hours or less of home help or home care and one visit per week), the proportion has fallen from 34 per cent in 1994 to 13 per cent in 2004.

Unpaid carers are people who provide unpaid help, looking after or supporting family members, friends or neighbours who have physical or mental ill-health, disability, or problems related to old age. In 2000/01 the General Household Survey found that three quarters of people who provide 20 or more hours of care per week in Great Britain were caring for someone living in the same household. The 2001 Census identified 1.9 million unpaid carers in the United Kingdom who were providing at least 20 hours of care a week. Overall, women were slightly more likely than men to provide this level of care (4 per cent compared with 3 per cent). The likelihood of women providing 20 or more hours of care increased with each ten-year age band to peak at the 55 to 64 age group, after which age the percentage providing care decreased. For men, the likelihood of providing 20 or more hours of care also increased with age, but peaked at the 75 to 84 age group.

## Map 8.7

### Population aged 16 and over providing care,[1] 2001[2]

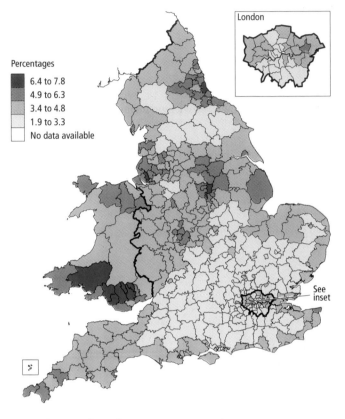

Percentages
- 6.4 to 7.8
- 4.9 to 6.3
- 3.4 to 4.8
- 1.9 to 3.3
- No data available

London

See inset

1 Providing care for 20 hours or more per week.
2 Unitary and local authorities in England and unitary authorities in Wales.

*Source: Census 2001, Office for National Statistics*

The areas with the highest prevalence of unpaid care were Merseyside, Durham, Tyne and Wear, and parts of Lincolnshire, South Yorkshire and Derbyshire and most of South and North Wales (Map 8.7). In London the highest rates of care were in Barking and Dagenham, Newham and Tower Hamlets. The areas with the lowest prevalence of unpaid care were South East Cumbria, North Yorkshire, Northumberland and the South East of England (other than London).

## Pensions

Much of central government expenditure on social protection for older people is through the provision of the state retirement pension. Nearly everyone over state pension age (women aged 60 and over and men aged 65 and over) receives this pension, though some also receive other state benefits, such as council tax or housing benefit, particularly if they are single. However there is an increasing emphasis on people making their own provision for retirement, and this can be through an occupational, personal or stakeholder pension.

In 2003/04, 55 per cent of single female pensioners in Great Britain had an occupational or personal pension in addition to the state pension, compared with 70 per cent of single male pensioners and 82 per cent of couples (Table 8.8). Much smaller proportions had a personal pension as well as the state pension. The lower percentages for women are partly because they have had lower employment rates than men and were less likely to have been in pensionable jobs (therefore they have accumulated lower pension funds). They were also less likely

## Table 8.8

### Pension receipt: by type of pensioner unit,[1,2] 2003/04

Great Britain

Percentages

| | Pensioner couples | Single male pensioners | Single female pensioners | All pensioners |
|---|---|---|---|---|
| Includes retirement pension/minimum income guarantee/pension credit only | 17 | 28 | 44 | 31 |
| *Plus* | | | | |
| Occupational, but not personal pension | 64 | 58 | 50 | 57 |
| Personal, but not occupational pension | 9 | 9 | 2 | 6 |
| Both occupational and personal pension | 8 | 3 | 2 | 4 |
| All including state pension | 99 | 98 | 98 | 98 |
| Other combinations, no retirement pension /minimum income guarantee/pension credit[3] | 0 | 1 | 0 | 0 |
| None | 1 | 1 | 2 | 1 |
| All people | 100 | 100 | 100 | 100 |

1 A pensioner unit is defined as either a single person over state pension age (60 for women, 65 for men), or a couple where the man is over state pension age.
2 Data are consistent with Pensioners' Incomes Series methodology.
3 People receiving some combination of an occupational or personal pension only.

*Source: Family Resources Survey, Department for Work and Pensions*

to have been self-employed and therefore to have had a personal pension.

In general, men are more likely than women to be members of a private pension scheme. In 2004/05, 66 per cent of male employees working full time, 63 per cent of female employees working full time and 41 per cent of female employees working part time in Great Britain were active members of a private pension scheme (Table 8.9). People in managerial and professional occupations were more likely to be active members than those in routine and manual occupations. A slightly higher proportion of female employees than male employees working full time were active members of an occupational pension scheme (56 per cent compared with 53 per cent), although the reverse was true for those members of personal pension schemes (23 per cent of men compared with 15 per cent of women).

## Older people

There is a range of state benefits available for older people. Pension credit replaced the minimum income guarantee in 2003. It provided a minimum income of £109 per week for single pensioners and £167 for couples in 2005/06. In addition

it provided an income top up for those with modest income above the level of the basic state pension – single pensioners with state pension and private income up to £151 per week, and couples with income up to £221.

Single pensioners are more likely than couples to receive any type of income-related benefits. In 2003/04, 33 per cent of single male pensioners and 43 per cent of single female pensioners in the United Kingdom received income-related benefits compared with 17 per cent of pensioner couples. Single female pensioners were almost twice as likely to be in receipt of income support/pension credit as single male pensioners (25 per cent compared with 13 per cent). The corresponding proportion for couples was 7 per cent (Table 8.10). Similar proportions (between a fifth and a quarter) of pensioners received disability-related benefits across all benefit units.

Older people are more likely than younger age groups to use health and social care services. The support they need can be provided formally by health and social services, voluntary organisations and community projects or informally by spouses,

## Table 8.9

### Current pension scheme membership of employees:[1] by sex and socio-economic classification,[2] 2004/05

Great Britain
Percentages

| | Managerial and professional | Intermediate | Routine and manual | All[3] |
|---|---|---|---|---|
| **Male full-time employees** | | | | |
| Occupational pension[4] | 67 | 63 | 37 | 53 |
| Personal pension[5] | 27 | 15 | 20 | 23 |
| Any pension | 82 | 68 | 51 | 66 |
| **Female full-time employees** | | | | |
| Occupational pension[4] | 68 | 55 | 34 | 56 |
| Personal pension[5] | 17 | 15 | 11 | 15 |
| Any pension | 76 | 62 | 40 | 63 |
| **Female part-time employees** | | | | |
| Occupational pension[4] | 58 | 46 | 25 | 34 |
| Personal pension[5] | 17 | 13 | 9 | 11 |
| Any pension | 69 | 54 | 32 | 41 |

1 Active membership of a pension scheme. Excluding those on youth training or employment training.
2 See Appendix, Part 1: National Statistics Socio-economic Classification.
3 Total includes a small number of employees for whom socio-economic classification could not be derived.
4 Includes a small number of people who were not sure if they were in a scheme but thought it possible.
5 Includes stakeholder pensions.

Source: General Household Survey, Office for National Statistics

## Table 8.10

### Receipt of selected social security benefits among pensioners: by type of benefit unit,[1] 2003/04

United Kingdom
Percentages

| | Single | | Couple |
|---|---|---|---|
| | Men | Women | |
| **Income-related** | | | |
| Council tax benefit | 29 | 38 | 15 |
| Housing benefit | 23 | 26 | 8 |
| Income support/ minimum income guarantee/pension credit | 13 | 25 | 7 |
| Any income-related benefit[2] | 33 | 43 | 17 |
| **Non-income-related[3]** | | | |
| Incapacity or disablement benefits[4] | 24 | 22 | 25 |
| Any non-income-related benefit[2] | 99 | 99 | 100 |
| **Any benefit[2]** | 99 | 99 | 100 |

1 Pensioner benefit units. See Appendix, Part 8: Benefit units.
2 Includes all benefits not listed here. Components do not sum to totals as each benefit unit may receive more than one benefit.
3 Includes state pension.
4 Includes incapacity benefit, disability living allowance (care and mobility components), severe disablement allowance, industrial injuries disability benefit, war disablement pension and attendance allowance.

Source: Family Resources Survey, Department for Work and Pensions

## Table **8.11**

### Reported sources of help for people aged 60 and over who have difficulty with daily activities or mobility:[1] by age, 2002/03

England                                             Percentages[2]

| | 60–74 | 75 and over | All respondents |
|---|---|---|---|
| No help | 64 | 46 | 56 |
| Spouse or partner | 23 | 16 | 20 |
| Son | 6 | 11 | 8 |
| Daughter | 9 | 17 | 12 |
| Son-in-law or daughter-in-law | 3 | 7 | 4 |
| Sibling | 1 | 2 | 2 |
| Grandchild | 2 | 5 | 3 |
| Friend or neighbour | 4 | 8 | 6 |
| Other unpaid[3] | 2 | 4 | 3 |
| Privately paid employee | 2 | 10 | 6 |
| Social or health service workers | 1 | 8 | 4 |
| All respondents (=100%) (numbers) | 2,760 | 1,942 | 4,702 |

1 See Appendix, Part 8: Activities of daily living (ADLs) and instrumental
  activities of daily living (IADLs).
2 Percentages do not add up to 100 per cent as respondents could give
  more than one answer.
3 Includes parents, other relatives, unpaid volunteers, other persons.

**Source: English Longitudinal Study of Ageing, University College London**

extended family, neighbours and friends. Assistance with activities of daily living is a significant step in this direction. This includes, among other things, help with dressing, bathing or showering, eating, getting in or out of bed, preparing a hot meal, shopping for groceries or taking medication (see Appendix, Part 8: Activities of daily living (ADLs) and instrumental activities of daily living (IADLs)).

People aged 75 and over in England who had difficulties with daily activities or mobility were more likely to receive help than those aged 60 to 74 in 2002/03 (Table 8.11). Family members accounted for most of the help provided to people aged 60 and over, with spouses or partners most likely to provide help to those aged 60 to 74. For those aged 75 and over caring is mostly provided by the younger generations such as children, children-in-law or grandchildren. In addition to family, some help is provided by privately-paid employees, social or health service workers and friends or neighbours. This may in part be explained by widowhood, which becomes more common as people grow older, so that their chances of living alone increase – this is particularly true for women. Twenty four per cent of

men and 58 per cent of women aged 75 to 84 were widowed in 2001 in the United Kingdom, increasing to 47 per cent and 79 per cent respectively of those aged 85 and over. Sixty two per cent of people aged 60 and over receiving help reported that it met their needs all the time, and a further 27 per cent thought that the help usually met their needs. Only 1 per cent thought that the help they received hardly ever met their needs.

In 2001/02, 52 per cent of older people in private households in Great Britain (those aged 65 and over) said they had seen a doctor at their surgery in the previous three months, while 24 per cent had seen a hospital doctor and 8 per cent a doctor at home. A higher proportion of women than men had seen a doctor at home, particularly those aged 85 and over. Of other health and social services, 29 per cent of people had seen a nurse at a surgery or health centre, 22 per cent had visited a dentist and 18 per cent had visited an optician. Sixty two per cent of women aged 85 and over had seen a chiropodist and 10 per cent a social worker or care manager.

## Sick and disabled people

There are a number of cash benefits available to sick and disabled people. Disability living allowance (DLA) is a benefit for people who are disabled, have personal care needs, mobility needs, or both and who are aged under 65. Attendance allowance (AA) is paid to people who become ill or disabled on or after their 65th birthday, or who are claiming it on or after this birthday, and, due to the extent or severity of their physical or mental condition, need someone to help with their personal care needs. Table 8.12 overleaf shows that, since the early 1990s, there has been an increase in the number of long-term sick and/or disabled people in Great Britain receiving either DLA or AA, reaching 4.1 million in 2004/05 compared with 1.8 million in 1991/92 (although these figures include people receiving both). This increase is a result of changes in entitlement conditions for benefits, demographic changes and increased take-up.

As at February 2005, 2.7 million people were in receipt of DLA and a further 1.4 million were receiving AA. The most common condition for which both were received was arthritis (526,000 and 422,000 respectively). For recipients of DLA, other common conditions included 'other mental health causes' such as psychosis and dementia, learning difficulties and back ailments. Other common conditions for people receiving AA included frailty, heart disease and mental health causes. Incapacity benefit (IB) and severe disablement allowance (SDA) are claimed by those who are unable to work because of illness and/or disability. The number of people receiving IB or SDA or their earlier equivalents (including those also in receipt of income support) was considerably higher than in the early 1980s, at over 1.7 million in 2004/05, although the number of such recipients has fallen since the mid-1990s.

Table **8.12**

## Recipients of benefits for sick and disabled people

Great Britain

Thousands

| | 1981/82 | 1991/92 | 1999/2000 | 2002/03 | 2003/04[1] | 2004/05[1] |
|---|---|---|---|---|---|---|
| **Long-term sick and people with disabilities** | | | | | | |
| Incapacity benefit[2,3]/severe disablement allowance | 747 | 1,438 | 1,372 | 1,324 | 1,304 | 1,274 |
| One of the above benefits plus income support[4] | 129 | 304 | 409 | 415 | 407 | 388 |
| Income support only[4] | .. | .. | 586 | 690 | 723 | 748 |
| **Short-term sick** | | | | | | |
| Incapacity benefit only[2,3] | 369 | 107 | 69 | 67 | 63 | 74 |
| Incapacity benefit[2,3] and income support[4] | 24 | 28 | 22 | 22 | 19 | 3 |
| Income support only[4] | .. | .. | 163 | 156 | 143 | 130 |
| **Disability living allowance/attendance allowance[5]** | 582 | 1,758 | 3,353 | 3,802 | 3,957 | 4,083 |

1 Income support 'over 60' cases, which transferred to pension credit in October 2003, are not included in 2003/04 and 2004/05 figures.
2 Incapacity benefit and severe disablement allowance figures are current at end-February from 1996/97.
3 Incapacity benefit was introduced in April 1995 to replace sickness and invalidity benefits.
4 Income-based jobseeker's allowance (JSA) replaced income support for the unemployed from October 1996. Income support includes some income-based JSA claimants.
5 People receiving both are counted twice. Before April 1992 includes mobility allowance.

*Source: Department for Work and Pensions*

The NHS offers a range of health and care services to sick and disabled people. Primary care services include those provided by GPs, dentists, opticians and the NHS Direct telephone, website and digital TV services, while NHS hospitals (secondary care services) provide acute and specialist services, treating conditions that normally cannot be dealt with by primary care specialists. Acute finished consultant episodes – those where the patient has completed a period of care under one consultant with one hospital provider (see Appendix, Part 8: In-patient activity) – rose by 55 per cent in the United Kingdom between

Table **8.13**

## NHS in-patient activity for sick and disabled people[1]

United Kingdom

| | 1981 | 1991/92 | 2000/01 | 2001/02 | 2002/03 | 2003/04 |
|---|---|---|---|---|---|---|
| **Acute[2]** | | | | | | |
| Finished consultant episodes[1] (thousands) | 5,693 | 6,974 | 8,164 | 8,209 | 8,395 | 8,829 |
| In-patient episodes per available bed (numbers) | 31.1 | 51.4 | 64.4 | 64.4 | 65.8 | 68.5 |
| Mean duration of stay (days) | 8.4 | 6.0 | 5.1 | 5.2 | 5.1 | 4.9 |
| **Mentally ill** | | | | | | |
| Finished consultant episodes[1] (thousands) | 244 | 281 | 270 | 262 | 254 | 240 |
| In-patient episodes per available bed (numbers) | 2.2 | 4.5 | 6.5 | 6.6 | 6.5 | 6.2 |
| Mean duration of stay (days) | .. | 114.8 | 58.5 | 57.7 | 56.2 | 58.3 |
| **People with learning disabilities** | | | | | | |
| Finished consultant episodes[1] (thousands) | 34 | 62 | 44 | 46 | 39 | 35 |
| In-patient episodes per available bed (numbers) | 0.6 | 2.4 | 5.5 | 6.4 | 6.2 | 5.5 |
| Mean duration of stay (days) | .. | 544.0 | 90.2 | 126.1 | 73.4 | 48.8 |

1 See Appendix, Part 8: In-patient activity.
2 General patients on wards, excluding elderly, maternity and neonatal cots in maternity units.

*Source: Health and Social Care Information Centre; National Assembly for Wales; National Health Service in Scotland; Department of Health, Social Services and Public Safety, Northern Ireland*

1981 and 2003/04 to reach 8.8 million (Table 8.13). The number of finished episodes for the mentally ill has fallen in recent years and in 2003/04 was 15 per cent lower than in 1991/92 and 2 per cent below the level in 1981.

Between 1991/92 and 2003/04 the average length of stay in hospital for the mentally ill almost halved (down by 49 per cent) to around 58 days. Over the same period the mean duration of stay for people with learning disabilities fell by 91 per cent to almost 49 days. This is possibly the result of a change in legislation to help people with such difficulties live with independence in the community, rather than keeping them in NHS hospitals.

An out-patient is a person who is seen by a hospital consultant for treatment or advice but who is non-resident at the hospital. In 2004/05, 14 per cent of people in Great Britain reported visiting an out-patient or casualty department at least once in the previous three months. With the exception of the youngest age group, which includes births and children aged under five, the percentage of people attending generally increased with age (Figure 8.14). Women in age groups between 16 and 64 were more likely than men in the same age groups to have attended although the reverse was true for those aged 65 and over.

People consult their GP for a number of services including vaccinations, general health advice and secondary care services, as well as for the diagnosis of illness and dispensing of prescriptions. On average, females visit their GP more than males. In 2004/05, 68 per cent of females and 65 per cent of males in Great Britain who had consulted their GP in the previous two

## Figure **8.14**

### Out-patient or casualty department attendance:[1] by sex and age, 2004/05

**Great Britain**
Percentages

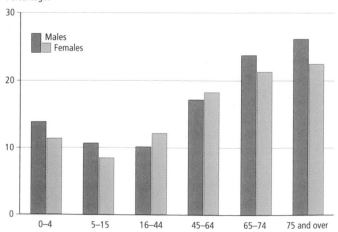

1 In the three months before interview.

*Source: General Household Survey, Office for National Statistics*

## Figure **8.15**

### NHS GP consultations where prescription was obtained: by socio-economic classification,[1] 2004/05

**Great Britain**
Percentages

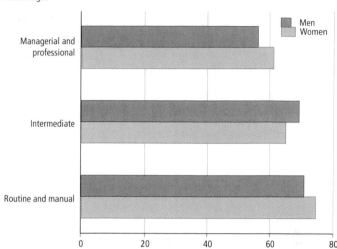

1 Based on the current or last job of the household reference person. See Appendix, Part 1: National Statistics Socio-economic Classification. Where the household reference person was a full-time student, had an inadequately described occupation, had never worked or was long-term unemployed they are excluded from the analysis.

*Source: General Household Survey, Office for National Statistics*

weeks had obtained a prescription. Those whose household reference person was in a routine or manual occupation were more likely to have obtained a prescription than those in a managerial or professional occupation (Figure 8.15). In both cases, a higher percentage of women than men were likely to have obtained a prescription.

The British Social Attitudes (BSA) survey includes information on attitudes towards various aspects of NHS care. The survey provides insights into views the general public has towards services. Satisfaction levels with NHS hospitals and GPs were generally higher in 2004 than in 2002 with the exception of the general condition of hospital buildings. In 2004, 55 per cent of adults in Great Britain aged 18 and over thought that waiting times for ambulances after 999 calls were satisfactory or very good, based on their own experience or from what they had heard (Table 8.16 overleaf). A further 52 per cent were of the same opinion about waiting areas for out-patients. In comparison, 22 per cent thought that waiting times in accident or emergency departments to see a doctor were satisfactory or very good, the same opinion as 17 per cent in respect of waiting times for appointments with hospital consultants. For GP services, the amount of time GPs gave to each patient was thought to be satisfactory or very good by 65 per cent of people, while 50 per cent held the same opinion about GP appointment systems.

Table **8.16**

### Satisfaction with NHS hospitals and GPs in their area, 2004[1]

Great Britain

Percentages

| | In need of a lot of improvement | In need of some improvement | Satisfactory | Very good |
|---|---|---|---|---|
| **Hospital services** | | | | |
| Waiting times for ambulance after 999 call | 12 | 33 | 45 | 10 |
| General condition of hospital buildings | 24 | 39 | 31 | 6 |
| Waiting areas for out-patients | 12 | 36 | 47 | 5 |
| Waiting areas in accident and emergency departments | 20 | 37 | 39 | 4 |
| Waiting times for seeing doctor in accident and emergency departments | 36 | 42 | 20 | 2 |
| Waiting times for appointments with hospital consultants | 40 | 43 | 15 | 2 |
| Waiting times in out-patient departments | 23 | 48 | 27 | 2 |
| Hospital waiting lists for non-emergency operations | 30 | 48 | 21 | 2 |
| **GP services** | | | | |
| Waiting areas at GP surgeries | 5 | 16 | 65 | 14 |
| GP appointment systems | 16 | 33 | 37 | 13 |
| Amount of time GP gives to each patient | 11 | 24 | 54 | 11 |

1 Respondents aged 18 and over were asked, 'From what you know or have heard, say whether you think the NHS in your area is, on the whole, satisfactory or in need of improvement'. Excludes those who responded 'Don't know' or did not answer.

*Source: British Social Attitudes Survey, National Centre for Social Research*

The NHS is increasingly using technology in patient care. NHS Direct, the telephone helpline in England and Wales, provides fast and convenient access to health advice and information and was launched in 1998. In 2004/05 the service handled over 6.6 million calls in England. In addition, the NHS Direct Online website provides a wealth of quality assured, evidence based health information. Since its launch in December 1999, usage has increased steadily year on year (Figure 8.17). In 2001/02 the average number of visits per month to the website was 169,000, but by 2004/05 this had risen to 774,000 visits. Usage is generally highest during January, February and March. The most visited areas of the website are its comprehensive health encyclopaedia and interactive self-help guide. The most popular topics accessed within the encyclopaedia during 2004/05 were under-active thyroid and mumps and, in the self-help guide, joint pains, backache and headaches in adults. In the health information enquiry service, the user profile has changed very little since it was launched in 2002, with 64 per cent of enquiries in 2004/05 from female patients and 63 per cent from people aged under 35. The most popular topics of enquiry were women's health and medicines (7.3 per cent and 6.8 per cent respectively). In December 2004 NHS Direct launched a new service, NHS Direct Interactive, extending access to health information to 7.9 million homes initially via digital satellite television.

Figure **8.17**

### Visits to NHS Direct Online website
Millions

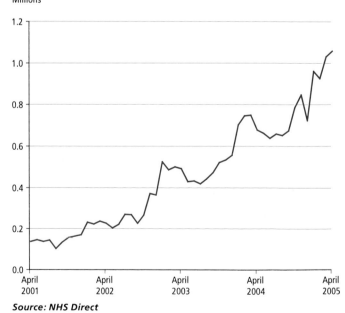

*Source: NHS Direct*

## Families and children

There are a number of benefits available to families with children. Not all are income-related, such as child benefit and incapacity or disablement benefits. Other benefits are income-related and paid to low-income families, such as housing and council tax benefit or income support. In 2003/04, 56 per cent of lone parents with dependent children and 10 per cent of couples in the United Kingdom were receiving income-related benefits. Among lone parents with children, 46 per cent received working tax credit or income support compared with 5 per cent of couples (Table 8.18). This may reflect the employment status of lone mothers, who head the majority of lone-parent families, as they are less likely to be employed than mothers with a partner (see also Table 4.6).

Childcare is essential in supporting parents to take up or return to employment. One of the Government's targets is a 50 per cent increase by 2008 in the take-up of formal childcare by lower-income families, using the average for 2003/04 and 2004/05 as a baseline. Childcare can be provided by formal paid sources such as nurseries/crèches, nursery schools/playgroups,

registered childminders and after school clubs/breakfast clubs or holiday play schemes. Parents can receive financial support from the Government if they use these services (provided they are registered and approved). In March 2005 there were 535,000 registered full day-care places and 366,000 out of school day-care places in England and Wales. Childcare can also be provided informally by grandparents, older children, partners/ex-partners and other relatives and friends. In 2003, 26 per cent of all dependent children in Great Britain received childcare from their grandparents, 12 per cent from other relatives and friends and 4 per cent from older siblings.

Around nine in ten children aged 0 to 2 and 3 to 4 in Great Britain received some form of childcare in 2003 (Table 8.19). Use of formal childcare reduces as children get older; over 40 per cent of children under five whose mothers were working received formal childcare. This fell to 23 per cent for children aged five to seven, when most start primary school, and decreased further when they started secondary education. Use of informal childcare remained relatively stable, with around two thirds of children up to the age of ten receiving it.

The hours a parent works on a weekly basis are related to the type of childcare used. In 2003 working lone parents and couples where both parents worked more than 16 hours per week in Great Britain were likely to use the same mixture of formal and informal childcare (between 21 and 22 per cent for formal childcare and between 50 and 54 per cent for informal childcare). Use of formal childcare in families where only one parent worked more than 16 hours per week was 10 per cent. This may be

## Table **8.18**

**Receipt of selected social security benefits among families below pension age: by type of benefit unit,[1] 2003/04**

United Kingdom                                              Percentages

|  | Single person with dependent children | Couple with dependent children |
| --- | --- | --- |
| **Income-related** | | |
| Council tax benefit | 48 | 8 |
| Housing benefit | 45 | 7 |
| Working tax credit or income support | 46 | 5 |
| Jobseeker's allowance | 1 | 2 |
| Any income-related benefit[2] | 56 | 10 |
| **Non-income-related** | | |
| Child benefit | 97 | 97 |
| Incapacity or disablement benefits[3] | 8 | 9 |
| Any non-income-related benefit[2] | 97 | 97 |
| **Any benefit or tax credit[2]** | 98 | 98 |

1 Families below pension age. See Appendix, Part 8: Benefit units.
2 Includes all benefits not listed here. Components do not sum to totals as each benefit unit may receive more than one benefit.
3 Includes incapacity benefit, disability living allowance (care and mobility components), severe disablement allowance, industrial injuries disability benefit, war disablement pension and attendance allowance.

**Source: Family Resources Survey, Department for Work and Pensions**

## Table **8.19**

**Childcare arrangements for children with working mothers:[1] by age of child, 2003**

Great Britain                                                Percentages[2]

|  | Formal childcare[3] | Informal childcare[4] | Childcare not required |
| --- | --- | --- | --- |
| 0–2 | 42 | 64 | 10 |
| 3–4 | 43 | 64 | 13 |
| 5–7 | 23 | 67 | 24 |
| 8–10 | 20 | 65 | 28 |
| 11–13 | 5 | 52 | 46 |
| 14–16 | 1 | 18 | 82 |

1 All children where the mother is in work.
2 Percentages do not add up to 100 per cent as respondents could give more than one answer.
3 Includes nurseries/crèches, nursery schools, playgroups, registered childminders, after school clubs/breakfast clubs, and holiday play schemes.
4 Provided by the main respondent's partners/ex-partners, parents/ parents-in-law, other relatives and friends, and older children.

**Source: Families and Children Study, Department for Work and Pensions**

because the other parent was at home looking after the child. Formal types of childcare were less likely to be used when parents (lone or couples) worked less than 16 hours per week.

Parental perceptions of the affordability of local childcare provision vary between lone parents and couples. In 2003 almost a third (31 per cent) of lone parents in Great Britain described their local childcare provisions as 'not at all affordable' compared with less than a quarter (23 per cent) of couples. A further 34 per cent of lone parents found the provisions 'fairly affordable' compared with 41 per cent of couples. Grandparents help their children by providing childcare and also financially. In 2001/02 the Millennium Cohort Study showed that families with a nine to ten month old baby received financial help from grandparents. Seventy two per cent of mothers reported that their parents bought gifts and extras for the baby, 25 per cent said their parents were buying essentials for the baby such as food, clothes or nappies, while 18 per cent said their parents had lent them money. The help received from the parents of the fathers followed a similar pattern.

In cases where parents are unable to look after their children properly, local authorities can take them into care. These children are usually described as being 'looked after'. In 2004, 68,000 children were being looked after by local authorities in England, Wales and Northern Ireland (Table 8.20). Over two thirds of them were cared for in foster homes. In Scotland, which has a different definition of looked after children, 12,000 children were being looked after and 3,500 were cared for in foster homes in the same year. Here, children who have committed offences or are in need of care and protection may be brought before a Children's Hearing, which can impose a supervision requirement if it thinks that compulsory measures are appropriate. Under these requirements, most children are allowed to remain at home under the supervision of a social worker, but some may live with foster parents or in a residential establishment while under supervision.

Children may be placed on a local authority child protection register when social services departments consider they are at continuing risk of significant harm. As at March 2005 there were 25,900 children on child protection registers in England, with 500 more boys than girls. Neglect was the most common reason to be placed on the register, affecting 45 per cent of boys and 43 per cent of girls. Emotional abuse was the second most common reason, with around a fifth of both boys and girls on the register suffering from this.

While some services are designed for them, children also make use of services available to the whole population. In 2004/05, 16 per cent of all children aged 0 to 4 in Great Britain visited an NHS GP in the 14 days before interview, with young girls

## Table **8.20**

### Children looked after by local authorities:[1] by type of accommodation[2]

England, Wales & Northern Ireland                    Thousands

|  | 1994 | 1999 | 2004 |
|---|---|---|---|
| Foster placements | 35.1 | 40.2 | 45.8 |
| Children's homes | .. | 6.8 | 7.6 |
| Placement with parents[3] | 5.5 | 7.1 | 7.0 |
| Placed for adoption[4] | 2.3 | 3.0 | 3.8 |
| Living independently or in residential employment[4] | 1.7 | 1.2 | 1.2 |
| Residential schools[4,5] | .. | 1.0 | 1.5 |
| Other accommodation | 1.9 | 1.8 | 1.0 |
| All looked after children | 55.2 | 61.1 | 67.9 |

1 In England and in Wales (except for 1994), excludes children looked after under an agreed series of short-term placements. In Northern Ireland, children looked after for respite care are included in 2004. At 31 March.
2 See Appendix, Part 8: Children looked after by local authorities.
3 In England, placed with parents or person with parental responsibility in 2004.
4 Not collected for Northern Ireland.
5 England only in 1994 and 1999.

**Source: Department of Health; Department for Education and Skills; National Assembly for Wales; Department of Health, Social Services and Public Safety, Northern Ireland**

slightly more likely to do so than boys (17 per cent and 15 per cent respectively). Six per cent of all children under five saw a health visitor at the GP surgery and a further 6 per cent visited a child health or welfare clinic. Visits to GPs or other health professionals are lower for older children, with only 7 per cent of children aged 5 to 15 having seen an NHS GP.

The majority of children in the United Kingdom visited the dentist at least once in 2003. Only 6 per cent of five year olds had never visited the dentist, compared with 14 per cent in 1983 (Table 8.21). However differences between socio-economic backgrounds were wider in 2003 for five year olds than they were 10 or 20 years earlier. Attendance levels for children with parents who had professional, managerial and technical, and non-manual skilled occupations improved at a faster rate (between 1993 and 2003 from 93 per cent to 98 per cent) than those whose parents worked in partly skilled and unskilled occupations (from 85 to 87 per cent over the same period). For eight year olds, only 2 per cent had never visited the dentist in 2003, compared with 4 per cent in 1993. Among this age group, the proportion of children who had never visited the dentist fell from 6 per cent in 1993 to 1 per cent in 2003 for those whose parents worked in partly skilled and unskilled occupations.

## Table 8.21

### Children who had never visited the dentist: by age and socio-economic classification[1]

United Kingdom

Percentages

| | Aged five | | | Aged eight | | |
|---|---|---|---|---|---|---|
| | 1983 | 1993 | 2003 | 1983 | 1993 | 2003 |
| Professional, managerial and technical, and non-manual skilled occupations | 10 | 7 | 2 | 3 | 2 | - |
| Manual skilled occupations | 15 | 10 | 5 | 4 | 3 | 2 |
| Partly skilled, and unskilled occupations | 18 | 15 | 13 | 9 | 6 | 1 |
| All households | 14 | 10 | 6 | 4 | 4 | 2 |

1 Of the household reference person. See Appendix, Part 1: National Statistics Socio-economic Classification. Data for 1983 and 1993 are based on Social Class. See Appendix, Part 8: Social Class.

Source: Children's Dental Health Survey, Office for National Statistics

Very few children (only 1 to 2 per cent in 2003) received dental treatment outside the NHS. Among those parents of five and eight year olds who reported difficulty in accessing NHS dental care at some point, around one in five were reporting current difficulties in 2003, mainly because their nearest family dentist would not accept any more NHS patients.

In 2004 one in ten children aged 5 to 16 had a clinically recognisable mental disorder (see Chapter 7: Mental health). Almost three in ten families had asked for help from a range of specialist and informal services because they were worried about their child's emotional behaviour or concentration in the year before the interview (Table 8.22). Around one in five (22 per cent) had contacted a professional service, 18 per cent had contacted a teacher, 6 per cent a GP or practice nurse and 4 per cent an educational psychologist. Informal sources of help were also used, with family and friends accounting for most (12 per cent). Parents of children with a hyperkinetic disorder (children whose behaviour is hyperactive, impulsive and inattentive) and those whose child had an autistic spectrum disorder were most likely to have sought help or advice (95 per cent and 89 per cent respectively) (see also Table 7.19 and Figure 7.20).

## Table 8.22

### Help sought in the last year for a child's[1] mental health problems: by type of mental disorder,[2] 2004

Great Britain

Percentages[3]

| | Type of disorder | | | | |
|---|---|---|---|---|---|
| | Emotional disorder | Conduct disorder | Hyperkinetic disorder | Autistic spectrum disorder | All children aged 5 to 16 |
| **Specialist services** | | | | | |
| Child/adult mental health specialist | 24 | 28 | 52 | 43 | 3 |
| Child physical health specialist | 8 | 7 | 15 | 36 | 2 |
| Social services | 10 | 16 | 15 | 23 | 2 |
| Education services | 18 | 24 | 37 | 51 | 4 |
| **Front line services** | | | | | |
| Primary health care | 29 | 32 | 46 | 33 | 6 |
| Teachers | 47 | 60 | 70 | 69 | 18 |
| **All professional services** | 64 | 76 | 93 | 86 | 22 |
| **Informal sources** | | | | | |
| Family member/friends | 34 | 34 | 35 | 22 | 12 |
| Internet | 5 | 6 | 11 | 10 | 1 |
| Telephone help line | 4 | 4 | 6 | 3 | 1 |
| Self-help group | 3 | 3 | 7 | 10 | 0 |
| Other type of help | 8 | 7 | 4 | 8 | 2 |
| **All sources** | 73 | 81 | 95 | 89 | 28 |
| No help sought | 27 | 19 | 5 | 11 | 72 |

1 Aged 5 to 16 and living in private households.
2 See Appendix, Part 7: Mental disorders.
3 Percentages do not add up to 100 per cent as respondents could give more than one answer.

Source: Mental Health of Children and Young People Survey, Office for National Statistics

# Crime and justice

- The British Crime Survey (BCS) showed that there were 10.9 million crimes committed against adults living in private households in England and Wales in 2004/05. (Figure 9.1)

- Vehicle-related theft was the most prevalent type of crime in the 2004/05 BCS with 1.9 million offences, 17 per cent of all offences in England and Wales. (Page 130)

- The total value of all card fraud in the UK in 2004 was £504.8 million, an increase of 20 per cent from 2003. (Page 133)

- Benefit fraud was nearly three and a half times as high in 2004 as it was in 1999, and was the second most commonly committed fraud offence in England and Wales after obtaining property by deception. (Table 9.7)

- Men in England and Wales were almost twice as likely as women to be a victim of violent crime (5 per cent compared with 3 per cent) with young men aged 16 to 24 most at risk in 2004/05. (Page 135)

- In 2004, 6 per cent of all 17 year old boys in England and Wales were found guilty of indictable offences, by far the highest rate for any age group, and five times the corresponding rate for girls. (Figure 9.12)

- Between 1993 and 2004 the average prison population in England and Wales rose by 67 per cent, to 75,000 – on 30 September 2005 it was 77,300. (Figure 9.21)

# Chapter 9

Many people will be affected by crime in the course of their lives. It can affect people's lives directly through loss and suffering, or indirectly, such as through the need for increased security measures. The fear of crime can have a restrictive effect on people's behaviour. Dealing with crime and its associated problems is an ever-present concern for society and the Government.

## Crime levels

The 2004/05 British Crime Survey (BCS) (see Measures of crime box) estimated that 10.9 million crimes were committed against adults living in private households in England and Wales, a 7 per cent decrease on the previous year and 8.5 million fewer crimes than the peak in 1995 (Figure 9.1). The number of BCS crimes rose steadily through the 1980s and into the 1990s before falling progressively back to the levels of the early 1980s. As well as a decrease in overall BCS crime in the last year, there was also a 6 per cent fall in the number of crimes recorded by the police over this period.

The 2003/04 Northern Ireland Crime Survey estimated that 300,000 offences were committed against adults living in private households in Northern Ireland, the same number as in the 2001 Survey.

Estimates from the Scottish Crime Survey suggest that over 1 million crimes were committed against individuals and households in Scotland in 2002, an increase of 30 per cent since 1999.

In 2004/05, 55 per cent of BCS offences involved some type of theft. Vehicle-related theft was the most prevalent type of crime accounting for 17 per cent of all offences. There were 1.9 million vehicle-related thefts in 2004/05. Between 1995 and 2004/05 vehicle-related theft fell by 57 per cent. The second most common BCS offence group was vandalism. Vandalism accounted for 24 per cent of all crime in 2004/05 and fell by 24 per cent from 3.4 million in 1995 to 2.6 million in 2004/05. Violent incidents were the third most common type of BCS crime, accounting for 22 per cent of all crime in 2004/05. Between 1995 and 2004/05 the number of violent offences fell by 43 per cent, from 4.3 million to 2.4 million.

Most BCS crimes (58 per cent) are not reported to the police (Table 9.2). Victims may not report a crime for a number of reasons, such as thinking the crime was too trivial, there was no loss, they believed the police would or could not do much about it, or that it was a private matter. The proportion of crimes reported to the police varied considerably according to the type of offence. Of the comparable crimes (see Appendix, Part 9: Comparing the British Crime Survey and police recorded crime) burglary was the most likely crime to be reported in

## Figure **9.1**

### British Crime Survey offences

England & Wales
Millions

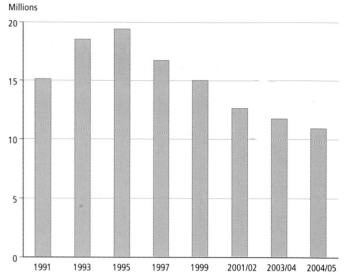

*Source: British Crime Survey, Home Office*

## Measures of crime

There are two main measures of the extent of crime in the United Kingdom: surveys of the public, and the recording of crimes by the police. The British Crime Survey (BCS) interviews adult members of households in England and Wales. The BCS, and similar surveys in Scotland and Northern Ireland, are thought to give a better measure of many types of crime than police recorded crime statistics. These surveys are able to find out about the large number of offences that are not reported to the police. They also give a more reliable picture of trends, as they are not affected by changes in levels of reporting to the police or by variations in police recording practice (see Appendix, Part 9: Types of offences in England and Wales).

Recorded crime data collected by the police are a by-product of the administrative procedure of completing a record for crimes that they investigate. A new National Crime Recording Standard (NCRS) was introduced in England and Wales in April 2002 with the aim of taking a more victim-centred approach and providing consistency between forces (see Appendix, Part 9: National Crime Recording Standard).

Police recorded crime and BCS measured crime have different coverage. Unlike crime data recorded by the police, the BCS is restricted to crimes against adults (aged 16 or over) living in private households and their property, and does not include some types of crime (for example, fraud, murder and victimless crimes such as drug use where there is not a direct victim).

## Table 9.2

### Crimes[1] committed within the last 12 months: by outcome, 2004/05

England & Wales                                                                       Percentages

|  | BCS crimes reported to the police | BCS crimes recorded by the police |
| --- | --- | --- |
| Burglary | 61 | 47 |
| Comparable property crime[2] | 48 | 38 |
| Vehicle thefts | 49 | 43 |
| Violence[3] | 45 | 30 |
| Theft from the person | 32 | 20 |
| Vandalism | 32 | 24 |
| All comparable crime | 42 | 32 |

1 BCS crimes that are comparable with those recorded in police statistics.
2 Comprises all acquisitive crime: all burglary, vehicle thefts, bicycle theft and theft from the person.
3 Does not include snatch theft.

**Source: British Crime Survey, Home Office**

2004/05 (61 per cent). Although around half of all vehicle-related thefts were reported (49 per cent), this rose to 95 per cent when the crime involved the actual theft of a vehicle. This could be because a formal record of such incidents is generally needed for insurance purposes.

Not all crimes that are reported to the police are recorded by them. The police recorded 32 per cent of all comparable BCS crimes in 2004/05. Police recording rates vary according to the type of offence, ranging from 47 per cent of burglaries to 20 per cent of theft from the person. Although the National Crime Recording Standard (see Appendix, Part 9: National Crime Recording Standard) has introduced a more victim-based approach to recording, the police are not required to record incidents and they may choose not to record a crime. They may consider that the incident is too minor or that there is insufficient evidence. Alternatively, the victim may not want the police to proceed.

The number of crimes recorded by the police in England and Wales decreased by 6 per cent between 2003/04 and 2004/05, to 5.6 million. Three quarters of these offences were property crimes. Theft and handling stolen goods comprised 36 per cent of all recorded crime, this includes thefts of, or from, vehicles, which comprised 13 per cent of all recorded crime. Criminal damage, burglary and fraud and forgery are the other property offences (Table 9.3).

In Scotland the term 'crime' is reserved for the more serious offences (roughly equivalent to 'indictable' and 'triable-either-way' offences in England and Wales), while less serious crimes

## Table 9.3

### Crimes recorded by the police: by type of offence,[1] 2004/05

Percentages

|  | England & Wales | Scotland | Northern Ireland |
| --- | --- | --- | --- |
| Theft and handling stolen goods | 36 | 34 | 26 |
| Theft of vehicles | 4 | 4 | 4 |
| Theft from vehicles | 9 | 6 | 5 |
| Criminal damage | 21 | 29 | 27 |
| Violence against the person | 19 | 4 | 25 |
| Burglary | 12 | 8 | 11 |
| Fraud and forgery | 5 | 5 | 4 |
| Drugs offences | 3 | 10 | 2 |
| Robbery | 2 | 1 | 1 |
| Sexual offences | 1 | 1 | 1 |
| Other offences[2] | 1 | 8 | 2 |
| All notifiable offences (=100%) (thousands) | 5,563 | 438 | 118 |

1 See Appendix, Part 9: Types of offences in England and Wales, and in Northern Ireland, and Offences and crimes.
2 Northern Ireland includes 'offences against the state'. Scotland excludes 'offending while on bail'.

**Source: Home Office; Scottish Executive; Police Service of Northern Ireland**

are called 'offences' (see Appendix, Part 9: Types of offences in England and Wales, and Offences and crimes). Crime in Scotland increased by 8 per cent between 2003 and 2004/05, when a total of 438,000 crimes were recorded by the police (Table 9.3). Theft and handling stolen goods comprised 34 per cent of recorded crime in Scotland, criminal damage 29 per cent, and drug offences 10 per cent. The rise in crime in Scotland recorded by the police can be ascribed to the introduction of the Scottish Crime Recording Standard (SCRS) implemented in April 2004. The introduction of the SCRS had no impact on the figures for the more serious crimes such as serious assault, sexual assault, robbery or housebreaking. However it did increase the number of minor crimes recorded by the police (including vandalism, minor thefts, petty assault, breach of the peace). The introduction of the NCRS in England and Wales in April 2002 had similarly resulted in an increase in certain crime categories.

The definitions used in Northern Ireland are broadly comparable with those used in England and Wales. Crime recorded by the police in Northern Ireland decreased by 8 per cent from 2003/04 to 2004/05 to 118,000 incidents. Criminal damage comprised over a quarter of recorded crime in Northern Ireland and violence against the person accounted for a similar proportion. These crimes made up a greater proportion of all crime in Northern Ireland than in England and Wales. Theft and handling stolen goods comprised 26 per cent of recorded crime in

Northern Ireland, a smaller proportion of all crime than in England and Wales (Table 9.3).

Perceptions on whether crime is rising or falling play a part in determining how concerned people are about crime. In 2004/05, two thirds of people interviewed in England and Wales said they believed that across the whole country the level of crime had risen a 'lot' or a 'little' over the last two years compared with one in twenty who believed crime rates were falling (Figure 9.4).

In 2002/03, when asked about their local area, more than half (54 per cent) thought local crime had increased in the previous two years. Eight out of ten people interviewed in the Northern Ireland Crime Survey in 2003/04 (80 per cent) believed that crime in Northern Ireland had risen over the two previous years, while 7 per cent believed the crime rates were falling.

Perceptions of crime vary by demographic and socio-economic characteristics. How people feel about the Criminal Justice System and their general feelings of safety also have an effect. In England and Wales older people were more likely than younger people, and women were more likely than men, to believe that crime rates had risen. In 2002/03 unskilled workers were more than twice as likely as professionals to think there was a lot more crime than two years ago. People who had confidence in the Criminal Justice System bringing offenders to justice were more likely to believe that the crime level had declined than those who were not confident. People who reported feeling unsafe about walking alone after dark and those who were worried about being a victim of burglary, violence or, car crime or being at home alone, were more likely to believe there had been an increase in crime, both locally and nationally.

## Offences

In line with the overall decline in offences, domestic burglary has fallen steadily since 1995 (Table 9.5). In 2004/05 there were 756,000 attempted burglaries in England and Wales; 469,000 of these involved entry into the house. Burglaries were more likely to result in no loss than in anything being taken and in general this was consistent over time. In 2004/05, 57 per cent of burglaries resulted in nothing being taken. The 2004/05 BCS estimated that 61 per cent of domestic burglaries were reported to the police, and of these three quarters were recorded. Burglaries were more likely to have been reported where there was a loss.

The risk of becoming a victim of burglary varied by the characteristics of the household. Households with no home security measures in place were much more likely to be victims of burglary; 15 per cent of these households were victims of one or more burglaries in 2004/05 compared with 1 per cent of households with security measures such as burglar alarms, security lights or window bars. Households with a reference person aged 16 to 24 were more likely to have experienced burglary (7 per cent) than those where the reference person was older (2 per cent of households where the household reference person was aged 45 to 64 were victims). Single parent families were at a high risk of burglary compared with other family types, as were households with a low income compared with households with a higher income. Households in council estates were at a higher risk of burglary than those in other areas and those in rented accommodation were at a higher risk than homeowners. The risk of burglary was also higher for those who had moved recently (within a year) than

## Figure **9.4**

### Perceptions about the change in the national crime rate[1]

England & Wales
Percentages

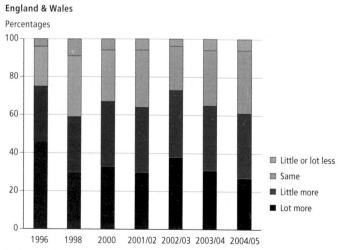

Little or lot less
Same
Little more
Lot more

1  Respondents were asked whether they thought the level of crime in the country as a whole had changed over the two previous years.

**Source: British Crime Survey, Home Office**

## Table **9.5**

### Trends in domestic burglary:[1] by type

England & Wales                                                   Thousands

|      | Burglary | | Burglary | | |
| --- | --- | --- | --- | --- | --- |
|      | With entry | No entry | With loss | No loss | All burglary |
| 1981 | 474 | 276 | 373 | 376 | 749 |
| 1991 | 869 | 511 | 712 | 668 | 1,380 |
| 1995 | 998 | 772 | 791 | 979 | 1,770 |
| 1997 | 852 | 768 | 651 | 970 | 1,621 |
| 1999 | 767 | 523 | 551 | 739 | 1,290 |
| 2001/02 | 552 | 416 | 396 | 573 | 969 |
| 2002/03 | 561 | 412 | 407 | 566 | 973 |
| 2003/04 | 533 | 410 | 417 | 526 | 943 |
| 2004/05 | 469 | 287 | 327 | 429 | 756 |

1  Burglary with no entry and with entry add up to all burglary. Burglary with no loss and with loss also add up to all burglary.

**Source: British Crime Survey, Home Office**

## Table **9.6**

### Vehicle crime: by type

England & Wales

Thousands

| | Theft from vehicles | Theft of vehicles | Attempted theft of and from | All vehicle crime |
|---|---|---|---|---|
| 1991 | 2,424 | 522 | 899 | 3,845 |
| 1995 | 2,544 | 510 | 1,297 | 4,350 |
| 1997 | 2,200 | 378 | 933 | 3,511 |
| 1999 | 1,849 | 336 | 825 | 3,009 |
| 2001/02 | 1,496 | 316 | 683 | 2,494 |
| 2002/03 | 1,425 | 278 | 662 | 2,365 |
| 2003/04 | 1,337 | 241 | 543 | 2,121 |
| 2004/05 | 1,210 | 214 | 462 | 1,886 |

*Source: British Crime Survey, Home Office*

for those who had lived at the address for a longer period of time.

The BCS definition of vehicle-related theft comprises theft, or attempted theft, of or from a vehicle. Theft from a vehicle is the most common type of vehicle-related theft and accounted for 64 per cent of vehicle crime in 2004/05 (Table 9.6). Recent years have seen a decrease in all categories of vehicle-related theft. Attempted thefts had the greatest decrease in the vehicle-related theft categories. They fell by 64 per cent between 1995 and 2004/05.

In 2004/05 most vehicle-related thefts occurred in areas around the home (67 per cent) with 41 per cent of all vehicle-related theft occurring on the street outside the home. Overall, 19 per cent of all vehicle thefts occurred in a car park. Households in areas with high levels of vandalism, graffiti, rubbish and litter, and where homes were in poor condition were more likely to have

been victims of vehicle-related thefts, as were those living in urban areas in comparison with rural areas and those living in council estates. People living in flats or terraced housing were at a higher risk of vehicle theft. This could be because they are more likely to park their cars on the street rather than in private areas.

The 2004/05 BCS estimated that there were 2.4 million violent incidents against adults in England and Wales, a fall of 11 per cent from 2003/04. However, the police recorded 1.2 million violent crimes, an increase of 7 per cent from 2003/04. This increase may be partly because of changes in recording and the more proactive policing of violence problems. Of these recorded violent incidents, 20 per cent were common assaults and 18 per cent were harassment, both of which involved no physical injury to the victim. Less serious woundings accounted for 41 per cent of recorded violent crime and included minor injuries such as bruising or black eyes. Provisional statistics show that the number of recorded firearm offences increased by 6 per cent in the last year to 10,979 in 2004/05 and the number of homicides increased by 1 per cent to 859 incidents.

In 2004/05, 280,000 fraud and forgery offences were recorded by the police in 2004/05, a decrease of 12 per cent from 2003/04 Of these, under half (43 per cent) were cheque and credit card frauds, a 7 per cent decrease from 2003/04. The Association for Payment and Clearing Services (APACS), the UK payments association, puts the total value of all card fraud at £504.8 million in 2004, an increase of 20 per cent from 2003.

Although data collected by APACS suggest the value of fraud is rising, the number of defendants found guilty of fraud-related offences has fallen over the past five years. A total of 14,800 defendants were found guilty of indictable fraud offences in England and Wales in 2004, a fall of 17 per cent compared with the peak in 1999 (Table 9.7). Obtaining property by deception was

## Table **9.7**

### Defendants found guilty of indictable fraud offences

England & Wales

Numbers

| | 1998 | 1999 | 2000 | 2001 | 2002 | 2003 | 2004 |
|---|---|---|---|---|---|---|---|
| Obtaining property by deception | 11,440 | 11,480 | 10,540 | 9,440 | 9,350 | 8,460 | 7,520 |
| Dishonest representation for obtaining benefit | 240 | 710 | 1,350 | 1,950 | 1,990 | 1,840 | 2,460 |
| Making off without payment | 1,250 | 1,440 | 1,410 | 1,320 | 1,300 | 1,810 | 1,690 |
| Obtaining services by deception | 980 | 1,030 | 880 | 880 | 830 | 800 | 750 |
| False accounting | 1,690 | 1,620 | 1,160 | 870 | 750 | 650 | 730 |
| Conspiracy to defraud | 470 | 420 | 430 | 450 | 410 | 450 | 520 |
| Other offences | 1,130 | 1,100 | 1,100 | 1,000 | 940 | 1,030 | 1,130 |
| All offences | 17,200 | 17,800 | 16,870 | 15,910 | 15,570 | 15,040 | 14,800 |

*Source: Home Office*

## Table 9.8

### Persons found guilty of, or cautioned for, drug offences: by type of drug

England & Wales

Thousands

|  | 1990 | 1992 | 1994 | 1995 | 1996 | 1997 | 1998 | 1999 | 2000 | 2001 | 2002 | 2003 | 2004 |
|---|---|---|---|---|---|---|---|---|---|---|---|---|---|
| Cocaine (excluding crack) | 0.9 | 0.9 | 1.6 | 1.8 | 2.2 | 2.9 | 4.0 | 4.6 | 4.2 | 4.7 | 5.8 | 7.0 | 8.1 |
| Heroin | 1.6 | 1.4 | 2.7 | 3.9 | 5.7 | 8.2 | 10.1 | 10.8 | 10.7 | 11.1 | 10.7 | 10.5 | 10.1 |
| LSD | 0.9 | 1.4 | 1.7 | 1.1 | 0.8 | 0.7 | 0.5 | 0.4 | 0.2 | 0.2 | 0.1 | 0.1 | 0.1 |
| Ecstasy type | 0.3 | 1.5 | 1.8 | 3.1 | 3.7 | 3.7 | 2.7 | 3.8 | 5.9 | 6.8 | 6.1 | 5.5 | 5.2 |
| Amphetamines | 2.3 | 5.7 | 7.8 | 9.6 | 12.3 | 12.4 | 13.2 | 10.6 | 5.9 | 4.6 | 5.6 | 5.9 | 5.8 |
| Cannabis[1] | 40.2 | 41.4 | 67.2 | 72.0 | 69.1 | 80.9 | 90.5 | 81.1 | 70.2 | 66.4 | 78.1 | 82.1 | 49.8 |
| All drugs[2] | 44.9 | 48.9 | 82.9 | 90.6 | 91.2 | 107.5 | 122.4 | 112.8 | 99.1 | 96.5 | 106.6 | 110.4 | 82.8 |

1 Cannabis was reclassified on 29 January 2004 from Class B to Class C. Data for 2004 does not include police formal warnings.
2 Individual components do not sum to the total because each person may appear in more than one category. The total includes all drugs but not all drug offences.

**Source: Home Office**

the most common offence, committed by 51 per cent of offenders found guilty of indictable fraud. The number of people found guilty of this offence has fallen by 35 per cent since 1999. Dishonest representation for obtaining benefit was nearly three and a half times higher than it was in 1999, and was the second most commonly committed fraud offence, increasing from 4 per cent of all indictable fraud offences in 1999 to 17 per cent in 2004.

Drug offences can cover a wide range of activities, including unlawful production, supply, import or export and possession of illegal substances. The number of people found guilty of, or cautioned for, drug offences in England and Wales rose from 80,390 in 1994 to a peak of 120,290 in 1998. The number of drug offenders has fluctuated since then, with 83,440 persons being dealt with in 2004. In 2004, 85 per cent of drug offences were for unlawful possession.

The number of people found guilty of, or cautioned for, drug offences varied by type of drug over time (Table 9.8). Most drug offences in 2004 were for cannabis (60 per cent), followed by heroin (12 per cent) and cocaine (10 per cent). In comparison, nine out of ten drug offences involved cannabis in 1990. Cannabis was re-classified from a Class B to Class C drug in January 2004 and this has led to fewer arrests. As such the number of cannabis offences for 2004 should not be directly compared with those for previous years. The number of persons found guilty of, or cautioned for, a drug offence involving cocaine has been increasing, from 860 persons in 1990 to 8,070 persons in 2004. Offences involving heroin increased throughout the 1990s and peaked in 2001 with 11,097 persons being found guilty or cautioned. The number of persons involved in ecstasy-related drug offences increased generally throughout the 1990s but has been decreasing since 2001.

## Victims

People's perception of crime is affected by their fear of being a victim of crime. Women are more worried about a range of crimes than men, with the exception of theft of, and from, a car, for which women and men have broadly similar levels of worry (Table 9.9). Women are almost three times as likely as men to be very worried about violent crime (being mugged, physically attacked, insulted, pestered or raped). Though young people were less likely than older people to believe there had been an increase in overall crime levels, a higher proportion of men and women in the youngest age group (16 to 24 years old) reported being worried about vehicle and violent crime compared with those in the older age groups. Most notably, almost a third of women aged 16 to 24 were very worried about violent crime. The percentage of people who reported being worried about crime was lowest among men and women aged 65 and over.

The BCS asks respondents whether worry about crime had affected their quality of life. In 2004/05, 30 per cent said that worrying about crime had a moderate impact on their quality of life and a further 6 per cent said it had a great impact. In Northern Ireland 43 per cent of respondents of the Northern Ireland Crime Survey said that worry about crime had a moderate or great effect on their quality of life.

Fear of crime does not necessarily reflect the likelihood of being a victim of crime. The risk of becoming a victim of crime fell from 40 per cent of the population in 1995 to 24 per cent in 2004/05 – the lowest recorded level since the BCS began in 1981. This fall represents almost 6 million fewer victims.

Although women were more worried than men about being a victim of violence (23 per cent compared with 8 per cent), men

## Table **9.9**

### Worry about crime:[1] by sex and age, 2004/05

England & Wales                                                Percentages

| | Vehicle crime[2] | Burglary | Worry about violence |
|---|---|---|---|
| **Men** | | | |
| 16–24 | 20 | 8 | 11 |
| 25–44 | 14 | 10 | 8 |
| 45–64 | 12 | 10 | 7 |
| 65–74 | 9 | 10 | 6 |
| 75 and over | 7 | 7 | 3 |
| All aged 16 and over | 13 | 10 | 8 |
| **Women** | | | |
| 16–24 | 21 | 14 | 32 |
| 25–44 | 14 | 15 | 24 |
| 45–64 | 14 | 15 | 23 |
| 65–74 | 11 | 15 | 18 |
| 75 and over | 6 | 11 | 14 |
| All aged 16 and over | 14 | 14 | 23 |

1 Percentages of people who were 'very worried' about selected types of crime.
2 Based on respondents residing in households owning, or with regular use of, a vehicle.
**Source: British Crime Survey, Home Office**

were almost twice as likely as women to be a victim of violent crime (5 per cent compared with 3 per cent). Men aged 16 to 24 were most at risk; 15 per cent had experienced a violent crime

according to the 2004/05 BCS, compared with 6 per cent of women in the same age group. Older people were less likely than younger people to be a victim of violent crime; less than 1 per cent of those aged 65 and over reported they had been victims of some sort of violence.

Just over a third (35 per cent) of all incidents of violent crime in the 2004/05 BCS were committed by strangers. A further third (34 per cent) were incidents of violence by acquaintances, and just under a fifth (17 per cent) were incidents of domestic violence. Men were more likely than women to experience violence committed by strangers (45 per cent compared with 19 per cent) and young men aged 16 to 24 were more likely to be victims of violence by strangers than men aged over 24. In contrast, women were more likely to be victims of domestic violence. Of those women who were victims of violent crime in the BCS, 32 per cent of women were victims of domestic violence (308,000) in 2004/05, compared with 6 per cent of men (92,000).

Just under half (46 per cent) of all BCS violent incidents in 2004/05 involved no injury. Of those who were injured, the most common injuries were minor bruisings or a black eye (32 per cent of males and 31 per cent of females). These were the most common injuries across the different categories of violent crime, for example victims of violence by strangers were around twice as likely to suffer from minor bruising or a black eye as they were to suffer from severe bruising (Table 9.10).

## Table **9.10**

### Type of injury from violent crime: by sex, 2004/05

England & Wales                                                                                     Percentages

| | Domestic | Mugging | Stranger | Acquaintance[1] | All violence |
|---|---|---|---|---|---|
| **Men** | | | | | |
| Minor bruise/black eye | 47 | 24 | 30 | 36 | 32 |
| Severe bruising | 23 | 14 | 14 | 12 | 14 |
| Scratches | 32 | 15 | 10 | 7 | 11 |
| Cuts | 18 | 15 | 16 | 18 | 17 |
| Broken bones | 3 | 1 | 3 | 2 | 2 |
| Concussion or loss of consciousness | 2 | 2 | 4 | 3 | 3 |
| Other | 2 | 2 | 10 | 12 | 9 |
| **Women** | | | | | |
| Minor bruise/black eye | 38 | 11 | 30 | 34 | 31 |
| Severe bruising | 27 | 9 | 14 | 19 | 19 |
| Scratches | 17 | 7 | 6 | 16 | 13 |
| Cuts | 14 | 3 | 7 | 19 | 13 |
| Broken bones | 1 | 1 | 2 | 2 | 2 |
| Concussion or loss of consciousness | 1 | 0 | 0 | 3 | 1 |
| Other | 4 | 3 | 6 | 7 | 5 |

1 Assaults in which the victim knew one or more of the offenders, at least by sight.
**Source: British Crime Survey, Home Office**

## Table **9.11**

### Anti-social behaviour indicators[1]

England & Wales
Percentages

| | 1992 | 1996 | 2000 | 2001/02 | 2002/03 | 2003/04 | 2004/05 |
|---|---|---|---|---|---|---|---|
| High level of perceived anti-social behaviour[2,3] | - | - | - | 19 | 21 | 16 | 17 |
| Abandoned or burnt-out cars[3] | - | - | 14 | 20 | 25 | 15 | 12 |
| Noisy neighbours or loud parties | 8 | 8 | 9 | 10 | 10 | 9 | 9 |
| People being drunk or rowdy in public places | - | - | - | 2 | 23 | 19 | 22 |
| People using or dealing drugs | 14 | 21 | 33 | 31 | 32 | 25 | 26 |
| Teenagers hanging around on the streets | 20 | 24 | 32 | 32 | 33 | 27 | 31 |
| Rubbish or litter lying around | 30 | 26 | 30 | 32 | 33 | 29 | 30 |
| Vandalism, graffiti and other deliberate damage to property | 26 | 24 | 32 | 34 | 35 | 28 | 28 |
| Total (=100%)[4] (thousands) | 10.1 | 8.0 | 9.7 | 32.8 | 36.5 | 37.9 | 45.1 |

1 People saying anti-social behaviour is a 'very/fairly big problem' in their area.
2 This measure is derived from responses to the seven individual anti-social behaviour strands reported in the table.
3 Question only asked of one-quarter of the sample in 2001/02 and 2002/03.
4 Percentages do not add up to 100 per cent as respondents could give more than one answer.

**Source: British Crime Survey, Home Office**

The number of incidents of violence by strangers and muggings have remained relatively constant since 1995. However there have been large and statistically significant falls in the number of incidents of acquaintance and domestic violence. This has led to a decrease in the proportion of violent crime incidents committed by someone known to the victim.

The *Crime and Disorder Act (1998)* defined anti-social behaviour as 'acting in a manner that caused or was likely to cause harassment, alarm or distress to one or more persons not of the same household (as the defendant)'. In the 2004/05 BCS, almost a third of people believed teenagers and young people hanging around on the streets (31 per cent) and rubbish or litter (30 per cent) were anti-social behaviour problems in their area (Table 9.11). A further quarter perceived vandalism and graffiti (28 per cent) and drug use or dealing (26 per cent) were a problem in their area. The proportion of people saying each of these behaviours were a very or fairly big problem in their area generally increased for all the behaviour indicators between 1992 and 2002/03. These proportions fell for most indicators in 2003/04. Between 2003/04 and 2004/05 the percentage of people who perceived people being drunk or rowdy and teenagers hanging around to be a problem increased significantly. The proportion of people who believed drug use or dealing was a problem increased from 14 per cent in 1992 to a peak in 2000 of 33 per cent, and then fell in recent years to 26 per cent in 2004/05. A similar increase was also seen for the proportion who believed teenagers hanging around was a problem reaching a peak in 2002/03 and then falling.

People's perceptions of anti-social behaviour vary by socio-demographic and socio-economic characteristics. The proportion perceiving high levels of anti-social behaviour in 2004/05 decreased with age from 22 per cent of those aged 16 to 24, to 5 per cent of people aged 75 and over. There was no real difference between men and women. People from a non-White background were more likely than those from a White background to perceive high levels of anti-social behaviour. A lower proportion of people in the professional and managerial social grades perceived high levels of anti-social behaviour in comparison with those in the other social classes. A higher proportion of people in households with an income of £10,000 or less perceived high levels of anti-social behaviour compared with people in households with an income of £30,000 or more. There was also a difference by housing tenure; 30 per cent of social renters perceived high levels of anti-social behaviour compared with 13 per cent of owner occupiers and 16 per cent of private renters.

## Offenders

In 2004, 1.8 million offenders were found guilty of, or cautioned for, indictable and summary offences in England and Wales, a rise of 4 per cent on the previous year. Most of the offenders were male (80 per cent), of whom around 11 per cent were aged 17 and under.

According to recorded crime figures based on administrative data collected by the police, the number of young offenders as a proportion of the population rises sharply for males between

# Figure **9.12**

**Offenders[1] as a percentage of the population: by sex and age,[2] 2004**

England & Wales
Percentages

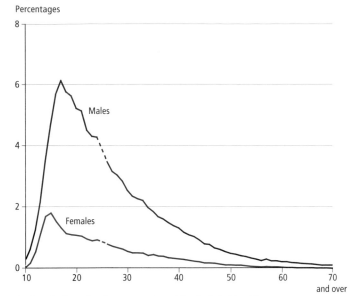

1 People found guilty or cautioned for indictable offences.
2 Age 25 is plotted as the mid-point between ages 24 and 26, as it is used for offenders who did not give an age.

**Source: Home Office**

the ages of 10 and 17. In 2004 in England and Wales, 6 per cent of all 17 year old males were found guilty of indictable offences, by far the highest rate for any age group, and five times the corresponding rate for females (Figure 9.12). As males and females entered their mid-20s, the proportion of offenders started to decline with age. Less than 1 per cent of males over the age of 43 and females over the age of 21 were found guilty of, or cautioned for, an indictable offence. There were negligible proportions of offenders aged 70 and above.

In 2004, 473,000 people were found guilty of, or cautioned for, an indictable offence in England and Wales, of whom four fifths were males. Theft and handling stolen goods was the most common offence committed by both male and female offenders (Figure 9.13). Although 70 per cent of these offences were committed by males, over half of the female offenders were found guilty of, or cautioned for, theft-related offences compared with almost a third of male offenders. Between 10 and 20 per cent of offenders found guilty of, or cautioned for, all other indictable offences were female, apart from burglary (6 per cent) and sexual offences (2 per cent). Offending patterns of behaviour are often established at an early age. Young people aged 16 to 24 years had the highest offending rates for both males and females in 2003. For men aged 25 to 34, the offending rate for theft was higher than for

# Figure **9.13**

**Offenders found guilty of, or cautioned for, indictable offences:[1] by sex and type of offence, 2004**

England & Wales
Thousands

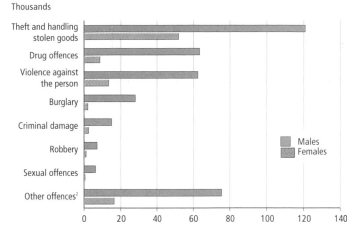

1 See Appendix, Part 9: Types of offences in England and Wales.
2 Includes fraud and forgery and indictable motoring offences.

**Source: Home Office**

males aged 10 to 15. In contrast females aged 10 to 15 had a higher offending rate than females aged 25 to 34.

A relatively small number of offenders are responsible for a disproportionately high number of offences. Eight in ten men and over seven in ten women previously convicted for theft and handling stolen goods were reconvicted within two years of discharge from prison in England and Wales in 2001 (Figure 9.14 overleaf). Over the same period, a similar proportion of men convicted for burglary were also reconvicted within two years. Around half of men were reconvicted for robbery and violence, and one in seven men were reconvicted for sexual offences. In Northern Ireland, 68 per cent of adults convicted of theft and 64 per cent convicted of burglary were reconvicted within two years of their discharge from custody into the community in 2001 (figures exclude those who received a non-custodial sentence in 2001). One in five people aged 17 and over previously convicted of sexual offences in Northern Ireland were reconvicted within two years of discharge.

In England and Wales reconviction rates for those with a first conviction were much lower than for those with previous convictions. The reconviction rate for people released from prison in 2001 was 17 per cent for first time offenders, 38 per cent for those with one or two previous convictions and 80 per cent for those with 11 or more convictions. For offenders released from prison or starting a community sentence in the first quarter of 2001 the reconviction rate was 19 per cent for offenders with no previous convictions, 39 per cent for those

## Figure **9.14**

### Prisoners reconvicted[1] within two years of discharge in 2001: by original offence

**England & Wales**
Percentages

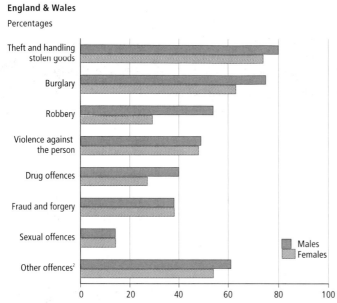

1 Reconvicted of a standard list offence. Standard list offences are all indictable offences and some of the more serious summary offences.
2 Includes criminal damage, motoring offences and other indictable and summary offences.

**Source: Home Office**

## Table **9.15**

### Recorded crimes detected by the police: by type of offence,[1] 2004/05[2]

Percentages

| | England & Wales | Scotland | Northern Ireland |
|---|---|---|---|
| Drug offences | 95 | 97 | 73 |
| Violence against the person | 53 | 77 | 53 |
| Sexual offences | 34 | 72 | 46 |
| Rape (including attempts) | 29 | 69 | 45 |
| Fraud and forgery | 26 | 80 | 36 |
| Robbery | 20 | 39 | 17 |
| Theft and handling stolen goods | 16 | 34 | 17 |
| Theft of vehicles | 15 | 37 | 17 |
| Theft from vehicles | 8 | 17 | 4 |
| Criminal damage | 14 | 21 | 14 |
| Burglary | 13 | 25 | 15 |
| Other offences[3] | 70 | 95 | 55 |
| All recorded crime | 26 | 45 | 28 |

1 See Appendix, Part 9: Types of offences in England and Wales, and in Northern Ireland, and Offences and crimes.
2 Some offences cleared up/detected may have been initially recorded in an earlier year.
3 The Northern Ireland figure includes 'offences against the state'.

**Source: Home Office; Scottish Executive; Police Service of Northern Ireland**

with 1 or 2 previous convictions and 78 per cent for those with 11 or more previous convictions.

The 2003 Crime and Justice Survey showed that around four in ten people aged 10 to 65 in England and Wales had committed at least one core offence (see Appendix, Part 9: Crime and Justice Survey core offences) at some time, with one in ten doing so in the year before the Survey. Young people aged between 10 and 25 commited two thirds of all core offences and four fifths of serious offences.

## Police and courts action

Under the National Crime Recording Standard counting rules, a crime is defined as 'detected' if a suspect has been identified and interviewed, and there is sufficient evidence to bring a charge. There does not have to be a prosecution; for example, the offender may accept a caution or ask for the crime to be taken into consideration by the court, or the victim may not wish to give evidence.

There were just over 1.4 million detected crimes in England and Wales in 2004/05, an increase of 2 per cent on the previous year. Detections are counted on the basis of crimes, rather than offenders (for example, one robbery is one detection, even if it involved ten offenders). Care must therefore be taken when

comparing detection rates with conviction data. The average number of detections per officer was just over ten detections per officer per year, and this has remained stable from 2003/04 to 2004/05. Not all officers are involved in the investigation of crime.

In England and Wales the overall detection rate increased from 23 per cent in 2003/04 to 26 per cent in 2004/05. This increase was observed for most offences. The main exception was for sexual offences where the rate fell by 5 percentage points. Detection rates vary according to the type of offence. Drug offences were the most likely type of crime to be detected in 2004/05, and theft from vehicles was the least likely (Table 9.15). The detection rate in Northern Ireland in 2004/05 was 28 per cent. There could be a time lapse between an offence being committed and the police clearing it up.

In Scotland detection rates are known as clear-up rates. The clear-up rates have been increasing steadily over the past quarter of a century, from 30 per cent in 1982 to 45 per cent in 2004/05. Detection rates followed a similar pattern to England and Wales, with drug offences the most likely to be detected. Fraud and forgery also had a high detection rate with eight out of ten offences being detected. Even with the introduction of

## Table **9.16**

### Ethnic[1] composition of stop and searches, 2003/04

England & Wales                                                                                                                      Percentages

|  | Drugs | Stolen property | Going equipped | Offensive weapons | Firearms | Other reasons | Total |
|---|---|---|---|---|---|---|---|
| White | 69 | 79 | 83 | 67 | 65 | 84 | 74 |
| Black | 18 | 13 | 10 | 19 | 23 | 5 | 15 |
| Asian | 10 | 5 | 4 | 9 | 8 | 4 | 7 |
| Other | 1 | 1 | 1 | 2 | 2 | 2 | 1 |
| Not recorded | 2 | 2 | 2 | 2 | 3 | 5 | 2 |
| Total (=100%) (thousands) | 322.8 | 214.4 | 87.8 | 59.3 | 10.6 | 43.1 | 738.0 |

1 Ethnicity of the person stopped and searched as perceived by the police officer concerned.

**Source: Home Office**

the new crime recording standards in Scotland and England and Wales (see Appendix, Part 9: National Crime Recording Standard), care should be taken when making comparisons between detection rates across countries, because of the different legal systems and crime recording practices.

The *Police and Criminal Evidence Act*, which was implemented in January 1986, gave the police certain powers covering stop and searches of people or vehicles, road checks, detention of people and intimate searches of people. Stop and searches in England and Wales rose from 118,000 in 1987 to a peak of nearly 1.1 million in 1998/99. In 2003/04 stop and searches of people and vehicles had fallen to 734,000. Looking for stolen property was the most common reason for a stop and search in the 1990s. In 2002/03 and 2003/04 looking for drugs became the most common reason.

Three quarters of people who were stopped and searched in 2003/04 in England and Wales were White (Table 9.16). The White population made up 91 per cent of the population in the 2001 Census. In 2003/04 the main reason for searching all ethnic groups was drugs, followed by stolen property. Previously White people were more likely to have been searched for stolen property than for drugs. Almost a quarter of people searched for firearms and just under a fifth of people searched for offensive weapons were Black. Overall Black people accounted for 15 per cent of those stopped and searched. In 2001, 2 per cent of the population were Black.

Anti-social behaviour orders (ASBOs) were introduced in England and Wales under the *Crime and Disorder Act 1998* and have been available since April 1999. They are civil orders that impose restrictions on the behaviour of individuals who have behaved in

an anti-social way, to protect communities from often longstanding and highly intimidating activity. They can be made against anyone aged ten and over. The number of ASBOs issued in England and Wales has increased from 135 from the period June to December 2000 to 2,652 in 2004, most notably from 2002 onwards (Figure 9.17). This increase was in line with the introduction of the *Anti-Social Behaviour Act* that came into effect in 2003. As well as strengthening the ASBO and banning spray paint sales to people under the age of 16, the Act gives local councils the power to order the removal of graffiti from private property. It also specifically addresses truancy, false reports of emergency, fireworks, public drunkenness and gang activity.

## Figure **9.17**

### Anti-social behaviour orders issued by all courts

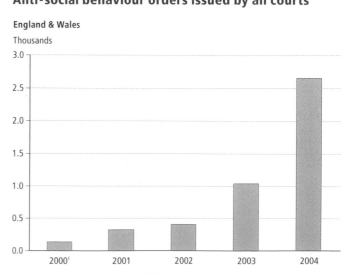

England & Wales
Thousands

1 Data available from 1 June 2000 only. For the period 1 April 1999 to 31 May 2000 data were collected by police force area on aggregate numbers only.

**Source: Home Office**

In England and Wales a formal caution may be given by a senior police officer when an offender has admitted his or her guilt, there is sufficient evidence for a conviction, and it is not in the public interest to institute criminal proceedings. Cautions are more severe than a reprimand and details remain on an individual's record. There must be sufficient evidence gathered by the police for the likelihood of a successful prosecution for a caution to be given. In 2004, 156,300 cautions for indictable offences in England and Wales were given, an increase of 5,600 (4 per cent) on 2003. The number of cautions has been rising since 2001 following a fall in the 1990s (Table 9.18). The offence category receiving the highest number of cautions was theft and handling stolen goods. For the first time since the 1980s a higher number of cautions were received for violence against the person than for drug offences. There was a rise of 88 per cent for those cautioned for violence between 2001 and 2004, from 19,500 to 36,600. In comparison, the number of offenders cautioned for drug offences peaked in 2003 before dropping by 29 per cent to 32,600 in 2004.

The Crown Prosecution Service (CPS) is the government agency that handles the bulk of prosecutions (charging individuals with committing a crime) in England and Wales. Most cases in the Crown Court are prosecuted by the CPS. The CPS alongside other authorities, including HM Revenue and Customs, the Driver and Vehicle Licensing Agency, and the Environment Agency, also prosecute in magistrates' courts. The Crown Court deals with more serious criminal offences that will be tried by judge and jury, appeals from the magistrates' courts,

and convictions in the magistrates' courts that are referred to the Crown Court for sentencing. Imprisonment and fines imposed by the Crown Court are more severe than in the magistrates' court. Magistrates' courts deal with criminal and some civil cases and usually only deal with cases that arise in their own area.

Almost 1.5 million defendant cases were prosecuted in magistrates' courts by the CPS in 2004 (excluding those committed for trial in the Crown Court). The majority of cases at magistrates' courts resulted in a conviction (74 per cent), while 20 per cent of cases were terminated early without trial and 2 per cent resulted in dismissal. The CPS completed 78,000 defendant cases in the Crown Court in 2004, three quarters of which resulted in a conviction.

When an offender has been charged, or summonsed, and then found guilty, the court will impose a sentence. Sentences in England, Wales and Northern Ireland can include immediate custody, a community sentence, a fine or, if the court considers that no punishment is necessary, a discharge. In 2004, 316,900 people were sentenced for indictable offences in England and Wales (Table 9.19). The form of sentence varied according to the type of offence committed. In 2004 a community sentence was the most common type of sentence; almost half of those sentenced for burglary, violence against the person or criminal damage were given a community sentence. Those sentenced for drug offences were the most likely to be fined, with 36 per cent receiving this form of sentence.

## Table **9.18**

### Offenders cautioned for indictable offences:[1] by type of offence

England & Wales

Thousands

|  | 1981 | 1991 | 2001 | 2003 | 2004 |
|---|---|---|---|---|---|
| Theft and handling stolen goods | 79.2 | 108.5 | 63.5 | 54.5 | 61.9 |
| Drug offences | 0.3 | 21.2 | 39.4 | 45.7 | 32.6 |
| Violence against the person | 5.6 | 19.4 | 19.5 | 28.8 | 36.6 |
| Burglary[2] | 11.2 | 13.3 | 6.4 | 5.6 | 5.6 |
| Fraud and forgery | 1.4 | 5.6 | 5.8 | 5.5 | 6.0 |
| Criminal damage | 2.1 | 3.8 | 3.4 | 3.7 | 5.5 |
| Sexual offences | 2.8 | 3.3 | 1.2 | 1.4 | 1.6 |
| Robbery | 0.1 | 0.6 | 0.5 | 0.4 | 0.5 |
| Other offences | 1.3 | 4.1 | 4.2 | 5.3 | 6.0 |
| All offenders cautioned | 103.9 | 179.9 | 143.9 | 150.7 | 156.3 |

1 Excludes motoring offences.
2 See Appendix, Part 9: Offenders cautioned for burglary.

**Source: Home Office**

## Table **9.19**

### Offenders sentenced for indictable offences: by type of offence[1] and sentence,[2] 2004

England & Wales

Percentages

| | Discharge | Fine | Community sentence | Fully suspended sentence | Immediate custody | Other | All sentenced (=100%) (thousands) |
|---|---|---|---|---|---|---|---|
| Theft and handling stolen goods | 21 | 17 | 38 | - | 21 | 3 | 110.2 |
| Drug offences | 18 | 36 | 23 | 1 | 20 | 2 | 39.1 |
| Violence against the person | 10 | 9 | 46 | 1 | 31 | 3 | 39.3 |
| Burglary | 4 | 2 | 48 | - | 45 | 1 | 24.1 |
| Fraud and forgery | 17 | 15 | 41 | 2 | 23 | 2 | 18.0 |
| Criminal damage | 20 | 14 | 48 | - | 11 | 7 | 11.6 |
| Motoring | 4 | 33 | 33 | 1 | 28 | 1 | 8.2 |
| Robbery | 1 | - | 31 | - | 67 | 1 | 7.5 |
| Sexual offences | 5 | 4 | 29 | 1 | 59 | 2 | 4.8 |
| Other offences | 9 | 39 | 21 | 1 | 19 | 11 | 54.0 |
| All indictable offences | 15 | 23 | 33 | 1 | 24 | 4 | 316.9 |

1  See Appendix, Part 9: Types of offences in England and Wales.
2  See Appendix, Part 9: Sentences and orders.

**Source: Home Office**

The proportion in the BCS who thought that sentencing was too lenient fell from just over a half in 1996 to just under a third in 2002/03 (32 per cent) but increased to 35 per cent in 2004/05. There was relatively little change in the proportion who thought that sentencing by the courts was about right, at around one in five people.

The BCS respondents were also asked about their confidence in the Criminal Justice System (CJS). In 2004/05, 78 per cent were confident that the CJS respects the rights of people accused of committing a crime and treats them fairly (Figure 9.20). Two thirds of people were confident that the CJS treats witnesses well. The least amount of confidence was with how effective the CJS was at dealing with young people accused of crime (72 per cent) and meeting the needs of victims (66 per cent). There was an increase in confidence of those who thought that the CJS was very or fairly effective at reducing crime, from 31 per cent in 2002/03 to 39 per cent in 2004/05.

Confidence in the CJS varies by ethnic group. People in the White group were more likely than those in the non-White groups to be confident that the CJS respects the rights of people accused of committing a crime and treats them fairly (White, 78 per cent; Asian, 76 per cent; Mixed, 69 per cent; Black, 67 per cent). In contrast, those in ethnic minority groups were more confident than the White group that the CJS was effective in bringing people to justice, was effective in reducing crime,

deals with cases promptly and efficiently, meets the needs of victims and was effective in dealing with young people. Only 26 per cent of the White group were confident in the way the CJS dealt with young people accused of crime, compared with around 40 per cent of the Asian, Black or Mixed ethnic groups.

## Figure **9.20**

### Confidence in the criminal justice system, 2004/05

England & Wales

Percentages

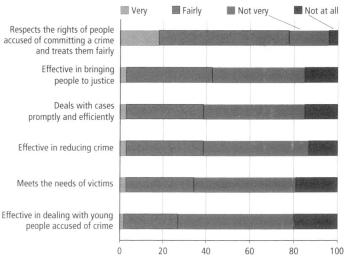

**Source: British Crime Survey, Home Office**

## Figure **10.12**

### Homeless households[1] in temporary accommodation[2]

England
Thousands

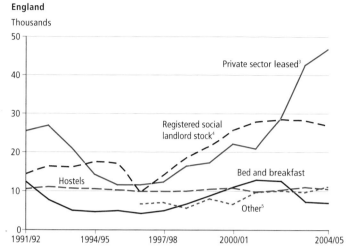

1 Excludes 'homeless at home' cases. See Appendix, Part 10: Homeless at home.
2 Data are as at 31 December, and include households awaiting the outcome of homeless enquiries.
3 Prior to March 1996, includes those accommodated directly with a private sector landlord.
4 Prior to March 1996, includes all 'Other' types of accommodation.
5 From March 1996, includes mobile homes (such as caravans and portacabins) or being accommodated directly with a private sector landlord.

**Source: Office of the Deputy Prime Minister**

## Table **10.13**

### Under-occupation[1] and overcrowding:[2] by selected types of household, 2004/05

Great Britain
Percentages

| | Under-occupied | Overcrowded |
|---|---|---|
| **One person** | | |
| Under pensionable age | 32 | . |
| Over pensionable age | 39 | . |
| **One family households[3]** | | |
| Couple | | |
| No children | 62 | - |
| Dependent children | 19 | 6 |
| Non-dependent children only | 20 | 4 |
| Lone parent | | |
| Dependent children | 5 | 8 |
| Non-dependent children only | 14 | 6 |
| **All households[4]** | 35 | 3 |

1 Two or more above bedroom standard. See Appendix, Part 10: Bedroom standard.
2 One or more below bedroom standard. See Appendix, Part 10: Bedroom standard.
3 Other individuals who were not family members may also be included.
4 Also includes two or more unrelated adults and multi-family households.

**Source: General Household Survey, Office for National Statistics**

temporary basis (Figure 10.12). Under the *Homelessness (Suitability of Accommodation) (England) Order 2003*, local authorities can no longer place families with children in B&B accommodation for longer than six weeks. Between March 2003 and March 2005 the total number of homeless households living in B&B hotels fell by 45 per cent to 6,800. Over the same period, the use of self-contained property leased from the private sector increased by 64 per cent, and by March 2005 accounted for almost half of all temporary accommodation.

### Housing condition and satisfaction with area

Overcrowding is an important indicator of housing conditions. This is commonly measured by the bedroom standard, which compares the number of bedrooms actually available to a household against the number required, given the household's size and composition (see Appendix, Part 10: Bedroom standard). Overall, only 3 per cent of households in Great Britain were below the bedroom standard and hence defined as overcrowded in 2004/05, compared with 7 per cent in 1971. Overcrowding was greatest among lone parent with dependent children households with nearly one in ten living in overcrowded housing (Table 10.13). In contrast, under-

occupation was most common for households comprising couples with no children and one-person households above pensionable age. These households include people whose children have grown up and left the home. Overcrowding varies according to the tenure of the household. In 2004/05 it was lowest among owner occupiers at 1 per cent. In contrast, 5 per cent of households renting from the social sector and 4 per cent of private-renter households lived in accommodation below the bedroom standard.

To be considered 'decent' a dwelling must meet the statutory minimum standard for housing: it must be in a reasonable state of repair; have reasonably modern facilities and services; and provide a reasonable degree of thermal comfort.

Between 1996 and 2003 the number of non-decent homes in England fell from 9.1 million to 6.7 million (from 45 per cent to 31 per cent of all dwellings) (Table 10.14). Over this period the proportion of non-decent homes in the social sector fell at a faster rate than in the private sector, halving the gap from 10 percentage points to 5 percentage points. The Government target, set out in the 2003 Sustainable Communities Plan, is to bring all social housing in England up to a decent standard by 2010. The Plan also includes action to improve conditions for

## Table **10.14**

### Non-decent homes:[1] by tenure

England                                                          Percentages

|                              | 1996 | 2001 | 2003 |
|------------------------------|------|------|------|
| **Private sector**           |      |      |      |
| Owner-occupied               | 40   | 29   | 28   |
| Privately rented             | 62   | 51   | 48   |
| All private sector           | 43   | 32   | 30   |
| **Social sector**            |      |      |      |
| Local authority              | 54   | 42   | 40   |
| Registered social landlords  | 48   | 33   | 29   |
| All rented from social sector| 53   | 39   | 35   |
| **All tenures**              | 45   | 33   | 31   |

1  See Appendix, Part 10: Decent home standard.

*Source: English House Condition Survey, Office of the Deputy Prime Minister*

## Table **10.15**

### Dwellings that fail the decent home standard:[1] by tenure and reason for failure, 2003

England                                                          Percentages

|                                | Reason for failure | | |
|                                | Thermal comfort only | Other[2] | Decent |
|--------------------------------|----------------------|----------|--------|
| **Owner-occupied**             |      |      |      |
| Owned outright                 | 19   | 11   | 71   |
| Owned with mortgage            | 15   | 11   | 75   |
| All owner-occupied             | 16   | 11   | 73   |
| **Rented from social sector**  |      |      |      |
| Local authority                | 22   | 16   | 61   |
| Registered social landlords    | 20   | 8    | 72   |
| All rented from social sector  | 21   | 13   | 66   |
| **Privately rented**           | 23   | 23   | 54   |
| **All tenures**                | 18   | 12   | 70   |

1  See Appendix, Part 10: Decent home standard.
2  Includes disrepair, fitness and modernisation.

*Source: English House Condition Survey, Office of the Deputy Prime Minister*

vulnerable people in private housing. Those living in vulnerable households (defined as those in receipt of the main means tested and disability-related benefits) are more likely than others to live in non-decent homes. In 2003, 36 per cent of vulnerable households in England were living in non-decent homes. However this was considerably lower than in 1996 when the proportion was 55 per cent. The 18 percentage point gap in 1996 between the proportion of vulnerable households and other households living in non-decent homes in the private sector halved to 9 percentage points in 2003.

The most common reason for dwellings to fail the decent home standard in 2003 was that they did not provide a reasonable level of thermal comfort. This affected 5.25 million dwellings in England. Between 2001 and 2003 the overall reduction in the number of non-decent homes mainly resulted from improvements to the level of thermal comfort, particularly in the social rented sector where there was a 20 per cent fall in the number of homes failing on this criterion. In 2003 compared with dwellings in other tenure groups, privately rented homes were the most likely to fail to meet the decent home standard either for thermal comfort or for other reasons including disrepair, fitness and modernisation. (Table 10.15).

Owner-occupied homes were the most likely to meet the decent home standard, with those that were owned with a mortgage being more likely to meet it than those that were owned outright. This difference in part reflects the likelihood that those people who are buying their home with a mortgage are more likely than those who own outright to be working

rather than retired and therefore better able financially to maintain their home. In 2003 around 75 per cent of owner-occupied homes where the oldest person in the household was aged 25 to 59 were decent, compared with just under 70 per cent where the oldest person was aged 75 to 84 and less than 60 per cent where they were aged 85 and over. There was also a relatively low proportion of decent owner-occupied homes among younger households where the reference person was aged 16 to 24, at just over 60 per cent.

The concentration of non-decent homes varies by the level of neighbourhood deprivation and tenure (see Appendix, Part 10: Index of Multiple Deprivation, which uses Super Output Area geographies). In 2003 social sector non-decent housing stock in England was highly concentrated in the more deprived areas with 30 per cent of all non-decent stock located in the 10 per cent most deprived areas identified by the Index. The proportion of social sector non-decent housing was very similar in each of the six most deprived areas ranging between 33 per cent and 38 per cent. Private sector (defined as those owned and privately rented) non-decent stock was found across a wider range of locations, including more affluent suburban areas, with 46 per cent being located in the 50 per cent least deprived areas. However in the 10 per cent most deprived areas in England, 44 per cent of private sector homes were non-decent,

## Figure **10.16**

### Concentration of non-decent homes: by area deprivation[1] and housing sector, 2003

England

Percentages

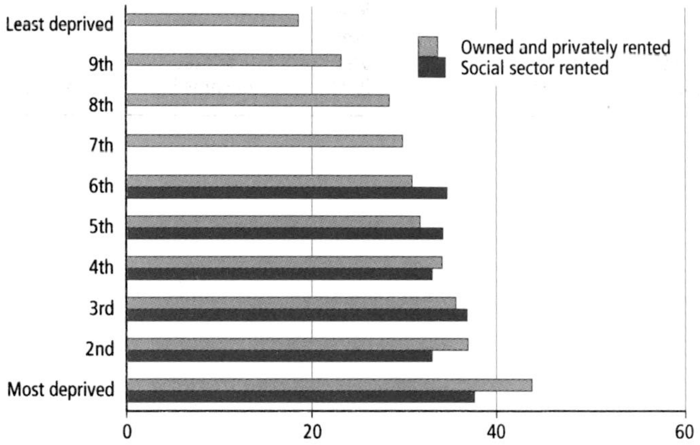

1  See Appendix, Part 10: Index of Multiple Deprivation.

**Source: English House Condition Survey, Office of the Deputy Prime Minister**

over twice the proportion of those in the 10 per cent least deprived neighbourhoods (Figure 10.16).

As well as the standard of housing, the quality of the immediate environment may also influence how content people are with their homes. A poor quality environment includes areas with significant problems related to the upkeep, management and misuse of the surrounding public and private buildings or space; significant problems related to road traffic and other forms of transport and problems associated with abandonment or intrusive use of property for non-residential purposes. In 2003, 3.3 million (16 per cent) households in England were assessed as living in homes with a poor quality environment. Areas with poor quality environments are particularly concentrated in urban areas and associated with high density of population and land use.

The environmental problems most frequently reported were fear of burglary, litter and rubbish in the street, problems with dogs or dog mess, the general level of crime and heavy traffic (Table 10.17). Residents living in neighbourhoods with poor quality environments were more likely to report these problems than those living in neighbourhoods whose environment was 'not poor'. Regardless of the quality of the environment, the fear of being burgled ranked as a major concern for all residents. Among those living in environments classified as not poor, problems with dogs and dog mess ranked third, higher than among residents of poor quality environments where it was ranked sixth.

## Table **10.17**

### Residents' views of problems in their neighbourhood: by whether living in a poor quality environment,[1] 2003

England

Percentages

| | Quality of environment | | All households |
| --- | --- | --- | --- |
| | Not poor | Poor | |
| Fear of being burgled | 41 | 50 | 43 |
| Litter and rubbish in the streets | 38 | 55 | 41 |
| Problems with dogs/dog mess | 35 | 39 | 36 |
| General level of crime | 33 | 44 | 35 |
| Heavy traffic | 32 | 46 | 34 |
| Vandalism and hooliganism | 28 | 40 | 30 |
| | | | |
| Troublesome teenagers/children | 25 | 34 | 26 |
| Pollution | 19 | 32 | 21 |
| Presence of drug dealers/users | 18 | 27 | 20 |
| Poor state of open space/gardens | 17 | 29 | 19 |
| Graffiti | 15 | 24 | 16 |
| Problems with neighbours | 12 | 17 | 13 |
| | | | |
| All households | 84 | 16 | 100 |

1  See Appendix, Part 10: Poor quality environments.

**Source: English House Condition Survey, Office of the Deputy Prime Minister**

## Housing mobility

In 2004/05 around a tenth of all households in Great Britain had been resident in their homes for less than 12 months. The most common types of move of such households in England was from one owned property to another or from one privately rented property to another (Table 10.18). Overall movement within each of the three most common types of tenure was more likely than movement between them; 55 per cent of households that owned their home outright had previously done so, while 1 per cent of such households had previously rented from a registered social landlord (RSL). Almost two fifths of all those moving had previously been in privately-rented accommodation, showing how important this sector is in facilitating mobility within the housing market. Among newly formed households, half moved into the private-rented sector, while just over a quarter became owner occupiers and just over a fifth social sector renters.

People have different reasons for moving. In 2004/05 the most common reasons given for moving in England in the year before interview were for personal reasons (21 per cent), of which 7 per cent of all moves were because of divorce or

## Table **10.18**

**Households resident under one year: current tenure by previous tenure, 2004/05**

England                                                                                                                          Percentages

|  | | | Previous tenure | | | | |
| --- | --- | --- | --- | --- | --- | --- | --- |
|  | New household | Owned outright | Owned with a mortgage | Rented from local authority | Rented from registered social landlord | Rented privately[1] | All tenures |
| **Current tenure** | | | | | | | |
| **Owner-occupied** | | | | | | | |
| Owned outright | 4 | 55 | 30 | 2 | 1 | 8 | 100 |
| Owned with a mortgage | 15 | 5 | 48 | 1 | 1 | 29 | 100 |
| **Rented from social sector** | | | | | | | |
| Local authority | 22 | 2 | 4 | 48 | 7 | 17 | 100 |
| Registered social landlord | 24 | 6 | 5 | 18 | 28 | 19 | 100 |
| **Rented privately** | | | | | | | |
| Unfurnished | 18 | 5 | 14 | 3 | 3 | 57 | 100 |
| Furnished | 28 | 3 | 5 | 2 | 2 | 60 | 100 |
| **All tenures** | 18 | 8 | 23 | 8 | 4 | 38 | 100 |

1  The split between privately rented unfurnished and privately rented furnished is not available for previous tenure.

*Source: Survey of English Housing, Office of the Deputy Prime Minister*

separation and 5 per cent marriage or cohabitation; the desire for different accommodation (20 per cent); to live independently (11 per cent); and to move to a better area (11 per cent) (Figure 10.19). Reasons for moving varied by tenure. Among owner occupiers, 24 per cent who owned outright had moved because they wanted a smaller or cheaper house or flat, reflecting the high proportion of this group who had retired. However among those buying with a mortgage, 21 per cent had moved because they wanted a larger or better home. A far higher proportion of private renters than any other tenure group gave job-related reasons for their move (17 per cent).

The mobility of owner occupiers is also linked to the housing market. Over the past 40 years the economy and the housing market have mirrored one another closely, with booms and slumps in one also occurring in the other. The number of residential property transactions that took place in England and Wales rose during the 1980s, mainly as a result of existing owner occupiers moving home (Figure 10.20 overleaf). Market activity by first-time buyers and public sector tenants (right to buy purchases) (see Figure 10.7) were also factors, but contributed to a lesser extent. Changes to the credit market in the 1980s may also have contributed to the 1980s property

## Figure **10.19**

**Main reasons for moving, 2004/05**

England

Percentages

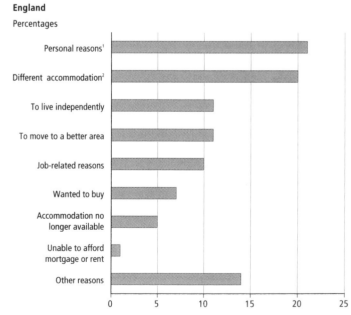

1  Includes divorce or separation, marriage or cohabitation, and other personal reasons.
2  Includes those wanting a larger or better house or flat, and those wanting a smaller or cheaper house or flat.

*Source: Survey of English Housing, Office of the Deputy Prime Minister*

## Figure **11.11**

### Discharges from the nuclear industry

United Kingdom
Indices (1985=100)

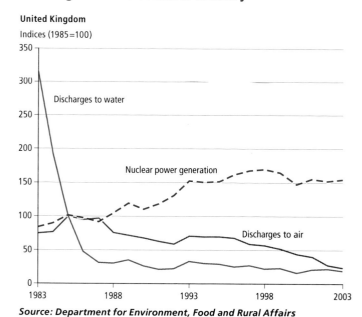

Source: Department for Environment, Food and Rural Affairs

## Figure **11.12**

### Emissions of selected air pollutants[1]

United Kingdom
Million tonnes

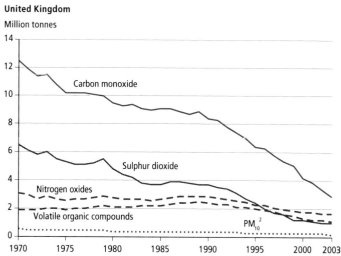

1  See Appendix, Part 11: Air pollutants.
2  Particulate matter that is less than 10 microns in diameter.

Source: Department for Environment, Food and Rural Affairs; National Environmental Technology Centre

detectors. The annual average dose is estimated to be around 0.4 millisieverts (mSv). In the United Kingdom, individual doses from artificial sources (excluding medical procedures such as radiography) must be below 1 mSv per year, by law.

Fallout accounts for a very small proportion (0.2 per cent) of total radioactive exposure in the United Kingdom. Before 1985 the main source of exposure to fallout was from nuclear weapons testing that took place between the late 1940s and early 1960s. The average annual dose from this source reached a peak of 0.14 mSv in the early 1960s. Following the implementation of the Partial Nuclear Test Ban Treaty of 1963, average annual dose fell steadily to 0.006 mSv in 1985. The Chernobyl reactor incident in 1986 caused a near fivefold increase in the average annual dose from fallout in that year, but by 1997 this had gone down to pre-Chernobyl levels.

Emissions of the major air pollutants in the United Kingdom have generally been falling since the 1970s, and the rate of decline has accelerated since 1989 (Figure 11.12). Carbon monoxide (CO) reduces the capacity of the blood to carry and deliver oxygen. Emissions of carbon monoxide fell by 33 per cent between 1970 and 1990, followed by a 67 per cent reduction between 1990 and 2003, mainly as a result of the introduction of catalytic converters in petrol-driven cars.

Sulphur dioxide ($SO_2$) is an acid gas that can affect both human health and vegetation. It affects the lining of the nose, throat and lungs, particularly among those with asthma and chronic lung disease. Sulphur dioxide emissions fell by 43 per cent between 1970 and 1990, and then by 74 per cent between 1990 and 2003, largely as a result of a reduction in coal use by

power stations and the introduction of the desulphurisation of flue gas at two power stations. However, the rate of decline slowed after 1999. Nitrogen oxides (NOx) are also acid gases and can have similar effects to sulphur dioxide. Emissions of nitrogen oxide pollutants fell by 44 per cent between 1990 and 2003.

Particulate matter that is less than 10 microns in diameter, known as $PM_{10}$, is generated primarily by combustion processes, as well as from processes such as stone abrasion during construction, mining and quarrying. Particulate matter can be responsible for causing premature deaths among those with pre-existing heart and lung conditions. Emissions fell by 51 per cent between 1990 and 2003.

Fossil fuel combustion is the main source of air pollution in the United Kingdom, with road transport and power stations the most important contributors. Emissions of other pollutants are more evenly spread among different sources, although road transport and electricity generation are, again, important contributors. In 2003, road transport accounted for 49 per cent of carbon monoxide emissions, and 40 per cent of nitrogen oxide emissions (Table 11.13). Although the level of road traffic has continued to grow over the last decade (see Figure 12.1), changes in vehicle technology have reduced the impact of emissions from this sector. In 1990 road transport accounted for 66 per cent of carbon monoxide emissions and for 47 per cent of nitrogen oxide emissions. Power stations produced 69 per cent of sulphur dioxide and 24 per cent of nitrogen oxide emissions in 2003, compared with 74 per cent and 27 per cent respectively in 1990.

## Table **11.13**

### Air pollutants:[1] by source, 2003

**United Kingdom**

Percentages

| | Carbon monoxide | Nitrogen oxides | Volatile organic compounds | Sulphur dioxide | $PM_{10}$[2] |
|---|---|---|---|---|---|
| Road transport | 49 | 40 | 15 | - | 27 |
| Power stations | 3 | 24 | 1 | 69 | 7 |
| Manufacturing and industry[3] | 28 | 18 | 16 | 16 | 26 |
| Solvent use | - | - | 35 | - | 4 |
| Domestic | 15 | 7 | 4 | 3 | 14 |
| Extraction and distribution of fossil fuels | 1 | - | 28 | 1 | 1 |
| Refineries | - | 2 | - | 7 | 1 |
| Commercial and institutional | - | 2 | - | 1 | 1 |
| Other | 4 | 7 | 2 | 3 | 18 |
| All sources (=100%) (million tonnes) | 2.8 | 1.6 | 1.4 | 1.0 | 0.2 |

1 See Appendix, Part 11: Air pollutants.
2 Particulate matter that is less than 10 microns in diameter.
3 Includes industrial processes and other energy industry.
**Source: National Environmental Technology Centre**

## Figure **11.14**

### Days when air pollution[1] is moderate or higher[2]

**United Kingdom**

Average number of days per site

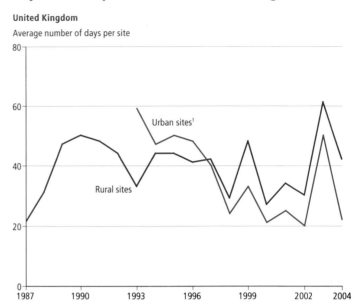

1 Any one of five pollutants: carbon monoxide, nitrogen dioxide, ozone, sulphur dioxide and particulate matter less than 10 microns in diameter.
2 Assessed against the Air Pollution Information Service bandings.
3 Data not available before 1993.

**Source: Department for Environment, Food and Rural Affairs; National Environmental Technology Centre**

Some pollutants, particularly sulphur dioxide, nitrogen oxides and ammonia ($NH_3$), can cause harm to the environment through acid deposition. This deposition consists of both wet processes (through polluted rainfall – 'acid rain') and dry processes (by removal of gases and particles from the atmosphere at the land surface) and can occur hundreds of kilometres away from the source of emissions. The percentage of areas of sensitive habitats where critical loads (the levels at which significant harm is caused) were exceeded in the United Kingdom fell between 1996 and 2002, from 73 per cent to 55 per cent. The largest reduction, from 68 per cent in 1996 to 43 per cent in 2002, was in Scotland.

One result of the reduction in emissions of air pollutants has been a fall in the average number of days when levels of any one of a basket of five pollutants (carbon monoxide, nitrogen dioxide, ozone, particulate matter and sulphur dioxide) were 'moderate or higher', according to the Air Pollution Information Service bandings (Figure 11.14). These five pollutants are recognised as the most important for causing short term health problems. In 1993 air pollution monitoring sites in urban areas recorded an average of 59 days per site when air pollution was moderate or higher, but by 2004 this figure had fallen to 22 days, largely because of a reduction in particles and sulphur dioxide.

There is no clear trend in pollution at rural sites and it is much more variable, largely due to fluctuations in levels of ozone, the main cause of pollution in such areas. The production of ozone at ground level is strongly influenced by the weather, as it is created on sunny days. This results in days of pollution in rural areas being concentrated in the warmer months, whereas those in urban areas are spread more evenly throughout the year. The impact of warm weather can been seen in Figure 11.14, when the hot summers of 1999 and 2003 resulted in a sharp increase in the numbers of days with average or higher pollution in both rural and urban areas.

## Waste management

The United Kingdom disposed of 74 per cent of its municipal waste (mainly household waste) by landfill in 2003. This was among the highest rates of landfill disposal of municipal waste in the EU-15, behind Greece, 92 per cent, and Portugal, 75 per cent (Table 11.15 overleaf). Comparisons between countries need to be treated with some care because of differences in definitions. 'Recycling and other' can be considered to be mainly recycling except in Germany where a large proportion of waste is used in the manufacture of fuel for energy use. The Netherlands, Austria, Germany and Belgium had the highest rates of recycling, while Denmark incinerated most of its municipal waste. However the

## Table **11.15**

### Municipal waste management: EU comparison,[1] 2003

Percentages

| | Landfill | Recycled and other | Incineration | Waste generated per head (=100%) (kilograms) |
|---|---|---|---|---|
| Ireland | 69 | 31 | 0 | 732 |
| Denmark | 5 | 41 | 54 | 675 |
| Luxembourg | 23 | 36 | 42 | 658 |
| Germany | 20 | 57 | 23 | 638 |
| Austria | 30 | 59 | 11 | 610 |
| Spain | 59 | 34 | 7 | 609 |
| Netherlands | 3 | 64 | 33 | 599 |
| United Kingdom | 74 | 18 | 8 | 592 |
| France | 38 | 28 | 34 | 561 |
| Italy | 62 | 29 | 9 | 523 |
| Sweden | 14 | 41 | 45 | 471 |
| Portugal | 75 | 4 | 22 | 452 |
| Finland | 63 | 28 | 9 | 450 |
| Belgium | 13 | 52 | 36 | 446 |
| Greece | 92 | 8 | 0 | 428 |

1 EU-15 countries.

*Source: Department for Environment, Food and Rural Affairs*

United Kingdom was ranked in the middle of all EU-15 countries in terms of the amount of waste produced per head. It is estimated that around 577 kilogrammes of municipal waste is produced on average by each person in the EU-15 countries every year.

Eurostat has estimated that a total of around 2 billion tonnes of waste is generated in the EU-15 every year. Almost a third comes from agriculture and forestry and broadly the same amount from construction and demolition. A similar proportion of waste comes from the mining and quarrying and the manufacturing sectors, with municipal waste accounting for only 6 per cent.

According to the Municipal Waste Management Survey, about 29.1 million tonnes of municipal waste were collected in England in 2003/04, a decrease of 1 per cent from the 29.4 million tonnes collected in 2002/03. Household waste accounted for 87 per cent of municipal waste in 2003/04. This represented about 25.4 million tonnes of waste, an average of 23.1 kilograms per household per week. Compared with 2002/03, total household waste decreased by 1.5 per cent.

The amount of household waste collected for recycling in England nearly trebled between 1996/97 and 2003/04 to 4.5 million tonnes (Table 11.16). This represented an average of 4.1 kilograms collected per household per week. It includes materials taken to civic amenity sites and other drop-off points provided by the local authority as well as those collected directly from households.

The Government target is for 25 per cent of household waste to be recycled by 2005/06. In 2003/04, 18 per cent was recycled, exceeding the interim 2003/04 recycling (including composting) target of 17 per cent. Compost, followed by paper and card, make up the largest proportions of recycled material, and accounted for 30 per cent and 28 per cent of recycled materials in 2003/04.

There was wide variation in household recycling rates across England in 2003/04. Each local authority was set individual

## Table **11.16**

### Materials collected from households for recycling[1]

England

Thousand tonnes

| | 1996/97 | 1998/99 | 2000/01 | 2002/03 | 2003/04 |
|---|---|---|---|---|---|
| Compost[2] | 278 | 454 | 798 | 1,189 | 1,360 |
| Paper and card | 554 | 783 | 910 | 1,126 | 1,271 |
| Glass | 308 | 347 | 396 | 470 | 568 |
| Scrap metal/white goods | 198 | 253 | 310 | 419 | 464 |
| Co-mingled and other materials[3] | 281 | 257 | 363 | 536 | 853 |
| Total | 1,619 | 2,094 | 2,777 | 3,740 | 4,516 |

1 Includes data from different types of recycling schemes collecting waste from household sources, including private/voluntary schemes such as kerbside and 'bring' systems.
2 Includes organic materials (kitchen and garden waste) collected for centralised composting. Home composting is not included.
3 Co-mingled materials are separated after collection. Other includes textiles, cans, plastics, oils, batteries and shoes.

*Source: Department for Environment, Food and Rural Affairs*

## Map **11.17**

**Household waste recycling:[1] by waste disposal authority,[2] 2003/04**

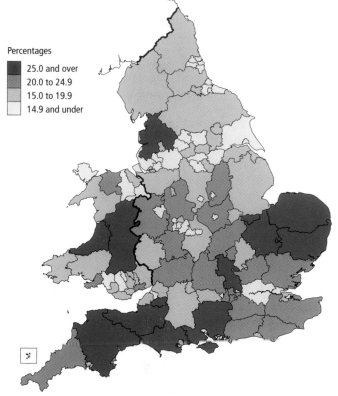

Percentages

- 25.0 and over
- 20.0 to 24.9
- 15.0 to 19.9
- 14.9 and under

1  Includes composting.
2  These boundaries generally match county or unitary authority boundaries, except for metropolitan districts in West Yorkshire, South Yorkshire, Tyne and Wear and West Midlands. Data are collected separately for Wigan metropolitan district and Isles of Scilly local authority district.

**Source: Department for Environment, Food and Rural Affairs; Welsh Assembly Government**

recycling targets as a means of achieving the national household recycling target of 17 per cent. The rates achieved varied from 2.5 to 46 per cent, with the majority of authorities achieving between 10 and 20 per cent. Fifteen per cent of authorities failed to achieve a rate of at least 10 per cent. Most of the authorities with relatively high recycling rates (20 per cent and above) were located in the South East and East of England, and there are pockets of authorities with low recycling rates (less than 10 per cent) in the North East, North West and London (Map 11.17). No waste disposal authority in England had a household waste recycling rate of less than 5 per cent.

Local authorities in the South East and East of England collected the largest amount of household waste for recycling in 2003/04, both collecting 5.4 kilograms per household per week. Local authorities in London collected the least, at 2.6 kilograms per household per week.

There has been an increase in the amount collected for recycling in each type of authority, with a slightly larger increase of 27 per cent between 2002/03 and 2003/04 in metropolitan authorities compared with London and non-metropolitan authorities. However non-metropolitan authorities still recycle more at 5.0 kilograms per household per week. A regional comparison of the composition of materials collected for recycling showed wide variation across the regions. For example, only 17 per cent of materials collected in London, and 20 per cent in the North East, were for composting, compared with 37 per cent in the North West and 35 per cent in the East Midlands.

## Land use

Demand for housing and associated infrastructure constitutes the main pressure for developing land in rural areas and for recycling land already in use in urban areas. In 2000 the Government set a target of 60 per cent of new housing to be built on previously developed land or converted from existing buildings. This target, to be achieved by 2008, aims to minimise the effect of house building on the countryside. In England 70 per cent of new homes (including the conversion of existing buildings, which are estimated to add about 3 percentage points to the national figure) were built on previously developed 'brownfield' land in 2004 (Figure 11.18).

The percentage of new homes built on previously developed land is much higher in urban areas, but there is also considerable regional variation. Over the period 2000–04, London had the

## Figure **11.18**

**New homes built on previously developed land[1]**

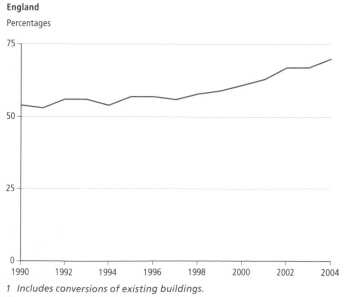

England

Percentages

1  Includes conversions of existing buildings.
**Source: Office of the Deputy Prime Minister**

## Figure **11.19**

### Inland area: by land use, 2004

**United Kingdom**
Percentages

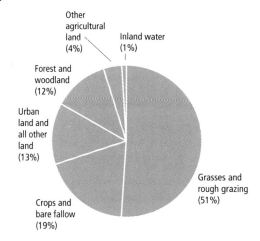

Other agricultural land (4%)

Inland water (1%)

Forest and woodland (12%)

Urban land and all other land (13%)

Grasses and rough grazing (51%)

Crops and bare fallow (19%)

*Source: Department for Environment, Food and Rural Affairs*

highest rate, generally over 90 per cent (excluding conversions), and the East Midlands and the South West had the lowest rates, both at around 50 per cent (see also Figure 10.4).

While 70 per cent of new homes were built on previously developed land, the proportion of previously developed land used for new housing was lower (58 per cent). This is largely because of the higher density of new dwellings which are mostly in urban areas (on average, 29 dwellings per hectare), and the lower density of building on land not previously developed (23 dwellings per hectare).

Land use is defined as the main activity taking place on an area of land. Over 70 per cent of the total UK land area is under agricultural uses (Figure 11.19), and so much of what many people consider 'natural' landscape is in fact the result of many centuries of human intervention. The total area of agricultural land fell by 1 per cent between 1998 and 2004. The area under crops fell by 8 per cent in the same period, mainly as a result of EC Set Aside Schemes – the amount of set aside land rose by 80 per cent between 1998 and 2004. Rough grazing land decreased by 5 per cent and grassland increased by 3 per cent, while urban and other land use increased by 10 per cent.

Between 1998 and 2004 there was a drop in the area covered by most crop types, in line with a fall in the overall area under crop production. However the area used for growing cereals other than wheat and barley has increased by 18 per cent over this period.

Over the past ten years, concerns about the possible impact that the use of pesticides, BSE in cattle, and the development of genetically modified (GM) crops may have on people's health

and the environment have led to an increased interest in organic farming. There has been an increase in the area of land under organic production since 1998. By December 2004, 635,500 hectares of land in the United Kingdom were under organic production, though this still only represented 4 per cent of total area (Figure 11.20). However this increase began to slow in 2002, and the amount of land converting to organic production – a process that takes two to three years – has fallen since 1999.

At December 2004, Scotland had the largest proportion of organically farmed land, at 7 per cent of its total area. Wales had 4 per cent, England 3 per cent, and Northern Ireland less than 1 per cent. Most land that is organically farmed (or is in the process of being converted to organic farming) in the United Kingdom is used for permanent or temporary pasture – 85 per cent in December 2004. In contrast, 67 per cent of all agricultural land in 2004 was grassland or used for rough grazing. Just 9 per cent of organic land was used for growing cereals and other crops in December 2004, and 2 per cent for fruit and vegetables.

The area of woodland in the United Kingdom fell to a low of around 1.1 million hectares at the beginning of the 20th century but has more than doubled since then, reaching 2.8 million hectares in 2005. This represented approximately 12 per cent of the land area of the United Kingdom. Ancient woodland, which has existed since the earliest reliable records began (over 400 years ago in England and Wales), covered around 2 per cent of the United Kingdom. These often contain complex and fragile ecosystems, and preserve historical features.

## Figure **11.20**

### Land under organic crop production[1]

**United Kingdom**
Thousand hectares

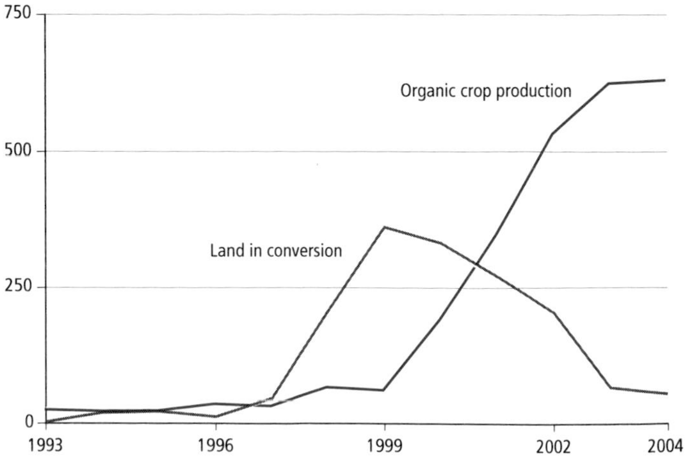

Organic crop production

Land in conversion

1 Figures for 1993 to 1999 use dates closest to December. From 2000 onwards, data are at December.

*Source: Department for Environment, Food and Rural Affairs*

Although there is a greater area of conifer than broadleaved forest and woodland in Great Britain, new broadleaved woodland creation on land not previously used for afforestation has exceeded that of conifers since 1993/94 (Figure 11.21). Between 1990/91 and 2004/05 the area of new land planted each year with conifers fell by 83 per cent, while planting of broadleaved trees rose by 36 per cent. Before the 1990s timber production remained the key priority, resulting in the planting of conifers that were suitable for timber but not usually native to Great Britain. Since then additional incentives for planting broadleaved trees and native pinewood, and for planting on former agricultural land, have led to a growth in the area planted with broadleaved trees, and the continued decline in the planting of new conifers, 8,900 and 2,100 hectares respectively in 2004/05.

Hedges, walls, fences and other boundary features are an integral part of the UK landscape. They provide habitats for many animal and plant species and act as a barrier against soil erosion and loss. They can also act as protective corridors for movement for some species and help maintain biodiversity. There are an estimated 1.8 million kilometres of these features in the United Kingdom. Although the Countryside survey in 1990 revealed a net loss of field boundaries in Great Britain, in particular of hedges, between 1984 and 1990 as a result of agricultural and other types of development, the results of the Countryside survey in 2000 indicate that these declines have been halted.

## Wildlife

Wild bird populations are considered to be good indicators of the broad state of the environment, as they tend to have a wide range of habitats and tend to be at or near the top of the food chain. The size of the total population of UK breeding birds has been relatively stable over the last two decades. In 2003 the population of 111 native bird species across the United Kingdom was 6 per cent higher than it was in 1970, similar to the level in 2000. However the trends for different species groups vary. The steepest decline has been in the population of farmland species, such as the turtledove, skylark and corn bunting, which almost halved between 1977 and 1993, but has been relatively stable since (Figure 11.22). The woodland bird population fell by around 20 per cent between 1974 and 1998, with the main decrease taking place in the late 1980s and early 1990s. The population of coastal birds has risen steadily and in 2003 was 37 per cent higher than 1970.

Although populations of the more common farmland and woodland birds have been declining, rare bird populations, which are not included in this index, have been stable or rising. This reflects conservation efforts focused on these rare species, and some species possibly benefiting from climate change in southern areas of the country.

### Figure **11.21**

#### New woodland creation[1]

Great Britain
Thousand hectares

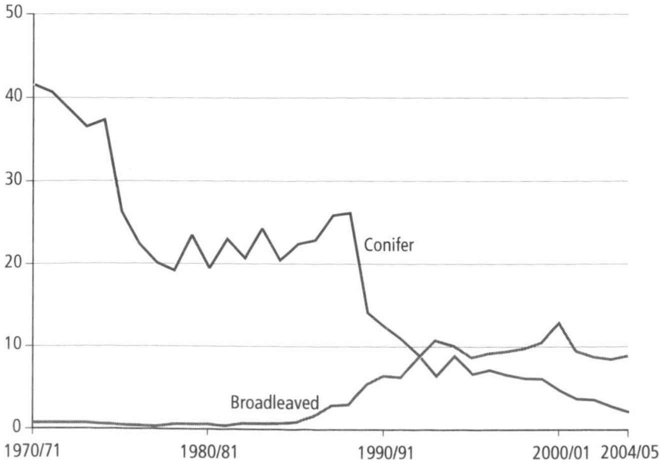

### Figure **11.22**

#### Population of wild birds[1]

**United Kingdom**
Indices (1970=100)

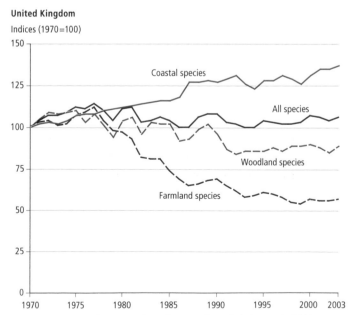

1 It was not possible to complete the Breeding Birds Survey in 2001 because of restrictions imposed during the outbreak of foot-and-mouth disease. Estimates for that year are based on the average for 2000 and 2002 for individual species.

**Source: British Trust for Ornithology; Royal Society for the Protection of Birds; Department for Environment, Food and Rural Affairs**

1 Figures exclude areas of new private woodland created without grant aid. See Appendix, Part 11: New woodland creation.

**Source: Forestry Commission**

# Figure **11.23**

## North Sea fish stocks

Thousand tonnes

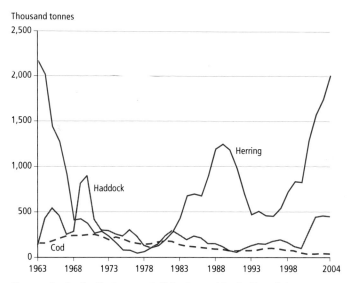

Source: Centre for Environment, Fisheries and Agriculture Science, International Council for the Exploration of the Sea, Department for Environment, Food and Rural Affairs

# Table **11.24**

## Threatened species and habitats,[1] 2002

United Kingdom                                                          Number

|                                  | Species | Habitats |
| -------------------------------- | ------- | -------- |
| Lost                             | 16      | 0        |
| Continued or accelerated decline | 67      | 3        |
| Slowed decline                   | 30      | 14       |
| Fluctuating/no clear trend       | 40      | 2        |
| Stable                           | 76      | 6        |
| Increase                         | 25      | 6        |
| Unknown[2]                       | 137     | 14       |
| All                              | 391     | 45       |

1 According to the UK Biodiversity Action Plan (BAP) published in 1994.
2 Not yet assessed.

Source: UK Biodiversity Partnership

Fish have traditionally formed an important food resource for many people in the United Kingdom, and they are vital elements of ocean ecosystems. Stocks of herring in the North Sea, after declining to very low levels in the 1970s, have recovered strongly (Figure 11.23). Haddock stocks have fluctuated since the 1960s, and continue to do so; they increased by more than four times between 2000 and 2005.

Stocks of cod in the North Sea and elsewhere are causing particular concern. After increasing in the 1960s, North Sea stocks have declined since the early 1970s, and in 2004 were 73 per cent lower than in 1980. There was, however, a small increase between 2001 and 2004. The depletion in numbers is thought to have occurred through a combination of overfishing, small numbers of fish surviving to a size where they are taken commercially, and possible environmental factors such as changing sea temperatures. Measures have been put in place that aim to halt and ultimately reverse the decline in cod stocks. These have included restrictions on cod fishing during the key spring spawning periods, cuts in the numbers that can be caught, and a limit to the number of days each month fishermen can spend at sea catching cod.

UK priority species and habitats are those that have been identified as being most threatened in response to the UN Convention on Biological Diversity. Biodiversity Action Plans have been put in place to establish the reasons for their decline and the work necessary for recovery. In 2002, of the 254 assessed priority species, 44 per cent were declining or had been lost, 10 per cent were found to be increasing, and 46 per cent were stable, fluctuating or showed no clear pattern since 1994 (Table 11.24). A further 137 species had not yet been assessed.

Of the 31 assessed priority habitats, 55 per cent were declining or lost, 19 per cent were found to be improving, and 26 per cent were stable, fluctuating or showed no clear pattern. A further 14 habitats had not yet been assessed.

Furthermore, the International Union for Conservation of Nature and Natural Resources produces a global 'red list' of plants and animals it considers to be threatened. In 2004 the United Kingdom had 42 species of animal, comprising 10 mammals, 10 birds, 12 fish, 2 molluscs and 8 invertebrate species, and 13 plant species that were considered to be critically endangered, endangered or vulnerable.

# Transport

- The total distance travelled by people within Great Britain grew between 1961 and 2004, from 295 billion to 797 billion passenger kilometres. (Page 176)

- Over 4.6 billion journeys in Great Britain were made by local bus in 2004/05, more than twice the number made by rail. (Page 180)

- In 2004/05 more than 1 billion passenger journeys were made on the national rail network for the second year running, the highest it has been since 1961. (Figure 12.12)

- Between 1980 and 2004, the number of air passengers travelling to or from overseas countries through UK airports (excluding those in transit) almost quadrupled from 43 million to 167 million. (Figure 12.16)

- Between 1991 and 2004/05, UK household expenditure on motoring increased by 30 per cent in real terms, while spending on fares and other travel costs rose by 20 per cent. (Table 12.19)

- According to the Organisation for Economic Co-operation and Development, the United Kingdom had one of the lowest road death rates in the EU-25, at 6.1 per 100,000 population in 2003. (Table 12.23)

The last ten years have seen the continuation of long-term trends in many areas of transport and travel, for example the increase in the distance each person travels in a year, the rising number of cars on the roads, and the ever-increasing reliance on those cars. Travel overseas, and particularly air travel, has increased substantially over the same period. There are however pronounced variations in people's travel patterns, depending, for example, on their age, sex, where they live, and their income.

## Travel patterns

The total distance travelled by people within Great Britain grew substantially between 1961 and 2004, from 295 billion to 797 billion passenger kilometres. Over this period, domestic air travel grew the most in terms of the distance covered by all passengers, so that in 2004 it was nearly 10 times the 1961 level (Figure 12.1). The data in Figure 12.1 have been converted from passenger kilometres travelled to an index in order to illustrate the relative growth between the different modes of transport. This means that although air travel showed the greatest percentage growth, the 10 billion passenger kilometres travelled by air in 2004 only represented 1 per cent of all passenger kilometres travelled within Great Britain.

Travel by car, van and taxi rose by nearly four and a half times between 1961 and 2004, and it was this form of transport that contributed most to the increase in total distance travelled because of the large numbers of journeys made this way. The rapid rates of increase that occurred particularly in the 1960s

### Figure **12.1**

### Passenger kilometres: by mode[1]

Great Britain

Indices (1961=100)

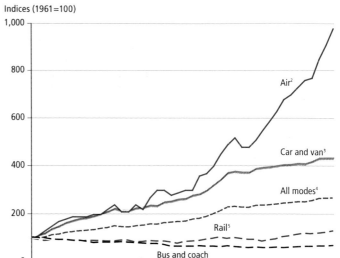

1  Road transport data from 1993 onwards are not directly comparable with earlier years. See Appendix, Part 12: Road traffic.
2  Includes Northern Ireland, Channel Islands and Isle of Man.
3  Includes taxis.
4  Includes motorcycles and bicycles.
5  Data relate to financial years.

*Source: Department for Transport*

and 1980s were replaced by more gradual growth from 1989, but the car has been the dominant means of transport since the early 1960s. It accounted for 85 per cent of all passenger kilometres travelled in 2004.

### Table **12.2**

### Trips per person per year: by main mode[1] and trip purpose,[2] 2004

Great Britain

Numbers

| | Car driver | Walk | Car passenger | Local bus | Rail[3] | Bicycle | Other[4] | All modes |
|---|---|---|---|---|---|---|---|---|
| Leisure | 93 | 48 | 91 | 12 | 4 | 5 | 9 | 262 |
| Shopping | 79 | 51 | 41 | 17 | 2 | 1 | 3 | 193 |
| Commuting/business | 111 | 20 | 17 | 12 | 11 | 6 | 5 | 181 |
| Education/escort education | 24 | 50 | 27 | 10 | 1 | 1 | 4 | 118 |
| Personal business | 41 | 28 | 24 | 5 | 1 | 1 | 2 | 102 |
| Other escort | 51 | 10 | 27 | 2 | - | - | 1 | 91 |
| Other[5] | - | 39 | - | - | - | - | - | 40 |
| All purposes | 399 | 246 | 226 | 59 | 19 | 15 | 24 | 988 |

1  Mode used for the longest part of the trip.
2  See Appendix, Part 12: National Travel Survey.
3  Includes London Underground.
4  Includes motorcycles, taxis, and other private and public transport.
5  Includes walking trips for pleasure or exercise.

*Source: National Travel Survey, Department for Transport*

Table **12.3**

**Purpose of next trip: by sex and previous trip made, 2003–04**

Great Britain

Percentages

| | Previous trip | | | | | | | |
| | Males | | | | Females | | | |
| Next trip to: | Work or business | Escort education | Shopping | All purposes | Work or business | Escort education | Shopping | All purposes |
| --- | --- | --- | --- | --- | --- | --- | --- | --- |
| Work or business | 13 | 8 | 3 | 13 | 9 | 8 | 3 | 9 |
| Education | - | 2 | - | 4 | - | 1 | - | 4 |
| Escort education | - | 3 | - | 2 | 2 | 2 | 1 | 4 |
| Shopping | 3 | 3 | 8 | 10 | 7 | 4 | 9 | 12 |
| Other personal business and escort | 3 | 9 | 3 | 10 | 6 | 7 | 4 | 11 |
| Visit friends | 3 | 2 | 5 | 9 | 4 | 3 | 7 | 10 |
| Other leisure | 2 | 1 | 2 | 9 | 2 | 1 | 2 | 8 |
| Home | 75 | 72 | 79 | 43 | 71 | 74 | 75 | 42 |
| All purposes | 100 | 100 | 100 | 100 | 100 | 100 | 100 | 100 |

*Shaded cells indicate the estimates are unreliable and any analysis using these figures may be invalid. Any use of these shaded figures must be accompanied by this disclaimer.*

**Source: National Travel Survey, Department for Transport**

Travel by rail accounted for 51 billion passenger kilometres in 2004/05, 31 per cent more than in 1961/62. There was a decline in the number of passenger kilometres travelled for much of the early part of this period, reaching a low point of 31 billion in 1982/83. Passenger kilometres then rose during most of the 1980s, before declining again in the early 1990s. Between 1994/95 and 2004/05, rail travel rose by an average of nearly 4 per cent a year.

Travel on buses and coaches declined steadily between 1961 and 1992 before recovering slightly. However the 48 billion passenger kilometres travelled in 2004 still represented an overall decrease of 37 per cent since 1961. Buses and coaches and the railways each accounted for just 6 per cent of all passenger kilometres in 2004.

The National Travel Survey (NTS) found that British residents travelled an average of nearly 10,900 kilometres (including walks) within Great Britain in 2004. This was 188 kilometres less than in 2002, but over 520 kilometres a year more than in 1992–94, and over 3,000 kilometres more than during the 1970s. Average trip length was approximately 11 kilometres, and the average trip time was 22 minutes. The average number of trips made per person in 2004 was 988. This was 6 per cent less than in 1993–95, and a continuation of the longer term decline.

The car accounts for the largest proportion of trips made in Great Britain (Table 12.2). In 2004, 40 per cent of all trips were made by car drivers, and 23 per cent were made by car

passengers. Walks accounted for 25 per cent of all trips. However, 61 per cent of all commuting or business trips for work were made by car drivers. Forty two per cent of trips to school or escorting others to school were made by walking and 43 per cent were made by car.

On public transport, the greatest proportion of bus journeys were made for shopping (30 per cent), while the majority of rail trips (56 per cent) were made for commuting or business. Most trips made by bicycle were made for commuting (38 per cent) and leisure (36 per cent).

Most trips start or finish in the home, but having left their home, many people make additional trips before returning there. In 2003–04, 13 per cent of work and business trips made by men were followed by a further trip for work or business, compared with 9 per cent for women (Table 12.3). Women however were more likely than men to follow a work or business trip with visits for shopping, escorting children to school or to visit friends. Overall women were less likely than men to return straight home from work or shopping.

Although men and women were equally likely to be going on to work having previously escorted children to school, women were twice as likely as men to be escorting children after having already made a trip. Around three quarters of men and women returned straight home after having escorted children to school.

## Table **12.4**

### Travel to work trips: by sex, age and mode, 2004[1]

Great Britain

Percentages

| | Car/van | Walk | Bus/coach | Rail | Bicycle | Other[2] | All trips (=100%) (millions) |
|---|---|---|---|---|---|---|---|
| **Males** | | | | | | | |
| 18–24 | 61 | 15 | 12 | 7 | 3 | 2 | 1.6 |
| 25–44 | 75 | 6 | 5 | 8 | 4 | 3 | 6.6 |
| 45–64 | 81 | 5 | 4 | 5 | 2 | 2 | 5.0 |
| 65 and over | 80 | 8 | 2 | 5 | 3 | 2 | 0.3 |
| All males aged 18 and over | 76 | 7 | 5 | 7 | 3 | 2 | 13.4 |
| **Females** | | | | | | | |
| 18–24 | 52 | 18 | 20 | 7 | 1 | 2 | 1.5 |
| 25–44 | 70 | 12 | 8 | 7 | 2 | 1 | 5.7 |
| 45–59 | 71 | 15 | 9 | 4 | 1 | 1 | 3.7 |
| 60 and over | 63 | 19 | 11 | 4 | 2 | 1 | 0.5 |
| All females aged 18 and over | 68 | 14 | 10 | 6 | 1 | 1 | 11.4 |

1 At autumn. Data are not seasonally adjusted and have been adjusted in line with population estimates published in spring 2003. See Appendix, Part 4: LFS reweighting.
2 Includes taxis and motorcycles.

**Source: Labour Force Survey, Office for National Statistics**

The majority of trips made to work in Great Britain for both men and women are made by car; 76 per cent and 68 per cent respectively in 2004 (Table 12.4). Walking is the next most common mode of travel to work for both sexes (along with rail for men), although a higher proportion of women than men walk to work. Young people aged 18 to 24 are the least likely to travel to work by car and the most likely to travel by bus or coach.

The average distance travelled for those commuting was 8.5 miles per trip in 2004, up from 7.5 miles in 1992–94. Similarly, average commuting time per trip increased from 24 minutes to 26 minutes over the same period. However the number of commuting trips has fallen by 6 per cent over the same period, which might be considered surprising during a period of overall economic growth and rising employment rates (see Figure 4.3). However increasingly people work from home (see Figure 4.15), work flexible hours over fewer days (see Table 4.17) and more workers are now entitled to longer leave entitlements. It should be noted that trips from home to work made by people with no fixed workplace are counted as business trips.

The ways in which children travel to school have changed over the last fifteen years. In general fewer are walking and more are travelling in cars (Figure 12.5). In 1989–91, 27 per cent of trips to school by 5 to 10 year olds were in a car; by 2004 this

## Figure **12.5**

### Trips[1] to and from school: by age of child and selected main mode[2]

Great Britain

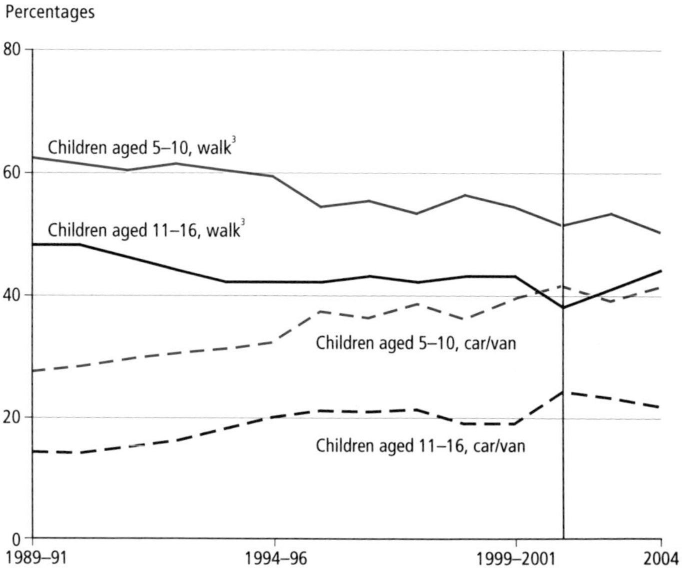

Percentages

1 Trips of under 80 kilometres (50 miles) only.
2 Data prior to 2002 are averages for three years combined.
3 Short walks are believed to be under-recorded in 2002 and 2003 compared with earlier years.

**Source: National Travel Survey, Department for Transport**

## Table **12.6**

### Older people's trips:[1] by sex, age and main mode, 2003–04

Great Britain

Percentages

| | Men | | | Women | | |
|---|---|---|---|---|---|---|
| | 60–69 | 70–79 | 80 and over | 60–69 | 70–79 | 80 and over |
| Car | 70 | 65 | 54 | 63 | 54 | 45 |
| Walk | 22 | 25 | 30 | 25 | 28 | 32 |
| Local bus | 4 | 6 | 10 | 8 | 13 | 16 |
| Other | 4 | 4 | 6 | 4 | 5 | 7 |
| Trips per person (=100%) (numbers) | 1,060 | 882 | 661 | 898 | 683 | 447 |

1 Per person per year.

**Source: National Travel Survey, Department for Transport**

figure had risen to 41 per cent. For 11 to 16 year olds the proportion rose from 14 per cent to 22 per cent over the same period. Private and local bus travel accounted for 7 per cent of journeys to and from school made by 5 to 10 year olds, and 29 per cent of 11 to 16 year olds in 2004. The average length of trips to school also increased over the same period – from 2.1 to 2.7 kilometres for children aged 5 to 10, and from 4.5 to 4.7 kilometres for those aged 11 to 16.

Since trips to and from school usually take place at the same time each morning and evening, they have a major impact on levels of congestion in residential areas. The peak time for school traffic in 2004 was 8.45am on weekdays during term time, when an estimated 23 per cent of all cars on urban roads were taking children to school.

People's use of transport and their travel patterns change as they get older. In 2003–04, those aged 60 and over made an average of 832 trips per year, compared with an average of 1,034 trips for those aged less than 60. It should be noted that the National Travel Survey is a household survey, so these figures exclude those people living in residential care – who may be less mobile. For men and women aged 60–69, 70 per cent and 63 per cent of trips respectively, were made by car (Table 12.6). For men and women aged 80 and over, 54 per cent and 45 per cent of trips respectively, were made by car.

As car use falls, the use of other modes of transport rises proportionately. Thirty per cent of trips made by men aged 80 and over, and 32 per cent of trips made by women of the same age, were by foot. Free or discounted bus passes are available to older people, but use will depend to a certain extent on the availability of local bus services. The number of bus trips made by people aged 60 and over in Great Britain fell between 1994 and 2004,

mainly because of the increased availability of cars. Men aged 80 and over made 10 per cent of their trips by local bus. Women of the same age made 16 per cent of their trips in this way.

## Road transport

There has been significant growth in the proportion of households with two or more cars – from 7 per cent in 1970 to 30 per cent in 2003 (Figure 12.7). The proportion of households with access to one car only has been stable at around 44 per cent since 1970, but the proportion with no car fell from 48 per cent to 26 per cent over the same period.

## Figure **12.7**

### Households with regular use of a car[1]

Great Britain

Percentages

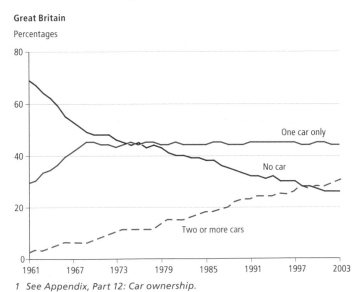

1 See Appendix, Part 12: Car ownership.

**Source: Family Expenditure Survey, General Household Survey, Office for National Statistics; National Travel Survey, Department for Transport**

The higher a household's income, the more likely it is to have access to a car. Forty six per cent of households in the bottom fifth of the income distribution had access to at least one car in 2004. This proportion rose to 63 per cent for those in the next fifth and reached 92 per cent for households in the highest fifth of the income distribution.

Having a car available to the household varies considerably between different household types. Over two thirds of people living alone who were aged 65 or over, and half of lone-parent families, did not have access to a car (Table 12.8). The households most likely to have access to a car were families with children and two or more adults (90 per cent) and households with two or more adults where the household reference person was under the age of 65. Among households with access to a car, it was more likely that there would be a non-driver where three or more adults lived together.

Historically men have been much more likely than women to hold full car driving licences. In 1975–76, 69 per cent of men in Great Britain held such a licence compared with only 29 per cent of women (Figure 12.9). However this gap between men and women is getting smaller. The proportion of men aged 17 and over with a driving licence was 81 per cent (17.9 million) in 2004, while among women the proportion was 61 per cent (14.4 million). The gap between the sexes is smallest in the youngest age groups and largest in the oldest. Twenty nine per

cent of men and 24 per cent of women aged 17 to 20 held licences in 2004, whereas among those aged 70 and over, 72 per cent of men held a licence compared with only 27 per cent of women. However the proportion of younger (17 to 20 year old) men and women holding a licence has decreased since the early 1990s.

Growth in the number of motor vehicles and the greater distances travelled by individuals have led to an increase in the average daily flow of vehicles on Great Britain's roads. Between 1993 and 2004 average traffic flows rose by 20 per cent, to 3,500 vehicles per day (Table 12.10). Motorways had the highest flow of any type of road at 74,900 vehicles a day in 2004. This was an increase of 29 per cent since 1993, but with nearly two thirds of this growth occurring between 1993 and 1998. Rural trunk roads had the greatest proportional increase in traffic flow between 1993 and 2003 (32 per cent), while urban trunk roads had an increase of only 1 per cent.

One consequence of increased traffic can be lower average speeds, especially in urban areas. Transport for London found the average traffic speed for all areas of London during 2000–03 was 15.7 miles per hour in the evening peak period, the lowest it has been since 1968–70.

Buses and coaches are the most widely used form of public transport. Over 4.6 billion journeys in Great Britain were made

## Table **12.8**

**Personal car access: by household type, 2003–04**

Great Britain

Percentages

| | Persons in households without a car | Persons in households with a car | | | | All persons |
| --- | --- | --- | --- | --- | --- | --- |
| | | Main driver | Other driver | Non-driver | All | |
| One person households | | | | | | |
| Aged 16–64 | 37 | 61 | 1 | - | 63 | 100 |
| Aged 65 and over | 69 | 31 | - | - | 31 | 100 |
| Two or more adults only households | | | | | | |
| 2 adults, household reference person aged 16–64 | 13 | 62 | 14 | 11 | 87 | 100 |
| 2 adults, household reference person aged 65 and over | 21 | 46 | 15 | 19 | 79 | 100 |
| 3 or more adults | 11 | 51 | 14 | 23 | 89 | 100 |
| Households with children | | | | | | |
| Lone-parent family | 50 | 49 | - | 1 | 50 | 100 |
| 2 or more adults with children | 10 | 61 | 14 | 15 | 90 | 100 |
| All households | 20 | 55 | 12 | 13 | 80 | 100 |

*Source: National Travel Survey, Department for Transport*

## Figure **12.9**

### Full car driving licence holders: by sex and age

Great Britain
Percentages

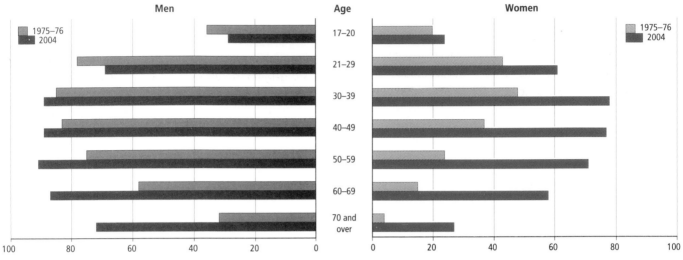

Source: National Travel Survey, Department for Transport

by local bus in 2004/05, more than twice the number of journeys made by rail. Just over a third of these journeys on local buses took place in London. After a long period of post-war decline, which continued into the 1990s, local bus use in terms of passenger journeys stabilised towards the end of the decade and

started to increase from 1999/2000 (Figure 12.11). There were substantial increases in passenger journeys on London buses, offsetting further declines in most other areas of Great Britain. The overall distance travelled by bus recovered from a low point in the mid-1980s until the mid-1990s, before it too stabilised.

## Table **12.10**

### Average daily flow[1] of motor vehicles: by class of road[2]

Great Britain                                               Thousands

|  | 1993 | 1998 | 2001 | 2004 |
|---|---|---|---|---|
| **Motorways[3]** | 58.2 | 68.7 | 71.6 | 74.9 |
| **Urban major roads** | 19.2 | 20.2 | 20.1 | 20.3 |
| Trunk | 32.4 | 34.6 | 27.5 | 32.6 |
| Principal | 17.6 | 18.6 | 19.6 | 19.7 |
| **Rural major roads** | 8.9 | 10.0 | 10.3 | 10.9 |
| Trunk | 14.3 | 16.4 | 17.0 | 18.9 |
| Principal | 6.5 | 7.2 | 7.4 | 8.3 |
| **All major roads** | 14.4 | 16.3 | 16.7 | 17.5 |
| **All minor roads** | 1.3 | 1.3 | 1.4 | 1.4 |
| **All roads** | 2.9 | 3.2 | 3.3 | 3.5 |

1 Flow at an average point on each class of road.
2 See Appendix, Part 12: Road traffic.
3 Includes motorways owned by local authorities.

Source: National Road Traffic Survey, Department for Transport

## Figure **12.11**

### Bus travel[1]

Great Britain
Indices (1981/82=100)

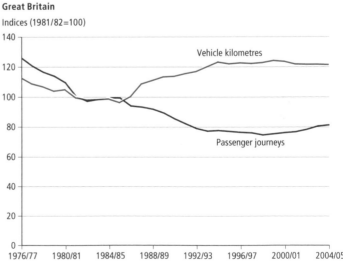

1 Local services only. Includes street-running trams but excludes modern 'supertram' systems. Financial years from 1985/86.

Source: Department for Transport

181

## The railways

The number of journeys made on Great Britain's railway network (including underground and metro systems) rose by 114 million between 2003/04 and 2004/05, to 2.2 billion. There were around 1.3 billion passenger journeys per year in the early 1980s and, apart from a period in the early 1990s, these numbers have generally increased. Between 1993/94 and 2004/05 passenger numbers rose by 44 per cent (Figure 12.12). In 2004/05 more than 1 billion passenger journeys were made on the national rail network for the second year running, the highest since 1961. This represented 42 billion passenger kilometres, the most since 1946. Overall, national rail and London Underground accounted for almost all rail journeys in 2004/05 (49 and 44 per cent respectively).

Several new light railways and tram lines have been built or extended during the last ten years. Over the next decade, further increases in route kilometres for the Docklands Light Railway are predicted, alongside possible new lines and extensions elsewhere in the United Kingdom. Passenger journeys by this mode of transport more than doubled between the mid-1990s and 2004/05, and rose by 8 per cent between 2003/04 and 2004/05.

Nearly half of all rail journeys made on the national rail network in Great Britain originated in London in both 1995–96 and 2003–04 (Figure 12.13). The South East and East of England regions surrounding London accounted for a further quarter of rail journeys. This has led to overcrowding on many commuter routes in and around London. The lowest proportion

### Figure **12.12**

**Passenger railway journeys**

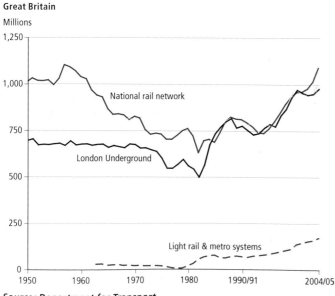

Great Britain

Millions

*Source: Department for Transport*

### Figure **12.13**

**Journeys made on national rail from each region**

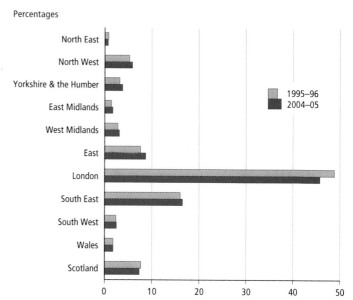

Percentages

*Source: Department for Transport*

of rail journeys originated in the North East even though this region has the lowest car ownership at less than 0.5 cars per adult in 2002/03.

According to the British Social Attitudes survey in 2003, 21 per cent of people aged 18 or over in Great Britain agreed, or strongly agreed, with the statement that 'trains generally run on time', and 16 per cent agreed or strongly agreed with the statement 'train fares are fairly reasonable'. However 57 per cent of those asked agreed or strongly agreed that 'trains are a fast way to travel' and 59 per cent agreed or strongly agreed that 'it is easy to find out what time trains run'.

## Freight transport

The volume of goods transported within Great Britain has grown over the last 30 years, although it has remained broadly stable since 2000. The volume of goods transported by road grew by 86 per cent between 1971 and 1998 and then stabilised so that in 2004, 160 billion tonne kilometres were transported in this way (Figure 12.14). The volume of freight carried by water (virtually all of it by sea) also rose over the period, although much of this growth occurred between the mid-1970s and early 1980s. In 2004/05, 21 billion tonne kilometres of goods were moved by rail. This was 5 per cent lower than in 1971/72, although it represents an increase since 1995/96 of 62 per cent.

The increase in the volume of goods moved by road has resulted from increases in both the weight of goods transported and the average distance carried. The weight

## Figure **12.14**

**Goods moved by domestic freight transport: by mode**

Great Britain

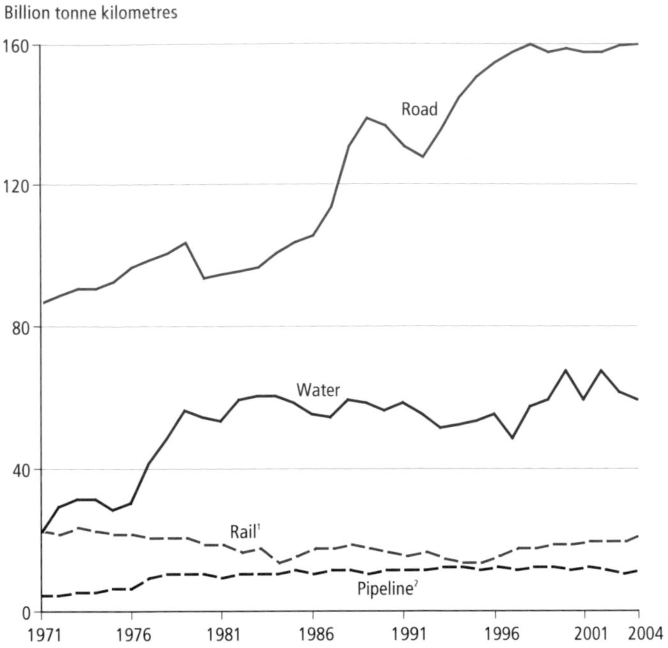

Billion tonne kilometres

1  Data are for financial years from 1991.
2  Carrying petroleum products.

**Source: Department for Transport**

## Table **12.15**

**Goods traffic[1] between the United Kingdom and EU-15 countries, 2004[2]**

| | Goods loaded in the United Kingdom | | Goods unloaded in the United Kingdom | |
|---|---|---|---|---|
| | Thousand tonnes | UK hauliers' share (percentages) | Thousand tonnes | UK hauliers' share (percentages) |
| Ireland | 12,697 | 59 | 7,236 | 42 |
| France | 3,746 | 52 | 5,682 | 44 |
| Germany | 1,800 | 50 | 2,855 | 37 |
| Belgium and Luxembourg | 1,615 | 64 | 2,682 | 57 |
| Netherlands | 1,245 | 58 | 2,309 | 43 |
| Spain | 1,135 | 39 | 2,049 | 26 |
| Italy | 984 | 61 | 1,593 | 43 |
| Austria | 254 | 7 | 329 | 3 |
| Portugal | 105 | 31 | 209 | 14 |
| Denmark | 61 | 26 | 124 | 9 |
| Sweden | 5 | 100 | 20 | 18 |
| Greece[3] | 29 | .. | 5 | .. |
| Finland | 2 | 100 | 1 | 100 |
| All | 23,676 | 56 | 25,093 | 41 |

1  Excluding 'cross trade', that is trade in vehicles registered elsewhere than in the country of loading or unloading.
2  Figures for goods carried in other countries' vehicles are for 2003.
3  Data are for UK hauliers only.

**Source: Department for Transport**

of freight loaded into vehicles that are over 3.5 tonnes, rose by 9 per cent to 1,831 million tonnes between 1994 and 2004. Similarly the average distance travelled by vehicles carrying this freight rose by 1 per cent, to 87 kilometres, although this was 5 kilometres less on average than in 2003.

Nearly 50 million tonnes of goods were loaded and unloaded in the United Kingdom and transported between the member countries of the EU-15 in 2004 (Table 12.15). Around 23.7 million tonnes of goods were loaded in the United Kingdom for dispatch to other EU-15 countries, and a slightly greater amount (25.1 million tonnes) was unloaded in the United Kingdom. More than half of the goods loaded in the United Kingdom and transported to other EU-15 countries were to Ireland, and much of this was across the border with Northern Ireland. France, which is close in proximity to the United Kingdom and has extensive links through port traffic and the Channel Tunnel, was the destination for 16 per cent of freight carried to the rest of the EU-15. Overall UK hauliers were responsible for carrying 56 per cent of freight transported from the United Kingdom to the rest of the EU-15, although this percentage varied widely with the destination.

The United Kingdom imported more goods by weight than it exported to the EU-15. Ireland and France were the origin of the greatest proportions of freight unloaded in the United

Kingdom, followed by Germany, Belgium and Luxembourg, and the Netherlands. Only two fifths of this freight was carried into the country by UK hauliers.

## International travel

Almost 90 per cent of all air terminal passengers (that is, excluding those in transit) through UK airports were travelling to or from overseas countries. The increase in the number of people travelling by plane over the last two decades is both a continuation, and a quickening, of a long-term trend. Between 1980 and 2004, the number of international terminal passengers at UK airports almost quadrupled from 43 million to 167 million (Figure 12.16 overleaf). The overall pattern is of rapid growth, but the numbers of passengers fell in 1991, the year of the Gulf war, before continuing upward. There was also a marked flattening of the upward trend in 2001 (the result of the outbreak of foot-and-mouth disease in the United Kingdom and the terrorist attacks of 11 September in the United States, both in that year) but numbers continued to rise in 2002. The increase in the number of domestic passengers

## Figure **12.16**

### Passengers at UK civil airports

United Kingdom
Millions

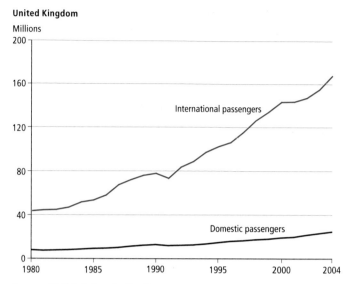

Source: Civil Aviation Authority

## Figure **12.17**

### Distance travelled on passenger flights: by type of flight

United Kingdom
Billion passenger kilometres

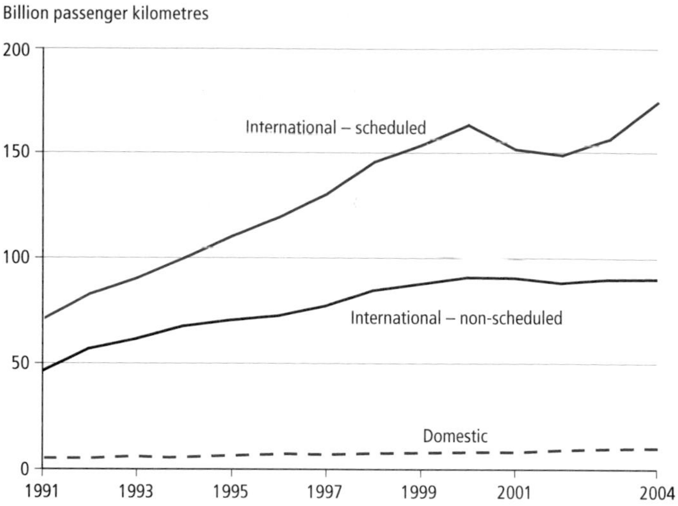

Source: Civil Aviation Authority

has been less erratic, tripling between 1980 and 2004 to 24 million.

The Department for Transport has forecasted that demand for air travel will continue rising in the 21st century. Mid-range estimates suggest that between 2005 and 2020, the number of international and domestic terminal passengers at UK airports will grow from 229 million to 401 million. The growth in international passengers (nearly 80 per cent) is expected to exceed growth in domestic passengers (around 70 per cent).

While more people are travelling by air, the total distance they travel is also increasing. There was an increase of nearly 150 per cent between 1991 and 2004 in the distance travelled by passengers on scheduled international flights by UK airlines departing and arriving at UK airports. In 2004 passengers

travelled 174 billion kilometres, following slight falls in 2001 and 2002 (as noted for passenger numbers) (Figure 12.17). The distance travelled on domestic flights has increased by 104 per cent to 10 billion kilometres over the same period. While the distance travelled on international non-scheduled flights, typically for package holidays, levelled off between 2000 and 2004, it increased by 97 per cent between 1991 and 2004, to 90 billion kilometres.

The increased availability and affordability of air travel has driven the rise in distance travelled, but this rise is not necessarily a result of an increase in the average length of air journeys. The growth in the number of journeys made has exceeded the growth in passenger kilometres flown, so passengers are travelling more often, rather than further afield.

## Table **12.18**

### International travel: by mode of travel and purpose of visit, 2004

United Kingdom

Percentages

| | UK residents[1] | | | | Overseas residents[2] | | | |
|---|---|---|---|---|---|---|---|---|
| | Air | Sea | Channel Tunnel | All modes | Air | Sea | Channel Tunnel | All modes |
| Holiday | 68 | 66 | 55 | 67 | 29 | 46 | 41 | 33 |
| Visiting friends and relatives | 16 | 13 | 10 | 15 | 31 | 20 | 20 | 28 |
| Business | 13 | 8 | 17 | 13 | 28 | 22 | 30 | 27 |
| Other | 3 | 13 | 18 | 5 | 12 | 11 | 9 | 11 |
| All purposes (=100%) (millions) | 50.4 | 9.0 | 4.8 | 64.2 | 20.0 | 4.8 | 3.0 | 27.8 |

1 Visits abroad by UK residents.
2 Visits to the United Kingdom by overseas residents.

Source: International Passenger Survey, Office for National Statistics

In 2004 holidays accounted for two thirds of the 64 million trips made abroad by UK residents (Table 12.18). Countries in the EU-25 were the destination for 70 per cent of visits made by air and 95 per cent of visits made by sea and the Channel Tunnel. Business trips accounted for a greater proportion of trips made through the Channel Tunnel than for other routes, 17 per cent in 2004. The number of trips made abroad by UK residents was nearly two and a half times the number of trips made by overseas residents to the United Kingdom. Additionally greater proportions of overseas residents visiting the United Kingdom than UK residents visiting overseas were travelling either for business or to visit relatives. Only around a third of overseas residents' journeys to the United Kingdom were for a holiday.

## Prices and expenditure

In 2004/05 transport and travel accounted for 17 per cent of all household expenditure in the United Kingdom. After taking into account the effect of inflation, UK household expenditure on transport and travel increased by 29 per cent between 1991 and 2004/05 to £72 per week (Table 12.19). This compares with a 19 per cent increase in household spending on all goods and services over the same period.

Between 1991 and 2004/05, household expenditure on motoring increased by 30 per cent in real terms, although within this total, spending on insurance and taxation increased by 65 per cent. Household expenditure on motoring was seven times the expenditure on fares and other travel costs. Bus and coach fares was the only area of transport expenditure that decreased, by 17 per cent between 1991 and 2004/05. However overall spending on fares and other travel costs increased by 20 per cent during this period.

Motoring costs as measured by the 'All motoring' component of the retail prices index (RPI) rose by 81 per cent between January 1987 and January 2005, compared with a rise in the RPI of 89 per cent. Therefore motoring was relatively less expensive in 2005 than it was in 1987 (Table 12.20 overleaf). This is mainly because the rise in the price of vehicles (11 per cent) was much less than the rate of inflation. Vehicle tax and insurance rose by 184 per cent and maintenance by 172 per cent, while the cost of petrol and oil rose by 133 per cent.

Bus and coach fares, and rail and tube fares both rose by more than the rate of inflation between 1987 and 2005, by 151 and 142 per cent respectively. Overall the 'All fares and other travel' index rose by 115 per cent.

## Table **12.19**

### Household expenditure on transport in real terms[1]

| United Kingdom | | | | | | £ per week |
|---|---|---|---|---|---|---|
| | 1981 | 1986 | 1991 | 1996/97[2] | 2001/02[2] | 2004/05 |
| **Motoring** | | | | | | |
| Cars, vans and motorcycle purchase | 13.50 | 16.50 | 22.20 | 19.90 | 27.90 | 25.10 |
| Repairs, servicing, spares and accessories | 5.70 | 5.20 | 6.00 | 7.30 | 7.60 | 7.70 |
| Motor vehicle insurance and taxation | 4.60 | 5.50 | 6.70 | 7.60 | 9.80 | 11.00 |
| Petrol, diesel and other oils | 12.40 | 12.00 | 11.90 | 14.70 | 16.00 | 16.20 |
| Other motoring costs | 1.00 | 1.00 | 1.20 | 2.10 | 1.90 | 2.60 |
| All motoring expenditure | 37.20 | 40.00 | 48.10 | 51.60 | 62.70 | 62.60 |
| **Fares and other travel costs** | | | | | | |
| Rail and tube fares | 1.90 | 1.40 | 1.40 | 1.70 | 2.00 | 2.00 |
| Bus and coach fares | 2.70 | 2.00 | 1.80 | 1.70 | 1.60 | 1.50 |
| Taxi, air and other travel costs[3] | 2.70 | 3.80 | 3.70 | 4.30 | 6.60 | 6.00 |
| All fares and other travel costs[4] | 7.70 | 7.90 | 7.90 | 9.40 | 10.10 | 9.50 |
| **Motoring and all fares** | 44.80 | 48.00 | 55.90 | 59.20 | 72.90 | 72.00 |
| **All expenditure groups** | 309.70 | 336.00 | 364.80 | 382.60 | 426.30 | 432.90 |

1 At 2004/05 prices deflated by the 'All items' retail prices index. Expenditure rounded to the nearest 10 pence. See Appendix, Part 6: Household expenditure.
2 Data prior to and including 1996/97 are unweighted and based on adult only expenditure. From 2001/02 onwards data include children's expenditure, and are weighted based on the population figures from the 2001 census.
3 Includes combined fares.
4 Includes expenditure on bicycles and boats – purchases and repairs.

*Source: Family Expenditure Survey and Expenditure and Food Survey, Office for National Statistics*

Table **12.20**

## Passenger transport prices[1]

United Kingdom

Indices (1987=100)

|  | 1987 | 1991 | 1996 | 2001 | 2004 | 2005 |
|---|---|---|---|---|---|---|
| **Motoring costs** | | | | | | |
| Vehicle tax and insurance | 100 | 136 | 184 | 264 | 287 | 284 |
| Maintenance[2] | 100 | 135 | 174 | 216 | 255 | 272 |
| Petrol and oil | 100 | 120 | 164 | 225 | 223 | 233 |
| Purchase of vehicles | 100 | 117 | 134 | 124 | 119 | 111 |
| All motoring expenditure | 100 | 123 | 154 | 180 | 183 | 181 |
| **Fares and other travel costs** | | | | | | |
| Bus and coach fares | 100 | 133 | 175 | 209 | 236 | 251 |
| Rail fares | 100 | 140 | 183 | 212 | 226 | 242 |
| Other | 100 | 122 | 140 | 163 | 179 | 182 |
| All fares and other travel | 100 | 131 | 161 | 188 | 207 | 215 |
| **Retail prices index** | 100 | 130 | 150 | 171 | 183 | 189 |

1 At January each year based on the retail prices index. See Appendix, Part 6: Retail prices index.
2 Includes spare parts and accessories, and roadside recovery services.

*Source: Office for National Statistics*

## Transport safety

The safety levels of most major forms of transport have improved since the early 1980s, and improvements in most areas have continued since the early 1990s. Despite improvements in road safety, other forms of transport, such as rail, air and sea, continue to have much lower death rates from accidents (Table 12.21). Conversely, motorcycling, walking and cycling

Table **12.21**

## Passenger death rates:[1] by mode of transport

Great Britain

Rate per billion passenger kilometres

|  | 1981 | 1991 | 1996 | 2001 | 2003 |
|---|---|---|---|---|---|
| Motorcycle | 115.8 | 94.6 | 108.4 | 112.1 | 114.4 |
| Walk | 76.9 | 74.6 | 55.9 | 47.5 | 43.3 |
| Bicycle | 56.9 | 46.8 | 49.8 | 32.6 | 25.3 |
| Car | 6.1 | 3.7 | 3.0 | 2.8 | 2.7 |
| Van | 3.7 | 2.1 | 1.0 | 0.9 | 0.9 |
| Bus or coach | 0.3 | 0.6 | 0.2 | 0.2 | 0.2 |
| Rail[2] | 1.0 | 0.8 | 0.4 | 0.2 | 0.1 |
| Water[3] | 0.4 | 0.0 | 0.8 | 0.4 | 0.0 |
| Air[3] | 0.2 | 0.0 | 0.0 | 0.0 | 0.0 |

1 See Appendix, Part 12: Passenger death rates.
2 Financial years. Includes train accidents and accidents occurring through movement of railway vehicles.
3 Data are for the United Kingdom.

*Source: Department for Transport*

are the most dangerous forms of transport per kilometre travelled. Death rates among motorcyclists were over 40 times greater than those among car users in 2003.

Almost all passenger deaths in transport accidents in Great Britain occur on the roads. In 2004 there were 3,221 deaths caused by road accidents, compared with an annual average of 3,578 in 1994–98, and 5,846 in 1981. In 2004, 51 per cent of those killed in road accidents were occupants of cars, 21 per cent were pedestrians, 18 per cent were riders or passengers of two-wheeled motor vehicles, and 4 per cent were pedal cyclists. Occupants of buses, coaches and goods vehicles accounted for the remaining 4 per cent of deaths.

The number of pedestrians killed each year has fallen steadily since the mid-1990s. There were 671 pedestrian fatalities in 2004, the lowest recorded figure since 1950. Conversely, the number of car users killed has remained fairly stable over the last decade. In 2004, 1,671 car users were killed, compared with 1,769 in 2003, 1,764 in 1994 and a low of 1,665 in 2000.

A total of 24,094 people were killed or seriously injured on Great Britain's roads on weekdays during 2004, or an average of 92 people each day. The incidence of people being killed or seriously injured in road accidents is not uniform throughout the day. Among pedestrians and car users most casualties occur in the morning and evening 'rush hours', with the highest number during the extended evening period (Figure 12.22).

## Figure **12.22**

**Average number of people killed or seriously injured in road accidents on weekdays: by road user type and time of day,[1] 2004**

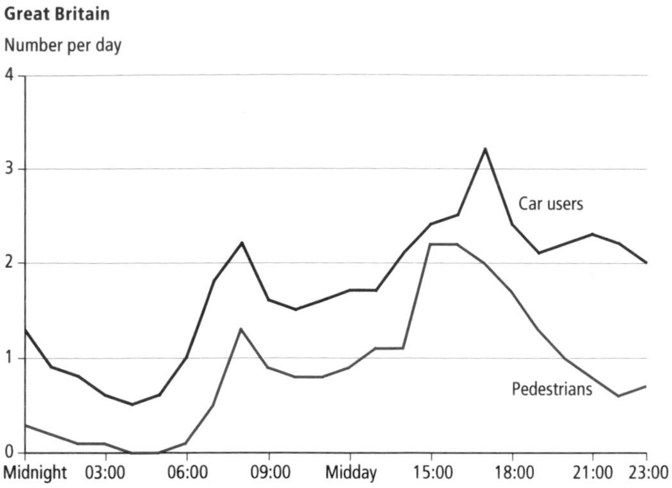

**Great Britain**
Number per day

1  For each hour beginning at time shown.

**Source: Department for Transport**

## Table **12.23**

**Road deaths: EU comparison, 2003**

|  | Rate per 100,000 population |  | Rate per 100,000 population |
| --- | --- | --- | --- |
| Malta | 4.1 | Cyprus | 12.8 |
| Sweden | 5.9 | Spain | 12.8 |
| United Kingdom | 6.1 | Hungary | 13.1 |
| Netherlands | 6.3 | Czech Republic | 14.2 |
| Finland | 7.3 | Belgium | 14.5 |
| Denmark | 8.0 | Greece | 14.6 |
| Germany | 8.0 | Poland | 14.8 |
| Ireland | 8.4 | Portugal | 14.8 |
| France | 10.2 | Lithuania | 20.4 |
| Italy | 10.5 | Latvia | 21.0 |
| Austria | 11.5 | EU-15 average | 9.5 |
| Luxembourg | 11.8 | EU-25 average | .. |
| Estonia | 12.0 |  |  |
| Slovakia | 12.0 |  |  |
| Slovenia | 12.1 |  |  |

**Source: Organisation for Economic Co-operation and Development**

The first peak occurs in the hour beginning at 08:00: 579 car users and 346 pedestrians were killed or seriously injured during this hour on weekdays in 2004. The number of pedestrians killed or seriously injured is highest during the hours starting at 15:00 and 16:00, during which many schools finish for the day. There were 580 deaths and 585 serious injuries respectively, during these hours in 2004. The number of car users killed or seriously injured reaches its highest in the hour starting at 17:00: 843 people in 2004, an average of over three each weekday.

The United Kingdom has a good record for road safety compared with most other EU-25 countries. According to the Organisation for Economic Co-operation and Development, the United Kingdom had one of the lowest road death rates in the EU-25, at 6.1 per 100,000 population in 2003 (Table 12.23).

Latvia had the highest recorded road death rate in the EU-25, at 21 per 100,000 population. The UK rate was also substantially lower than those for other industrialised nations such as Japan (7.0 per 100,000 population), Australia (8.2) and the United States (14.7).

The United Kingdom also has a relatively good record in terms of road accidents involving children and older people. In 2003 the UK road accident death rate for children aged 0 to 14, at 1.3 per 100,000 of population, was the equal second lowest of the EU-15 countries. Luxembourg had the lowest rate, at 1.2 per 100,000 population, while Portugal had the highest (3.3). The UK road accident death rate for those aged 65 and over was 6.9 per 100,000, the lowest rate for all EU-15 countries.

# Lifestyles and social participation

- A digital television service was received by 57 per cent of households with a television in Great Britain in May 2005. This was up from 43 per cent in April 2003. (Table 13.2)

- In Great Britain, the proportion of households with a broadband connection rose from 8 per cent to 31 per cent between April 2003 and July 2005. (Figure 13.3)

- Nearly nine in ten adult viewers in the United Kingdom watched television every day of the week in 2003, with nearly a quarter of viewers watching it for two to three hours a day. (Page 192)

- The most borrowed authors from libraries in the UK were Danielle Steel (contemporary adult fiction), Jacqueline Wilson (contemporary children's) and JRR Tolkien (classic) between July 2003 and June 2004. (Page 194)

- UK residents made a record 42.9 million holiday trips abroad in 2004, an increase from 6.7 million in 1971; Spain was the most popular destination, followed by France. (Figure 13.13)

- Just under two thirds of adults in the UK gave money to charity in 2003. The average monthly donation was £12.32. (Page 199)

# Chapter 13

People engage in many different activities in their spare time. Some visit places of entertainment and cultural activity, such as the theatre and museums, or go away on holidays. Other activities involve interaction with technology, such as watching television or listening to the radio, and more recently the Internet. Although modern technology seems ever present, traditional forms of leisure, such as reading books or newspapers, remain popular. Many individuals participate in sports or exercise in their leisure time or use their free time for purposes other than entertainment, such as helping other people, participating in politics, or religious worship.

## Media and use of information technology

A period of technological change has brought about the widening application of information and communication technology (ICT). Home ownership of CD players, DVD players, computers, Internet access, and mobile phones has risen substantially over the last five or six years (Figure 13.1). Ownership of some products has grown more than others. The proportion of UK households with a DVD player has risen from 31 per cent in 2002/03 to 67 per cent in 2004/05, an average increase of 18 percentage points a year. Growth in ownership of CD players has occurred more slowly. In 1996/97, 59 per cent of households had a CD player compared with 87 per cent in 2004/05, an average increase of 3 percentage points a year. The spread of Internet connections and mobile phone ownership slowed in the last three years after a sharp rise in the late 1990s. Between 1998/99 and 2002/03 the percentage of households that had an Internet connection and a mobile phone grew, on average, 9 percentage points and 11 percentage points a year respectively. Between 2002/03 and 2004/05, the annual increase in home Internet connection and mobile phone ownership was 4 percentage points for both technologies.

There has been a sharp rise in the number of homes that receive a digital television service. The proportion of households with a television that did so in Great Britain rose from 43 per cent in April 2003 to 57 per cent in May 2005 (Table 13.2). Most of this increase came from greater access to digital terrestrial television, which rose from 6 per cent to 19 per cent of households. Satellite is the most widely used means to receive digital television. In May 2005, 32 per cent of households with a television had access to a satellite service, an increase of 3 percentage points since April 2003. The percentage receiving digital cable services has remained approximately the same. The highest growth in household digital television ownership occurred between the months of October and February, rising by 7 percentage points between October 2002 and February 2003, 5 percentage points

### Figure **13.1**

**Households with selected durable goods[1]**

United Kingdom

Percentages

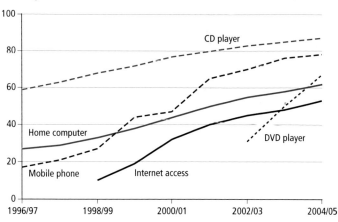

1 Based on weighted data. Data for 1998/99 onwards include children's expenditure.

Source: Family Expenditure Survey and Expenditure and Food Survey, Office for National Statistics

### Table **13.2**

**Household television service:[1] by type**

Great Britain                                                    Percentages

|  | April 2003 | April 2004 | May 2005 |
|---|---|---|---|
| Analogue terrestrial | 52 | 46 | 36 |
| Analogue cable | 5 | 5 | 6 |
| Digital terrestrial | 6 | 12 | 19 |
| Digital cable | 7 | 7 | 6 |
| Satellite | 29 | 30 | 32 |
| Any digital service | 43 | 49 | 57 |

1 See Appendix, Part 13: Television service.

Source: Omnibus Survey, Office for National Statistics

between October 2003 and February 2004, and 8 percentage points between October 2004 and February 2005. Together, these three periods accounted for almost three quarters of the increase in household digital television use over the period between October 2002 and February 2005.

Home broadband connections have almost quadrupled since 2003. The proportion of households in Great Britain with a broadband connection rose from 8 per cent to 31 per cent between April 2003 and July 2005 (Figure 13.3). Over the same period, the percentage of households with a dial-up (or narrow band) connection fell from 40 per cent to 25 per cent. Overall, households with an Internet connection of any type

# Figure **13.3**

## Household Internet connection: by type

**Great Britain**
Percentages

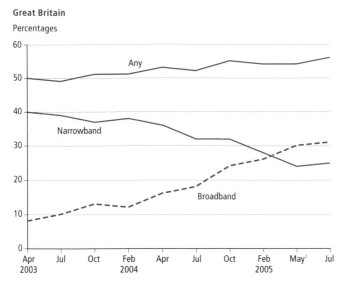

1 From 2005 Internet access data was collected in May instead of April.

*Source: Omnibus Survey, Office for National Statistics*

# Figure **13.4**

## Selected online activities: by home connection, February 2005

**Great Britain**
Percentages

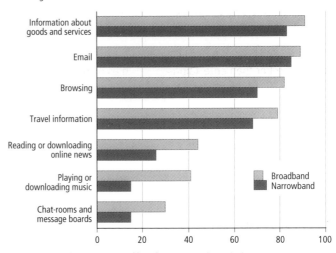

*Source: Omnibus Survey, Office for National Statistics*

have increased, from 50 per cent to 56 per cent of all households. In July 2005 broadband connections accounted for over half of household Internet connections.

When people go online, there are many activities they can engage in, of which the most popular in February 2005 were email and looking for information about goods and services (both 85 per cent) and general browsing (72 per cent). Broadband Internet users take part in a wider variety of online activities than users with a dial-up connection, although for many online activities the difference is quite small (Figure 13.4). Dial-up users accessed email at slightly lower levels (85 per cent) than broadband users (89 per cent). A smaller proportion of dial-up users (83 per cent) looked online for goods and services than broadband users (91 per cent). Differences in participation between broadband and dial-up users were greater for activities that can involve downloading larger material. Fewer dial-up users (15 per cent) downloaded or played music online compared with broadband users (41 per cent). Similarly, 26 per cent of dial-up users downloaded or read news online, compared with 44 per cent of broadband users.

Although the proportion of homes with an Internet connection has grown, in 2004/05 almost half of households in the United Kingdom did not have one. Higher income households are more likely to have a home Internet connection than lower income households (Figure 13.5). Among households in the top 20 per cent for income (or quintile group – see analysing income distribution box on page 76), 87 per cent had an Internet connection. This compared with 18 per cent of

households in the lowest quintile, a difference of 69 percentage points. The gap between the highest and lowest quintiles has widened since 1998/99 when it was 24 percentage points.

Younger people are more likely to go online. Of people aged between 16 and 24 in Great Britain, 89 per cent were Internet users (defined as having gone online in the three months prior to interview) in 2004/05. This compared with 16 per cent of those aged 65 and over. Although the rates of Internet use have been

# Figure **13.5**

## Home internet connection: by household income quintile group

**United Kingdom**
Percentages

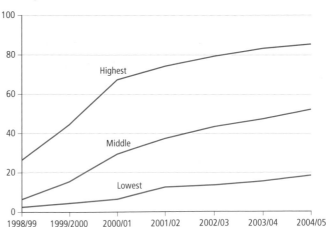

*Source: Family Expenditure Survey and Expenditure and Food Survey, Office for National Statistics*

## Figure **13.6**

### Most frequently viewed TV channels,[1] 2003

**United Kingdom**
Percentages

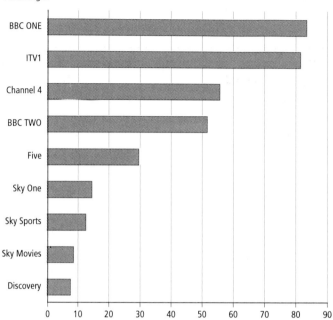

1 'Other', 'None of these' and 'Don't know' are not shown.
**Source: The Public's View, Ofcom**

growing among all age groups, the gap in Internet use between younger and older adults has widened. Between 2001/02 and 2004/05 Internet use grew by around 15 percentage points among all age groups under 65 years old. For those aged 65 and over, Internet use rose by 7 percentage points.

Internet security has become a widespread concern for people who go online. In 2004/05, 46 per cent of Internet users in Great Britain said they had received too many junk emails, 24 per cent had received emails they considered obscene or offensive, and 36 per cent had received a computer virus. Only a small proportion of Internet users (3 per cent) suffered either a financial problem, such as fraudulent card use, or were aware of the unauthorised use of personal information by another person as a result of going online.

Television has traditionally played an important part in people's leisure time occupying around half of that time. According to the Broadcasters Audience Research Board (BARB) television viewing in the United Kingdom has increased slightly over the past decade from 25.6 hours per household per week in 1993 to 26.1 hours in 2003. Nearly nine in ten adults in the United Kingdom watched television every day of the week in 2003 according to Ofcom's The Public's View survey, with nearly a quarter of viewers watching it for two to three hours a day and

one in ten viewing for over seven hours. Over half of adults stated that they have one or two sets at home, while nearly one in ten said that they have five or more.

The top five channels watched most often by adults in 2003 in the United Kingdom were the major terrestrial channels, BBC ONE, ITV1, Channel 4, BBC TWO and Five (Figure 13.6). BBC ONE was the most watched channel with 84 per cent of adult viewers stating they watched it most often compared with the most popular digital only channel, Sky One, which was watched by 15 per cent of viewers. The annual share of viewers for each channel has changed over the last 20 years as more channels become available. According to BARB, 48 per cent of viewing was to ITV1 (including GMTV) and 36 per cent of viewing was to BBC ONE in 1984. The remaining share of viewing was to BBC TWO (11 per cent) and Channel 4 (4 per cent) as there were no other channels available. With the introduction of digital and cable channels in the mid-1990s there has been a gradual shift away from the traditional channels. By 2004 the annual share of viewing to BBC ONE and ITV1 (including GMTV) had dropped to 25 per cent and 23 per cent respectively. The other terrestrial channels (BBC TWO, Channel 4 and Five) had a viewing share of 27 per cent between them. The digital or cable channels had the remaining 26 per cent share.

According to Ofcom's The Public's View survey, nearly three quarters of adults in the United Kingdom in 2003 stated that television was their main source of national news. This was followed by 13 per cent stating that newspapers were their main source of national news and 10 per cent the radio. Nearly four out of five people (78 per cent) stated that television was their main source of world news followed by newspapers (10 per cent) and radio (7 per cent).

Radio is a secondary medium; it is listened to while people do other things such as commuting or working. According to a research study conducted by MORI on behalf of Ofcom in 2004, nearly six in ten people in the United Kingdom listened to the radio while getting up or having breakfast on weekdays. Other most popular times for listening to the radio on weekdays were travelling in the car (56 per cent) and travelling to and from work (46 per cent and 43 per cent respectively).

According to the Radio Joint Audience Research Limited (RAJAR), nine in ten people in the United Kingdom listened to a radio station for at least five minutes during an average week between June and September 2005. BBC Radio 2 was the most popular station, followed by BBC Radio 4 and BBC Radio 1 (Table 13.7). The BBC attracted just over half the audience share (55 per cent), while commercial radio stations together had an audience share of 44 per cent.

## Table **13.7**

### Share of radio listening: by station, 2005[1]

| United Kingdom | Percentages |
| --- | --- |
| | All aged 15 and over |
| **BBC** | |
| BBC Radio 1 | 9.4 |
| BBC Radio 2 | 15.6 |
| BBC Radio 3 | 1.2 |
| BBC Radio 4 | 11.5 |
| BBC Radio Five Live | 4.6 |
| BBC World Service | 0.7 |
| 1Xtra from the BBC | 0.3 |
| BBC 7 | 0.3 |
| BBC Asian Network UK | 0.3 |
| FIVE LIVE SPORTS EXTRA | 0.1 |
| BBC 6Music | 0.1 |
| BBC local/regional | 10.7 |
| All BBC | 54.6 |
| **Commercial** | |
| Classic FM | 4.1 |
| Total Virgin Radio (AM/FM) | 1.5 |
| talkSPORT (Talk Radio) | 1.8 |
| All national commercial | 10.5 |
| All local commercial | 33.5 |
| All commercial | 43.5 |
| **Other listening[2]** | 1.9 |
| **All radio stations** (=100%) (hours listened) | 1,071,871 |

1 Quarter 3 fieldwork carried out between 27 June and 18 September.
2 Other listening includes non-subscribers to RAJAR, including student/hospital stations, foreign and pirate stations.

**Source: RAJAR/IPSOS**

Digital radio is growing in popularity as new stations launch and listening on new devices (such as the Internet) grows. At the end of 2004 there were 210 stations broadcasting on Digital Audio Broadcasting (DAB), 85 on digital satellite television, 30 on digital terrestrial television and thousands available over the Internet. According to RAJAR in June 2005, 19 per cent of adults in the United Kingdom stated that they had listened to the radio online, compared with 14 per cent in the same period two years earlier. Just under a third (32 per cent) of adults had listened to the radio through a digital television in June 2005, compared with 20 per cent in June 2003.

## Table **13.8**

### Readership of national daily newspapers: by sex, 2004–2005[1]

| Great Britain | | | Percentages |
| --- | --- | --- | --- |
| | Men | Women | All aged 15 and over |
| The Sun | 20 | 14 | 17 |
| Daily Mirror/Record | 13 | 11 | 12 |
| Daily Mail | 11 | 12 | 11 |
| Daily Telegraph | 5 | 4 | 5 |
| Daily Express | 5 | 4 | 4 |
| Daily Star | 6 | 2 | 4 |
| The Times | 4 | 3 | 4 |
| The Guardian | 3 | 2 | 2 |
| The Independent | 2 | 1 | 1 |
| Financial Times | 1 | 1 | 1 |
| Any national daily newspaper | 70 | 54 | 62 |

1 Data are for the period July 2004 to June 2005.

**Source: National Readership Survey Limited**

Almost two thirds of all people aged 15 and over in Great Britain read a national daily newspaper in the year to June 2005 (Table 13.8). The Sun was the most read paper with nearly one in five people reading it, followed by the Daily Mail. Men tended to read newspapers more than women; however the Daily Mail had a slightly larger proportion of women readers. The newspaper that had the greatest difference in readership between men and women was The Sun (20 per cent and 14 per cent respectively). The national daily newspapers with the smallest readerships were The Independent and the Financial Times (both had 1 per cent readership share). A larger proportion of people read Sunday newspapers compared with daily national papers (75 per cent). The News of the World was the most read Sunday newspaper with 19 per cent of people aged 15 and over reading it, followed by The Mail on Sunday (14 per cent).

Television guides such as What's on TV and the Radio Times made up six of the top ten most-read general weekly magazines. Private Eye was the most read fortnightly magazine in 2004–2005. The top weekly women's magazine was Take a Break, which was read by 12 per cent of women, followed by OK! and Hello! (8 per cent and 7 per cent of women respectively). The top three most-read women's monthly magazines were all supermarket titles; Asda Magazine was read by 16 per cent of women and Sainsbury Magazine and

*Somerfield Magazine*, both read by 8 per cent of women, followed by *Cosmopolitan* (7 per cent of women) and *Good Housekeeping* (5 per cent of women). *FHM* was the most read monthly men's periodical with just over one in ten males aged over 15 reading it, the majority being in the 15 to 44 age group.

Although the number of visits made to public libraries in the United Kingdom in 2003/04 increased by 4.3 per cent over the previous year to 337 million, there has been a decline in book lending according to LISU Annual Library Statistics. In 2003/04, 341 million books were issued, a fall of 38 per cent since 1993/94. The proportion of children's books issued since 1993/94 has increased by 6 percentage points to 26 per cent of all books issued compared with adult fiction, which has declined by 6 percentage points to 49 per cent. In 2003 nearly half of adult library users were female and aged 55 and over. The most popular activity undertaken by library visitors was borrowing books (73 per cent), followed by browsing (28 per cent) and seeking information (21 per cent) (Figure 13.9). Using the Internet in libraries more than doubled between 2001 and 2003 (6 per cent to 13 per cent). In 1997/98, 12 per cent of libraries offered Internet services; this had risen to 96 per cent of libraries in 2002/03.

The most borrowed adult fiction books between July 2003 and June 2004 were *The King of Torts* by John Grisham and *Quentin's* by Maeve Binchy. The most borrowed children's books were *Harry Potter and the Order of the Phoenix* by JK Rowling and *The Story of Tracy Beaker* by Jacqueline Wilson. Overall the most borrowed authors were Danielle Steel (contemporary adult fiction), Jacqueline Wilson (contemporary children's) and JRR Tolkien (classic).

## Social and cultural activities

Nearly half of people in England who attended an arts or cultural event or venue in the 12 months before interview in 2003 visited a library. Nine out of ten people visiting a library did so at least twice in the previous year, and six out of ten people visited six or more times (Table 13.10). The most attended event was film, with almost nine out of ten film visitors going to the cinema or other film venues at least twice in the 12 months before interview. About three in five of those attending plays or drama (61 per cent), art, photography or sculpture exhibitions (59 per cent), and craft exhibitions (58 per cent) had done so more than once in the last 12 months. The main reasons given for attending at least one of the selected events were that people liked going to the specific event (36 per cent), they went to see a specific performer or event (19 per cent) or they went as a social event (18 per cent). The main reasons for not attending events were the difficulty of finding time (48 per cent) and cost (34 per cent).

### Figure **13.9**

**Reasons for visiting a library,[1] 2003**

United Kingdom
Percentages

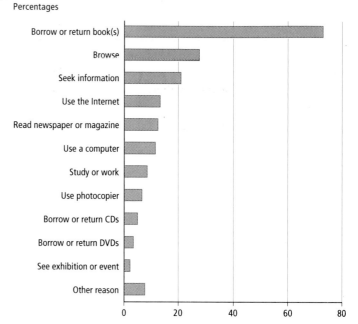

1 Percentages are of those who visited a library and do not add up to 100 per cent as respondents could give more than one answer.

**Source: Chartered Institute of Public Finance and Accountancy**

Overall younger people were more likely than older people to have gone to at least one arts event or cultural venue in the last 12 months. Over nine out of ten people aged 16 to 24 attended events compared with nearly five out of ten people aged 75 and over. People aged under 55 were most likely to have visited a cinema or other film venues, watched videos or electronic arts events or attended other live music events and carnivals in the 12 months before interview in 2003. People aged 55 to 64 were more likely than other age groups to have gone to musicals, craft exhibitions, classical music and opera.

The National Lottery which started in 1994 has funded around 185,000 social or cultural projects. Just over four in ten adults aged 16 and over in Great Britain participated in any of the National Lottery games every week in 2002 according to the National Lottery Commission. Levels of participation varied by age, with younger people aged 16 to 24 least likely to participate weekly in any of the National Lottery games (Table 13.11). Almost half (47 per cent) of people aged 16 to 24 had never played any National Lottery game compared with around a third (or less) of people aged between 25 and 64 .

The most common reason people gave for not playing any National Lottery game was that the chances of winning are so small (65 per cent). Over a third (39 per cent) believed that gambling could be harmful; this was more common among

## Table 13.10

### Number of attendances at selected arts or cultural events in the last 12 months, 2003

England                                                                                                        Percentages

|  | Once | Twice | 3 to 5 | 6 to 10 | 11 or more | All (=100%) (numbers) |
|---|---|---|---|---|---|---|
| Library | 8 | 11 | 19 | 17 | 44 | 2,649 |
| Film | 14 | 19 | 32 | 20 | 15 | 3,354 |
| Event connected with books or writing | 43 | 23 | 20 | 8 | 6 | 494 |
| Museum | 26 | 28 | 29 | 11 | 5 | 2,208 |
| Event including video or electronic art | 57 | 23 | 12 | 3 | 4 | 409 |
| Art, photography or sculpture exhibition | 41 | 27 | 21 | 9 | 3 | 1,284 |
| Play or drama | 39 | 29 | 23 | 7 | 2 | 1,510 |
| Musical | 51 | 28 | 16 | 3 | 2 | 1,489 |
| Culturally specific festival | 61 | 24 | 13 | 1 | 2 | 474 |
| Craft exhibition | 42 | 26 | 23 | 7 | 1 | 1,134 |
| Street arts or circus | 66 | 22 | 8 | 3 | 1 | 652 |
| Carnival | 76 | 18 | 6 | - | - | 1,131 |

*Source: Arts Council England*

women (43 per cent) than men (34 per cent). Two in ten people (22 per cent) did not play the National Lottery because there were too many games to choose from. The National Lottery games were 'too expensive' for 17 per cent of people with the highest proportion (32 per cent) in the 16 to 24 age group.

The United Kingdom has almost 6,500 visitor attractions, including country parks and farms, historic properties, theme parks, zoos, gardens, museums and galleries, and places of worship. The top two visitor attractions that charged admission in England in 2004 were the British Airways London Eye, which had 3.7 million visitors, and the Tower of London, with

2.1 million visitors. The top visitor attractions that charged admission in Scotland in 2004 were Edinburgh Castle (1.2 million visitors) and Edinburgh Zoo (600,000 visitors), while in Wales it was Portmeirion (254,000 visitors) and Caernarfon Castle (202,000 visitors). The top attractions in Northern Ireland excluding country parks or gardens that charged admission were the Giants Causeway Visitor Centre (445,000 visitors) and the W5 interactive discovery centre (246,000 visitors).

Overall visits to free attractions in England rose by 3 per cent in the year to 2004, while visits to paid attractions remained stable. Museums and art galleries represent around a third of all attractions and recorded visits rose by 4 per cent in 2004,

## Table 13.11

### Participation in the National Lottery:[1] by age, 2002

Great Britain                                                                                                  Percentages

|  | 16–24 | 25–34 | 35–44 | 45–54 | 55–64 | 65 and over | All aged 16 and over |
|---|---|---|---|---|---|---|---|
| Every week | 17 | 31 | 47 | 50 | 49 | 47 | 41 |
| Two or three times a month | 8 | 7 | 8 | 7 | 10 | 4 | 7 |
| Once a month | 10 | 9 | 5 | 5 | 3 | 5 | 6 |
| Less than once a month | 19 | 21 | 10 | 12 | 9 | 7 | 13 |
| Never | 47 | 32 | 30 | 27 | 30 | 37 | 33 |
| All age 16 and over (=100%) (numbers) | 275 | 379 | 381 | 331 | 260 | 398 | 2,024 |

1 Includes Lotto, Thunderball, Hotpicks, Lotto extra and Instants.

*Source: National Lottery Commission*

## Table **13.12**

### Annual change in visits to attractions: by type

England
Percentages

| | 2002 to 2003 | 2003 to 2004 |
|---|---|---|
| Country parks | 9 | 4 |
| Museums/art galleries | 1 | 4 |
| Steam/heritage railways | 3 | 3 |
| Other historic properties | -2 | 3 |
| Farms | 13 | 2 |
| Visitor/heritage centres | 7 | 2 |
| Wildlife attractions/zoos | 1 | 1 |
| Places of worship | -5 | 1 |
| Historic houses/castles | 4 | -1 |
| Leisure/theme parks | 3 | -1 |
| Gardens | 6 | -6 |

Source: Visit Britain, British Tourist Authority

after remaining level between 2002 and 2003 (Table 13.12). Visits to country parks rose by 4 per cent and continued their recovery after their decline in 2001 following the outbreak of foot and mouth disease. Visits to gardens fell by 6 per cent between 2003 and 2004; this was probably due to the unusually hot summer of 2003, which made visits to gardens very popular.

According to the 2002/03 Great Britain Day Visits Survey, eight out of ten adults had made a leisure day visit within the two weeks before interview. Half had taken a day trip to a town or city, while just over one in five had visited the countryside. Around one in ten people had visited the seaside and coast, or forests or woodland.

Residents of the United Kingdom made a record 42.9 million holiday trips abroad in 2004. Most holiday trips were taken between July and September, when more than twice as many were taken than during January to March. The number of holiday trips taken in 2004 increased by 17 per cent since 2000 and was a continuation of the rise in overseas holidays over the last three decades from 6.7 million in 1971. Nearly half (46 per cent) of the holiday trips abroad in 2004 were package holidays. Spain has been UK residents' favourite holiday destination since 1994. This continued in 2004 when Spain hosted 28 per cent of all holidays abroad, followed by France (17 per cent) (Figure 13.13). As in previous years, nine out of the ten most popular countries UK residents visited in 2004 were in Europe. The exception was the United States, which accounted for 6 per cent of all holidays (2.6 million visits). Trips to European countries were the shortest on

## Figure **13.13**

### Holidays abroad by UK residents: by selected destination, 2004

United Kingdom
Percentages

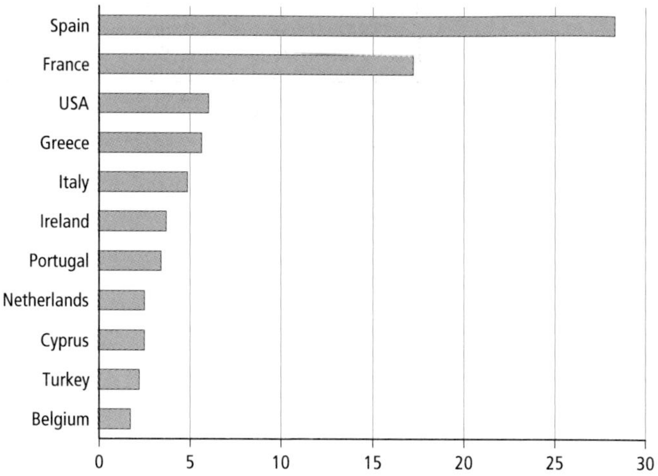

Source: International Passenger Survey, Office for National Statistics

average, because UK residents made more day trips here. A large proportion of day trips to France and Belgium were for shopping (48 per cent for both).

## Sporting activities

In 2002 three quarters of adults in Great Britain had taken part in a sport, game or physical activity in the 12 months before interview and three fifths had done so in the previous four weeks. When walking is excluded these proportions fall to two thirds and two fifths respectively. Over the 12 month period before interview walking (46 per cent) was the most popular sports activity followed by swimming (35 per cent), keep fit/yoga including aerobics and dance exercise (22 per cent), cycling (19 per cent) and cue sports (17 per cent).

Men were more likely than women to have participated in at least one sport, game or physical activity, in either the 4 weeks or 12 months before interview. Four in ten men participated in an organised competition in the 12 months before interview, compared with one in seven women. Women participating in sports were more likely than men to have received tuition to improve their performance in a sport, game or physical activity in the 12 months before interview (45 per cent compared with 31 per cent).

There was a clear relationship between socio-economic status and participation rates in sports, games and physical activities in the four weeks before interview. In households where the household reference person was in a large employers and higher managerial occupation, 59 per cent of adults took part

Table **13.14**

**Top ten sports, games and physical activities[1] among adults: by socio-economic classification,[2] 2002/03**

Great Britain

Percentages

| | Large employers and higher managerial occupations | Higher professional occupations | Lower managerial and professional occupations | Intermediate occupations | Small employers and own account workers | Lower supervisory and technical occupations | Semi-routine occupations | Routine occupations | Never worked and long-term unemployed | All aged 16 and over |
|---|---|---|---|---|---|---|---|---|---|---|
| Walking | 46 | 48 | 43 | 34 | 31 | 29 | 29 | 25 | 22 | 35 |
| Swimming | 24 | 20 | 17 | 13 | 12 | 11 | 9 | 8 | 8 | 14 |
| Keep fit/yoga | 20 | 18 | 15 | 15 | 11 | 9 | 7 | 6 | 4 | 12 |
| Snooker/pool/billiards | 9 | 9 | 10 | 10 | 9 | 9 | 8 | 7 | 6 | 9 |
| Cycling | 12 | 13 | 11 | 7 | 8 | 7 | 6 | 7 | 8 | 9 |
| Weight training | 11 | 9 | 7 | 7 | 5 | 4 | 4 | 3 | 3 | 6 |
| Running (jogging etc) | 10 | 9 | 6 | 5 | 4 | 3 | 2 | 2 | 3 | 5 |
| Football | 6 | 6 | 6 | 4 | 5 | 5 | 3 | 4 | 4 | 5 |
| Golf | 10 | 9 | 7 | 4 | 5 | 4 | 2 | 2 | 0 | 5 |
| Tenpin bowls/skittles | 4 | 4 | 4 | 4 | 3 | 3 | 3 | 2 | 1 | 3 |

1 Includes activities in which more than one per cent of all adults participated in the four weeks before interview.
2 Of the household reference person. See Appendix, Part 1: National Statistics Socio-economic Classification.

*Source: General Household Survey, Office for National Statistics*

in at least one activity (excluding walking) in the four weeks before interview. This compared with 30 per cent of adults in households headed by someone in a routine occupation. Walking was the most popular activity among all socio-economic classifications, but there were still large differences between the participation rates of adults within each occupation (Table 13.14). Those in large employers and higher managerial occupations were nearly twice as likely as those in routine occupations to go for a walk of two miles or more in the four weeks before interview (46 per cent compared with 25 per cent).

On average, women make up around one in four members of sporting organisations across England and Great Britain (Figure 13.15). There are large differences between organisations. Women dominate British gymnastics, accounting for 78 per cent of members, while less than 0.5 per cent of members in the Amateur Boxing Association are female. Football is the most popular female sport in England and in the 2002–03 season there were nearly 85,000 girls and women playing regular 11-a-side football affiliated to the Football Association; this was a rise from the 11,000 female players in the early 1990s. However men still dominate in the traditional male sports such as football, rugby, cricket, basketball and boxing where they make up over 90 per cent of the membership.

Figure **13.15**

**Membership of selected sporting organisations: by sex, 2004[1]**

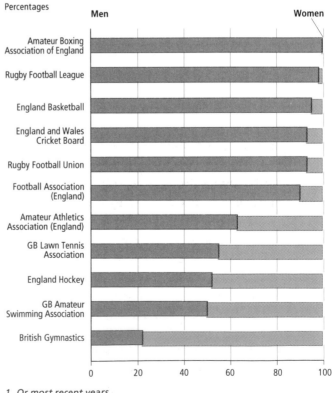

1 Or most recent years.

*Source: Governing bodies; Sport England*

## Political and social participation

The official turnout in the May 2005 General Election was 61 per cent, a small increase on the 59 per cent turnout recorded in 2001. The Labour Party retained control of Parliament after gaining 355 seats; they received 35 per cent of the vote, lower than any previously recorded share for a winning party. The Conservative Party won 198 seats and the Liberal Democrat Party, 62 seats. In 2005 turnout at the general election increased with age. Opinion poll data suggest that those aged 65 and over were twice as likely to vote as those under 25.

While there have been female Members of Parliament (MPs) since 1918, the numbers remained low for most of the last century. In 2005 a record 128 (20 per cent) of the 646 MPs elected were women; more than three quarters of these (98) represented the Labour Party. In the last three elections the number of female MPs has been around double the previous high of 60 in 1992 (Figure 13.16). The 15 minority ethnic MPs of both sexes elected in 2005 was also a record, but they still only represent 2 per cent of the total.

The Home Office Citizenship Survey (HOCS) records people's participation in civic activity in England and Wales. The survey found that the participation rates remained unchanged between 2001 and 2003. Nearly one in four (38 per cent) people had undertaken one form of civic participation in the previous 12 months, although only 3 per cent had done so at least once a month. The most common form of civic participation was signing a petition (68 per cent), followed by contacting a local councillor (27 per cent).

Those aged 25 to 64 had the highest rates of participation (43 per cent). It was lowest among young people aged 16 to 24 and older people aged between 65 and 74; participation among both groups was 30 per cent. There were differences in participation between ethnic groups, with those of mixed race being most civically active (42 per cent), followed by the White and Bangladeshi groups. Those of Chinese origin were the least active (24 per cent).

Civic participation was also associated with people's socio-economic classification. Participation among professional and managerial groups averaged 47 per cent, while for those in routine occupations averaged 31 per cent. Among people who had never worked or were long-term unemployed 21 per cent had taken part in at least one form of civic activity in the previous 12 months.

Volunteering is one of the ways in which individuals help their community, from formal volunteering activities such as organising an event to informal activities such as looking after a pet for someone. According to the 2003 HOCS, 62 per cent of people had taken part in at least one form of volunteering in the previous 12 months while 37 per cent had volunteered at least once a month. The most common types of informal volunteering were giving advice (44 per cent) and looking after

## Figure **13.16**

### Female Members of Parliament elected at general elections

**United Kingdom**

Numbers

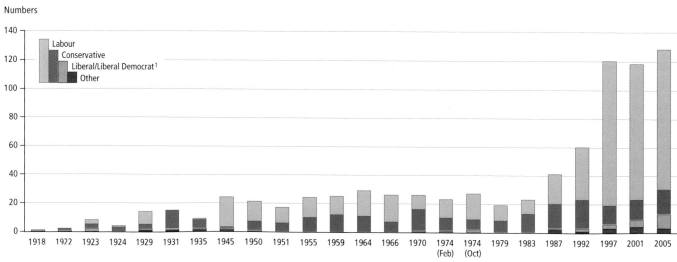

1  Liberal Democrat from 1992.

*Source: House of Commons*

## Figure **13.17**

**Participation in volunteering at least once in the 12 months before interview: by socio-economic classification,[1] 2003**

**England and Wales**
Percentages

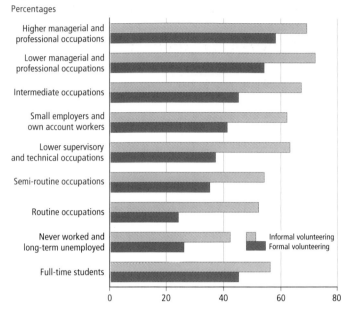

1 Of respondents aged 16 and over. See Appendix, Part 1: National Statistics Socio-economic Classification. The data excludes respondents who had been unemployed for less than one year.

**Source: Citizenship Survey, Home Office**

## Figure **13.18**

**Voluntary income of the top charities, 2003/04**

**United Kingdom**
£ million

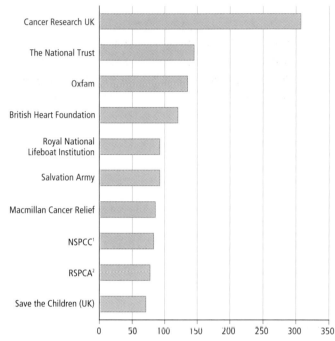

1 National Society for the Prevention of Cruelty to Children.
2 Royal Society for the Prevention of Cruelty to Animals.

**Source: Charities Aid Foundation**

a property or pet while someone was away (38 per cent). The most frequently reported types of formal volunteering were raising or handling money/taking part in sponsored events (53 per cent) and organising or helping to run an activity or event (49 per cent).

Rates of volunteering did not vary much by age, although participation in informal activities were higher among people aged 16 to 34. Participation overall fell for people aged 65 and over. Those in professional and managerial occupations had the highest rates of volunteering (Figure 13.17). They were a third more likely to participate in informal volunteering than those in routine occupations. Similarly people with higher educational qualifications were more likely to volunteer than those with no qualifications.

Charities derive their income in several ways, one of which is from individual donations. At the end of 2004 there were 166,129 registered charities in England and Wales and a further 17,864 active charities in Scotland. According to the Charity Commission the total annual income for all registered charities in the United Kingdom for 2003/04 was nearly £35 billion, £7.1 billion was received in individual voluntary donation for

2003. Nearly 90 per cent of the money is raised by just over 7 per cent of the charities. The most popular charity was Cancer Research UK, which received £306 million, followed by the National Trust with £144 million (Figure 13.18).

Just under two thirds of adults gave money to charity in 2003. The average monthly donation was £12.32. Women were more likely to give than men, 71 per cent of women gave an average monthly donation of £13.55 per month compared with 60 per cent of men with an average £10.81. Less than 5 per cent of individuals gave more than £50 to charity each month, although these contributions account for more than half of the monies donated.

There are a variety of different ways to give to charity. The most popular was through street or door-to-door collections, while the most income was obtained from voluntary donations and grants. Gift aid allows charities to recover the income tax paid on a donation, thereby increasing the amount of the donation. Overall a third of the £7.1 billion in individual charitable giving was given tax-efficiently, although half of the Disasters Emergency Committee Tsunami donations were tax-efficient.

## Religion

Attendance at religious services varies across Europe. Figure 13.19 shows the percentage of individuals who attended a religious service irrespective of faith at least once a month for the EU nations surveyed. In 2002 the highest attendance was by people resident in Poland (75 per cent) and the lowest by people of Denmark (9 per cent). The countries with the highest rates of attendance all followed the Catholic or Orthodox religion, while the Protestant Scandinavian countries recorded the lowest rates. The United Kingdom is placed 13th with 19 per cent of residents attending religious services at least once a month. See Table 1.6 for further information on the religious groups in Great Britain.

### Figure **13.19**

**Attendance at religious services: EU comparison,[1] 2002**

Percentages

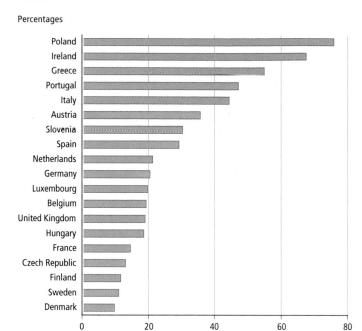

1 Respondents who replied 'at least once a month' when asked 'How often do you attend religious services apart from special occasions'.

***Source: European Social Survey***

# Websites and contacts

## Chapter 1: Population

### Websites

National Statistics
www.statistics.gov.uk

Eurostat
www.europa.eu.int/comm/eurostat

General Register Office for Scotland
www.gro-scotland.gov.uk

Government Actuary's Department
www.gad.gov.uk

Home Office Immigration and Asylum Statistics
www.homeoffice.gov.uk/rds/immigration1.html

National Assembly for Wales
www.wales.gov.uk/keypubstatisticsforwales

Northern Ireland Statistics and Research Agency
www.nisra.gov.uk

Scottish Executive
www.scotland.gov.uk

United Nations Population Fund (UNFPA)
www.unfpa.org

### Contacts

#### Office for National Statistics

Chapter author
**020 7533 5778**

Internal Migration
**01329 813872**

International Migration
**01329 813255**

Labour Market Statistics Helpline
**020 7533 6094**

Population Estimates
**01329 813318**

Population Projections
**020 7533 5222**

#### Other organisations

Eurostat
**00352 4301 35336**

General Register Office for Scotland
**0131 314 4254**

Government Actuary's Department
**020 7211 2622**

Home Office
**020 8760 8274**

Northern Ireland Statistics and Research Agency
**028 9034 8160**

Welsh Assembly Government Statistical Directorate
**029 2082 5058**

## Chapter 2: Households and families

### Websites

National Statistics
www.statistics.gov.uk

Department of Health
www.dh.gov.uk/publicationsAndStatistics/statistics

ESRC Research Centre for Analysis of Social Exclusion
http://sticerd.lse.ac.uk/case

Eurostat
www.europa.eu.int/comm/eurostat

General Register Office for Scotland
www.gro-scotland.gov.uk

Home Office
www.homeoffice.gov.uk

Institute for Social and Economic Research
www.iser.essex.ac.uk

National Assembly for Wales
www.wales.gov.uk/keypubstatisticsforwales

National Centre for Social Research
www.natcen.ac.uk

Northern Ireland Statistics and Research Agency
www.nisra.gov.uk

Northern Ireland Statistics Research Agency,
  General Register Office for Northern Ireland
www.groni.gov.uk

Office of the Deputy Prime Minister
www.odpm.gov.uk

Scottish Executive
www.scotland.gov.uk

Teenage Pregnancy Unit
www.teenagepregnancyunit.gov.uk

### Contacts

#### Office for National Statistics

Chapter author
**020 7533 5204**

Fertility and Birth Statistics
**01329 813758**

General Household Survey
**01633 813441**

Labour Market Statistics Helpline
**020 7533 6094**

Marriages and Divorces
**01329 813758**

#### Other organisations

Department of Health, Abortion Statistics
**020 7972 5533**

ESRC Research Centre for Analysis of Social Exclusion
**020 7955 6679**

Eurostat
**00352 4301 35427**

General Register Office for Scotland
**0131 314 4243**

Home Office, Family Policy Unit
**020 7217 8393**

Institute for Social and Economic Research
**01206 872957**

National Centre for Social Research
**020 7549 8520**

Northern Ireland Statistics and Research Agency,
General Register Office for Northern Ireland
**028 9025 2020**

Office of the Deputy Prime Minister
**020 7944 3303**

Welsh Assembly Government
**029 2082 5058**

## Chapter 3: Education and training

### Websites

National Statistics
**www.statistics.gov.uk**

Department for Education and Skills (DfES)
**www.dfes.gov.uk**

DfES: Research and Statistics Gateway
**www.dfes.gov.uk/rsgateway**

DfES: Trends in Education and Skills
**www.dfes.gov.uk/trends**

Higher Education Statistics Agency
**www.hesa.ac.uk**

Learning and Skills Council
**www.lsc.gov.uk**

National Assembly for Wales
**www.wales.gov.uk/keypubstatisticsforwales**

National Centre for Social Research
**www.natcen.ac.uk**

National Foundation for Educational Research
**www.nfer.ac.uk**

Northern Ireland Department of Education
**www.deni.gov.uk**

Northern Ireland Department for Employment and Learning
**www.delni.gov.uk**

Office for Standards in Education
**www.ofsted.gov.uk**

Scottish Executive
**www.scotland.gov.uk**

### Contacts

#### Office for National Statistics

Chapter author
**020 7533 6174**

#### Other organisations

Department for Education and Skills
**01325 392754**

Learning and Skills Council
**0870 900 6800**

National Assembly for Wales
**029 2082 3507**

Northern Ireland Department of Education
**028 9127 9279**

Northern Ireland Department for Employment and Learning
**028 9025 7592**

Scottish Executive
**0131 244 0442**

## Chapter 4: Labour market

### Websites

National Statistics
**www.statistics.gov.uk**

Department of Trade and Industry
**www.dti.gov.uk**

Department for Work and Pensions
**www.dwp.gov.uk**

Employment Tribunals Service
**www.ets.gov.uk**

Eurostat
**www.europa.eu.int/comm/eurostat**

Jobcentre Plus
**www.jobcentreplus.gov.uk**

Learning and Skills Council
**www.lsc.gov.uk**

Nomis
**www.nomisweb.co.uk**

National Centre for Social Research
**www.natcen.ac.uk**

### Contacts

#### Office for National Statistics

Chapter author
**020 7533 6174**

Labour Market Statistics Helpline
**020 7533 6094**

#### Other organisations

Eurostat, European Statistical Data Support in the UK
**01633 813369**

Jobcentre Plus (Jobseekers direct)
**0845 606 0234**

Learning and Skills Council
**0870 900 6800**

New Deal
**0114 209 8229**

## Chapter 5: Income and wealth

### Websites

National Statistics
**www.statistics.gov.uk**

Department for Work and Pensions
**www.dwp.gov.uk**

Eurostat
**www.europa.eu.int/comm/eurostat**

HM Revenue and Customs
**www.hmrc.gov.uk**

HM Treasury
**www.hm-treasury.gov.uk**

Institute for Fiscal Studies
**www.ifs.org.uk**

Institute for Social and Economic Research
**www.iser.essex.ac.uk**

National Centre for Social Research
**www.natcen.ac.uk**

Women and Equality Unit
**www.womenandequalityunit.gov.uk**

## Contacts

### Office for National Statistics

Chapter author
020 7533 5778

Annual Survey of Hours and Earnings
01633 819024

Average Earnings Index
01633 819024

Effects of Taxes and Benefits
020 7533 5770

National Accounts
020 7533 5938

New Earnings Survey
01633 819024

Regional Accounts
020 7533 5809

### Department for Work and Pensions

Families and Children Study
020 7712 2090

Family Resources Survey
020 7962 8092

Households Below Average Income
020 7962 8232

Individual Income
020 7712 2258

Pensions
020 7712 2721

Pensioners' Incomes
020 7962 8975

### Other organisations

Eurostat, Data Shop London UK
020 7533 5676

Inland Revenue
020 7147 3082

Institute for Fiscal Studies
020 7291 4800

Institute for Social and Economic Research
01206 872957

National Centre for Social Research
020 7250 1866

## Chapter 6: Expenditure

### Websites

National Statistics
www.statistics.gov.uk

Association for Payment Clearing Services
www.apacs.org.uk

Bank of England
www.bankofengland.co.uk

Department for Trade and Industry
www.dti.gov.uk

Eurostat
www.europa.eu.int/comm/eurostat

Organisation for Economic Co-operation and Development
www.oecd.org

## Contacts

### Office for National Statistics

Chapter author
020 7533 5770

Comparative Price Levels
020 7533 5818

Expenditure and Food Survey
020 7533 5752

Harmonised Index of Consumer Prices
020 7533 5818

Household Expenditure
020 7533 6058

Retail Prices Index
020 7533 5840

Retail Sales Index
01633 812713

### Other organisations

Association for Payment Clearing Services
020 7711 6265

Bank of England
020 7601 4166

Department for Trade and Industry
020 7215 3286

## Chapter 7: Health

### Websites

National Statistics
www.statistics.gov.uk

Department for Environment, Food and Rural Affairs
www.defra.gov.uk

Department of Health
www.dh.gov.uk/publicationsAndStatistics/statistics

Department of Health, Social Services and Public Safety, Northern Ireland
www.dhsspsni.gov.uk/stats&research/index.asp

Eurostat
www.europa.eu.int/comm/eurostat

General Register Office for Scotland
www.gro-scotland.gov.uk

Government Actuary's Department
www.gad.gov.uk

Health Protection Agency
www.hpa.org.uk

Home Office Research, Development and Statistics
www.homeoffice.gov.uk/rds

NHS Health and Social Care Information Centre
www.ic.nhs.uk

NHS Scotland, Information Services Division
www.isdscotland.org

National Assembly for Wales
www.wales.gov.uk/keypubstatisticsforwales

Northern Ireland Cancer Registry
www.qub.ac.uk/nicr

Northern Ireland Statistics and Research Agency
www.nisra.gov.uk

Northern Ireland Statistics and Research Agency, General Register Office for Northern Ireland
www.groni.gov.uk

Scottish Executive
www.scotland.gov.uk

Welsh Cancer Intelligence and Surveillance Unit
www.velindre-tr.wales.nhs.uk/wcisu

## Contacts

### Office for National Statistics

Chapter author
020 7533 5081

Cancer Statistics
020 7533 5230

Condom Use
020 7533 5391

General Household Survey
01633 813441

General Practice Research Database
020 7533 5240

Life Expectancy by Deprivation Group
020 7533 5241

Mortality Statistics
01329 813758

Psychiatric Morbidity Survey
020 7533 5305

Sudden Infant Death Syndrome
020 7533 5198

### Department of Health

Key Health Indicators
020 7972 1036/3734

Prescription Cost Analysis
020 7972 5515

### NHS Health and Social Care Information Centre

Health Survey for England
020 7972 5718/5660

Immunisation and Cancer Screening
020 7972 5533

Smoking, Misuse of Alcohol and Drugs
0113 254 7062

### Northern Ireland Statistics and Research Agency

Continuous Household Survey
028 9034 8243

General Register Office for Northern Ireland
028 9025 2031

### Other organisations

Department for Environment, Food and Rural Affairs,
Expenditure and Food Survey
01904 455077

Department of Health, Social Services and Public Safety,
Northern Ireland
028 9052 2800

Eurostat
00352 4301 32056

General Register Office for Scotland
0131 314 4227

Government Actuary's Department
020 7211 2635

Health Protection Agency
020 8200 6868

Home Office
020 7035 0422

National Centre for Social Research
020 7250 1866

NHS National Services Scotland, Information Services Division
0131 275 7777

Northern Ireland Cancer Registry
028 9026 3136

Welsh Assembly Government
029 2082 5080

Welsh Cancer Intelligence and Surveillance Unit
029 2037 3500

## Chapter 8: Social protection

### Websites

National Statistics
www.statistics.gov.uk

Charities Aid Foundation
www.cafonline.org

Department of Health
www.dh.gov.uk/publicationsAndStatistics/statistics

Department of Health, Social Services and Public Safety,
Northern Ireland
www.dhsspsni.gov.uk/stats&research/index.asp

Department for Education and Skills
www.dfes.gov.uk

Department for Social Development, Northern Ireland
www.dsdni.gov.uk

Department for Work and Pensions
www.dwp.gov.uk/asd/frs

Economic and Social Research Council (ESRC)
www.esrc.ac.uk

Eurostat
www.europa.eu.int/comm/eurostat

Local Government Data Unit – Wales
www.dataunitwales.gov.uk

National Assembly for Wales
www.wales.gov.uk/keypubstatisticsforwales

National Centre for Social Research
www.natcen.ac.uk

NHS Direct
www.nhsdirect.nhs.uk

NHS in Scotland
www.show.scot.nhs.uk/isd

Northern Ireland Statistics and Research Agency
www.nisra.gov.uk

Scottish Executive
www.scotland.gov.uk

### Contacts

### Office for National Statistics

Chapter author
020 7533 5778

General Household Survey
01633 813441

Labour Force Survey
020 7533 6094

## Department for Education and Skills

Children's Services
020 7972 3804

Day Care for Children
01325 392827

## Department of Health

Acute Services Activity
0113 254 5522

Adults' Services
020 7972 5582

Community and Cross-sector Services
020 7972 5524

General Dental and Community Dental Service
020 7972 5392

General Medical Services Statistics
0113 254 5911

Mental Illness/Handicap
020 7972 5546

NHS Expenditure
0113 254 6012

NHS Medical Staff
0113 254 5892

NHS Non-medical Manpower
0113 254 5744

Non-psychiatric Hospital Activity
020 7972 5529

Personal Social Services Expenditure
020 7972 5595

Residential Care and Home Help
020 7972 5585

Social Services Staffing and Finance Data
020 7972 5595

## Department of Health, Social Services and Public Safety, Northern Ireland

Community Health and Personal Social Services Activity
028 9052 2960

Health and Personal Social Services Manpower
028 9052 2468

## Department for Work and Pensions

Family Resources Survey
020 7962 8092

Number of Benefit Recipients
0191 225 7373

## Scottish Executive

Adult community care
0131 244 3777

Children's Social Services
0131 244 3551

Social Work Staffing
0131 244 3740

## Other organisations

Charities Aid Foundation
01732 520 000

Department for Social Development, Northern Ireland
028 9052 2280

ESRC Centre for Longitudinal Studies
020 7612 6860

Eurostat
00352 4301 34122

National Assembly for Wales
029 2082 5080

National Centre for Social Research
020 7250 1866

National Health Service in Scotland
0131 551 8899

Northern Ireland Statistics and Research Agency
028 9034 8209

## Chapter 9: Crime and justice

### Websites

National Statistics
www.statistics.gov.uk

Community Legal Service
www.clsdirect.org.uk

Crime Statistics for England and Wales
www.crimestatistics.org.uk

Crown Office and Procurator Fiscal Service
www.crownoffice.gov.uk

Crown Prosecution Service
www.cps.gov.uk

Department for Constitutional Affairs
www.dca.gov.uk

HM Courts Service
www.hmcourts-service.gov.uk

Home Office
www.homeoffice.gov.uk

Criminal Justice System
www.cjsonline.gov.uk

Legal Services Commission
www.legalservices.gov.uk

National Assembly for Wales
www.wales.gov.uk/keypubstatisticsforwales

Northern Ireland Court Service
www.courtsni.gov.uk

Northern Ireland Office
www.nio.gov.uk

Northern Ireland Prison Service
www.niprisonservice.gov.uk

Police Service of Northern Ireland
www.psni.police.uk

Police Services of the United Kingdom
www.police.uk

Prison Service for England and Wales
www.hmprisonservice.gov.uk

Scottish Executive
www.scotland.gov.uk

Scottish Prison Service
www.sps.gov.uk

The Bar Council
www.barcouncil.org.uk

The Law Society of England and Wales
www.lawsociety.org.uk

## Contacts

### Office for National Statistics

Chapter author
020 7533 5204

### Other organisations

Department for Constitutional Affairs
020 7210 8500

Home Office
0870 000 1585

Northern Ireland Office
028 9052 7538

Northern Ireland Statistics and Research Agency,
  Continuous Household Survey
028 9034 8243

Police Service of Northern Ireland
028 9065 0222 ext. 24865

Scottish Executive Justice Department
0131 244 2228

Welsh Assembly Government
029 2080 1388

## Chapter 10: Housing

### Websites

National Statistics
www.statistics.gov.uk

Council of Mortgage Lenders
www.cml.org.uk

Department for Social Development, Northern Ireland
www.dsdni.gov.uk

Department for Work and Pensions
www.dwp.gov.uk

Eurostat
www.europa.eu.int/comm/eurostat

HM Courts Service
www.hmcourts-service.gov.uk

Land Registry
www.landreg.gov.uk

National Assembly for Wales
www.wales.gov.uk/keypubstatisticsforwales

Northern Ireland Statistics and Research Agency
www.nisra.gov.uk

Office of the Deputy Prime Minister
www.odpm.gov.uk

Scottish Executive
www.scotland.gov.uk

Social Exclusion Unit
www.socialexclusionunit.gov.uk

### Contacts

### Office for National Statistics

Chapter author
020 7533 5081

Expenditure and Food Survey
020 7533 5752

General Household Survey
01633 813441

### Office of the Deputy Prime Minister

Housing Data and Statistics
020 7944 3317

Planning and Land Use Statistics
020 7944 5533

### Other organisations

Council of Mortgage Lenders
020 7440 2251

Court Service
020 7210 1773

Department for Social Development, Northern Ireland, Statistics
and Research Branch
028 9052 2762

Eurostat
00352 4301 32056

Land Registry
0151 473 6008

Northern Ireland Statistics and Research Agency
028 9034 8209

Scottish Executive
0131 244 7236

Welsh Assembly Government
029 2082 5063

## Chapter 11: Environment

### Websites

National Statistics
www.statistics.gov.uk

Centre for Ecology and Hydrology, Wallingford
www.ceh-nerc.ac.uk

Department for Environment, Food and Rural Affairs
www.defra.gov.uk/environment/statistics/index.htm

Department of the Environment Northern Ireland
www.doeni.gov.uk

Department of the Environment Northern Ireland.
  Environment and Heritage Service
www.ehsni.gov.uk

Department of Trade and Industry
www.dti.gov.uk/energy

Environment Agency
www.environment-agency.gov.uk

European Environment Agency
www.eea.eu.int

Eurostat
www.europa.eu.int/comm/eurostat

Forestry Commission
www.forestry.gov.uk/statistics

Joint Nature Conservation Committee
www.jncc.gov.uk

National Assembly for Wales
www.wales.gov.uk/keypubstatisticsforwales

Northern Ireland Statistics and Research Agency
www.nisra.gov.uk

Office of the Deputy Prime Minister
www.odpm.gov.uk/planning

Scottish Environment Protection Agency
www.sepa.org.uk

Scottish Executive
www.scotland.gov.uk

Sustainable Development
www.sustainable-development.gov.uk

## Contacts

### Office for National Statistics

Chapter author
020 7533 5283

Environment and Heritage Service
028 9023 5000

### Other organisations

Centre for Ecology and Hydrology
01491 838800

Department of the Environment Northern Ireland
028 9054 0540

Department of Trade and Industry
020 7215 2697

Environment Agency
0845 9333 111

European Environment Agency
0045 3336 7100

Eurostat
00352 4301 33023

Forestry Commission
0131 314 6337

Joint Nature Conservation Committee
01733 562626

Office of the Deputy Prime Minister
020 7944 5534

Scottish Environment Protection Agency
01786 457700

Scottish Executive
0131 244 0445

Welsh Assembly Government
029 2082 5111

## Chapter 12: Transport

### Websites

National Statistics
www.statistics.gov.uk

Civil Aviation Authority, Economic Regulation Group
www.caaerg.co.uk

Department for Transport
www.dft.gov.uk/transtat

Department of the Environment Northern Ireland
www.doeni.gov.uk

Department of Trade and Industry
www.dti.gov.uk

European Commission Directorate-General Energy
and Transport
http://europa.eu.int/comm/dgs/energy_transport/index_en.html

National Centre for Social Research
www.natcen.ac.uk

Office of Rail Regulation
www.rail-reg.gov.uk

Scottish Executive
www.scotland.gov.uk

## Contacts

### Office for National Statistics

Chapter author
020 7533 5283

Census Customer Services
01329 813800

Expenditure and Food Survey
020 7533 5752

Household Expenditure
020 7533 6001

International Passenger Survey
020 7533 5765

Retail Prices Index
020 7533 5874

### Department for Transport

General Enquiries
020 7944 8300

National Travel Survey
020 7944 3097

### Other organisations

Civil Aviation Authority, Economic Regulation Group
020 7453 6213

Department of the Environment Northern Ireland
028 9054 0540

Department of Trade and Industry
020 7215 5000

Driving Standards Agency
0115 901 2852

National Centre for Social Research
020 7250 1866

Office of Rail Regulation
020 7282 2192

Police Service of Northern Ireland
028 9065 0222 ext. 24135

Scottish Executive
0131 244 7255/7256

## Chapter 13: Lifestyles and social participation

### Websites

National Statistics
www.statistics.gov.uk

Arts Council England
www.artscouncil.org.uk

British Audience Research Board
www.barb.co.uk

Charities Aid Foundation
www.cafonline.org

European Social Survey
www.europeansocialsurvey.org

Home Office
www.homeoffice.gov.uk

National Lottery Commission
www.natlotcomm.gov.uk

National Readership Survey
www.nrs.co.uk

Ofcom
www.ofcom.org.uk

Radio Joint Audience Research Ltd
**www.rajar.co.uk**

UK Parliament
**www.parliament.uk**

VisitBritain
**www.visitbritain.com**

Contacts

Office for National Statistics

Chapter author
**020 7533 5418**

Expenditure and Food Survey
**020 7533 5756**

International Passenger Survey
**020 7533 5765**

Omnibus Survey (Internet access module)
**01633 813116**

Other organisations

Arts Council England
**0845 300 6200**

Countryside Agency
**01242 521381**

European Social Survey
**020 7040 4901**

Home Office
**020 7035 4848**

House of Commons (Information Office)
**020 7219 4272**

National Council for Voluntary Organisations
**020 7713 6161**

National Lottery Commission
**020 7016 3400**

National Readership Survey
**020 7242 8111**

Northern Ireland Tourist Board
**028 9023 1221**

Ofcom
**020 7981 3000**

Radio Joint Audience Research Ltd
**020 7292 9040**

VisitBritain
**020 8846 9000**

Visit Scotland
**0131 472 2349**

Visit Wales
**0870 830 0306**

# References and further reading

From January 2005 Office for National Statistics (ONS) products published by TSO are now available from Palgrave Macmillan. Many can also be found on the National Statistics website: **www.statistics.gov.uk**

## General

*Regional Trends*, (ONS), Palgrave Macmillan, also available at: www.statistics.gov.uk/regional trends

*Focus on Ethnicity and Identity*, Internet only publication, ONS: www.statistics.gov.uk/focuson/ethnicity

*Focus on Families*, Internet only publication, ONS: www.statistics.gov.uk/focuson/families

*Focus on Gender*, Internet only publication, ONS: www.statistics.gov.uk/focuson/gender

*Focus on Health* (ONS), Palgrave Macmillan, also available at: www.statistics.gov.uk/focuson/health

*Focus on Older People*, (ONS), Palgrave Macmillan, also available at: www.statistics.gov.uk/focuson/olderpeople

*Focus on People and Migration*, (ONS), Palgrave Macmillan, also available at: www.statistics.gov.uk/focuson/migration

*Focus on Religion*, Internet only publication, ONS: www.statistics.gov.uk/focuson/religion

*Focus on Social Inequalities*, (ONS), Palgrave Macmillan, also available at: www.statistics.gov.uk/focuson/socialinequalities

*UK 2005: The Official Yearbook of the United Kingdom of Great Britain and Northern Ireland*, Palgrave Macmillan

## Chapter 1: Population

*Annual Report of the Registrar General for Northern Ireland*, Northern Ireland Statistics and Research Agency

*Annual Report of the Registrar General for Scotland*, General Register Office for Scotland

*Asylum Statistics – United Kingdom*, Home Office

*Birth Statistics, England and Wales* (Series FM1), Internet only publication, ONS: www.statistics.gov.uk/statbase/Product.asp?vlnk=5768

*Census 2001: First results on population for England and Wales*, (ONS), TSO

*Control of Immigration: Statistics, United Kingdom*, TSO

*European Social Statistics – Population*, Eurostat

*Health Statistics Quarterly*, (ONS), Palgrave Macmillan

*International Migration Statistics* (Series MN), Internet only publication, ONS: www.statistics.gov.uk/statbase/Product.asp?vlnk=507

*Key Population and Vital Statistics* (Series VS/PP1), (ONS), TSO

*Mid-year Population Estimates for England and Wales*, Internet only publication, ONS: www.statistics.gov.uk/statbase/product.asp?vlnk=601

*Mid-year Population Estimates, Northern Ireland*, Northern Ireland Statistics and Research Agency

*Mid-year Population Estimates, Scotland*, General Register Office for Scotland

*Migration Statistics*, Eurostat

*Mortality Statistics for England and Wales* (Series DH1, 2,3,4), Internet only publications, ONS:
www.statistics.gov.uk/statbase/Product.asp?vlnk=620
www.statistics.gov.uk/statbase/Product.asp?vlnk=618
www.statistics.gov.uk/statbase/Product.asp?vlnk=6305
www.statistics.gov.uk/statbase/Product.asp?vlnk=621

*National Population Projections*, UK (Series PP2), TSO

*Patterns and Trends in International Migration in Western Europe*, Eurostat

*Persons Granted British Citizenship – United Kingdom*, Home Office

*Population and Projections for areas within Northern Ireland*, Northern Ireland Statistics and Research Agency

*Population Projections, Scotland (for Administrative Areas)*, General Register Office for Scotland

*Population Projections for Wales (sub-national)*, Welsh Assembly Government / Welsh Office Statistical Directorate www.wales.gov.uk/keypubstatisticsforwales/topicindex/topicindex-e.htm#P

*Population Trends*, (ONS), Palgrave Macmillan, also available at: www.statistics.gov.uk/statbase/Product.asp?vlnk=6303

## Chapter 2: Households and families

*Abortion Statistics* (Series AB), TSO (to 2001)

*Abortion Statistics Statistical Bulletin*, Department of Health (from 2002)

*Annual Report of the Registrar General for Northern Ireland*, TSO

*Annual Report of the Registrar General for Scotland*, General Register Office for Scotland

*Birth Statistics, England and Wales*, (Series FM1), Internet only publication, ONS: www.statistics.gov.uk/statbase/Product.asp?vlnk=5768

*Birth Statistics: Historical Series*, 1837–1983 (Series FM1), TSO

*British Social Attitudes*, National Centre for Social Research

*Choosing Childlessness*, Family Policy Studies Centre

*European Social Statistics – Population*, Eurostat

*Focus on Families*, Internet only publication, ONS: www.statistics.gov.uk/focuson/families

*General Household Survey* 2004/05, Internet only publication, ONS: www.statistics.gov.uk/ghs/

*Health Statistics Quarterly*, (ONS), Palgrave Macmillan, also available at: www.statistics.gov.uk/statbase/Product.asp?vlnk=6725&More=N

*Key Population and Vital Statistics* (Series VS/PP1), (ONS), TSO

*Marriage and Divorce Statistics 1837–1983* (Series FM2), (ONS), TSO

*Marriage, Divorce and Adoption Statistics, England and Wales*, (Series FM2), Internet only publication, ONS: www.statistics.gov.uk/statbase/Product.asp?vlnk=581

*Population Trends*, (ONS), Palgrave Macmillan, also available at: www.statistics.gov.uk/statbase/Product.asp?vlnk=6303, particularly Penn R and Lambert P, Attitudes towards ideal family size of different ethnic/nationality groups in Great Britain, France and Germany, Population Trends 108

*Projections of Households in England to 2021*, Office of the Deputy Prime Minister

*Recent Demographic Developments in Europe*, Council of Europe

*Survey of English Housing: Housing in England 2000/01*, TSO

*Teenage Pregnancy, Report by the Social Exclusion Unit*, TSO

*The British Population*, Oxford University Press

## Chapter 3: Education and training

*British Social Attitudes*, National Centre for Social Research

*Education at a Glance*, OECD Indicators 2005, Organisation for Economic Co-operation and Development, 2005

*ICT in Schools Survey 2004*, Department for Education and Skills

*Knowledge and Skills for Life*, Organisation for Economic Co-operation and Development, 2001

*Learning and Training at Work 2002*, IFF Research Ltd, for the Department for Education and Skills, Research Report 399, 2003, TSO

*National Adult Learning Survey 2002*, National Centre for Social Research, for the Department for Education and Skills, Research Report 415, 2003, TSO

*National Employers Skills Survey 2003*, Learning and Skills Council, 2004

*Skills in England 2004*, Learning and Skills Council, 2005

*Statistical Volume: Education and Training Statistics for the United Kingdom*, Department for Education and Skills, 2005, TSO

## Chapter 4: Labour market

*British Social Attitudes*, National Centre for Social Research

*Employment Tribunals Service. Annual Report & Accounts 2004–05*, Employment Tribunals Service

*European Social Statistics – Labour Force Survey Results*, Eurostat

*Factors affecting the labour market participation of older workers*, Department for Work and Pensions

*How Exactly is Unemployment Measured?*, ONS: www.statistics.gov.uk/statbase/Product.asp?vlnk=2054

*Inside the Workplace. First findings from the 2004 Workplace Employment Relations Survey*, Department of Trade and Industry

*Labour Force Survey Historical Supplement*, ONS: www.statistics.gov.uk/statbase/Product.asp?vlnk=11771

*Labour Force Survey Quarterly Supplement*, ONS: www.statistics.gov.uk/statbase/Product.asp?vlnk=545

*Labour Market Trends*, (ONS), Palgrave Macmillan

*Local area labour market statistics: statistical indicators*, ONS: www.statistics.gov.uk/Statbase/Product.asp?vlnk=14160

*National Employers Skills Survey 2003*, Learning and Skills Council

*Northern Ireland Labour Force Survey*, Department of Enterprise, Trade and Investment, Northern Ireland

*Results of the second flexible working employee survey*, Department of Trade and Industry

*The State of the Labour Market*, ONS

*Trade Union Membership 2004*, Department of Trade and Industry

*What exactly is the Labour Force Survey?*, ONS: www.statistics.gov.uk/statbase/Product.asp?vlnk= 4756

## Chapter 5: Income and wealth

*Annual Survey of Hours and Earnings*, Internet only publication, ONS: www.statistics.gov.uk/statbase/Product.asp?vlnk=5750

*Attitudes to inheritance*, Joseph Rowntree Foundation

Berthoud R, Bryan M and Bardasi E, The dynamics of deprivation: the relationship between income and material deprivation over time, *DWP Research Report 219* (2004)

Brewer M, Goodman A, Myck M, Shaw J and Shephard A, Poverty and Inequality in Britain: 2004, Commentary no. 96, The Institute for Fiscal Studies

*British Social Attitudes*, National Centre for Social Research

*Changing Households: The British Household Panel Survey*, Institute for Social and Economic Research

*Distribution of Income and Wealth 1975*; report by Royal Commission, quoted in book by Atkinson A B and Harrison A J, *Distribution of Personal Wealth in Britain*, Cambridge University Press 1978, Table 6.1

*Economic Trends*, (ONS), Palgrave Macmillan, also available at: www.statistics.gov.uk/statbase/product.asp?vlnk=308

*European Community Finances: Statement on the 2005 EC Budget and Measures to Counter Fraud and Financial Mismanagement*, TSO (Cm 6580 (ISBN 0-10-165802-8)

*Eurostat National Accounts ESA*, Eurostat

*Family Resources Survey*, Department for Work and Pensions

*Fiscal Studies*, The Institute for Fiscal Studies, particularly Clark T and Leicester A, Inequality and two decades of British tax and benefit reforms (2004), *Fiscal Studies*, vol. 25, pp. 129–58

*For Richer, For Poorer*, The Institute for Fiscal Studies

*Households Below Average Income, 1994/95–2003/04*, Department for Work and Pensions

*Income and Wealth. The Latest Evidence*, Joseph Rowntree Foundation

*Individual Incomes 1996/97–2003/04*, Women and Equality Unit

*Labour Market Trends*, Palgrave Macmillan

*Monitoring Poverty and Social Exclusion*, Joseph Rowntree Foundation

*Opportunity for All Annual Report*, Department for Work and Pensions

*Pension Trends*, (ONS), Palgrave Macmillan, also available at: www.statistics.gov.uk/pensiontrends

*The Distribution of Wealth in the UK*, The Institute for Fiscal Studies

*The Pensioners' Incomes Series*, Department for Work and Pensions

*United Kingdom National Accounts (The Blue Book)*, (ONS), Palgrave Macmillan

## Chapter 6: Expenditure

*Consumer Trends*, Internet only publication, ONS: www.statistics.gov.uk/consumertrends

*Economic Trends*, (ONS), Palgrave Macmillan, also available at: www.statistics.gov.uk/statbase/product.asp?vlnk=308

*Family Spending*, (ONS), Palgrave Macmillan

*Financial Statistics*, (ONS), Palgrave Macmillan

*Focus on Consumer Price Indices (formerly the Business Monitor MM23)*, ONS, www.statistics.gov.uk

Relative Regional Consumer Price Levels in 2004, *Economic Trends, no. 615*, ONS: www.statistics.gov.uk/cci/article.asp?id=1016

*Retail Sales Business Monitor (SDM28)*, Internet only publication, ONS: www.statistics.gov.uk/rsi

*United Kingdom National Accounts (The Blue Book)*, (ONS), Palgrave Macmillan

## Chapter 7: Health

*Alcohol Harm Reduction Strategy for England*, The Cabinet Office

*Annual Report of the Registrar General for Northern Ireland*, Northern Ireland Statistics and Research Agency

*Annual Report of the Registrar General for Scotland*, General Register Office for Scotland

*At Least Five a Week – Evidence on the Impact of Physical Activity and its Relationship to Health, A Report from the Chief Medical Officer*, Department of Health

*Cancer Atlas of the United Kingdom and Ireland 1991–2000*, (ONS), Palgrave Macmillan

*Cancer Trends in England and Wales 1950–1999*, (ONS), TSO

*Choosing Health – Making Healthy Choices Easier*, Cm 6374, TSO

*Community Statistics*, Department of Health, Social Services and Public Safety, Northern Ireland

*Drug Misuse Declared: Findings from the 2003/04 British Crime Survey*, Home Office

*General Household Survey 2004/05*, Internet only publication, ONS: www.statistics.gov.uk/ghs/

*Geographic Variations in Health*, (ONS), TSO

*Health in Scotland. The Annual Report of the Chief Medical Officer on the State of Scotland's Health*, Scottish Executive

*Health Statistics Quarterly*, (ONS), Palgrave Macmillan, also available at: www.statistics.gov.uk/statbase/Product.asp?vlnk=6725&More=N, particularly Results of the ICD-10 bridge coding study, England and Wales, 1999, *Health Statistics Quarterly 14*, Palgrave Macmillan

*Health Statistics Wales*, National Assembly for Wales

*Health Survey for England*, TSO

*Key Health Statistics from General Practice 1998*, ONS

*Mapping the Issues HIV and other Sexually Transmitted Infections in the United Kingdom: 2005*, Health Protection Agency Centre for Infections

*Mental Health of Children and Young People in Great Britain 2004*, (ONS), Palgrave Macmillan

*Mortality Statistics for England and Wales* (Series DH1, 2,3,4) Internet only publications, ONS:
www.statistics.gov.uk/statbase/Product.asp?vlnk=620
www.statistics.gov.uk/statbase/Product.asp?vlnk=618
www.statistics.gov.uk/statbase/Product.asp?vlnk=6305
www.statistics.gov.uk/statbase/Product.asp?vlnk=621

*On the State of the Public Health – The Annual Report of the Chief Medical Officer of the Department of Health*, TSO

*Population Trends*, (ONS), Palgrave Macmillan, also available at:
www.statistics.gov.uk/statbase/Product.asp?vlnk=6303

*Psychiatric Morbidity Survey Among Adults Living in Private Households 2000*, (ONS), TSO

*Report of the Chief Medical Officer*, Department of Health, Social Services and Public Safety, Northern Ireland

*Scottish Health Statistics*, Information Services Division, NHS Scotland

*Smoking, Drinking and Drug Use among Young People in England in 2004*, Health and Social Care Information Centre

*Smoking Kills – A White Paper on Tobacco*, TSO

*Smoking-related Behaviour and Attitudes, 2004*, (ONS), TSO

*Statistical Publications on Aspects of Health and Personal Social Services Activity in England* (various), Department of Health

*Tackling Health Inequalities: Status Report on the Programme for Action*, Department of Health

*Welsh Health: Annual Report of the Chief Medical Officer*, National Assembly for Wales

*World Health Statistics*, World Health Organisation

## Chapter 8: Social protection

Annual News Releases (various), Scottish Executive

*British Social Attitudes*, National Centre for Social Research

*Charity Trends 2005*, CAF (Charities Aid Foundation)

*Chief Executive's Report to the NHS*, Department of Health

*Children's social service statistics*, Department for Education and Skills

*Community Statistics for Northern Ireland*, Department of Health, Social Services and Public Safety, Northern Ireland

*Continuous Household Survey*, Northern Ireland Statistics and Research Agency

*ESSPROS Manual 1996*, Eurostat

*Family Resources Survey*, Department for Work and Pensions

*General Household Survey 2004/05*, Internet only publication, ONS: www.statistics.gov.uk/ghs/

*Health and Personal Social Services Statistics*, Department of Health

*Health Statistics Wales*, National Assembly for Wales

*Hospital Activity Statistics*, Department of Health

*Hospital Episode Statistics for England*, Department of Health

*Hospital Statistics for Northern Ireland*, Department of Health, Social Services and Public Safety, Northern Ireland

Lessof C and Nazroo J, *Health, wealth and lifestyles of the older population in England: The 2002 English Longitudinal Study of Ageing*, The Institute of Fiscal Studies

*Millennium Cohort Study First Survey: A User's Guide to Initial Findings*, ESRC Centre for Longitudinal Studies

*Occupational Pension Schemes 2000*, Government Actuary's Department

*Poverty and Inequality in Britain: 2005*, The Institute of Fiscal Studies

*Scottish Community Care Statistics*, Scottish Executive

*Scottish Health Statistics*, National Health Service in Scotland, Common Services Agency

*Social Protection Expenditure and Receipts*, Eurostat

*Social Security Departmental Report*, TSO

*Social Services Statistics Wales*, Local Government Data Unit – Wales

*Statistical Publications on Aspects of Community Care in Scotland* (various), Scottish Executive Health Department

*Statistical Publications on Aspects of Health and Personal Social Services Activity in England* (various), Department of Health

*Work and Pension Statistics*, Department for Work and Pensions

## Chapter 9: Crime and justice

*A Commentary on Northern Ireland Crime Statistics 2004*, Northern Ireland Office

*Civil Judicial Statistics Scotland* (2001), TSO

*Costs, Sentencing Profiles and the Scottish Criminal Justice System*, Scottish Executive

*Crime and the Quality of Life: Public Perceptions and Experiences of Crime in Scotland*, Scottish Executive

*Crime in England and Wales 2004/05*, Home Office

*Criminal Statistics, England and Wales 2004*, Home Office

*Crown Prosecution Service, Annual Report 2004/05*, TSO

*Digest 4: Information on the Criminal Justice System in England and Wales*, Home Office

*Digest of Information on the Northern Ireland Criminal Justice System 4*, Northern Ireland Office

*HM Prison Service Annual Report and Accounts*, TSO

*Home Office Departmental Report 2005*, TSO

*Home Office Research Findings*, Home Office

*Home Office Statistical Bulletins*, Home Office

*Judicial Statistics*, England and Wales, TSO

*Legal Services Commission Annual Report 2004/05*, TSO

*Northern Ireland Judicial Statistics*, Northern Ireland Court Service

*Offender Management Caseload Statistics*, The Home Office

*Police Service of Northern Ireland Statistical Report, 2003/2004*, Police Service of Northern Ireland

*Police Statistics, England and Wales*, CIPFA

*Prison Statistics, England and Wales 2002*, TSO

*Prison Statistics Scotland 2004/05*, Scottish Executive

*Prisons in Scotland Report*, TSO

*Race and the Criminal Justice System*, Home Office

*Recorded crime in Scotland 2004/05,* Scottish Executive

*Report of the Chief Constable 2003–04,* Police Service of Northern Ireland

*Report of the Parole Board for England and Wales,* TSO

*Report on the work of the Northern Ireland Prison Service,* TSO

*Scottish Crime Survey,* Scottish Executive

*Scottish Executive Statistical Bulletins: Criminal Justice Series,* Scottish Executive

*Statistics on Women and the Criminal Justice System,* Home Office

*Review of Crime Statistics: a Discussion Document,* Home Office

*Review of Police Forces' Crime Recording Practices,* Home Office

*The Criminal Justice System in England and Wales,* Home Office

*The Work of the Prison Service,* TSO

## Chapter 10: Housing

*A Review of Flexible Mortgages,* Council of Mortgage Lenders

*Becoming a Home-owner in Britain in the 1990s – The British Household Panel Survey,* ESRC Institute for Social and Economic Research

*Bringing Britain Together: A National Strategy for Neighbourhood Renewal,* Social Exclusion Unit, Cabinet Office

*Changing Households: The British Household Panel Survey,* Institute for Social and Economic Research

*Divorce, Remarriage and Housing: The Effects of Divorce, Remarriage, Separation and the Formation of New Couple Households on the Number of Separate Households and Housing Demand Conditions,* Department of the Environment, Transport and the Regions

*Economic Trends,* (ONS), Palgrave Macmillan, also available at: www.statistics.gov.uk/statbase/product.asp?vlnk=308, particularly Methodological improvements to UK foreign property investment statistics, Economic Trends 619

*English House Condition Survey 2003,* TSO

*General Household Survey 2004/05,* Internet only publication, ONS: www.statistics.gov.uk/ghs/

*Housing Finance,* Council of Mortgage Lenders

*Housing in England: Survey of English Housing,* TSO

*Living conditions in Europe – Statistical Pocketbook,* Eurostat

*Local Housing Statistics,* TSO

*My Home Was My Castle: Evictions and Repossessions in Britain,* ESRC Institute of Social and Economic Research and Institute Local Research

*Northern Ireland House Condition Survey,* Northern Ireland Housing Executive

*Northern Ireland Housing Statistics, 2004/05,* Department for Social Development, Northern Ireland

*Office of the Deputy Prime Minister Annual Report 2005,* TSO

*On the Move: The Housing Consequences Migration,* YPS

*Private Renting in England,* TSO

*Private Renting in Five Localities,* TSO

*Projections of Households in England to 2021,* TSO

*Scottish House Condition Survey 2002,* Communities Scotland

*Statistical Bulletins on Housing,* Scottish Executive

*Statistics on Housing in the European Community,* Eurostat

*The Social Situation in the European Union,* Eurostat

*Welsh House Condition Survey 1998,* National Assembly for Wales

*Welsh Housing Statistics,* National Assembly for Wales

## Chapter 11: Environment

*Accounting for Nature: Assessing Habitats in the UK Countryside,* Department for Environment, Food and Rural Affairs

*Achieving a Better Quality of Life, 2003,* Department for Environment, Food and Rural Affairs

*Agriculture in the United Kingdom 2003,* TSO

*Air Quality Strategy for England, Scotland, Wales and Northern Ireland,* TSO

*Air Quality Strategy for England, Scotland, Wales and Northern Ireland: Addendum,* Department for Environment, Food and Rural Affairs

*Biodiversity: The UK Action Plan,* TSO

*Digest of United Kingdom Energy Statistics,* TSO

*e-Digest of Environmental Statistics,* Internet only publication, Department for Environment, Food and Rural Affairs: www.defra.gov.uk/environment/statistics/index.htm

*Forestry Facts and Figures 2005,* Forestry Commission

*Forestry Statistics 2005,* Forestry Commission

*GM Nation. The Findings of the Public Debate,* Department for Environment, Food and Rural Affairs

*General Quality Assessment,* Environment Agency

*Hydrological Summaries for the United Kingdom,* Centre for Hydrology and British Geological Survey

*Land Use Change Statistics,* Office of the Deputy Prime Minister

*Municipal Waste Management Survey,* Department for Environment, Food and Rural Affairs

*OECD Environmental Data Compendium,* OECD

*Organic Statistics,* Department for Environment, Food and Rural Affairs

*Planning Public Water Supplies,* Environment Agency

*Pollution Incidents in England and Wales, 2002,* Environment Agency

*Quality of life counts – indicators for a strategy for sustainable development for the United Kingdom: a baseline assessment,* Department of the Environment, Transport and the Regions

*Scottish Environment Protection Agency Annual Report 2001–2002,* SEPA

*Survey of Public Attitudes to Quality of Life and to the Environment - 2001,* Department for Environment, Food and Rural Affairs

*Sustainable Development Indicators in your Pocket 2004,* Department for Environment, Food and Rural Affairs

*The Environment in your Pocket,* Department for Environment, Food and Rural Affairs

## Chapter 12: Transport

*A New Deal for Transport: Better for Everyone,* TSO

*A Strategy for Sustainable Development for the United Kingdom,* TSO

*Annual Report,* Central Rail Users Consultative Committee

*British Social Attitudes,* National Centre for Social Research

*Driving Standards Agency Annual Report and Accounts,* TSO

*European Union Energy and Transport in Figures, 2002,* European Commission

*Focus on Personal Travel,* TSO

*Focus on Public Transport,* TSO

*International Passenger Transport,* TSO

*National Rail Trends,* Strategic Rail Authority

*National Travel Survey Bulletins,* Department for Transport

*Rail Complaints*, Office of the Rail Regulator

*Road Casualties Great Britain – Annual Report*, TSO

*Road Accidents*, Scotland, Scottish Executive

*Road Accidents: Wales*, National Assembly for Wales

*Road Traffic Accident Statistics Annual Report*, Police Service of Northern Ireland

*Road Traffic Statistics Great Britain*, Department for Transport

*Scottish Transport Statistics*, Scottish Executive

*Transport Statistical Bulletins*, Scottish Executive

*Transport Statistics Bulletins and Reports*, Department for Transport

*Transport Statistics Great Britain*, TSO

*Transport Trends*, TSO

*Travel Trends*, (ONS), Palgrave Macmillan, also available at: www.statistics.gov.uk/statbase/Product.asp?vlnk=1391

*Vehicle Licensing Statistics*, Department for Transport

*Vehicle Speeds in Great Britain*, Department for Transport

*Welsh Transport Statistics*, National Assembly for Wales

## Chapter 13: Lifestyles and social participation

*Arts in England 2003: attendance, participation and attitudes*, Arts Council England

*BG Leisure Day Visits 2002/03*, The Countryside Agency

*Charity Trends 2005*, CarisData Ltd

*2003 Home Office Citzenship Survey: people families and communities*, Home Office

*LISU Annual Library Statistics 2005*, Loughborough University

*Report on Participation, Expenditure and Attitudes*, National Lottery Commision: www.natlotcomm.gov.uk/Publications/

*Sport and leisure – Results from the sport and leisure module*, 2002 General Household Survey, ONS

*The Communications Market 2004*, Ofcom

*Travel Trends*, (ONS), Palgrave Macmillan, also available at: www.statistics.gov.uk/statbase/Product.asp?vlnk=1391

*Visitor Attraction Monitor 2004*, VisitScotland

*Visitor Attraction Trends England*, VisitBritain

*Visits to Tourist Attractions 2004*, Wales Tourist Board

# Geographical areas

## The European Union, 1 May 2004

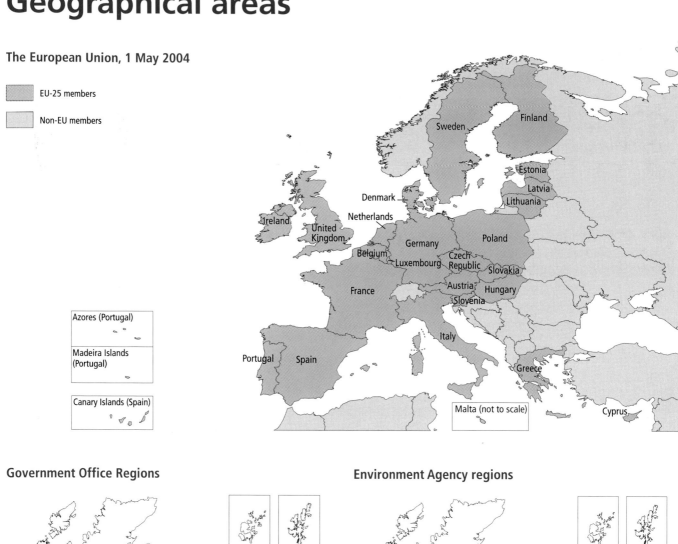

EU-25 members

Non-EU members

Azores (Portugal)

Madeira Islands (Portugal)

Canary Islands (Spain)

Sweden
Finland
Estonia
Latvia
Lithuania
Denmark
Ireland
Netherlands
United Kingdom
Germany
Poland
Belgium
Luxembourg
Czech Republic
Slovakia
France
Austria
Hungary
Slovenia
Italy
Portugal
Spain
Greece
Malta (not to scale)
Cyprus

## Government Office Regions

## Environment Agency regions

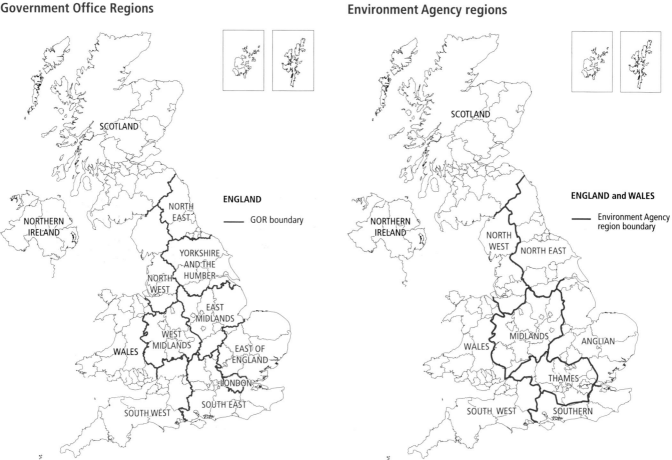

SCOTLAND

NORTHERN IRELAND

ENGLAND
— GOR boundary

NORTH EAST
YORKSHIRE AND THE HUMBER
NORTH WEST
EAST MIDLANDS
WEST MIDLANDS
WALES
EAST OF ENGLAND
LONDON
SOUTH WEST
SOUTH EAST

SCOTLAND

NORTHERN IRELAND

ENGLAND and WALES
— Environment Agency region boundary

NORTH WEST
NORTH EAST
MIDLANDS
WALES
ANGLIAN
THAMES
SOUTH WEST
SOUTHERN

# Health areas, 2001

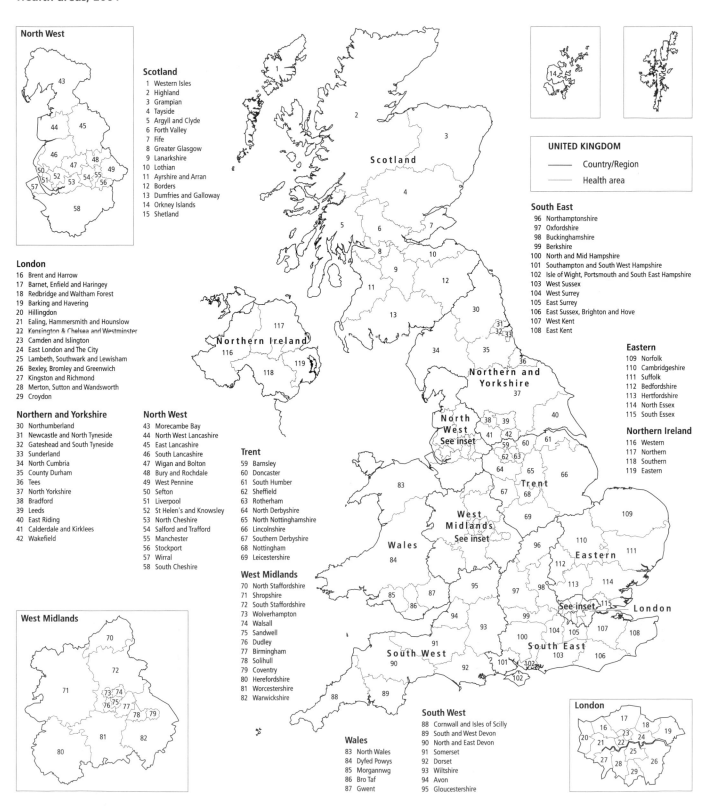

**North West**

43 Morecambe Bay

**Scotland**

1 Western Isles
2 Highland
3 Grampian
4 Tayside
5 Argyll and Clyde
6 Forth Valley
7 Fife
8 Greater Glasgow
9 Lanarkshire
10 Lothian
11 Ayrshire and Arran
12 Borders
13 Dumfries and Galloway
14 Orkney Islands
15 Shetland

**London**

16 Brent and Harrow
17 Barnet, Enfield and Haringey
18 Redbridge and Waltham Forest
19 Barking and Havering
20 Hillingdon
21 Ealing, Hammersmith and Hounslow
22 Kensington & Chelsea and Westminster
23 Camden and Islington
24 East London and The City
25 Lambeth, Southwark and Lewisham
26 Bexley, Bromley and Greenwich
27 Kingston and Richmond
28 Merton, Sutton and Wandsworth
29 Croydon

**Northern and Yorkshire**

30 Northumberland
31 Newcastle and North Tyneside
32 Gateshead and South Tyneside
33 Sunderland
34 North Cumbria
35 County Durham
36 Tees
37 North Yorkshire
38 Bradford
39 Leeds
40 East Riding
41 Calderdale and Kirklees
42 Wakefield

**North West**

43 Morecambe Bay
44 North West Lancashire
45 East Lancashire
46 South Lancashire
47 Wigan and Bolton
48 Bury and Rochdale
49 West Pennine
50 Sefton
51 Liverpool
52 St Helen's and Knowsley
53 North Cheshire
54 Salford and Trafford
55 Manchester
56 Stockport
57 Wirral
58 South Cheshire

**Trent**

59 Barnsley
60 Doncaster
61 South Humber
62 Sheffield
63 Rotherham
64 North Derbyshire
65 North Nottinghamshire
66 Lincolnshire
67 Southern Derbyshire
68 Nottingham
69 Leicestershire

**West Midlands**

70 North Staffordshire
71 Shropshire
72 South Staffordshire
73 Wolverhampton
74 Walsall
75 Sandwell
76 Dudley
77 Birmingham
78 Solihull
79 Coventry
80 Herefordshire
81 Worcestershire
82 Warwickshire

**Wales**

83 North Wales
84 Dyfed Powys
85 Morgannwg
86 Bro Taf
87 Gwent

**South West**

88 Cornwall and Isles of Scilly
89 South and West Devon
90 North and East Devon
91 Somerset
92 Dorset
93 Wiltshire
94 Avon
95 Gloucestershire

**UNITED KINGDOM**

—— Country/Region
—— Health area

**South East**

96 Northamptonshire
97 Oxfordshire
98 Buckinghamshire
99 Berkshire
100 North and Mid Hampshire
101 Southampton and South West Hampshire
102 Isle of Wight, Portsmouth and South East Hampshire
103 West Sussex
104 West Surrey
105 East Surrey
106 East Sussex, Brighton and Hove
107 West Kent
108 East Kent

**Eastern**

109 Norfolk
110 Cambridgeshire
111 Suffolk
112 Bedfordshire
113 Hertfordshire
114 North Essex
115 South Essex

**Northern Ireland**

116 Western
117 Northern
118 Southern
119 Eastern

*The 2001 health area boundaries shown are specific to the analysis presented in Map 7.18. More recent health boundaries are available.*

# Major surveys

| | Frequency | Sampling frame | Type of respondent | Coverage | Effective sample size[1] (most recent survey included in *Social Trends*) | Response rate (percentages) |
|---|---|---|---|---|---|---|
| Annual Population Survey | Continuous | Postcode Address File | All adults in household | UK | 515,000 individuals | [2] |
| Annual Survey of Hours and Earnings | Annual | Inland Revenue PAYE records | Employee | UK | 240,000 | 85 |
| British Crime Survey | Annual | Postcode Address File | Adult in household | EW | 45,000 addresses | 75 |
| British Household Panel Survey | Annual | Postal addresses in 1991, members of initial wave households followed in subsequent waves | All adults in households | GB | 5,798 households | 88.5[3] |
| British Social Attitudes Survey | Annual | Postcode Address File | One adult per household | GB | 5,660 addresses | 56.5[4] |
| Census of Population | Decennial | Detailed local | Adult in household | UK | Full count | 98 |
| Children's Dental Health Survey, 2003 | Decennial | Government-maintained and independent schools | Children aged 5, 8, 12, 15 and parents | UK | 12,698 children | 82[5] |
| Continuous Household Survey | Continuous | Valuation and Lands Agency Property | All adults in household | NI | 3,987 addresses | 70 |
| English House Condition Survey | Annual[6] | Postcode Address File | Any one householder | E | 32,825 addresses | 51[6] |
| English Longitudinal Study of Ageing | Biennial | 1998 and 1999 core sample and 2001 Health Survey for England | People aged 50 and over living in private households | E | 11,392 individuals | 67 |
| Expenditure and Food Survey | Continuous | Postcode Address File in GB, Rating and Valuation lists in NI | All adults in households aged 16 or over[7] | UK | 11,053 addresses[7] | 57[7] |
| Families and Children Study | Annual | Child benefit records[8] | Recipients of child benefit (usually mothers) | GB | 9,508[8] families | 82[8] |
| Family Resources Survey | Continuous | Postcode Address File | All members in household | UK | 45,210 households | 63 |
| General Household Survey | Continuous | Postcode Address File | All adults in household | GB | 12,149 households | 69[9] |
| Health Survey for England | Continuous | Postcode Address File | All household members | E | 13,680 addresses | 73[9] |
| Home Office Citizenship Survey | Biennial | Postcode Address File | One adult per household | EW | 14,057 interviews | 64[10] |
| International Passenger Survey | Continuous | International passengers | Individual traveller | UK[11] | 258,642 individuals | 87 |
| Labour Force Survey | Continuous | Postcode Address File | All adults in household | UK | 53,000 households | 73[12] |
| Mental Health of Children and Young People, 2004 | Ad hoc[13] | Child benefit records | Parents, children if aged 11–16, teachers | GB | 7,977 families | 76[13] |
| Millennium Cohort Study | Biennial[14] | Electoral wards | Parents of living babies born between specific dates[14] | UK | 18,553 families[14] | 72 |
| Monthly Wages and Salaries Survey | Monthly | Inter Departmental Business Register[15] | Employers | GB | 8.700 companies covering 12 million employees | 80 |
| National Employers Skills Survey | Annual | Experian Business Database | Employers | E | 72,100 interviews achieved | 42 |
| National Travel Survey | Continuous | Postcode Address File | All household members | GB | 13,611 households per year | 60[16] |
| New Earnings Survey | Annual | Inland Revenue PAYE records | Employee | GB | [17] | [17] |
| National Statistics Omnibus Survey | Continuous | Postcode Address File | Adults aged 16 or over living in private households | GB | Approximately 12,000[18] | 66 |
| Psychiatric Morbidity Survey | Ad hoc | Postcode Address File | Adults aged 16 to 74 years living in private households | GB | 15,804 addresses | 69 |
| Retail Sales Inquiry | Continuous | Inter Departmental Business Register[15] | Retailers | GB | Approximately 5,000 | 64[19] |
| Smoking, Drinking and Drug Use Among Young People In England 2004 | Annual | English schools[20] | Pupils in years 7 to 11 | E | 9,715 pupils | 62[20] |
| Survey of English Housing | Continuous | Postcode Address File | Household | E | 29,400 households | 72 |
| Youth Cohort Study | Annual[21] | School records | Young people (aged 16–19) | EW | 30,000 individuals | 47[21] |

1   Effective sample size includes non-respondents but excludes ineligible households.
2   The Annual Population Survey includes the English Local Labour Force Survey, Welsh Local Labour Force Survey, Scottish Labour Force Survey, Annual Population Survey 'Boost' and waves 1 and 5 of the Quarterly Labour Force Survey.
3   Wave on wave response rate at wave 12. Around 57 per cent of eligible wave 1 sample members were respondents in wave 12.
4   Response rate refers to 2003 survey.
5   The 82 per cent figure refers to the children who were examined. Questionnaires were also sent to the parents of a random sub-sample of 5,480 examined children. The response rate was 61 per cent.
6   Although the EHCS runs on a continuous basis, its reporting is based on a rolling two year sample. The EHCS response combines successful outcomes from two linked surveys where information is separately gathered about the household and the dwelling for each address.
7   There is an optional diary for children aged 7 to 15 in Great Britain. Basic sample for Great Britain only. Response rate refers to Great Britain.
8   For 2003 (wave 4) the panel sample was 7,901 cases and booster cases totalled 1,401. The overall response rate is given, which is the number of interviews as a proportion of the total initial sample.
9   Response rate for fully and partially responding households.
10  Response rate refers to the core sample of the 2003 survey.
11  Includes UK and overseas residents.
12  Response rate to first wave interviews of the quarterly LFS averages over the period March 2004 to February 2005.
13  A similar survey was carried out in 1999. Response rate based on number of families approached for interview.
14  The first two sweeps of the study were completed during 2001–02 and 2003–04 when the children were aged approximately nine months and three years. Two more surveys are scheduled for 2006–07 and 2008–09 when the children will be aged five and seven years respectively. Follow-up surveys are expected to take place in the future. Between 1 September 2000 and 31 August 2001 in England and Wales and between 22 November 2000 and 11 January 2002 in Scotland and Northern Ireland. Achieved sample size for sweep 1.
15  GB companies with 20 or more employees.
16  Sixty per cent of households were recorded as being 'fully productive'. However, a further 7 per cent co-operated partially with the survey, and the data from these households can be used on a limited basis.
17  In the New Earnings Survey employers supply data on a 1 per cent sample of employees who are members of PAYE schemes. For the 2003 sample approximately 239,000 were selected and there was an 88 per cent response, but some 48,000 returned questionnaires were not taken onto the results file for various reasons.
18  Achieved sample size per Omnibus interviews at one household per sampled address and one adult per household. Data are weighted to account for the fact that respondents living in smaller households would have a greater chance of selection.
19  Average response rate for 2005.
20  Excludes special schools. Based on overall response rate. In 2004, 70 per cent of schools and 89 per cent of selected pupils responded to the survey.
21  New samples are drawn every two years and each of these cohorts is then surveyed annually over four years. Based on cohort 12, sweep 1, spring 2004 survey.

# Symbols and conventions

**Reference years**  Where, because of space constraints, a choice of years has to be made, the most recent year or a run of recent years is shown together with the past population census years (2001, 1991, 1981, etc) and sometimes the mid-points between census years (1996, 1986, etc). Other years may be added if they represent a peak or trough in the series.

**Rounding of figures**  In tables where figures have been rounded to the nearest final digit, there may be an apparent discrepancy between the sum of the constituent items and the total as shown.

**Billion**  This term is used to represent a thousand million.

**Provisional and estimated data**  Some data for the latest year (and occasionally for earlier years) are provisional or estimated. To keep footnotes to a minimum, these have not been indicated; source departments will be able to advise if revised data are available.

**Seasonal adjustment**  Unless otherwise stated, unadjusted data have been used.

**Financial year**  – eg 1 April 2003 to 31 March 2004 would be shown as 2003/04.

**Academic year**  – eg September 2003 to July 2004 would be shown as 2003/04.

**Combined years**  – eg 2001–04 shows data for more than one year that have been combined.

**Units on tables**  Where one unit predominates it is shown at the top of the table. All other units are shown against the relevant row or column. Figures are shown in italics when they represent percentages.

**Household reference person**  Sometimes it is necessary to select one person in a household to indicate the general characteristics of the household. For this purpose the household reference person has replaced the head of household in all government-sponsored household surveys after 2000–01. The household reference person is identified during the interview and is:

a. the householder (in whose name the accommodation is owned or rented); or

b. in households with joint householders, the person with the highest income or, if both householders have the same income, the oldest householder.

**Dependent children**  Those aged under 16, or single people aged 16 to 18 and in full-time education unless otherwise indicated.

**EU**  Unless otherwise stated, data relate to the enlarged European Union of 25 countries (EU-25) as constituted since 1 May 2004. EU-15 refers to the 15 members of the EU before enlargement.

**Germany**  Unless otherwise stated, data relate to Germany as constituted since 3 October 1990.

**Ireland**  Refers to the Republic of Ireland and does not include Northern Ireland.

**Symbols**  The following symbols have been used throughout *Social Trends:*

..  not available

.  not applicable

-  negligible (less than half the final digit shown)

0  nil

# Appendix

## Part 1: Population

### Population estimates and projections

The estimated and projected populations are of the resident population of an area, i.e. all those usually resident there, whatever their nationality. Members of HM Forces stationed outside the United Kingdom are excluded; members of foreign forces stationed in the United Kingdom are included. Students are taken to be resident at their term-time addresses. Figures for the United Kingdom do not include the population of the Channel Islands or the Isle of Man.

The population estimates for mid-2001 to mid-2004 are based on results from the 2001 Census and have been updated to reflect subsequent births, deaths, net migration and other changes. The estimates used in this publication were released on 25 August 2005.

The most recent set of national population projections published for the United Kingdom are based on the populations of England, Wales, Scotland and Northern Ireland at mid-2004. These were released on 20 October 2005 and further details can be found on the Government Actuary's Department's website (www.gad.gov.uk).

### Classification of ethnic groups

The recommended classification of ethnic groups for National Statistics data sources was changed in 2001 to bring it broadly in line with the 2001 Census.

There are two levels to this classification. Level 1 is a coarse classification into five main ethnic groups. Level 2 provides a finer classification of Level 1. The preference is for the Level 2 (detailed) categories to be adopted wherever possible. The two levels and the categories are in the box below.

Direct comparisons should not be made between the figures produced using this new classification and those based on the previous classification.

Further details can be found on the National Statistics website: www.statistics.gov.uk/about/classifications/downloads/ns_ethnicity_statement.doc

### Religion

The Census in England and Wales asked one question about religion, 'What is your religion?' The responses to this question were very similar to answers given to the Labour Force Survey question, 'What is your religion, even if you are not currently practising?' – suggesting that despite slight differences in the wording, the two questions were answered on the same basis.

The Census in Scotland asked two questions about religion, 'What religion, religious denomination or body do you belong to?' and 'What religion, religious denomination or body were you brought up in?' The two questions produced different results, the main difference being the proportion with no religion, which was much greater on the current religion question. Answers given to the second question, religion of upbringing, were similar to those given by Labour Force Survey respondents in Scotland – again suggesting that respondents were answering on the same basis. Since the England and Wales question and the Scotland Religion of Upbringing question appear to have been answered on a similar basis, these two questions were combined to produce GB level data. The exact questions underlying all analyses were as follows:

## Classification of ethnic groups

| Level 1 | Level 2 |
| --- | --- |
| White | White |
| | British |
| | Irish |
| | Other White background |
| | All White groups |
| Mixed | White and Black Caribbean |
| | White and Black African |
| | White and Asian |
| | Other Mixed background |
| | All Mixed groups |
| Asian or Asian British | Indian |
| | Pakistani |
| | Bangladeshi |
| | Other Asian background |
| | All Asian groups |
| Black or Black British | Caribbean |
| | African |
| | Other Black background |
| | All Black groups |
| Chinese or other ethnic Group | Chinese |
| | Other ethnic group |
| | All Chinese or other groups |
| All ethnic groups | All ethnic groups |
| Not stated | Not stated |

### In England and Wales:

'What is your religion?'

None

Christian (including Church of England, Catholic, Protestant, and all other Christian denominations)

Buddhist

Hindu

Jewish

Muslim

Sikh

Any other religion (please write in)

### In Scotland:

'What religion, religious denomination or body were you brought up in?'

None

Church of Scotland

Roman Catholic

Other Christian (please write in)

Buddhist

Hindu

Jewish

Muslim

Sikh

Any other religion (please write in)

## National Statistics Socio-economic Classification (NS-SEC)

From 2001 the National Statistics Socio-economic Classification (NS-SEC) was adopted for all official surveys, in place of Social Class (see Appendix, Part 8: Social class) based on Occupation and Socio-economic Group. NS-SEC is itself based on the Standard Occupational Classification 2000 (SOC2000) and details of employment status.

The NS-SEC is an occupationally-based classification designed to provide coverage of the whole adult population. The version of the classification, which will be used for most analyses, has eight classes, the first of which can be subdivided. These are:

1. Higher managerial and professional occupations, sub-divided into:

   1.1  Large employers and higher managerial occupations

   1.2  Higher professional occupations

2. Lower managerial and professional occupations

3. Intermediate occupations

4. Small employers and own account workers

5. Lower supervisory and technical occupations

6. Semi-routine occupations

7. Routine occupations

8. Never worked and long-term unemployed

The classes can be further grouped into:

| | | |
|---|---|---|
| i. | Managerial and professional occupations | 1,2 |
| ii. | Intermediate occupations | 3,4 |
| iii. | Routine and manual occupations | 5,6,7 |
| | Never worked and long-term unemployed | 8 |

Users have the option to include them in the overall analysis or keep them separate. The long-term unemployed are defined as those unemployed and seeking work for 12 months or more. Members of HM Forces, who were shown separately in tables of social class, are included within the NS-SEC classification. Residual groups that remain unclassified include students and those with inadequately described occupations.

For the purposes of family spending in Chapter 6: Expenditure, retired individuals are not assigned an NS-SEC category.

Further details can be found on the National Statistics website: www.statistics.gov.uk/ methods_quality/ns_sec/default.asp

## Internal migration estimates

The estimates of internal migration presented in this volume are based on data provided by the NHS Central Register (NHSCR), which records movements of patients between former Health Authority areas (HAs). Using this data source, the definition of a migrant is therefore someone who changes their doctor and moves from one former HA to another. Historically, internal

migration estimates were only available at the former HA level; these were equivalent to shire counties, metropolitan districts and groupings of London boroughs. HA-level migration estimates are available from 1975 on a quarterly rolling year basis.

Internal migration estimates by age and sex became available for all local authority areas in 1999. By obtaining a download from each patient register and by combining all the patient register extracts together, ONS creates a total register for the whole of England and Wales. Comparing records in one year with those of the previous year enables identification of people who have changed their postcode. A migrant in the Patient Register Data System is therefore defined as a person who, between one year and the next, changes their area of residence. Estimates at local authority level are made by constraining the migration estimates from the patient registers with the NHSCR estimates at the former HA level.

It has been established that internal migration data under-report the migration of men aged between 16 and 36. Currently, however, there are no suitable sources of data available to enable adjustments or revisions to be made to the estimates. Further research is planned on this topic and new data sources may become available in the future. However, for the present, historical estimates will not be revised and future estimates will not be adjusted.

## International migration estimates

An international migrant is defined as someone who changes his or her country of usual residence for a period of at least a year, so that the country of destination becomes the country of usual residence. The richest source of information on international migrants comes from the International Passenger Survey (IPS), which is a sample survey of passengers arriving at, and departing from, the main UK air and sea ports and the Channel Tunnel. This survey provides migration estimates based on respondents' intended length of stay in the United Kingdom or abroad.

Adjustments are made to account for people who do not realise their intended length of stay. An estimate is made for the number of people who initially come to or leave the United Kingdom for a short period but subsequently stay for a year or longer ('visitor switchers'). The number of people who intend to be migrants, but who in reality stay in the United Kingdom or abroad for less than a year ('migrant switchers') are also estimated.

Data from other sources are used to supplement the IPS migration estimates. Home Office asylum seeker data are used to estimate the number of asylum seekers and their dependants who enter or leave the country without being counted in the IPS. Estimates of migration between the United Kingdom and Ireland are made using information from the Irish Central Statistics Office.

## Part 2: Households and families

Although definitions differ slightly across surveys and the Census, they are broadly similar.

## Households

A household: is a person living alone or a group of people who have the address as their only or main residence and who either share one meal a day or share the living accommodation.

*Students:* those living in halls of residence are recorded under their parents' household and included in the parents' family type in the Labour Force Survey (LFS), although some surveys/projections include such students in the institutional population.

In the General Household Survey (GHS), children aged 16 or over who live away from home for purposes of either work or study and come home only for holidays are not included at the parental address.

## Families

*Children:* are never-married people of any age who live with one or both parent(s). They include stepchildren and adopted children (but not foster children) and also grandchildren (where the parent(s) are absent).

*Dependent children:* in the 1971 and 1981 Census, dependent children were defined as never-married children in families who were either under 15 years of age, or aged 15 to 24 and in full-time education. In the 1991 Census, the Labour Force Survey (LFS) and the General Household Survey (GHS), dependent children are childless never-married children in families who are aged under 16, or aged 16 to 18 and in full-time education and living in the household (and, in the 1991 Census, economically inactive). In the 2001 Census a dependent child is a person aged under 16 in a household (whether or not in a family) or aged 16 to 18, in full-time education and living in a family with their parent or parents.

*A family:* is a married or cohabiting couple, either with or without their never-married child or children (of any age), including couples with no children or a lone parent together with his or her never-married child or children provided they have no children of their own. A family could also consist of a grandparent or grandparents with their grandchild or grandchildren if the parents of the grandchild or grandchildren are not usually resident in the household. In the LFS, a family unit can also comprise a single person. LFS family units include non-dependent children (who can in fact be adult) those aged 16 or over and not in full-time education provided they are never married and have no children of their own in the household.

*One family and no others:* A household comprises one family and no others if there is only one family in the household and there are no non-family people.

*Multi family household:* A household containing two or more people who cannot be allocated to a single family as defined in 'a family' above. This includes households with two or more unrelated adults and can also include a grandparent or grandparents with their child or children and grandchild or grandchildren in one household.

*A lone parent family:* in the Census is a father or mother together with his or her never-married child or children. A lone parent family in the LFS consists of a lone parent, living with his or her never-married children, provided these children have no children of their own living with them. A lone parent family in the GHS consists of a lone parent, living with his or her never-married dependent children, provided these children have no children of their own. Married lone mothers whose husbands are not defined as resident in the household are not classified as lone parents. Evidence suggests the majority are separated from their husband either because he usually works away from home or for some other reason that does not imply the breakdown of the marriage.

## Conceptions

Conception statistics used in Table 2.20 include pregnancies that result in one or more live or still births, or a legal abortion under the 1967 Act. Conception statistics do not include miscarriages or illegal abortions. Dates of conception are estimated using recorded gestation for abortions and still births, and assuming 38 weeks gestation for live births.

## True birth order

At registration, the question on previous live births is not asked where the birth occurred outside marriage. At the registration of births occurring within marriage, previous live births occurring outside marriage and where the woman had never been married to the father are not counted. The information collected on birth order, therefore, has been supplemented to give estimates of overall true birth order, which includes births both within and outside marriage. These estimates are obtained from details provided by the General Household Survey.

## Part 3: Education and training

### Stages of education

Education takes place in several stages: nursery (now part of the foundation stage in England), primary, secondary, further and higher education, and is compulsory for all children between the ages of 5 (4 in Northern Ireland) and 16. The non-compulsory fourth stage, further education, covers non-advanced education, which can be taken at both further (including tertiary) education colleges, higher education institutions and increasingly in secondary schools. The fifth stage, higher education, is study beyond GCE A levels and their equivalent, which, for most full-time students, takes place in universities and other higher education institutions.

### Nursery education

In recent years there has been a major expansion of pre-school education. Many children under five attend state nursery schools or nursery classes within primary schools. Others may attend playgroups in the voluntary sector or in privately run nurseries. In England and Wales many primary schools also operate an early admissions policy where they admit children under five into what are called 'reception classes'. The Education Act 2002 extended the National Curriculum for England to include the foundation stage. The foundation stage was introduced in September 2000 and covers children's education from the age of three to the end of the reception year, when

most are just five and some almost six years old. The 'Curriculum guidance for the foundation stage' supports practitioners in their delivery of the foundation stage.

Figure 3.1 reflects those children in early years education in maintained nursery and primary schools. Other provision also takes place in independent and special schools and in non-school education settings in the private and voluntary sector, such as nurseries (which usually provide care, education and play for children up to the age of five), playgroups and pre-schools (which provide childcare, play and early years education usually for children aged between two and five), and combined/family centres.

### Primary education

The primary stage covers three age ranges: nursery (under 5), infant (5 to 7 or 8) and junior (up to 11 or 12) but in Scotland and Northern Ireland there is generally no distinction between infant and junior schools. Most public sector primary schools take both boys and girls in mixed classes. It is usual to transfer straight to secondary school at age 11 (in England, Wales and Northern Ireland) or 12 (in Scotland), but in England some children make the transition via middle schools catering for various age ranges between 8 and 14. Depending on their individual age ranges middle schools are classified as either primary or secondary.

### Secondary education

Public provision of secondary education in an area may consist of a combination of different types of school, the pattern reflecting historical circumstances and the policy adopted by the local authority. Comprehensive schools largely admit pupils without reference to ability or aptitude and cater for all the children in a neighbourhood, but in some areas they co-exist with grammar, secondary modern or technical schools. In Northern Ireland, post primary education is provided by secondary intermediate and grammar schools. In England, the Specialist Schools Programme helps schools, in partnership with private sector sponsors and supported by additional government funding, to establish distinctive identities through their chosen specialisms. Specialist schools have a focus on their chosen subject area but must meet the National Curriculum requirements and deliver a broad and balanced education to all pupils. Any maintained secondary school in England can apply to be designated as a specialist school in one of ten specialist areas: arts, business and enterprise, engineering, humanities, language, mathematics and computing, music, science, sports, and technology. Schools can also combine any two specialisms.

### Special schools

Special schools (day or boarding) provide education for children who require specialist support to complete their education, for example because they have physical or other difficulties. Many pupils with special educational needs are educated in mainstream schools. All children attending special schools are offered a curriculum designed to overcome their learning difficulties and to enable them to become self-reliant.

### Pupil referral units

Pupil referral units (PRUs) are legally a type of school established and maintained by a local authority to provide education for children of compulsory school age who may otherwise not receive suitable education. The aim of such units is to provide suitable alternative education on a temporary basis for pupils who may not be able to attend a mainstream school. The focus of the units should be to get pupils back into a mainstream school. Pupils in the units may include: teenage mothers, pupils excluded from school, school phobics and pupils in the assessment phase of a statement of special educational needs (SEN).

### Further education

The term further education may be used in a general sense to cover all non-advanced courses taken after the period of compulsory education, but more commonly it excludes those staying on at secondary school and those in higher education, i.e. courses in universities and colleges leading to qualifications above GCE A level, Higher Grade (in Scotland), GNVQ/NVQ level 3, and their equivalents. Since 1 April 1993 sixth form colleges in England and Wales have been included in the further education sector.

### Higher education

Higher education (HE) is defined as courses that are of a standard that is higher than GCE A level, the Higher Grade of the Scottish Certificate of Education/National Qualification, GNVQ/NVQ level 3 or the Edexcel (formerly BTEC) or SQA National Certificate/Diploma. There are three main levels of HE courses:

1. Postgraduate courses leading to higher degrees, diplomas and certificates (including postgraduate certificates of education and professional qualifications) that usually require a first degree as entry qualification.

2. Undergraduate courses, which include first degrees, first degrees with qualified teacher status, enhanced first degrees, first degrees obtained concurrently with a diploma, and intercalated first degrees.

3. Other undergraduate courses, which include all other HE courses, for example HNDs and Diplomas in HE.

As a result of the 1992 Further and Higher Education Act, former polytechnics and some other HE institutions were designated as universities in 1992/93. Students normally attend HE courses at HE institutions, but some attend at further education colleges. Some also attend institutions that do not receive public grants (such as the University of Buckingham) and these numbers are excluded from the tables.

Up to 2000/01, figures for HE students in Table 3.8 are annual snapshots taken around November or December each year, depending on the type of institution, except for Scotland further education colleges from 1998/99, for which counts are based on the whole year. From 2001/02, figures for HE institutions are based on the Higher Education Statistics Agency (HESA) July 'standard registration' count, and are not directly comparable with previous years. The Open University is included in these estimates.

## Main categories of educational establishments

Educational establishments in the United Kingdom are administered and financed in several ways. Most schools are controlled by local authorities (LAs), which are part of the structure of local government, but some are 'assisted', receiving grants direct from central government sources and being controlled by governing bodies that have a substantial degree of autonomy. Completely outside the public sector are non-maintained schools run by individuals, companies or charitable institutions.

Up to March 2001, further education (FE) courses in FE sector colleges in England and in Wales were largely funded through grants from the respective Further Education Funding Councils. In April 2001, however, the Learning and Skills Council (LSC) took over the responsibility for funding the FE sector in England, and the National Council for Education and Training for Wales (part of Education and Learning Wales – ELWa) did so for Wales. The LSC in England is also responsible for funding provision for FE and some non-prescribed higher education in FE sector colleges; it also funds some FE provided by LA maintained and other institutions referred to as 'external institutions'. In Wales, the National Council – ELWa, funds FE provision made by FE institutions via a third party or sponsored arrangements. The Scottish FEFC (SFEFC) funds FE colleges in Scotland, while the Department for Employment and Learning funds FE colleges in Northern Ireland.

Higher education (HE) courses in HE establishments are largely publicly funded through block grants from the HE funding councils in England and Scotland, the Higher Education Council – ELWa in Wales, and the Department for Employment and Learning in Northern Ireland. In addition, some designated HE (mainly HND/HNC Diplomas and Certificates of HE) is also funded by these sources. The FE sources mentioned above fund the remainder.

Numbers of school pupils are shown in Table 3.3. Nursery school figures for Scotland prior to 1998/99 only include data for local authority pre-schools. Data thereafter include partnership pre-schools. Secondary 'Other' schools largely consist of middle schools in England, and secondary intermediate schools in Northern Ireland. 'Special schools' include maintained and non-maintained sectors, while 'public sector schools' and 'non-maintained schools' totals exclude special schools. The 'All schools' total includes pupil referral units, which accounted for around 15,000 pupils in 2004/05.

## Qualifications

In England, Wales and Northern Ireland the main examination for school pupils at the minimum school leaving age is the General Certificate of Secondary Education (GCSE), which can be taken in a wide range of subjects. This replaced the GCE O Level and CSE examinations in 1987 (1988 in Northern Ireland). In England, Wales and Northern Ireland the GCSE is awarded in eight grades, A* to G, the highest four (A* to C) being regarded as equivalent to O level grades A to C or CSE grade 1.

GCE A level is usually taken after a further two years of study in a sixth form or equivalent,

passes being graded from A (the highest) to E (the lowest).

For achievement at GCE A level shown in Figure 3.15, data are for pupils in schools and students in further education institutions generally aged 16 to 18 at the start of the academic year as a percentage of the 17 year old population. Data prior to 1995/96, and for Wales and Northern Ireland from 2002/03, are for school pupils only. In Scotland pupils generally sit Highers one year earlier than the rest of the United Kingdom sit A levels.

Following the Qualifying for Success consultation in 1997, a number of reforms were introduced to the 16 to 19 qualifications structure in September 2000. Under these reforms, students were encouraged to follow a wide range of subjects in their first year of post-16 study, with students expected to study four Advanced Subsidiaries before progressing three of them on to full A levels in their second year. In addition, students are encouraged to study a combination of both general and vocational advanced level examinations.

The Advanced Subsidiary (AS) qualification covers the first half of the full A level. New specifications introduced in 2001 are now in place and A levels now comprise units, normally six for a full A level (now A2) and three for the AS level, which is half a full A level. The full A level is normally taken either over two years (modular) or as a set of exams at the end of the two years (linear). The AS is a qualification in its own right, whereas A2 modules do not make up a qualification in their own right.

In Scotland, National Qualifications (NQs) are offered to students, which include Standard Grades, National Courses and National Units. The Standard Grade is awarded in seven grades, through three levels of study: Credit (1 or 2), General (3 or 4) and Foundation (5 or 6). Students who do not achieve a grade 1 to 6, but do complete the course, are awarded a grade 7. Standard Grade courses are made up of different parts called 'elements', with an exam at the end. National Courses are available at Intermediate, Higher and Advanced Higher, and consist of National Units that are assessed by the school/college, plus an external assessment. Grades are awarded on the basis of how well a student does in the external assessment, having passed all of the National Units. Pass grades are awarded at A, B and C. Grade D is awarded to a student who just fails to get a grade C. Intermediate courses can be taken as an alternative to Standard Grade or as a stepping stone to Higher. Access units are assessed by the school/college, with no exam involved. Groups of units in a particular subject area can be built up at Access 2 and 3 to lead to 'Cluster Awards'.

After leaving school, people can study towards higher academic qualifications such as degrees. However, a large number of people choose to study towards qualifications aimed at a particular occupation or group of occupations – these qualifications are called vocational qualifications.

Vocational qualifications can be split into three groups, namely National Vocational Qualifications (NVQs), General National Vocational Qualifications (GNVQs) and vocationally related qualifications.

NVQs are based on an explicit statement of competence derived from an analysis of employment requirements. They are awarded at five levels. Scottish Vocational Qualifications (SVQs) are the Scottish equivalent.

GNVQs are a vocational alternative to GCSEs and GCE A levels. They are awarded at three levels: Foundation, Intermediate and Advanced. Advanced GNVQs were redesigned and relaunched as Vocational A levels or, more formally, Advanced Vocational Certificates of Education (VCEs) and, as well as being available at AS level and A level, there are also double awards (counting as 12 units). General Scottish Vocational Qualifications (GSVQs) are the Scottish equivalent.

There are also a large number of other vocational qualifications, which are not NVQs, SVQs, GNVQs or GSVQs, for example, a BTEC Higher National Diploma or a City & Guilds craft award.

Other qualifications (including academic qualifications) are often expressed as being equivalent to a particular NVQ level so that comparisons can be made more easily.

An NVQ level 5 is equivalent to a Higher Degree.

An NVQ level 4 is equivalent to a First Degree, a HND or HNC, a BTEC Higher Diploma, an RSA Higher Diploma, a nursing qualification or other Higher Education.

An NVQ level 3 is equivalent to two A levels, an advanced GNVQ, International Baccalaureate, an RSA advanced diploma, a City & Guilds advanced craft, an OND or ONC or a BTEC National Diploma.

An NVQ level 2 is equivalent to five GCSEs at grades A* to C, an Intermediate GNVQ, an RSA diploma, a City & Guilds craft or a BTEC first or general diploma.

An NVQ level 1 is equivalent to one or more GCSEs at grade G (but less than five grades A* to C), BTEC general certificate, a Youth Training certificate, other RSA, City & Guilds qualifications.

## The National Curriculum

Under the *Education Reform Act 1988* a National Curriculum has been progressively introduced into primary and secondary schools in England and Wales. This consists of English (or the option of Welsh as a first language in Wales), mathematics and science. The second level of curriculum additionally comprises the so-called 'foundation' subjects, such as history, geography, art, music, information technology, design and technology, and physical education (and Welsh as a second language in Wales). The *Education Act 2002* extended the National Curriculum for England to include the foundation stage. It has six areas of learning namely, personal, social and emotional development; communication, language and literacy; mathematical development; knowledge and understanding of the world; physical development; and creative development.

Measurable targets have been defined for four key stages, corresponding to ages 7, 11, 14 and 16. Pupils are assessed formally at the ages of 7, 11 and 14 by a mixture of teacher assessments and by national tests in the core subjects of English, mathematics and science (and in Welsh speaking schools in Wales, Welsh), though the method varies between subjects and countries. Sixteen year olds are assessed by means of the GCSE examination. Statutory authorities have been set up for England and for Wales to advise the Government on the National Curriculum and promote curriculum development generally. Northern Ireland has its own common curriculum that is similar but not identical to the National Curriculum in England and Wales. Assessment arrangements in Northern Ireland became statutory from September 1996 and Key Stage 1 pupils are assessed at age eight.

| England | Attainment expected |
|---------|--------------------|
| Key Stage 1 | Level 2 or above |
| Key Stage 2 | Level 4 or above |
| Key Stage 3 | Level 5/6 or above |
| Key Stage 4 | GCSE |

In Scotland there is no statutory national curriculum and responsibility for the management and delivery of the curriculum belongs to education authorities and head teachers. Pupils aged 5 to 14 study a broad curriculum based on national guidelines, which set out the aims of study, the ground to be covered and the way the pupils' learning should be assessed and reported. Progress is measured by attainment of six levels based on the expectation of the performance of the majority of pupils on completion of certain stages between the ages of 5 and 14: Primary 3 (age 7/8), Primary 4 (age 8/9), Primary 7 (age 11/12) and Secondary 2 (age 13/14). It is recognised that pupils learn at different rates and some will reach the various levels before others. The 5 to 14 curriculum areas are language; mathematics; environmental studies; expressive arts; and religious and moral education with personal and social development and health education. In Secondary 3 and 4, it is recommended that the core curriculum of all pupils should include study within the following eight modes: language and communication; mathematical studies and applications; scientific studies and applications; social and environmental studies; technological activities and applications; creative and aesthetic activities; physical education; and religious and moral education. For S5 and S6 these eight modes are important in structuring the curriculum, although it is not expected that each pupil will study under each mode but that the curriculum will be negotiated. At present the Scottish curriculum 3 to 18 is being reviewed under *A Curriculum for Excellence*.

### Adult education

Local authorities (LAs) provide a range of learning opportunities for adults. In November 2002 opportunities fell into two categories – those that did not lead to academic or vocational qualifications and those that did. LAs offered the former provision in response to their statutory duty to secure adequate provision for further education. Although not leading to a qualification, these courses could cover a wide range of topics including vocational, social,

physical and recreational training, as well as organised leisure-time occupation provided in association with such activities. They were normally designated non-Schedule 2 courses to distinguish them from those courses set out in Schedule 2 to the *Further and Higher Education Act 1992*, for which the Further Education Funding Council (FEFC) had statutory responsibility for securing provision. LAs also had the power, although not the duty, to provide courses that fell within Schedule 2 and many authorities chose to do so. *The Learning and Skills* Act transferred LAs' duties to the Learning and Skills Council (LSC) and removed from the legislation the distinction between learning opportunities that lead to qualifications and those that do not.

The establishment of the LSC in March 2001 led to changes in the arrangements for planning and funding learning opportunities for adults as well as data collection. Since 2003/04, adult and community learning data have been collected by the LSC and incorporated into the Individualised Learner Record (ILR). The ILR already covers learners in further education and on work based learning for young people.

### National Employers Skills Survey

The National Employers Skills Survey (NESS) is an annual series of employer surveys to investigate skills deficiencies and the role of workforce development among employers in England.

Learning and training information was previously collected in the Learning and Training at Work (LTW) survey in 2000 and in an Employer Skills Survey in 1999 and 2001. Prior to that learning and training information, along with information on recruitment difficulties, skill shortages and skill gaps, was collected in the annual Skill Needs in Britain (SNIB) surveys carried out between 1990 and 1998.

The aim of the NESS study is to provide the Learning and Skills Council (LSC) and its partners with information on the current and future skills needs of employers in England, and how these needs vary by size of industry, occupation, region and local LSC areas.

In Figure 3.21 employers who had experienced skills gaps were asked to define what skills they felt needed improving for an occupation where staff were considered not fully proficient (if an establishment had at least two occupations with skills gaps then the occupation was chosen at random).

## Part 4: Labour market

### Labour Force Survey (LFS) reweighting

The results from the 2001 Census, published in September 2002, showed that previous estimates of the total UK population were around 1 million too high. As a result, the Office for National Statistics (ONS) published interim revised estimates of the population for the years 1982 to 2001, which were consistent with the 2001 Census population findings.

The interim mid-year population estimates (MYEs) and projections, see Appendix, Part 1: Population estimates and projections, are available by age and sex and these have been used to produce interim revised LFS estimates of

employment, unemployment and inactivity by age and sex. Other LFS analyses, for example, full/part-time, have been produced by scaling to these age/sex adjusted data. This scaling has been applied to the existing LFS data and summed to obtain new aggregate LFS totals.

In spring (February and March) 2003 slightly revised population estimates were published and these were incorporated into the April 2003 LFS national and regional interim estimates and, later, the LFS microdata (see below).

In autumn (September and October) 2004, ONS published the 2003 MYEs along with revised MYEs for 2001 and 2002. These revised population estimates took into account the census matching studies for Manchester and Westminster; population studies in 15 local authorities; and refinements to the method for allocating migration estimates. MYEs for 1992 to 2000, consistent with these revised estimates were also published. Also in autumn 2004 the Government Actuary's Department (GAD) published revised population projections for 2004 and later years, based on the revised population estimates. In August 2005 ONS published the MYEs for 2004 and these latest estimates were incorporated into LFS estimates published on 14 September 2005.

LFS data in this edition of *Social Trends* that have been adjusted in line with population estimates published in spring 2003 are calculated using the LFS microdata, whereas data that have been adjusted in line with population estimates published in August 2005 are taken from published ONS sources such as the Labour Market Statistics First Release.

It is planned that modernised LFS processing systems will be introduced that will enable future population data to be incorporated into revised LFS microdata to the same sort of timetable now achieved for the LFS time series by using the interim adjustment procedure. The aim is to complete this work as part of ONS's statistical modernisation work by late 2006/ early 2007.

For more information, see:
**www.statistics.gov.uk/cci/nugget.asp?id=207**
and 'Labour Force Survey reweighting and seasonal adjustment review', pp 167–72, *Labour Market Trends,* April 2004
**www.statistics.gov.uk/cci/article.asp?id=887**

### Historical LFS-consistent time series

The Office for National Statistics (ONS) has produced a set of historical estimates covering the period 1971–91, which are fully consistent with post-1992 Labour Force Survey (LFS) data. The data cover headline measures of employment, unemployment, economic activity, economic inactivity and hours worked. These estimates were published on an experimental basis in 2003, but following further user consultation and quality assurance, these estimates have now been made National Statistics. As such, they represent ONS's best estimate of the headline labour market series over this period. The labour market chapter uses data from these estimates only where headline data are reported (Figures 4.1, 4.3, 4.19 and 4.24) since the historical estimates are not yet available for subgroups of the population, other than by sex and for key age groups. Therefore, tables and figures showing further breakdowns of headline data are not fully consistent with the historical estimates.

For more information, see:
www.statistics.gov.uk/cci/nugget.asp?id=419

## Eurostat rates

There are differences between Eurostat and the Office for National Statistics (ONS) in the age bases used in calculating published employment and unemployment rates.

The employment rates published by Eurostat, are based on the population aged 15 to 64 including the employment rate for the United Kingdom. It is different from the employment rate for the United Kingdom published by the ONS, which is based on the working age population aged 16 to 64 (men) and 16 to 59 (women) and therefore takes account of both the school leaving age and the state pension age in the United Kingdom.

The unemployment rate for the United Kingdom published by Eurostat is based on the population aged 16 to 74 while the unemployment rate for the United Kingdom published by the ONS is based on those aged 16 and over. There are other minor definitional differences.

Unemployment rates published by Eurostat for most EU countries (but not for the United Kingdom) are calculated by extrapolating from the most recent LFS data using monthly registered unemployment data. A standard population basis (15 to 74) is used by Eurostat except for Spain and the United Kingdom (16 to 74).

## Annual Population Survey

The Annual Population Survey (APS) is a new survey that includes the annual Labour Force Survey (LFS) plus a new sample boost aimed at achieving a minimum sample of 500 economically active adults in local authority districts in England. The size of the total APS sample is approximately 500,000 people.

The first APS data published are for the period January to December 2004. Subsequently, APS data will be published quarterly with each publication covering a year's data. The APS data presented here have been weighted to be consistent with the population estimates published in February 2003.

Like the local area LFS data set, the APS data is published by local authority area. However, it contains an enhanced range of variables providing a greater level of detail about the resident household population of an area. In particular, more variables are provided on ethnic group, health and gender.

For more information see
www.nomisweb.co.uk/articles/195.aspx

## Homeworkers and teleworkers

In the Labour Force Survey (LFS) the concept of teleworking is intimately linked to the concept of homeworking. Since spring 1992, the LFS has asked respondents who are employees, self-employed, or unpaid family workers whether they work mainly:

- in their own home,

- in the same grounds or building as their home,

- in different places using home as a base,

- somewhere quite separate from home.

People who work mainly from home (either in their own home, or in different places using home as a base) are classified as homeworkers. The LFS also asks respondents whether they ever do any paid or unpaid work at home, and whether they spent at least one full day during the week before the LFS interview (the reference week) working in the locations listed above. Since spring 1997 the LFS has asked homeworkers and those people who worked from home during the reference week:

- whether they use both a telephone and a computer to carry out their work at home; and

- whether it would be possible to work at home (or use home as a base) without using both a telephone and a computer.

The wording and routing of the LFS questions enable the following definitions of teleworking to be used when analysing the data: People who work mainly in their own home or mainly in different places using home as a base, who use both a telephone and a computer to carry out their work at home.

For more information, see: 'Home-based working using communication technologies', pp 417–426, Labour Market Trends, October 2005.
www.statistics.gov.uk/cci/article.asp?id=1284

## Unemployment

The UK definition of unemployment is based on International Labour Organisation (ILO) guidelines and refers to people without a job who were available to start work within two weeks and had either looked for work in the previous four weeks or were waiting to start a job they had already obtained.

The former GB/UK Labour Force definition of unemployment, the only one available for estimates up to 1984, counted people not in employment and seeking work in a reference week (or prevented from seeking work by a temporary sickness or holiday, or waiting for the results of a job application, or waiting to start a job they had already obtained) whether or not they were available to start (except students not able to start because they had to complete their education).

Following a quality review of its labour market statistics, the Office for National Statistics re-labelled 'ILO unemployment' as 'unemployment'. This emphasises that the Labour Force Survey figures provide the official, and only internationally comparable, measure of unemployment in the United Kingdom. Claimant count data continue to be published monthly to provide further information about the labour market, but these are not presented as an alternative measure of UK unemployment.

## Job separations

The job separation rate is the number of working-age people who separated from a paid job in the three months before interview divided by the number of people who said they were in employment for more than three months plus those who had separated from a paid job. The Labour Force Survey (LFS) asks respondents whether they have left a paid job in the past three months and then finds out the reasons for leaving that job. These reasons are usually grouped into two employee-centric categories: voluntary separations; and involuntary separations (see box) to reflect the dynamics of labour supply and demand.

### Involuntary separations

Dismissed

Made redundant/voluntary redundancy

Temporary job finished

### Voluntary separations

Resigned

Gave up work for health reasons

Gave up work for family or personal reasons

Early retirement/retirement

Other reason

Voluntary redundancy and the termination of a temporary job are seen as involuntary separations as they are symptoms of a contraction in labour demand. Early retirement is a slightly ambiguous category to place in the voluntary group, as in some cases it may also be used by employers as a tool to destroy jobs in times of labour demand contraction. However, it is assumed that in the majority of cases it is the normal retirement age of the organisation which is early and therefore not related to labour demand (for example, public sector areas such as the police, civil service, fire brigade, armed forces).

For more information, see 'Job separations in the UK', pp 231–238, Labour Market Trends, June 2005. www.statistics.gov.uk/cci/article.asp?ID=1179

## Labour disputes

Statistics of stoppages of work caused by labour disputes in the United Kingdom relate to disputes connected with terms and conditions of employment. Small stoppages involving fewer than ten workers or lasting less than one day are excluded from the statistics unless the aggregate number of working days lost in the dispute is 100 or more. Disputes not resulting in a stoppage of work are not included in the statistics.

Workers involved and working days lost relate to persons both directly and indirectly involved (unable to work although not parties to the dispute) at the establishments where the disputes occurred. People laid off and working days lost at establishments not in dispute, because of resulting shortages of supplies for example, are excluded.

There are difficulties in ensuring complete recording of stoppages, in particular near the margins of the definition; for example, short disputes lasting only a day or so, or involving only a few workers. Any under-recording would affect the total number of stoppages much more than the number of working days lost.

For more information, see 'Labour disputes in 2004', pp 239–252, *Labour Market Trends*, June 2005. www.statistics.gov.uk/cci/article.asp?ID=1177

## Part 5: Income and wealth

### Household income data sources

The data for the household sector as derived from the National Accounts have been compiled according to the definitions and conventions set out in the European System of Accounts 1995 (ESA95). At present, estimates for the household sector cannot be separated from the sector for non-profit institutions serving households and so the data in *Social Trends* cover both sectors. The most obvious example of a non-profit institution is a charity. This sector also includes many other organisations of which universities, trade unions and clubs and societies are the most important. The household sector differs from the personal sector, as defined in the National Accounts prior to the introduction of ESA95, in that it excludes unincorporated private businesses apart from sole traders. More information is given in *United Kingdom National Accounts Concepts, Sources and Methods* published by The Stationery Office.

In ESA95, household income includes the value of national insurance contributions and pension contributions made by employers on behalf of their employees. It also shows property income (that is, income from investments) net of payments of interest on loans. In both these respects, national accounts' conventions diverge from those normally used when collecting data on household income from household surveys. Employees are usually unaware of the value of the national insurance contributions and pension contributions made on their behalf by their employer, and so such data are rarely collected. Payments of interest are usually regarded as items of expenditure rather than reductions of income.

Survey sources differ from the National Accounts in a number of other important respects. They cover the population living in households and some cover certain parts of the population living in institutions such as nursing homes, but all exclude non-profit making institutions. Survey sources are also subject to under-reporting and non-response bias. In the case of household income surveys, investment income is commonly underestimated, as is income from self-employment. All these factors mean that the survey data on income used in most of this chapter are not entirely consistent with the National Accounts household sector data.

### Individual income

Net individual income refers to the weekly personal income of women and men after deduction of income tax and national insurance contributions as reported in the Family Resources Survey. Income is from all sources received by an individual, including earnings, income from self-employment, investments and occupational pensions/annuities, benefit income, and tax credits. Income that accrues at household level, such as council tax benefit, is excluded. Income from couples' joint investment accounts is assumed to be received equally.

Benefit income paid in respect of dependants, such as Child Benefit, is included in the individual income of the person nominated for the receipt of payments. Full details of the concepts and definitions used may be found in *Individual Income 1996/97 to 2003/04* available on the Women and Equality Unit website: www.womenandequalityunit.gov.uk/indiv_incomes or from the Information and Analysis Division, Department for Work and Pensions.

### Earnings surveys

The Annual Survey of Hours and Earnings (ASHE) replaced the New Earnings Survey (NES) from October 2004. ASHE improves on the NES by extending the coverage of the survey sample, introducing weighting and publishing estimates of quality for all survey outputs. The new survey methodology produces weighted estimates, using weights calculated by calibrating the survey responses to totals from the Labour Force Survey by occupation, sex, region and age. The survey sample has been increased to include employees in businesses outside the PAYE system and those changing jobs between the survey sample identification and the survey reference date. The new survey design also produces outputs that focus on median rather than mean levels of pay. Full details of the methodology of ASHE can be found on the ONS website at: www.statistics.gov.uk/articles/nojournal/ASHEMethod_article.pdf

Back series using the ASHE methodology applied to the NES data sets are available for 1997 to 2004 at: www.statistics.gov.uk/statbase/Product.asp?vlnk=13101.

### Households Below Average Income (HBAI )

Information on the distribution of income based on the Family Resources Survey is provided in the Department for Work and Pensions publication *Households Below Average Income: 1994/95 –2003/04*, available both in hard copy and on the DWP website: www.dwp.gov.uk/asd/hbai.asp. This publication provides estimates of patterns of personal disposable income in Great Britain, and of changes in income over time. It attempts to measure people's potential living standards as determined by disposable income. Although as

the title would suggest, HBAI concentrates on the lower part of the income distribution, it also provides estimates covering the whole of the income distribution.

In 2002/03, the Family Resources Survey was extended to cover Northern Ireland. However, because inclusion of these data into the main HBAI may result in an inconsistent time series, results on a UK basis are presented separately in Appendix 4 of *Households Below Average Income: 1994/95–2003/04*.

Disposable household income includes all flows of income into the household, principally earnings, benefits, occupational and private pensions, and investments. It is net of tax, employees' national insurance contributions, council tax, contributions to occupational pension schemes (including additional voluntary contributions), maintenance and child support payments, and parental contributions to students living away from home.

Two different measures of disposable income are used in HBAI: before and after housing costs are deducted. This is principally to take into account variations in housing costs that do not correspond to comparable variations in the quality of housing. Housing costs consist of rent, water rates, community charges, mortgage interest payments, structural insurance, ground rent and service charges.

### Equivalisation scales

The Department for Work and Pensions (DWP), the Office for National Statistics (ONS), the Institute for Fiscal Studies (IFS) and the Institute for Social and Economic Research (ISER) all use McClements equivalence scales in their analysis of the income distribution, to take into account variations in the size and composition of households. This reflects the common sense notion that a household of five adults will need a higher income than will a single person living alone to enjoy a comparable standard of living. An overall equivalence value is calculated for each household by summing the appropriate scale values for each household member. Equivalised household income is then calculated by dividing household income by the household's equivalence value. The scales conventionally take a married couple as the reference point with an

**McClements equivalence scales:**

| Household member | Before housing costs | After housing costs |
|---|---|---|
| First adult (head) | 0.61 | 0.55 |
| Spouse of head | 0.39 | 0.45 |
| Other second adult | 0.46 | 0.45 |
| Third adult | 0.42 | 0.45 |
| Subsequent adults | 0.36 | 0.40 |
| **Each dependant aged:** | | |
| 0 – 1 | 0.09 | 0.07 |
| 2 – 4 | 0.18 | 0.18 |
| 5 – 7 | 0.21 | 0.21 |
| 8 – 10 | 0.23 | 0.23 |
| 11 – 12 | 0.25 | 0.26 |
| 13 – 15 | 0.27 | 0.28 |
| 16 or over | 0.36 | 0.38 |

equivalence value of one; equivalisation therefore tends to increase relatively the incomes of single person households (since their incomes are divided by a value of less than one) and to reduce incomes of households with three or more persons. For further information see *Households Below Average Income 1994/95–2003/04* available on the DWP website: www.dwp.gov.uk/asd/hbai.asp. There are two McClements equivalence scales, one for adjusting incomes before housing costs and one for adjusting income after housing costs, see table.

The DWP and IFS both use different scales for adjustment of income before and after the deduction of housing costs.

## Gini coefficient

The Gini coefficient is the most widely used summary measure of the degree of inequality in an income distribution. The first step is to rank the distribution in ascending order. The coefficient can then best be understood by considering a graph of the cumulative income share against the cumulative share of households – the Lorenz curve. This would take the form of a diagonal line for complete equality where all households had the same income, while complete inequality where one household received all the income and the remainder received none would be represented by a curve comprising the horizontal axis and the right-hand vertical axis. The area between the Lorenz curve and the diagonal line of complete equality and inequality gives the value of the Gini coefficient. As inequality increases (and the Lorenz curve bellies out) so does the Gini coefficient until it reaches its maximum value of 1 with complete inequality.

## Material hardship

The DWP Families and Children Study (FACS) examines the living standards of families with children according to their material deprivation – measured as the ability to purchase essential goods and to participate in leisure activities. Families were asked whether they possessed or took part in each of 34 items or activities, and if not, whether this was because they could not afford to or because they did not want or need the item. In addition, questions are asked about aspects of financial stress. From these data, the Policy Studies Institute has developed an index of hardship consisting of nine specific indicators:

Reports two plus problems with accommodation and cannot afford to repair (if owner)

Lives in over-crowded accommodation

Cannot afford to keep home warm

Worries about money almost all the time and runs out of money most weeks

Has no bank account and has two or more problem debts

Lacks food items

Lacks clothing items

Lacks consumer durables

Lacks social/leisure activities

Counting the number of these adverse indications recorded by each family provides a score of between zero and nine which is then used to define the levels of hardship used in Table 5.21:

| Not in hardship | No indicators |
| Moderate hardship | 1 or 2 indicators |
| Severe hardship | 3 to 9 indicators |

For more details see *DWP Research Report no. 219 The dynamics of deprivation: the relationship between income and material deprivation over time* by Richard Berthoud, Mark Bryan and Elena Bardasi www.dwp.gov.uk/asd/asd5/rports2003-2004/rrep219.asp.

## Net wealth of the household sector

Revised balance sheet estimates of the net wealth of the household (and non-profit institutions) sector were published in an article in *Economic Trends* November 1999. These figures are based on the new international system of national accounting and incorporate data from new sources. Quarterly estimates of net financial wealth (excluding tangible and intangible assets) are published in *Financial Statistics*.

## Distribution of personal wealth

Estimates of the distribution of individual marketable wealth of relate to all adults in the United Kingdom. They are produced by combining HM Revenue and Customs (HMRC) estimates of the distribution of wealth identified by the estate multiplier method with independent estimates of total personal wealth derived from the Office for National Statistics (ONS) National Accounts balance sheets. Estimates for 1995 onwards have been compiled on the basis of the new System of National Accounts, but estimates for earlier years are on the old basis. The methods used were described in an article in *Economic Trends* October 1990 entitled 'Estimates of the Distribution of Personal Wealth'. Net wealth of the personal sector differs from marketable wealth for the following reasons:

*Difference in coverage:* the ONS balance sheet of the personal sector includes the wealth of non-profit making bodies and unincorporated businesses, while the HMRC estimates exclude non-profit making bodies and treat the bank deposits and debts of unincorporated businesses differently from the ONS;

*Differences in timing:* the ONS balance sheet gives values at the end of the year, whereas HMRC figures are adjusted to mid-year;

*HMRC figures:* exclude the wealth of those under 18;

*Funded pensions:* are included in ONS figures (including personal pensions) but not in the HMRC marketable wealth. Also the ONS balance sheet excludes consumer durables and includes non-marketable tenancy rights, whereas the HMRC figures include consumer durables and exclude non-marketable tenancy rights.

## Household satellite account

The ONS has developed a household satellite account (HHSA) that measures and values the outputs produced by households in the United Kingdom. This provides a means by which the influence of changing patterns of unpaid work on the economy can be measured.

The HHSA brings together estimates of the output of housing, transport, nutrition, clothing, laundry, childcare, adult care and voluntary activity, and shows the related inputs of intermediate consumption and household capital, and the calculation of gross and net value added.

A variety of sources have been used to estimate the volume of output (number of journeys provided, number of meals produced, etc) and value them using the price of an equivalent good or service provided by the market. The value of inputs of purchased goods and services is then subtracted.

Adjustments have to be made to avoid double-counting. For example, the price of a meal in a restaurant includes the cost of the premises and any transport required for food shopping. The household production of these elements is valued in the housing and transport elements respectively. Thus a proportion of total housing and transport output must therefore be deducted from the nutrition output to avoid double-counting.

Removing the inputs of purchased goods and services and making the adjustment for inputs of household production gives the gross value added by households.

More information on the concepts and methodology may be found on the ONS website: www.statistics.gov.uk/hhsa

# Part 6: Expenditure

## Household expenditure

The National Accounts definition of household expenditure, within household final consumption expenditure, consists of: personal expenditure on goods (durable, semi-durable and non-durable) and services, including the value of income in kind; imputed rent for owner-occupied dwellings; and the purchase of second-hand goods less the proceeds of sales of used goods. Excluded are interest and other transfer payments; all business expenditure; and the purchase of land and buildings (and associated costs).

In principle, expenditure is measured at the time of acquisition rather than actual disbursement of cash. The categories of expenditure include that of non-resident as well as resident households and individuals in the United Kingdom.

Estimates of household expenditure valued in £ million are deflated used price indicators to provide a measure of growth in the volume of household expenditure. These chained volume measures show how household expenditure changes in real terms, i.e. after the effect of price changes have been removed.

For further details see *Consumer Trends* at: www.statistics.gov.uk/consumertrends

From April 2001, the Family Expenditure Survey (FES) was replaced by the Expenditure and Food Survey (EFS). This was formed by merging the FES with the National Food Survey (NFS). It continues to produce the information previously provided by the FES.

The EFS definition of household expenditure represents current expenditure on goods and services. This excludes those recorded payments that are savings or investments (for example, life assurance premiums). Similarly, income tax payments, national insurance contributions, mortgage capital repayments and other payments for major additions to dwellings are excluded. For further details see *Family Spending* at: **www.statistics.gov.uk/StatBase/ Product.asp?vlnk=361**

## Classification of Individual Consumption by Purpose

From 2001/02, the Classification Of Individual COnsumption by Purpose (COICOP) was introduced as a new coding frame for expenditure items in the Expenditure and Food Survey. COICOP has been adapted to the needs of Household Budget Surveys (HBS) across the European Union and, as a consequence, is compatible with similar classifications used in National Accounts and consumer price indices. This allows the production of indicators that are comparable Europe-wide, such as the Harmonised Indices of Consumer Prices (see below).

Twelve categories are used in this edition of *Social Trends,* labelled as food and non-alcoholic drink; alcohol and tobacco; clothing and footwear; housing, water and fuel; household goods and services; health; transport; communication; recreation and culture; education; restaurants and hotels; and miscellaneous goods and services.

A major difference also exists in the treatment of rent and mortgages that were included as part of 'housing' expenditure in the previous editions of *Social Trends* in the Family Expenditure Survey (FES) coding frame. Rent and mortgages are now excluded from the COICOP 'housing, water and fuel' category and are recorded under 'other expenditure items'.

## Retired households

Retired households are those where the household reference person is over state pension age (65 years for men and 60 years for women) and economically inactive. Hence if, for example, a male household reference person is over 65 years old, but working part time or waiting to take up a part-time job, this household would not be classified as a retired household. For analysis purposes two categories are used:

a. 'A retired household mainly dependent upon state pensions' is one in which at least three quarters of the total income of the household is derived from national insurance retirement and similar pensions, including housing and other benefits paid in supplement to or instead of such pensions. The term 'national insurance retirement and similar pensions' includes national insurance disablement and war disability pensions, and income support in conjunction with these disability payments.

b. 'Other retired households' are retired households that do not fulfil the income conditions of 'retired household mainly dependent upon state pensions' because more than a quarter of the household's income derives from occupational retirement pensions and/or income from investments, annuities, etc.

## Harmonised index of consumer prices

The harmonised index of consumer prices (HICP) has been known as the consumer prices index (see below) in the United Kingdom since 10 December 2003. HICPs are calculated in each Member State of the European Union for the purposes of European comparisons, as required by the Maastricht Treaty. From January 1999 the HICP has been used by the European Central Bank (ECB) as the measure for its definition of price stability across the euro area. Further details are contained in an ECB Press Notice released on 13 October 1998: *A stability oriented monetary policy strategy for the ESCB.*

A guide to the HICP can be found on the National Statistics website: **www.statistics.gov.uk/hicp**

Before 1996 the HICP had to be estimated using available data sources. For the period 1988 to 1995 inclusive, the HICP was estimated from archived RPI price quotes and historical weights data, and aggregated up to the published Classification Of Individual COnsumption by Purpose (COICOP) weights. Therefore, the estimated HICP is based on the RPI household population and not all private households, and it does not account for all items included in the official HICP. Between 1975 and 1987 the estimated HICP was based on published RPI section indices and weights, and unpublished item indices and weights for items excluded from the HICP. This estimated HICP can only be considered as a broad indicator of the official HICP.

For more information about how the HICP was estimated see the 'Harmonised Index of Consumer Prices: Historical Estimates' paper in *Economic Trends,* no. 541.

The HICP started in January 1996 and the first 12-month inflation figures were for January 1997.

## Retail prices index

The retail prices index (RPI) is the most familiar general purpose measure of inflation in the United Kingdom. It measures the average change from month to month in the prices of goods and services purchased by most households in the United Kingdom. The spending pattern on which the index is based is revised each year, mainly using information from the Expenditure and Food Survey (EFS). The RPI comprises all private households (i.e. not those living in institutions such as prisons, retirement homes or in student accommodation) excluding:

a. high income households, defined as those households with a total income within the top 4 per cent of all households, as measured by each quarter's EFS; and

b. 'pensioner' households that derive at least three quarters of their total income from state pensions and benefits.

It is considered that such households are likely to spend their money on atypical things and including them in the scope of the RPI would distort the overall average. Expenditure patterns of one-person and two-person 'pensioner' households differ from those of the households

upon which the RPI is based. Separate indices have been compiled for such pensioner households since 1969, and quarterly averages are published on the National Statistics website, *Focus on Consumer Price Indices* (formerly known as the *Consumer Price Indices (CPI) Business Monitor MM23).* They are chained indices constructed in the same way as the RPI. It should, however, be noted that the pensioner indices exclude housing costs.

A guide to the RPI can be found on the National Statistics website: **www.statistics.gov.uk/rpi**

## Consumer prices index

The consumer prices index (CPI) is the main UK domestic measure of inflation for macro-economic purposes. Prior to 10 December 2003 this index in the United Kingdom was published as the harmonised index of consumer prices (HCIP) and the two are the same (i.e. one) index. See also Appendix, Part 6: Harmonised index of consumer prices.

The methodology of the CPI is similar to that of the RPI but differs in the following ways:

1. In the CPI, the geometric mean is used to aggregate the prices at the most basic level whereas the RPI uses arithmetic means.

2. A number of RPI series are excluded from the CPI, in particular, those mainly relating to owner occupiers' housing costs (for example, mortgage interest payments, house depreciation, council tax and buildings insurance).

3. The coverage of the CPI is based on the international classification system, Classification of Individual Consumption by Purpose (COICOP), whereas the RPI uses its own bespoke classification.

4. The CPI includes series for university accommodation fees, foreign students' university tuition fees, unit trust and stockbrokers charges, none of which are included in the RPI.

5. The index for new car prices in the RPI is imputed from movements in second hand car prices, whereas the CPI uses a quality adjusted index based on published prices of new cars.

6. The CPI weights are based on expenditure by all private households, foreign visitors to the United Kingdom and residents of institutional households. In the RPI, weights are based on expenditure by private households only, excluding the highest income households, and pensioner households mainly dependent on state benefits.

7. In the construction of the RPI weights, expenditure on insurance is assigned to the relevant insurance heading. For the CPI weights, the amount paid out in insurance claims is distributed among the COICOP headings according to the nature of the claims expenditure with the residual (i.e. the service charge) being allocated to the relevant insurance heading.

All published CPI series were rebased from 1996=100 to 2005=100 from 14 February 2006.

A guide to the CPI can be found on the National Statistics website: **www.statistics.gov.uk/cpi**

## Retail sales index

The retail sales index (RSI) is a measurement of monthly movements in the average weekly retail turnover of retailers in Great Britain. All retailers selected for the retail sales inquiry are asked to provide estimates of total retail turnover, including sales from stores, e-commerce (including internet), mail order, stalls and markets, and door-to-door sales. Retail turnover is defined as the value of sales of goods to the general public for personal and household use.

The sample is addressed to approximately 5,000 retailers of all sizes every month. All of the largest 900 retailers are included in the sample together with a random sample of smaller retailers. Estimates are produced for each type of store by size-band. These detailed estimates are aggregated to produce estimates of weekly sales for 17 retail sectors, the main industry aggregates and retailing as a whole.

Headline data are presented in constant prices (volume) seasonally adjusted and at current prices (value) not seasonally adjusted.

For further details see *Retail Sales* at www.statistics.gov.uk/rsi

## Part 7: Health

### Expectation of life

The expectation of life is the average total number of years that a person of that age could be expected to live, if the rates of mortality at each age were those experienced in that year. The mortality rates that underlie the expectation of life figures are based, up to 2004, on total deaths occurring in each year for England and Wales and the total deaths registered in each year in Scotland and Northern Ireland.

### Area deprivation

Analysis published in *Health Statistics Quarterly,* spring 2005 was used for Figure 7.2. The deprivation scores were calculated for all 8,595 electoral wards in England as at the 1991 Census, using the index of deprivation developed by Carstairs et al. The index is an unweighted combination of four indicators of material deprivation: the proportions of people in households headed by a person in a semi-skilled or unskilled manual occupation (Social Class IV or V, see Appendix, Part 8: Social class), economically active men seeking work; persons with no car; and persons living in overcrowded accommodation. The main advantage of using the Carstairs index is that it is a population-based rather than a household-based measure, and therefore more appropriate for a study of population health inequalities. A deprivation score based on 1991 ward boundaries was used to facilitate matching to the available ward-level mortality and population data for the period 1994–1999. Because wards vary enormously in population size (mean: 5,475; minimum: 78; maximum 31,612), with larger populations in the most deprived wards, they have been grouped into equal population deciles in ascending order of deprivation. The following table shows the number of wards and people in each deprivation decile based on 1991 Census populations.

| Deprivation decile | Number of wards | Persons (thousands) | Population (percentages) |
|---|---|---|---|
| 1 Least deprived | 1,257 | 4,705 | 10.0 |
| 2 | 1,209 | 4,699 | 10.0 |
| 3 | 1,072 | 4,710 | 10.0 |
| 4 | 959 | 4,706 | 10.0 |
| 5 | 905 | 4,706 | 10.0 |
| 6 | 772 | 4,708 | 10.0 |
| 7 | 707 | 4,704 | 10.0 |
| 8 | 617 | 4,702 | 10.0 |
| 9 | 578 | 4,703 | 10.0 |
| 10 Most deprived | 519 | 4,713 | 10.0 |

### Healthy life expectancy

Health expectancies provide summary measures of the lifelong experience of health, illness and death. They combine together into a single index estimates of years lived in states of full health and the average number of years a person may expect to remain alive (life expectancy). Health expectancies are independent of the age structure of the population and represent the average health expectation of a synthetic birth cohort experiencing current rates of mortality and morbidity over their lifetime.

For Figure 7.2 from analysis in *Health Statistics Quarterly,* spring 2005, the measures of health status used for calculating health expectancies have been derived from the Health Survey for England (HSE) series. The HSE is a continuous survey of the general (non-institutional) population of England. Over the six years (1994–1999) of HSE data used for this study, the aggregated sample size was 100,686 of whom 47 per cent were male. The response rate to the HSE varied between 76 per cent and 78 per cent over the period of the study.

Self-assessed general health was measured in the HSE using a five-point scale recommended by the World Health Organisation for national health interview surveys, which ranges from 'very good', 'good', 'fair', 'bad' and 'very bad' health. The five-point scale improves the international comparability of the results and has also been found to provide a sensitive measure of the underlying variation in health between areas. For the calculation of healthy life expectancy, age-specific rates of good health were based on the proportion of respondents who reported their health as 'very good' or 'good'.

The electoral ward of residence of informants in the survey was assigned using a look-up table matching postcode of residence to 1991 Census ward geography. The distribution of the sample was evenly spread across the ward deprivation deciles (see below) and there is no evidence of a systematic response bias by deprivation.

### Standardised rates

Directly age-standardised incidence rates have been used to enable comparisons to be made between geographical areas over time, and between the sexes, which are independent of changes in the age structure of the population.

For each year, the crude rates in each five-year age group were multiplied by the European standard population for that age group. These were then summed and divided by the total standard population for these age groups to give an overall standardised rate.

### International Classification of Diseases

The International Classification of Diseases (ICD) is a coding scheme for diseases and causes of death. The Tenth Revision of the ICD (ICD10) was introduced for coding the underlying cause of death in Scotland from 2000 and in the rest of the United Kingdom from 2001. The causes of death included in Figure 7.4 correspond to the following ICD10 codes: circulatory diseases I00–I99: cancer C00–D48: and respiratory diseases J00–J99. Rates for 2000 are for England and Wales only.

The data presented in Figure 7.4 cover three different revisions of the ICD. Although they have been selected according to codes that are comparable, there may still be differences between years that are due to changes in the rules used to select the underlying cause of death. This can be seen in deaths from respiratory diseases where different interpretation of these rules were used to code the underlying cause of death from 1983 to 1992, and from 2001 onwards in England and Wales, and 2000 onwards in Scotland.

### Body mass index

Figure 7.7 uses the UK national body mass index (BMI) percentile classification to describe childhood overweight and obesity. This classification uses the 85th and 95th percentiles of the 1990 UK data as cut-off points for overweight and obesity respectively. This means that when the reference data was compiled in 1990, the prevalence of overweight and obesity among children of each age was held to be 15 per cent and 5 per cent of children respectively. This provides a benchmark against which to compare prevalence data from that point forward. In terms of categorising children's BMI status it means, for example, that a child whose BMI corresponds to the 65th BMI percentile of the reference data will be classified as having a normal weight, a child at the 89th BMI percentile will be classified as overweight and a child at the 97th BMI percentile will be classed obese.

Using the UK national BMI percentile classification provides a reference point that is derived from information about the UK population. The national BMI percentile classification was used to present obesity trends estimates in the Chief Medical Officer's *2002 Annual Report*. However, there are alternative methods for measuring childhood obesity. Specifically, the International Obesity Task Force (IOTF) has developed an international classification, using data collected from six countries (the United Kingdom, Brazil, Hong Kong, The Netherlands, Singapore and the United States). The IOTF definition may be better for comparing obesity rates between countries as the reference dataset is more ethnically diverse. There is ongoing debate regarding which classification of childhood obesity is more robust. For a more detailed examination of these issues, see the *Health Survey for England 2002: The Health of Children and Young People*.

## Alcohol-related causes of death

The ONS definition of alcohol-related deaths includes only those causes regarded as being most directly a result of alcohol consumption. Apart from deaths from accidental poisoning with alcohol the definition excludes other external causes of deaths, such as road traffic deaths and other accidents.

For the years 1980–2000 the cause of death was defined using the International Classification of Diseases, Ninth Revision (ICD-9). The codes used by ONS to define alcohol-related deaths for those years are listed below:

| | |
|---|---|
| 291 | – Alcoholic psychoses |
| 303 | – Alcohol dependence syndrome |
| 305.0 | – Non-dependent abuse of alcohol |
| 425.5 | – Alcoholic cardiomyopathy |
| 571 | – Chronic liver disease and cirrhosis |
| E860 | – Accidental poisoning by alcohol |

For the years 2001–03 the International Classification of Diseases, Tenth Revision (ICD-10) was used. To maintain comparability with earlier years the following codes were used:

| | |
|---|---|
| F10 | – Mental and behavioural disorders due to use of alcohol |
| I42.6 | – Alcoholic cardiomyopathy |
| K70 | – Alcoholic liver disease |
| K73 | – Chronic hepatitis, not elsewhere classified |
| K74 | – Fibrosis and cirrhosis of liver |
| X45 | – Accidental poisoning by and exposure to alcohol |

## Mental disorders

The data presented in Table 7.19, Figure 7.20 and Table 8.22 were coded using the term 'mental disorder' as defined by the ICD-10 to imply a clinically recognisable set of symptoms or behaviours associated in most cases with considerable distress and substantial interference with personal functions.

# Part 8: Social protection

## Benefit units

A benefit unit is a single adult or couple living as married and any dependent children, where the head is below state pension age (60 and over for females and 65 and over for males). A pensioner benefit unit is where the head is over state pension age, although couples where the woman is over state pension age but the man is under are currently excluded. The head of the benefit unit is either the household reference person, where he or she belongs to the benefit unit, or the first person listed at interview in the benefit unit – for couples this is usually the male.

## Activities of daily living (ADLs) and instrumental activities of daily living (IADLs)

In Table 8.11, to assess whether a respondent had any problems with mobility, ADLs and IADLs, they were asked to assess their abilities from a range of activities on a showcard (see boxes below). Respondents were asked to exclude any difficulties that they expected would last less than three months.

### Mobility – leg and arm function showcard

1. Walking 100 yards
2. Sitting for about two hours
3. Getting up from a chair after sitting for long periods
4. Climbing several flights of stairs without resting
5. Climbing one flight of stairs without resting
6. Stooping, kneeling or crouching
7. Reaching or extending your arms above shoulder level
8. Pulling or pushing large objects like a living room chair
9. Lifting or carrying weights over 10 pounds, like a heavy bag of groceries
10. Picking up a 5p coin from a table
96. None of these.

### ADLs and IADLs showcard

1. Dressing, including putting on shoes and socks
2. Walking across a room
3. Bathing or showering
4. Eating, such as cutting up food
5. Getting in or out of bed
6. Using the toilet, including getting up or down
7. Using a map to figure out how to get around in a strange place
8. Preparing a hot meal
9. Shopping for groceries
10. Making telephone calls
11. Taking medications
12. Doing work around the house or garden
13. Managing money such as paying bills and keeping track of expenses
96. None of these.

## In-patient activity

In Table 8.13 in-patient data for England are based on finished consultant episodes (FCEs). Data for Wales, Scotland and Northern Ireland are based on deaths and discharges and transfers between specialities (between hospitals in Northern Ireland). An FCE is a completed period of care of a patient using a bed, under one consultant, in a particular NHS Trust or directly managed unit. If a patient is transferred from one consultant to another within the same hospital, this counts as an FCE but not a hospital discharge. Conversely if a patient is transferred from one hospital to another provider, this counts as an FCE and a hospital discharge.

Data for England, Wales and Northern Ireland exclude NHS beds and activity in joint-user and contractual hospitals. For Scotland, data for joint-user and contractual hospitals are included.

## Children looked after by local authorities

In England and Wales children's homes include homes, hostels and secure units. In Northern Ireland this category includes homes and secure units but excludes hostels, which are included in the other accommodation category.

In Northern Ireland, data for the 'placement with parents' category used in Great Britain are collected as 'placed with family'.

## Social class

Social class is based on occupation and is a classification system that has grown out of the original Registrar-General's social class classification. These are defined in the Classification of Occupations 1990 (SOC90), which was revised and updated in SOC2000, prepared by the Office for National Statistics. The five categories are:

| |
|---|
| I. Professional, etc. occupations |
| II. Managerial and technical occupations |
| III. Skilled occupations |
| (N) non-manual |
| (M) manual |
| IV. Partly skilled occupations |
| V. Unskilled occupations. |

From 2001, the National Statistics Socio-economic Classification (NS-SEC) was adopted for all official surveys, in place of social class based on occupation, see Appendix, Part 1: National Statistics Socio-economic Classification (NS-SEC).

# Part 9: Crime and justice

## National Crime Recording Standard

Changes in the counting rules for recorded crime on 1 April, 1998 affected both the methods of counting and the coverage for recorded crime and had the effect of inflating the number of crimes recorded. For some offence groups – homicide, violence against the person and burglary – there was likely to be little effect on numbers recorded. However the changes will have had more effect on figures for minor violence and criminal damage.

In April 2002 a new National Crime Recording Standard (NCRS) was introduced in England and Wales with the aim of taking a more victim centred approach and providing more consistency between forces. Prior to 2002 police forces in England and Wales did not necessarily record a crime that was reported if there was no evidence to support the claim of the victim. Therefore recorded crime rates have been adjusted to allow comparison between recent years and pre-2002 statistics.

It is not possible to assess the effect of the NCRS on recorded firearm crimes. The NCRS inflated the overall number of violence against the person and criminal damage offences, but has less effect on the number of robberies. Many firearm offences are among the less serious categories, and these types of offences are among those most affected by the NCRS.

The introduction of the NCRS may have had an effect on the recorded crime detection rate, but this is difficult to quantify.

## Types of offences in England and Wales

The figures are compiled from police returns to the Home Office or directly from court computer systems.

In England and Wales, indictable only offences cover those offences that can only be tried at the Crown Court and include the more serious offences. Summary offences are those for which a defendant would normally be tried at a magistrates' court and are generally less serious – the majority of motoring offences fall into this category. Triable-either-way offences are triable either on indictment or summarily.

Recorded crime statistics broadly cover the more serious offences. Up to March 1998 most indictable and triable-either-way offences were included, as well as some summary ones; from April 1998, all indictable and triable-either-way offences were included, plus a few closely related summary ones.

Recorded offences are the most readily available measures of the incidence of crime, but do not necessarily indicate the true level of crime. Many less serious offences are not reported to the police and cannot, therefore, be recorded. Moreover, the propensity of the public to report offences to the police is influenced by a number of factors and may change over time.

From 2000 some police forces have changed their systems to record the allegations of victims unless there is credible evidence that a crime has not taken place. In April 2002, the new National Crime Recording Standard (NCRS) formalised these changes across England and Wales.

### The British Crime Survey

There have been changes to the methodology of the British Crime Survey. Between 1982 and 2001 the survey was carried out every two years, and reported on victimisation in the previous calendar year. From 2001/02 the survey covers the financial year of interviews and reports on victimisation in the 12 months before the interview.

This change makes the survey's estimates more comparable with figures collected by the police. Because of these significant changes taking place in both measures of crime, direct comparisons with figures for previous years cannot be made.

## Comparing the British Crime Survey with police recorded crime

To compare the British Crime Survey (BCS) with police recorded crime figures it is necessary to limit both to a set of offences that are covered by both series, the comparable subset, which comprises vandalism, burglary, vehicle-related theft, bicycle theft, theft from the person, robbery, common assault and wounding.

The BCS excludes so-called victimless crimes (e.g. drug dealing), crimes such as murder, where the victim is no longer available for interview, and fraud. BCS estimates also exclude sexual offences (because of the small number reported to the survey and concerns about the willingness of respondents to disclose such offences).

BCS thefts involving household and personal property cannot be compared because while they might be included in police figures they would fall into a miscellaneous category of thefts, which will also include thefts of business property, shoplifting and other crimes.

Various adjustments are also made to police figures to take account of the fact that the BCS does not cover offences against non-domestic targets (e.g. businesses) and those under 16.

## Types of offences in Northern Ireland

In recording crime, the Police Service of Northern Ireland broadly follow the Home Office rules for counting crime. As from 1 April 1998 notifiable offences are recorded on the same basis as those in England and Wales. Prior to the revision of the rules, criminal damage offences in Northern Ireland excluded those where the value of the property damaged was less than £200.

## Offences and crimes

There are a number of reasons why recorded crime statistics in England and Wales, Northern Ireland and Scotland cannot be directly compared:

*Different legal systems:* The legal system operating in Scotland differs from that in England and Wales, and Northern Ireland. For example, in Scotland child offenders aged under 16 are normally dealt with by the Children's Hearings system rather than the courts.

*Differences in classification:* There are significant differences in the offences included within the recorded crime categories used in Scotland and the categories of notifiable offences used in England, Wales and Northern Ireland. Scottish figures of 'crime' have therefore been grouped in an attempt to approximate to the classification of notifiable offences in England, Wales and Northern Ireland.

*Counting rules:* In Scotland each individual offence occurring within an incident is recorded whereas in England, Wales and Northern Ireland only the main offence is counted.

*Burglary:* This term is not applicable to Scotland where the term used is 'housebreaking'.

*Theft from vehicles:* In Scotland data have only been separately identified from January 1992. The figures include theft by opening lock fast places from a motor vehicle and other theft from a motor vehicle.

## Crime and Justice Survey 'core' offences

The 2003 Crime and Justice Survey presents the key results on 20 core offences.

*Property offences:*
Burglary (domestic, commercial)

Vehicle related thefts (theft of vehicles, attempted theft of a vehicle, theft from outside a vehicle, theft from inside a vehicle, attempted thefts from a vehicle)

Other thefts (from work, from school, shoplifting, thefts from person, other theft)

Criminal damage (to a vehicle, to other property)

*Violent offences:*
Robbery (of an individual, of a business)

Assaults (with injury, without injury)

*Drug offences:*
Selling drugs (Class A drugs, other drugs).

## Offenders cautioned for burglary

In England and Wales offenders cautioned for going equipped for stealing, etc were counted against burglary offences until 1986 and against other offences from 1987. Historical data provided in Table 9.18 have been amended to take account of this change.

## Sentences and orders

The following are the main sentences and orders that can be imposed upon those persons found guilty. Some types of sentence or order can only be given to offenders in England and Wales in certain age groups. Under the framework for sentencing contained in the *Criminal Justice Acts 1991, 1993* and the *Powers of Criminal Courts (Sentencing) Act 2000* the sentence must reflect the seriousness of the offence. The following sentences are available for adults (a similar range of sentences is available to juveniles aged 10 to 17):

*Absolute and conditional discharge:* A court may make an order discharging a person absolutely or (except in Scotland) conditionally where it is inexpedient to inflict punishment and, before 1 October, 1992, where a probation order was not appropriate. An order for conditional discharge runs for such period of not more than three years as the court specifies, the condition being that the offender does not commit another offence within the period so specified. In Scotland a court may also discharge a person with an admonition.

The term *'community sentence'* refers to attendance centre orders, reparation orders, action plan orders, drug treatment and testing orders, community rehabilitation orders, community punishment orders, community punishment and rehabilitation orders, supervision orders, curfew orders and referral orders. Under the *Criminal Justice and Courts Services Act 2000,* certain community orders current at 1 April, 2001 were renamed. Probation orders were renamed community rehabilitation orders, community service orders were renamed community punishment orders and combination orders were renamed community punishment and rehabilitation orders.

*Attendance Centre Order:* Available in England, Wales and Northern Ireland for young offenders and involves deprivation of free time.

*Reparation Order:* Introduced under the *Powers of Criminal Courts (Sentencing) Act 2000.* This requires the offender to make an apology to the victim or apologise in person. Maximum duration of the order is 24 hours and is only available to youngsters aged 10 to 18 in England and Wales.

*Action Plan Order:* An order imposed for a maximum of three months in England, Wales and Northern Ireland to address certain behavioural problems. This is again available for the younger age groups and is considered as early intervention to stop serious offending.

*Drug Treatment and Testing Order:* This is imposed as a treatment order to reduce the person's dependence on drugs and to test if the offender is complying with treatment. Length of order can run from six months to three years in England, Wales and Northern Ireland. This was introduced under the *Powers of Criminal Courts (Sentencing) Act 2000* for persons aged 16 years and over.

*Community Rehabilitation Order:* An offender sentenced to a Community Rehabilitation Order is under the supervision of a probation officer (social worker in Scotland), whose duty it is (in England and Wales and Northern Ireland) to advise, assist and befriend him or her but the court has the power to include any other requirement it considers appropriate. A cardinal feature of the order is that it relies on the co-operation of the offender. Community rehabilitation orders may be given for any period between six months and three years.

*Community Punishment Order:* An offender who is convicted of an offence punishable with imprisonment may be sentenced to perform unpaid work for not more than 240 hours (300 hours in Scotland), and not less than 40 hours. A minimum of 20 hours community service are given for persistent petty offending or fine default. In Scotland the *Law Reform (Miscellaneous Provisions) (Scotland) Act 1990* requires that community service can only be ordered where the court would otherwise have imposed imprisonment or detention. Probation and community service may be combined in a single order in Scotland.

*Community Punishment and Rehabilitation Order:* The *Criminal Justice Act 1991* introduced the Combination Order in England and Wales only, which combines elements of both probation supervision and community service. Meanwhile, Article 15 of the Criminal Justice (NI) Order 1996 introduced the combination order to Northern Ireland. The *Powers of Criminal Courts (Sentencing) Act 2000* brought into effect the Community Punishment and Rehabilitation Order, known as the Combination Order, which requires an offender to be under a probation officer and to take on unpaid work.

*Detention and Training Order:* This was introduced for youths aged 10 to 18 under the *Powers of Criminal Courts (Sentencing) Act 2000.* It is for youths who have committed a serious crime. They can serve the sentence at a Young Offender Institution or at a Local Authority Establishment, or Local Authority Secure Training Centre. The sentence is given from 4 to 24 months, but sentences can run consecutively.

*Imprisonment:* is the custodial sentence for adult offenders. In the case of mentally disordered offenders, hospital orders, which may include a Restriction Order, may be considered appropriate.

Home Office or Scottish Executive consent is needed for release or transfer. A new disposal, the 'hospital direction', was introduced in 1997. The court, when imposing a period of imprisonment, can direct that the offender be sent directly to hospital. On recovering from the mental disorder, the offender is returned to prison to serve the balance of their sentence.

The *Criminal Justice Act 1991* abolished remission and substantially changed the parole scheme in England and Wales. Those serving sentences of under four years, imposed on or after 1 October 1992, are subject to Automatic Conditional Release and are released, subject to certain criteria, halfway through their sentence. Home Detention Curfews result in selected prisoners being released up to two months early with a tag that monitors their presence during curfew hours. Those serving sentences of four years or longer are considered for Discretionary Conditional Release after having served half their sentence, but are automatically released at the two thirds point of sentence.

The *Crime (Sentences) Act 1997,* implemented on 1 October 1997, included for persons aged 18 or over, an automatic life sentence for a second serious violent or sexual offence unless there are exceptional circumstances.

All offenders serving a sentence of 12 months or more are supervised in the community until the three quarter point of sentence. A life sentence prisoner may be released on licence subject to supervision and is always liable to recall.

In Scotland the *Prisoners and Criminal Proceedings (Scotland) Act 1993* changed the system of remission and parole for prisoners sentenced on or after 1 October 1993. Those serving sentences of less than four years are released unconditionally after having served half of their sentence, unless the court specifically imposes a Supervised Release Order that subjects them to social work supervision after release. Those serving sentences of four years or more are eligible for parole at half sentence. If parole is not granted then they will automatically be released on licence at two thirds of sentence subject to days added for breaches of prison rules. All such prisoners are liable to be 'recalled on conviction' or for breach of conditions of licence, i.e. if between the date of release and the date on which the full sentence ends a person commits another offence that is punishable by imprisonment, or breaches his/her licence conditions, then the offender may be returned to prison for the

remainder of that sentence whether or not a sentence of imprisonment is also imposed for the new offence.

*Fully suspended sentences:* These may only be passed in exceptional circumstances. In England, Wales and Northern Ireland, sentences of imprisonment of two years or less may be fully suspended. A court should not pass a suspended sentence unless a sentence of imprisonment would be appropriate in the absence of a power to suspend. The result of suspending a sentence is that it will not take effect unless during the period specified the offender is convicted of another offence punishable with imprisonment. Suspended sentences are not available in Scotland.

*Fines:* The *Criminal Justice Act 1993* introduced new arrangements on 20 September 1993 whereby courts are now required to fit an amount for the fine that reflects the seriousness of the offence and that takes account of an offender's means. This system replaced the more formal unit fines scheme included in the *Criminal Justice Act 1991.* The Act also introduced the power for courts to arrange deduction of fines from income benefit for those offenders receiving such benefits. *The Law Reform (Miscellaneous Provision) (Scotland) Act 1990* as amended by the *Criminal Procedure (Scotland) Act 1995* provides for the use of supervised attendance orders by selected courts in Scotland. *The Criminal Procedure (Scotland) Act 1995* also makes it easier for courts to impose a supervised attendance order in the event of a default and enables the court to impose a supervised attendance order in the first instance for 16 and 17 year olds.

*Custody Probation Order:* An order unique to Northern Ireland reflecting the different regime that applies in respect of remission and the general absence of release on licence. The custodial sentence is followed by a period of supervision for a period of between 12 months and 3 years.

## Civil courts

*England and Wales*

The main civil courts are the High Court and the county courts. The High court is divided into three divisions:

• The *Queen's Bench Division* deals with disputes relating to contracts, general commercial matters and breaches of duty – known as 'liability in tort' – covering claims of negligence, nuisance or defamation.

• The *Chancery Division* deals with disputes relating to land, wills, companies and insolvency.

• The Family Division deals with matrimonial matters, including divorce, and the welfare of children.

Magistrates' courts also have some civil jurisdiction, mainly in family proceedings. Most appeals in civil cases go to the Court of Appeal (Civil Division) and may go from there to the House of Lords. Since July 1991, county courts have been able to deal with all contract and tort cases and actions for recovery of land, regardless of value. Cases are presided over by a judge who almost always sits without a jury. Jury trials are limited to specified cases, for example, actions for libel.

*Scotland*

The Court of Session is the supreme civil court. Any cause, apart from causes excluded by statute, may be initiated in, and any judgment of an inferior court may be appealed to, the Court of Session. The Sheriff Court is the principal local court of civil jurisdiction in Scotland. It also has jurisdiction in criminal proceedings. Apart from certain actions the civil jurisdiction of the Sheriff Court is generally similar to that of the Court of Session.

## Civil representation certificates

A civil representation certificate gives authority for work to be carried out in cases where civil court proceedings are in prospect. The certificate defines the preparatory work to be carried out and sets an initial costs limit for that work. Both the work authorised and the costs limit can be amended on application, subject to the satisfactory completion of the initial work, up to and including the proceedings themselves and subsequent appeals to the higher courts.

## Legal professionals

To qualify as a barrister, it is necessary to complete three stages of training:

1. *Academic:* To fulfil the academic stage one of the following must be achieved. Pass an approved law degree (minimum grade 2:2) or pass a non-law degree (minimum grade 2:2) followed by a law conversion course, known as the Common Professional Examination (CPE) or a Graduate Diploma in Law (GDL), or a Senior Status Law degree. Exceptionally, mature people with a professional qualification considered equivalent to a degree may be granted a certificate of academic standing that allows them to take the CPE or GDL.

2. *Vocational:* When the academic stage has been completed, the vocational stage is undertaken – this involves joining one of the four Inns of Court. Once the Bar Vocational Course (BVC) is completed students are 'called to the bar' by their Inn of Court. They remain a member of their Inn for the rest of their career.

3. *On the job training:* Pupillage is the final stage of training in which the student carries out a funded full-time 12-month period of on the job training, under the guidance of an approved pupil supervisor.

In the first three years of practice, barristers must obtain a tenancy in a set of chambers, or work with another barrister who has at least five years' experience. Barristers may then set up their own practice. Once qualified, barristers are subject to certain requirements to keep their practicing certificates. This is called Continuing Professional Development (CPD) and is usually in the form of courses or lectures.

## Part 10: Housing

### Dwelling stock

The definition of a dwelling follows the census definition applicable at that time. Currently the 2001 Census is used, which defined a dwelling as a self-contained unit of accommodation. Self-containment is where all the rooms in a household are behind a door, which only that household can use. Non-self-contained household spaces at the same address are counted together as a single dwelling. A dwelling can consist of one self-contained household space or two or more non-self-contained spaces at the same address.

In all stock figures vacant dwellings are included but non-permanent dwellings are generally excluded. For housebuilding statistics, only data on permanent dwellings are collected.

Estimates of the total dwelling stock, stock changes and the tenure distribution in the United Kingdom are made by the Office of the Deputy Prime Minister (ODPM) for England, the Scottish Executive, the National Assembly for Wales, and the Northern Ireland Department for Social Development. These are primarily based on census output data for the number of dwellings (or households converted to dwellings) from the censuses of population for the United Kingdom. Adjustments were carried out if there were specific reasons to do so. Census year figures are based on outputs from the censuses. For years between censuses, the total figures are obtained by projecting the base census year's figure forward annually. The increment is based on the annual total number of completions plus the annual total net gain from other housing flows statistics, i.e. conversions, demolitions and changes of use.

Estimates of dwelling stock by tenure category are primarily based on the census except where it is considered that for some specific tenure information, there are other more accurate sources. In this situation it is assumed that the other data sources contain vacant dwellings also, but it is not certain and it is not expected that these data are very precise. Thus the allocation of vacant dwellings to tenure categories may not be completely accurate. This means that the margin of error for tenure categories are wider than for estimates of total stock.

For the 2001 Census, a comparison with other available sources indicated that for local authority stock, figures supplied by local authorities are more reliable. Similarly, it was found that the Housing Corporation's own data are more accurate than those from the census for the registered social landlord (RSL) stock. Hence only the rented privately or with a job or business tenure data were used directly from the census. The owner-occupied data were taken as the residual of the total from the census. For non-census years, the same approach was adopted except for the privately rented or with a job or business, for which Labour Force Survey results were used.

In the Survey of English Housing, data for privately rented unfurnished accommodation include accommodation that is partly furnished.

For further information on the methodology used to calculate stock by tenure and tenure definitions, see Appendix B Notes and Definitions in the ODPM annual volume *Housing Statistics* or the housing statistics page of the ODPM website at: **www.odpm.gov.uk**

### Dwellings completed

In principle a dwelling is regarded as completed when it becomes ready for occupation whether it is in fact occupied or not. In practice there are instances where the timing could be delayed and some completions are missed, for example, because no completion certificates were requested by the owner.

Tenure definition for housebuilding is only slightly different from that used for stock figures. For further information on the methodology used to calculate stock by tenure and tenure definitions, see Appendix B Notes and Definitions in the ODPM annual volume *Housing Statistics* or the housing statistics page of the ODPM website.

### Sales and transfers of local authority dwellings

Right to buy was established by the *Housing Act 1980* and was introduced across Great Britain in October 1980. In England, large scale voluntary transfers (LSVTs) of stock have been principally to housing associations/registered social landlords; figures include transfers supported by estate renewal challenge funding (ERCF). The figures for 1993 include 949 dwellings transferred under Tenants' Choice. In Scotland LSVTs to registered social landlords and trickle transfers to housing associations are included.

### Ownership of second homes abroad

Figures presented in Table 10.8 are based on data collected by the Office of the Deputy Prime Minister's (ODPM) Survey of English Housing (SEH). Questions concerning second home ownership were introduced in the 1994/95 survey. The SEH asks whether households in England have a second home, whether the second home is located in Great Britain or elsewhere and what the tenure is (rented, owner-occupied, timeshare or otherwise). From 2003/04 the SEH provided a geographical breakdown of where foreign second homes were located. Second homes were categorised into Spain, France, Portugal, Italy, other European countries, the United States and other non-European countries. A time series of the geographical breakdown has been estimated by applying the same geographical proportions identified in the 2003/04 SEH to the earlier totals.

The methodology used to produce the data in Table 10.8 assumes that the number of properties that are owned abroad is equal to the number of households that own property abroad. If a household owns more than one property abroad, the SEH only records the main property. Moreover, this methodology does not attempt to measure the number or value of properties owned by several households (for example, timeshare accommodation). As the SEH records the number of English households that own second homes outside Great Britain the data have been adjusted to represent the number of UK households that own property outside the United Kingdom.

### Homeless at home

Homeless at home refers to any arrangement where a household for whom a duty has been accepted (eligible for assistance, unintentionally homeless and in priority need) is able to remain in, or return to the accommodation from which they are being made homeless, or temporarily stay in other accommodation found by the applicant. Such schemes may locally be referred to as: Direct Rehousing, Prevention of Homelessness;

Concealed Household Schemes; Prevention of Imminent Homelessness Schemes; Impending Homeless Schemes and Pre-eviction Schemes.

## Bedroom standard

The concept is used to estimate occupation density by allocating a standard number of bedrooms to each household in accordance with its age/sex/marital status composition and the relationship of the members to one another. A separate bedroom is allocated to each married or cohabiting couple, any other person aged 21 or over, each pair of adolescents aged 10 to 20 of the same sex, and each pair of children under 10. Any unpaired person aged 10 to 20 is paired if possible with a child under 10 of the same sex, or, if that is not possible, is given a separate bedroom, as is any unpaired child under 10. This standard is then compared with the actual number of bedrooms (including bedsitters) available for the sole use of the household, and deficiencies or excesses are tabulated. Bedrooms converted to other uses are not counted as available unless they have been denoted as bedrooms by the informants; bedrooms not actually in use are counted unless uninhabitable.

## Decent home standard

The Government's key housing target is for all housing rented from social landlords in England to meet the decent home standard by 2010. A decent home is one that:

a. meets the current statutory minimum for housing, which at present is the 'fitness standard';

b. is in a reasonable state of repair;

c. has reasonably modern facilities and services; and

d. provides a reasonable degree of thermal comfort.

## Index of Multiple Deprivation

In summer 2004, the Office of the Deputy Prime Minister updated and revised the Index of Multiple Deprivation 2000. The Index of Multiple Deprivation 2004 (IMD 2004) is a Super Output Area (SOA) level index and comprises seven dimensions/domains of deprivation: income; employment; health deprivation and disability; education, skills and training deprivation; barriers to housing and services; crime; and the living environment deprivation. SOAs are typically smaller than wards – each SOA comprises an average of 1,500 people – and thus allows a better identification and targeting of small pockets of deprivation. The Index ranks 32,482 SOAs in England with 1 being the most deprived and 32,482 being the least deprived.

## Poor quality environments

The identification of poor quality environments is based on surveyors' observed assessments of the severity of problems in the immediate environment of the home. The problems assessed fall into three groups:

• the upkeep, management or misuse of private and public buildings and space (scruffy or neglected buildings; poor condition housing; graffiti; scruffy gardens or landscaping; litter; rubbish or dumping; vandalism; dog or other excrement; nuisance from street parking);

• road traffic or other transport (presence of intrusive motorways and main roads; railway or aircraft noise; heavy traffic; ambient air quality);

• abandonment or non-residential use (vacant sites; vacant or boarded up buildings; intrusive industry; nonconforming use of domestic premises such as running car repair, scrap yard or haulage business).

A home is regarded as having a poor quality environment of a given type if it is assessed to have 'significant' or 'major' problems in respect of any of the specific environmental problems assessed and grouped under that type. The overall assessment of households with poor quality environments is based on whether the home has any of the three types of problems.

## Property transactions

The figures are based on the number of particular delivered (PD) forms processed and stamp duty land tax certificates issued. They relate to the transfer or sale of any freehold interest in land or property, or the grant or transfer of a lease of at least 21 years and 1 day. In practice there is an average lag of about one month between the transaction and the date when the PD form is processed.

## Mix adjusted prices

Information on dwelling prices at national and regional levels are collected and published by the Office of the Deputy Prime Minister (ODPM) on a monthly basis from a sample survey of mortgage completions, the Survey of Mortgage Lenders (SML). The SML covers about 50 banks and building societies that are members of the Council of Mortgage Lenders.

Data prior to the first quarter of 2002 were derived from a 5 per cent sample of completions data and were calculated on an old mix adjusted methodology. As a consequence of a significantly increased sample (to an average 25,000 cases per month), the ODPM has recently been able to introduce a monthly series. The mix adjusted methodology has also been enhanced. The monthly series are available back to February 2002 and annual figures have been derived as an average of these monthly prices. The annual change in price is shown as the average percentage change over the year and is calculated from the house price index.

A simple average price will be influenced by changes in the mix of properties bought in each period. This effect is removed by applying fixed weights to the process at the start of each year, based on the average mix of properties purchased during the previous three years, and these weights are applied to prices during the year.

The mix adjusted average price excludes sitting tenant (right to buy) purchases, cash purchases, remortgages and further loans.

## Housing expenditure

Housing expenditure data presented in Chapter 6: Expenditure, are based on the Classification Of Individual COnsumption by Purpose (COICOP) definition (see Appendix, Part 6: Classification of Individual Consumption by Purpose). Housing costs that are included in the COICOP classification are:

– net rent for housing (gross rent less housing benefit, rebates and allowances received);

– second dwelling rent;

– maintenance and repair of dwelling;

– water supply and miscellaneous services relating to dwelling;

– household insurances.

Under COICOP classification expenditure on mortgage interest payments, mortgage protection premiums, council tax and Northern Ireland domestic rates are included in 'other expenditure items'.

Data presented in Table 10.23 are based on a comprehensive definition of housing costs. In addition to the housing costs included within the COICOP classifications of housing expenditure and other expenditure items outlined above, this also includes the following non-consumption expenditure on the purchase or alteration of dwellings and mortgages:

– outright purchase of dwelling including deposits;

– capital repayment of mortgage;

– central heating installation;

– DIY improvements;

– home improvements (contracted out);

– bathroom fittings;

– purchase of materials for capital improvements;

– purchase of second dwelling.

# Part 11: Environment

## Global warming and climate change

In Figure 11.2, the Kyoto reduction targets cover a basket of six gases: carbon dioxide ($CO_2$), methane ($CH_4$), nitrous oxide ($N_2O$), hydrofluorocarbons (HFCs), perfluorocarbons (PFCs) and sulphur hexafluoride ($SF_6$). For the latter three gases signatories to the Protocol may choose to use 1995, rather than 1990, as the base year from which to calculate targets, since data for 1995 for these gases tend to be more widely available and more reliable than for 1990. The United Kingdom announced in its Climate Change Programme that it would use 1995 as the base year for the fluorinated gases – therefore the 'base year' emissions for the UK target differ slightly from UK emissions in 1990. Limited allowance is given in the Protocol for the absorption of $CO_2$ by forests, which act as so-called carbon sinks.

## Fuels for energy use

Energy use of fuel mainly comprises use for lighting, heating or cooling, motive power and power for appliances. Non-energy uses of fuel include chemical feedstock, solvents, lubricants, and road making material.

Coal includes other solid fuels. Petroleum excludes marine bunkers. Natural gas includes colliery methane and non-energy use of natural gas up to 1998. Primary electricity includes nuclear, hydroelectric and renewable energy, and imports of electricity via interconnections.

## Rivers and canals

The chemical quality of rivers and canal waters in the United Kingdom are monitored in a series of separate national surveys in England and Wales, Scotland and Northern Ireland. In England, Wales and Northern Ireland the General Quality Assessment (GQA) Scheme provides a rigorous and objective method for assessing the basic chemical quality of rivers and canals based on three factors: dissolved oxygen, biochemical oxygen demand (BOD) and ammoniacal nitrogen. The GQA grades river stretches into six categories (A – F) of chemical quality. For Table 11.9 these have been grouped into four broader groups – good (classes A and B), fair (classes C and D), poor and bad. Classification of biological quality is based on the River Invertebrate Prediction and Classification System (RIVPACS).

The length of rivers monitored in Northern Ireland increased by more than 40 per cent between 1991 and 2001.

In Scotland water quality is based upon the Scottish River Classification Scheme of 20 June 1997, which combines chemical, biological, nutrient and aesthetic quality using the following classes: excellent (A1), good (A2), fair (B), poor (C) and seriously polluted (D). In 1999 a new Digitised River Network was introduced.

## Bathing waters

Directive 76/160/EEC concerning the quality of bathing waters sets the following mandatory standards for the coliform parameters:

1. for total coliforms, 10,000 per 100 millilitres; and

2. for faecal coliforms 2,000 per 100 millilitres.

The directive requires that at least 95 per cent of samples taken for each of these parameters over the bathing season must meet the mandatory values. In practice this has been interpreted in the following manner: where 20 samples are taken only one sample for each parameter may exceed the mandatory values for the water to pass the coliform standards; where less than 20 samples are taken, none may exceed the mandatory values for the water to pass the coliform standards.

The bathing season is from mid-May to end-September in England and Wales, but is shorter in Scotland and Northern Ireland. Bathing waters that are closed for a season are excluded for that year.

The boundaries of the Environment Agency regions are based on river catchment areas and not county borders. In particular, the figures shown for Wales are for the Environment Agency Welsh Region, the boundary of which does not correspond to the boundary of Wales. See Geographic Maps on page 214.

## Air pollutants

Volatile organic compounds (VOCs) comprise a wide range of chemical compounds including hydrocarbons, oxygenates and halogen containing species. Methane ($CH_4$) is an important component of VOCs but its environmental impact derives principally from its contribution to global warming, see Appendix, Part 11: Global warming and climate change.

The major environmental impact of non-methane VOCs lies in their involvement in the formation of ground level ozone. Most VOCs are non-toxic or are present at levels well below guideline values. Others, such as benzene and 1,3-butadiene, are of concern because of their potential impact on human health.

$PM_{10}$ is airborne particulate matter. Specifically, it is the fraction of 'black smoke' which is thought most likely to be deposited in the lungs. It can be defined as the fraction resulting from a collection from black smoke by a size selective sampler which collects smaller particles preferentially, capturing 50 per cent of 10 micron aerodynamic diameter particles, more than 95 per cent of 5 micron particles, and less than 5 per cent of 20 micron particles.

## New woodland creation

For Figure 11.21, areas receiving grant aid are allocated to years by date of payment.

# Part 12: Transport

## Road traffic

The figures from 1993 to 2002 have been produced on a new basis and are not directly comparable with earlier figures. In 2001/02, steps were taken to improve the quality of the Department for Transport's major road network database. The net result of these improvements has been little change to the estimates of total motor vehicle traffic for Great Britain for after 1993, but some changes to the composition of the overall figure. In general, from 1993 to 1999 the new motorway traffic estimates are higher than before, while those for other major roads are lower, with the reverse being true for 2000 and 2001.

## National Travel Survey

The National Travel Survey (NTS) has been conducted on a small scale continuous basis since July 1988. The last of the previous ad hoc surveys was carried out in 1985–86.

Information was collected from about 3,000 households in Great Britain each year up to 2001, 7,400 households in 2002 and over 8,000 in 2003 and 2004. Each member of the household provides personal information (for example, age, sex, working status, driving licence, season ticket) and details of trips carried out in a sample week, including the purpose of the trip, method of travel, time of day, length, duration, and cost of any tickets bought.

Travel included in the NTS covers all trips by British residents within Great Britain for personal reasons, including travel in the course of work.

A trip is defined as a one-way course of travel having a single main purpose. It is the basic unit of personal travel defined in the survey. A round trip is split into two trips, with the first ending at a convenient point about half-way round as a notional stopping point for the outward destination and return origin. A stage is that portion of a trip defined by the use of a specific method of transport or of a specific ticket (a new stage being defined if either the mode or ticket changes). The main mode of a trip is that used for the longest stage of the trip. With stages of equal length the mode of the latest stage is used.

*Walks:* of less than 50 yards are excluded.

*Car:* includes light vans, 4x4 vehicles and privately owned lorries.

*Rail:* includes both surface rail (former British Rail) and London Underground services, but not any other rail service.

*Light Rail:* includes the Tyne & Wear Metro, Docklands Light Railway, Manchester Metrolink, Glasgow Underground System, South Yorkshire Supertram, Blackpool Trams, Croydon Tramlink, Leeds Supertram, Greater Nottingham Light Rapid Transit and Midlands Metro. It has been possible to distinguish these modes since 1998, but the number of cases is small and they are included in tables under 'other public' transport.

*Local bus:* includes all 'local' services, but excludes express services, excursions and tours.

*A bicycle:* is any pedal cycle capable of use on the public road, but not children's bicycles or tricycles that are intended as toys.

*Other:* modes depend on the context, but may include other types of bus (works or school bus, private hire, express bus, and tours and excursions), two-wheeled motor vehicles, motorcaravans, dormobiles, taxis/minicabs, domestic air travel and other private and public transport.

Cars are regarded as household cars if they are either owned by a member of the household, or available for the private use of household members. Company cars provided by an employer for the use of a particular employee (or director) are included, but cars borrowed temporarily from a company pool are not.

The main driver of a household car is the household member who drives the furthest in that car in the course of a year.

The purpose of a trip is normally taken to be the activity at the destination, unless that destination is 'home', in which case the purpose is defined by the origin of the trip. The classification of trips to 'work' is also dependent on the origin of the trip. The following purposes are distinguished:

*Commuting:* trips to a usual place of work from home, or from work to home.

*Business:* personal trips in the course of work, including a trip in the course of work back to work. This includes all work trips by people with no usual place of work (for example, site workers) and those who work at or from home.

*Education:* trips to school or college, etc, by full-time students, students on day-release and part-time students following vocational courses.

*Escort:* used when the traveller has no purpose of his or her own, other than to escort or accompany another person; for example, taking a child to school. Escort commuting is escorting or accompanying someone from home to work or from work to home.

*Shopping:* all trips to shops or from shops to home, even if there was no intention to buy.

*Personal business:* visits to services, for example, hairdressers, launderettes, dry-cleaners, betting shops, solicitors, banks, estate agents, libraries, churches; or for medical consultations or treatment, or for eating and drinking, unless the main purpose was social or entertainment.

*Social or entertainment:* visits to meet friends, relatives, or acquaintances, both at someone's home or at a pub, restaurant, etc; all types of entertainment or sport, clubs, and voluntary work, non-vocational evening classes, political meetings, etc.

*Holidays or day trips:* trips (within Great Britain) to or from any holiday (including stays of four nights or more with friends or relatives) or trips for pleasure (not otherwise classified as social or entertainment) within a single day.

*Just walk:* walking pleasure trips along public highways including taking the dog for a walk and jogging.

## Car ownership

The figures for household ownership include four-wheeled and three-wheeled cars, off-road vehicles, minibuses, motorcaravans, dormobiles, and light vans. Company cars normally available for household use are also included.

## Passenger death rates

Passenger fatality rates given in Table 12.21 can be interpreted as the risk a traveller runs of being killed, per billion kilometres travelled. The coverage varies for each mode of travel and care should be exercised in drawing comparisons between the rates for different modes.

The table provides information on passenger fatalities and where possible travel by drivers and other crew in the course of their work has been excluded. Exceptions are for private journeys and those in company owned cars and vans where drivers are included.

Figures for all modes of transport exclude confirmed suicides and deaths through natural causes. Figures for air, rail and water exclude trespassers, and rail excludes attempted suicides. Accidents occurring in airports, seaports and railway stations that do not directly involve the mode of transport concerned are also excluded, for example, deaths sustained on escalators or falling over packages on platforms.

The figures are compiled by the Department for Transport. Further information is available in the annual publications *Road Casualties Great Britain: Annual Report,* and *Transport Statistics Great Britain.* Both are published by The Stationery Office and are available at: **www.dft.gov.uk/transtat**

The following definitions are used:

*Air:* accidents involving UK registered airline aircraft in UK and foreign airspace. Fixed wing and rotary wing aircraft are included but air taxis are excluded. Accidents cover UK airline aircraft around the world not just in the United Kingdom.

*Rail:* train accidents and accidents occurring through movement of railway vehicles in Great Britain. As well as national rail the figures include accidents on underground and tram systems, Eurotunnel and minor railways.

*Water:* figures for travel by water include both domestic and international passenger carrying services of UK registered merchant vessels.

*Road:* figures refer to Great Britain and include accidents occurring on the public highway (including footways) in which at least one road vehicle or a vehicle in collision with a pedestrian is involved and which becomes known to the police within 30 days of its occurrence. Figures include both public and private transport.

*Bus or coach:* figures for work buses are included. From 1 January 1994, the definition was revised to include only those vehicles equipped to carry 17 or more passengers regardless of use. Prior to 1994 these vehicles were coded according to construction, whether or not they were being used for carrying passengers. Vehicles constructed as buses that were privately licensed were included under 'bus and coach' but Public Service Vehicles (PSV) licensed minibuses were included under cars.

*Car:* includes taxis, invalid tricycles, three-wheeled and four-wheeled cars and minibuses. Prior to 1999 motor caravans were also included.

*Van:* vans mainly include vehicles of the van type constructed on a car chassis. From 1 January 1994 these are defined as those vehicles not over 3. 5 tonnes maximum permissible gross vehicle weight. Prior to 1994 the weight definition was not over 1.524 tonnes unladen.

*Two-wheeled motor vehicle:* mopeds, motor scooters and motorcycles (including motorcycle combinations).

*Pedal cycle:* includes tandems, tricycles and toy cycles ridden on the carriageway.

*Pedestrian:* includes persons riding toy cycles on the footway, persons pushing bicycles, pushing or pulling other vehicles or operating pedestrian controlled vehicles, those leading or herding animals, occupants of prams or wheelchairs, and people who alight safely from vehicles and are subsequently killed.

## Part 13: Lifestyles and social participation

### Television service

The categories in Table 13.2 are based on the main television receiver in the household. As many households have more than one television, respondents have had difficulty in deciding which television should be counted as their main receiver. As such these results are based on a subjective decision by the respondents and should be treated with caution. It should also be noted that each household may have more than one type of television receiver, but will only be reporting for their main television.

# Articles published in previous editions

**No.1 1970**

Some general developments in social statistics Professor C A Moser, CSO

Public expenditure on the social services Professor B Abel-Smith, London School of Economics and Political Science

The growth of the population to the end of the century Jean Thompson, OPCS

A forecast of effective demand for housing in Great Britain in the 1970s A E Holmans, MHLG

**No.2 1971**

Social services manpower Dr S Rosenbaum, CSO

Trends in certificated sickness absence F E Whitehead, DHSS

Some aspects of model building in the social and environmental fields B Benjamin, CSC

Social indicators – health A J Culyer, R J Lavers and A Williams, University of York

**No.3 1972**

Social commentary: change in social conditions CSO

Statistics about immigrants: objectives, methods, sources and problems Professor C A Moser, CSO

Central manpower planning in Scottish secondary education A W Brodie, SED

Social malaise research: a study in Liverpool M Flynn, P Flynn and N Mellor, Liverpool City Planning Department

Crimes of violence against the person in England and Wales S Klein, HO

**No.4 1973**

Social commentary: certain aspects of the life cycle CSO

The elderly D C L Wroe, CSO

Subjective social indicators M Abrams, SSRC

Mental illness and the psychiatric services E R Bransby, DHSS

Cultural accounting A Peacock and C Godfrey, University of York

Road accidents and casualties in Great Britain J A Rushbrook, DOE

**No.5 1974**

Social commentary: men and women CSO

Social security: the European experiment E James and A Laurent, EC Commission

Time budgets B M Hedges, SCPR

Time budgets and models of urban activity patterns N Bullock, P Dickens, M Shapcott and P Steadman, Cambridge University of Architecture

Road traffic and the environment F D Sando and V Batty, DOE

**No.6 1975**

Social commentary: social class CSO

Areas of urban deprivation in Great Britain: an analysis of 1971 Census data S Holtermann, DOE

Note: Subjective social indicators M Abrams, SSRC

**No.7 1976**

Social commentary: social change in Britain 1970–1975 CSO

Crime in England and Wales Dr C Glennie, HO

Crime in Scotland Dr Bruce, SHHD

Subjective measures of quality of life in Britain: 1971 to 1975 J Hall, SSRC

**No.8 1977**

Social commentary: fifteen to twenty-five: a decade of transition CSO

The characteristics of low income households R Van Slooten and A G Coverdale, DHSS

**No.9 1979**

Housing tenure in England and Wales: the present situation and recent trends A E Holmans, DOE

Social forecasting in Lucas B R Jones, Lucas Industries

**No.10 1980**

Social commentary: changes in living standards since the 1950s CSO

Inner cities in England D Allnutt and A Gelardi, DOE

Scotland's schools D Wishart, SED

**No.14 1984**

Changes in the life-styles of the elderly 1959–1982 M Abrams

**No.15 1985**

British social attitudes R Jowell and C Airey, SCPR

**No.16 1986**

Income after retirement G C Fiegehen, DHSS

**No.17 1987**

Social Trends since World War II Professor A H Halsey, University of Oxford

Household formation and dissolution and housing tenure: a longitudinal perspective A E Holmans and S Nandy, DOE; A C Brown, OPCS

**No.18 1988**

Major epidemics of the 20th century: from coronary thrombosis to AIDS Sir Richard Doll, University of Oxford

**No.19 1989**

Recent trends in social attitudes L Brook, R Jowell and S Witherspoon, SCPR

**No.20 1990**

Social Trends, the next 20 years T Griffin, CSO

**No.21 1991**

The 1991 Census of Great Britain: plans for content and output B Mahon and D Pearce, OPCS

**No.22 1992**

Crime statistics: their use and misuse C Lewis, HO

**No.24 1994**

Characteristics of the bottom 20 per cent of the income distribution N Adkin, DSS

**No.26 1996**

The OPCS Longitudinal Study J Smith, OPCS

British Household Panel Survey J Gershuny, N Buck, O Coker, S Dex, J Ermish, S Jenkins and A McCulloch, ESRC Research Centre on Micro-social Change

**No.27 1997**

Projections: a look into the future T Harris, ONS

**No.28 1998**

French and British societies: a comparison P Lee and P Midy, INSEE and A Smith and C Summerfield, ONS

**No.29 1999**

Drugs in the United Kingdom – a jigsaw with missing pieces A Bradley and O Baker, Institute for the Study of Drug Dependence

**No.30 2000**

A hundred years of social change A H Halsey, Emeritus Fellow, Nuffield College, Oxford

**No.31 2001**

200 hundred years of the census of population M Nissel

**No.32 2002**

Children B Botting, ONS

**No.33 2003**

Investing in each other and the community: the role of social capital P Haezewindt, ONS

**No.34 2004**

Ageing and gender: diversity and change S Arber and J Ginn, University of Surrey

**No.35 2005**

35 years of social change L Cook and J Martin, ONS

# Index

The references in this index relate to chapters, to table, figure and map numbers, or to Appendix entries. Analyses by sex and or age will generally be found under their main entries.